What Is Religion?

What Is Religion?

A Theological Answer

Nigel Ajay Kumar

☞PICKWICK *Publications* • Eugene, Oregon

WHAT IS RELIGION?
A Theological Answer

Copyright © 2013 Nigel Ajay Kumar. All rights reserved. Except for brief quotations in critical publications or reviews, no part of this book may be reproduced in any manner without prior written permission from the publisher. Write: Permissions, Wipf & Stock, 199 W. 8th Ave., Suite 3, Eugene, OR 97401.

Pickwick Publications
A imprint of Wipf and Stock Publishers
199 W. 8th Ave., Suite 3
Eugene, OR 97401

ISBN 13: 978-1-62032-794-4

Cataloging-in-Publication data:

Kumar, Nigel Ajay.

    What is religion? : a theological answer / Nigel Ajay Kumar.

    x + 310 p. ; 23cm ; Includes bibliography

    ISBN 13: 978-1-62032-794-4

    1. Religion. 2. Religions. 3. Theology of religion (Christian theology). 4. Chenchiah, Pandipeddi, 1886–. I. Title.

BL48 K85 2013

Manufactured in the U.S.A.

Contents

Preface • vii

1 Introduction: The Need for a Theology of Religion • 1
2 The Context of Chenchiah's Theology of Religion • 49
3 Chenchiah's Theology of Religion • 117
4 Evaluation of Chenchiah's Theology of Religion • 192
5 A Critical Framework to Formulate a Theological Answer • 219
6 Conclusion • 275

Bibliography • 285

Preface

IN A CONTEXTUAL THEOLOGY class during my theological studies at the graduate level, I was struck by Aloysius Pieris's challenge that Asian theologians must address one of two vital issues facing our context—poverty or religion. My own urbanized middle-class context had limited my experience of the abject poverty facing our nation. Nevertheless, I had grown up in an India that was deeply religious in both poor and non-poor contexts. I had seen that spirituality, gods, rituals, religious traditions—however we commonly understand these terms—were within India's cultural core. In fact, when I left my job at Filmfare magazine in 1998 to join SAIACS, one of the first supporters of my journey into theological education was a Hindu colleague who presented me with the Bhagavad Gita. In it she wrote: "When you find the truth, tell me." I chose to focus my research on religion because my own experience of a religious India took me there.

While the above-stated exposure to Pieris explains my choice of religion, it was working on my MTh dissertation that drew my attention to the problems in the "theology of religions." In that 2005 study, I investigated some Indian receptions of Karl Barth's theology of religion. Particularly focusing on Chenchiah, Chakkarai, and Devanandan, I began with the assumption that Indian theologians disagreed with Karl Barth's theology of religion, especially with his infamous reference to religion as *unbelief*. I also presumed that the Indian theologians would offer views significantly different from Barth's proposal, considering that they themselves had claimed to reject Barth. In the course of study, however, these assumptions were rectified: I discovered that, while fundamental differences between Barth and early Indian theologians remained, these Indian theologians also held views quite similar to Karl Barth, even about religion.

To find such similarity of views between Indian theologians and Barth surprised me, and I investigated its possible causes. I found that, to the point that the Indian theologians viewed Christ above religions, they were similar to Barth. Yet to the point that they viewed religions functionally, with the ability to positively impact culture, the Indian theologians were contrary to Barth.

An important reason for the perceived confusion and rejection of Karl Barth's view of religion was that the Indian theologians and Karl Barth were talking at cross purposes. Barth primarily attempted a theology of religion, the theological perspective of religion. The Indian theologians were largely concerned with a theology of religions, the theological interaction between multiple religious traditions. Hence, Indian theologians found Barth's judgment of religion offensive; in Barth's universal criticism of religion, the Indian theologians perceived a rejection of particular religious faiths. I concluded that a "positive" view of religion was not necessary for a positive interaction with/within religions. So, I proposed that Barth's "negative" theology of religion offered the possibility of a positive theology of religions.

Despite the prevailing confusion between a "theology of religion" and a "theology of religions," it was beyond the scope of my MTh thesis sufficiently to explore and clarify the two. Nevertheless, since then I noticed how there was general ignorance about the internal contradictions within a theology of religions about what religion meant. Not surprisingly, theologians of religions were hardly alert to the contemporary discussions about the use and misuse of religion, and thus they were in danger of uncritically reflecting contradictory concepts of religion in their work.

It was evident that a much deeper study than my initial MTh thesis was needed to address these issues. My subsequent study for my doctoral research pursued clarity within these two theological fields.

As for the reason for choosing to focus on Indian theologian Chenchiah, the beginnings are in another class. While attending the Doctoral Methodology course at SATHRI, Bangalore, in May 2006, I was surprised to see that most of the research proposals by the doctoral candidates focused upon Western theologians. In reaction, the teacher asserted that Indian students must interact with Indian theologians because we had an obligation to Indian theology. He stated that while Western theologians and theologies had been often dealt with from various angles, as Indian scholars we must dialogue with our own to improve our discipline. For indeed, if we did not interact with our own scholars, who would?

I remember that I resisted the normative nature of the comment because I found that the scholarly divide between West and East was unhelpful. Yet I noted that there was something to be said about the value of dialoguing with scholars from our own tradition, especially when dealing with concerns that deeply affected the Indian context. I myself had benefited from scholars, such as Alyosius Pieris, who were similarly affected by issues and realities as my own. Thus, while it was not then that I decided to focus upon Chenchiah, I know that a seed was sown.

All this could have followed a dangerously unproductive track had it not been for the timely intervention of Kiran Sebastian, a faculty member at UTC, who warned me not to study religion until I had read a book by S. N. Balagangadhara. Through Balagangadhara's work I began to look at the concept of religion more critically. In response to his and similar critiques of religion, however, I was drawn to approach the concept of religion more theologically.

During my dissertation proposal drafting stage, I spent a lot of time examining the methodologies behind the theologies of religions in the context of contemporary and theological debates about religion. It was eventually clear that a key problem in the 'theology of religions' discipline lay in the confusion over what religion was and to what it could be applied. Nevertheless, theologians rarely spent time exploring theological definitions of what religion was and instead were more focused on the implications of the confluence of one religion with another. As my exploration led me to look for scholars who had offered a theological definition of religion, I was drawn back to the Indian lay thinker who addressed the concept of religion even before the 'theology of religions' discipline became prevalent.

Pandipeddi Chenchiah, a Hindu convert and a lawyer, was the epitome of a lay theologian. He wrote several important articles that challenged his generation to rethink its Christianity in the pre-Independence era. Chenchiah was also one of the earliest Indian theologians to make a theological assertion about what religion was. Of course he did not consciously write a theology of religion or a theology of religions, because its formal discourse did not exist back in his day. Furthermore, Chenchiah's concerns were primarily theological in that his effort was to seek and understand Christ and what he means to humanity rather than provide a framework for discourse between multiple religions. Nevertheless, I saw that Chenchiah was not only interested in theology, but was acutely aware of the 'religious' context within which theology existed. Chenchiah used his 'theology of religion' as a stepping stone for his Christological formulations and his views of religion provided a unique access to the theological discourse about religion. For an Indian theologian who discussed the problem of religion, I no longer needed to look further. The results of my dissertation were drawn over several pages of long and arduous research. Thankfully, despite several edits in this book, my conclusion from my dissertation remains largely the same.

Before I proceed to present my case, I have a few people who I wish to thank. I would like to thank Dr. Chris Barrigar. He has been my supervisor, counselor, and friend over many years. I thank the members of St. Peters'

Anglican Church, Montreal, who graciously hosted my family in Montreal. A special thanks to the Faculty of Presbyterian College, my host institution in Montreal, especially to Dr. John Vissers and Dr. Dan Shute.

I also thank the financial supporters of our trip to Canada—in particular Dr. Chris Hancock and AMO. Their assistance sustained us long enough for me to make the best use of the academic resources available there.

At SAIACS, I would like to thank Dr. Graham and Carol Houghton, Dr. Ashish Chrispal, Dr. Ian Payne, and Dr. Cor Bennema. I especially thank Dr. Dieter Kemmler, who helped me to translate a German book into English. My many thanks to the library staff of SAIACS, UTC, and McGill.

I would like to thank Shilpa Waghmare for her editorial assistance for this book. I also thank the editors at Wipf and Stock Publishers for both the opportunity to publish with them and getting my work print ready.

I thank my parents, who supported me unconditionally. I thank our friends Abhra and Sandy, Sandeep and Airy, and Arpit and Shilpa, who stood by my family in difficult times.

I thank my daughter, Taarika, who reminded me to focus on what was important. And finally I thank my wife, Selena, who stood by me and supported me through it all.

My hope is that this work will contribute to the academic discussion about religion, particularly for those willing to engage with theological voices. Similarly, I hope that the Church in India will take notice, to be both inspired by predecessors like Chenchiah but also to take learning and research about religion more seriously—for the sake of the Gospel.

1

Introduction
The Need for a Theology of Religion

When soccer games are seen as religious phenomena and the recitation of Buddhist sutras is not, something has obviously gone wrong.[1]

PREAMBLE

For a concept as pervasive as religion, it is surprising that there is no consensus on what religion is. Neither is there any agreement about what the concept applies to or even to what it does not. It is common to hear both, that Christianity is the true religion[2] as well as that Christianity is not a religion at all.[3] Nor is it difficult to find instances where Communism is shown to be both antireligious[4] as well as religious.[5] In India, while most are able to unquestionably refer to Hinduism as a religion,[6] some do so with

---

1. Riesebrodt, *The Promise of Salvation*, xi.
2. For instance, the Christian Apologetics & Research Ministry (CARM), a US-based Christian Apologetics center, unequivocally declares that "Christianity is the one true religion."
3. Fowler, *Christianity is Not a Religion*.
4. Kolarz, "Religion and Communism in Africa," 223.
5. Zeldin, "The Religious Nature of Russian Marxism," 100–111.
6. Singh, *In Defence of Religion and Other Essays*.

qualification,[7] and a few find it problematic to refer to Hinduism as a religion at all.[8] Furthermore, the Indian Supreme Court has said that Hindutva is not a religious but a cultural system, by using the Hindu Vedas as textual support![9] Added to this problematic is the current and popular view that prefers spirituality over religion.[10]

In view of these obvious discrepancies, it is surprising that there is a general confidence over the notion of religion. People talk about religion without fearing that they are being misunderstood. This applies not only to popular discourse, but also to the academic study of religion in universities as well as within the interreligious discourse of the religions themselves. Many institutions have invested a huge amount of resources to encourage comparative religious studies, interreligious dialogue and even, in the case of some Christian denominations, interreligious worship. Almost all these initiatives assume that religion exists in all cultures, is knowable (even if in a limited sense), and at its core is essentially good.

The purpose of this introductory chapter is threefold. First, I establish that a definitional problem in the category 'religion' does exist. This I do by showcasing the increasingly influential scholarly voices that are critiquing the foundations of religious studies and highlighting the uncritical uses of religion, particularly within the Christian theology of religions. Second, I emphasize the need for a Christian theological definition of religion that is useful for Christian interaction with that which is considered to be the religious and interreligious spaces. Third, I end this chapter by outlining the trajectory of my project. This includes establishing what a "theology of religion" is—I conceive of a theology of religion as the theological method for defining and engaging with definitions of religion—and how one would do it. In particular, I explain my choice of the Indian theologian Pandipeddi Chenchiah, showing that Chenchiah is a helpful entry point for this discussion.

First, we explore the problem of religion facing the academic study of religion today.

---

7. Aleaz, *Dimensions of Indian Religion*, 1–5.

8. Sugirtharajah, *Imagining Hinduism*, ix–xii.

9. For instance, see the newspaper editorials by Jois, "Supreme Court Judgment on 'Hindutva': An Important Landmark"; and Tarkunde, "Supreme Court Judgment: A Blow to Secular Democracy."

10. Pearce, *The Death of Religion and the Rebirth of Spirit*.

THE PROBLEM OF RELIGION IN THE ACADEMIC STUDY OF RELIGION

In contemporary scholarship regarding the concept of religion, there are primarily two challenges. One challenge pertains to the difficulty of defining religion, which makes it almost impossible to differentiate between religion and nonreligion. The other challenge comes from scholars who argue that religion is not a universal cross-cultural reality but a localized (usually Western) and ideological category, making its application to India and the East problematic.

In his 1926 lectures, Alfred North Whitehead stated that "there is no agreement as to the definition of religion in its most general sense, including true and false religion; nor is there any agreement as to valid religious beliefs, nor even as to what we mean by the truth of religion."[11] Almost eighty years later, Mark Taylor opines that the field of religious studies is "in a perpetual state of crisis because it can neither define its object of study nor agree on distinctive methods or strategies of interpretation."[12] Taylor goes on to say, "It has never been more important or more difficult to study religion critically than it is today" because the "resurgence of old orthodoxies and emergence of new fundamentalisms in multiple traditions pose both implicit and explicit threats that make critical reflection on religion imperative."[13]

These scholars are certainly not saying that there is a lack of theoretical reflection on the nature of religion. In fact, there are so many definitions of religion that it seems as if there are "as many definitions as there are scholars."[14] Similarly, there are numerous *approaches* to religion[15] which represent entirely different ways of looking at the subject matter. Neither the definitions nor the approaches correlate easily with one another. It is evident that while it is not so difficult for scholars to come up with definitions or approaches, it is harder to find agreement over their validity.[16]

---

11. Despite this, Whitehead ironically went on to offer his own universally-intended definition of religion as "a system of general truths which have the effect of transforming character when they are sincerely held and vividly apprehended." Whitehead, *Religion in the Making*, 14–15.

12. Taylor, *Defining Religion*, B4.

13. Ibid.

14. Kunin, *Theories of Religion*, 1.

15. Whaling lists at least eleven approaches to religion. See Whaling, *Contemporary Approaches to the Study of Religion*.

16. While a definition and approach refers to two separate things, they are related. As a result, while I focus here on the definition *of* religion, I am also mindful that it

Bloch for instance raises certain pertinent questions when he notes the difficulty anthropologists face in identifying what is religious. On one level, it seems straightforward—"there are special places for it." Yet, in some religions, "sleeping, waking, eating" all have a religious character to it so that "it is not clear where religion begins and where it ends."[17]

Bloch sees a greater complexity within what he calls traditional societies, who lack the "concept of religion as a distinct phenomenon."[18] He goes on to criticize definitions of religion that dichotomize between natural and supernatural knowledge, or even between the sacred and the profane, because he is skeptical of the criteria that accords greater value to some aspects of culture than to others.[19] In addition, Lash critiques preconceived notions about religion that suggest that it is "a territory quite distinct from those we know as 'politics' and 'art,' as 'science' and 'law' and 'economics.'"[20] "This view of things," Lash says emphatically, "is now coming to an end."[21]

Kunin explores three definitional strategies—essentialist, substantialist and functionalist—that have dominated the study of religion, but remain extremely problematic.[22] He highlights that these definitional strategies tend to force commonalities that do not necessarily exist, and do not safely establish the boundaries of what constitutes a religion.[23] Essentialist definitions are those that attempt to define religion through some religious nature or trait shared by humanity across cultures.[24] Such universals can include psychological or biological traits in humanity.[25] These kinds of definitions tend to be founded on extended claims about the human person, assuming some universal anthropology. For instance, the *belief* that all human beings have a God-shaped vacuum which religion tries to fill[26] is an example of an

---

implies an approach *to* religion.

17. Bloch, "Religion and Ritual," 732–36.
18. Ibid., 732.
19. Ibid., 732–33.
20. Lash, *The Beginning and the End of 'Religion,'* ix.
21. Ibid.
22. Kunin adds that many definitions reflect traits of more than one type. Kunin, *Theories of Religion*, 2.
23. For more in-depth critique of each position see ibid., 3–7.
24. Ibid., 3.
25. Ibid.
26. For instance, Smith says, "As long as there are human beings, there will be religion for the sufficient reason that the self is a theomorphic creature ... God encased within it. Having been created in the *imago Dei* ... all human beings have a God-shaped vacuum built into their hearts. Since nature abhors a vacuum, people keep trying to fill the one inside them." Smith, *Why Religion Matters*, 148.

essentialist definition that attempts to find a spiritual core within humanity.[27] However, these claims may not actually be universal and their universality cannot be demonstrated scientifically.

An example of the essentialist position is the cognitive theory of religion—which focuses upon the biological component, particularly on the brain activity which generates and interprets religious beliefs and experiences.[28] The chief concern is to explain the religious phenomena we have before us within a scientific (evolutionary) paradigm. Religious beliefs and behaviors are even shown to be the possible key to the survival of the human species.[29] However, it is difficult to derive the concept of religious activity in the cognitive function without first having a theory of what that religious activity actually is. To look for what portions of the brain are activated when a person prays, tends to ignore the fact that the scientist has categorized the act of closing eyes and speaking as a religious act. In effect, scientists who look for naturalistic explanations of religion often fail to see the ideological roots of their hypotheses about religion.

Substantialist definitions are those which, like essentialist positions, identify a core essence of religion. However they do not find that core *in* humanity but in a particular trait that is common to all religions.[30] Examples of these are Tylor's minimalist definition that all religion has "belief in Spiritual Beings,"[31] Karan Singh's suggestion that all religion "is simply that inner search for the truth of one's being, often called the spiritual quest,"[32] and more recently, Robin Horton's attempts to identify the "real" within religion by offering that religion is "an extension of the field of people's social relationships beyond the confines of purely human society."[33] The problem with these kinds of definitions is that when faced with *religions* that do not fit neatly within these categories—like Buddhism—scholars are tempted to go out of their way to change their theory to force a commonality.[34]

27. A more "secular" version of this same theory could be the view that humanity has deep psychological needs or anxieties that needs to be filled by purpose.

28. See, for instance, Boyer, *The Naturalness of Religious Ideas*, and several essays in Schloss and Murray, *The Believing Primate*.

29. See Johnson and Bering, who argue that religious belief played an essential role in the evolutionary development and survival of the human species, especially in "human social development." Johnson and Bering, "Hand of God, Mind of Man," 42.

30. Kunin, *Theories of Religion*, 4.

31. Tylor, *Primitive Culture*, 424.

32. Singh, *In Defence of Religion and Other Essays*, v.

33. Horton, *Patterns of Thought in Africa and the West*, 31–32.

34. For instance, Almond documents how Buddhism was constructed primarily as a textual religion. Almond, *The British Discovery of Buddhism*.

Functionalist definitions, by contrast, focus upon a certain role (function) religion has for society or the individual.[35] For instance, Clifford Geertz's popular, yet by now much maligned,[36] definition offers that: "Religion is (1) a system of symbols which acts to (2) establish powerful, pervasive, and long-lasting moods and motivations in men by (3) formulating conceptions of a general order of existence and (4) clothing these conceptions with such an aura of actuality that (5) the moods and motivations seem uniquely realistic."[37]

The functional focus is evident when Geertz promotes religion as *establishing* and *causing* "long-lasting moods."[38] Yet the question remains: how indeed is Geertz to identify without doubt the "system of symbols" that establishes "long-lasting moods"? How can he guarantee that his definition will help us differentiate between what we normally consider a "religious activity" (like going to the temple during Diwali), from what we call "patriotism" (saluting the National Flag on Independence Day)? Also, even with Geertz's definition, a theoretical stance about what religious is in culture must already be assumed in order to highlight what we are looking for in other cultures.

The above definitional strategies all require scholars to operate with a theory of religion already in place, which they subconsciously apply to the study of diverse cultures. To further highlight these problems, consider Paul Hiebert's definition of religion, which employs all three definitional strategies. He offers that religion "encompasses all specific beliefs about the ultimate nature of reality and the origins, meaning, and destiny of life, as well as the myths and rituals that symbolically express them ... Religion is also based on the person's ability to transcend the self, to step 'outside' of and contemplate oneself, one's fellows, and the universe. It is based on the human need to 'make sense' out of the human experience and find some order and significance in the whole human situation."[39]

Hiebert is an essentialist in identifying the "human need" which attempts to "make sense" and "find some order."[40] Even if we accept that, with his vast anthropological experience, Hiebert *saw* this to be true, a fellow social scientist could ask whether Hiebert had a belief about human need and thus saw it expressed in other cultures, or whether Hiebert actually

---

35. Kunin, *Theories of Religion*, 6.
36. See Asad, *Genealogies of Religion*.
37. Geertz, *The Interpretation of Cultures*, 90.
38. Ibid.
39. Hiebert, *Cultural Anthropology*, 372.
40. Ibid.

went into other cultures with absolutely no prior expectation about human commonality and found the need represented in every single culture.[41] Hiebert is substantive in identifying religion as encompassing "specific beliefs about the ultimate nature of reality and the origins, meaning, and destiny of life."[42] Obviously, questions can be raised about whether all that is called religion fits neatly within Hiebert's categories. Also, it could be asked whether Hinduism, for instance, is a religion when it hardly has the same concern (as Christianity) for ultimate origins. The functionalism of Hiebert's definition is evident in the power of religion to help the person to "transcend the self," though it is not hard to see its lack of definitional power when even movies and music can achieve a similar effect. Thus, Hiebert's definition is perspectival. His definition is conditioned by presuppositions of what religion should be.

In view of the difficulties of finding an objective reference to what religion is, it has become popular to promote a polythetic definitional strategy known as "family resemblance."[43] This approach, associated sometimes with Wittgenstein, offers an alternative to how we can begin to identify what religions are. Thus, religion is viewed as a family of similarities but not sameness, making it easier to talk about religions that share mutual relations. Thus, Southwold recognizes that "religions" like Buddhism escape the traditional categorization of religion and offers a polythetic definition of religion.[44] He asserts that "anything which we would call a religion must have at least some of the following attributes" which include, though are not exhausted by:

1. A central concern with godlike beings and men's relations with them.
2. A dichotomization of elements of the world into sacred and profane, and a central concern with the sacred.
3. An orientation towards salvation from the ordinary conditions of worldly existence.

---

41. Anthropologists could argue against observer neutrality. Yet this example still shows that assertions about human commonality are difficult to establish scientifically and, oftentimes, represent *a priori* belief of the observer.

42. Hiebert, *Cultural Anthropology*, 372.

43. Bryne's list is similar to Kunin's except that he includes family resemblance and uses the label of experiential instead of essentialist. Byrne, "Religion: Definition and Explanation" in Smelser and Baltes, *International Encyclopedia of Social & Behavioral Sciences*, 13060–62. For another helpful survey on the theories of religion, see Strenski, *Thinking about Religion*.

44. Southwold, "Buddhism and the Definition of Religion," 371.

4. Ritual practices.

5. Beliefs which are neither logically nor empirically demonstrable or highly probable, but must be held on the basis of faith . . .

6. An ethical code, supported by such beliefs.

7. Supernatural sanctions on infringements of that code.

8. A mythology.

9. A body of scriptures, or similarities exalted by oral traditions.

10. A priesthood, or similar specialist religious elite.

11. Association with a moral community, a church . . .

12. Association with an ethnic or similar group.[45]

Importantly, while what we conceive of as religion will have at least some of these above attributes, there need not be unanimity about all. In effect, these overlapping similarities allow Buddhism to be in the same religious class as Christianity.[46]

Yet scholars like Fitzgerald have found two significant problems with family resemblance; namely, that they "smuggle in" an idea of religion to distinguish it from other families and also that they use definitional similarities so broad that they cease to be useful in identifying what they refer to.[47] Evidently, here too an *a priori* theory of religion is needed to form a definition of religion.

With even the family resemblance method unable to provide a conclusive definition of religion, it is safe to say that there are currently no universally accepted definitions of religion. From current scholarship, it is near impossible to objectively (and without presuppositions) identify what religion is and what it is not.

Against Universal Religion

The above problem reveals yet another challenge facing religious studies, namely the question of whether religion is an ideology imposed by a particular culture. A growing number of scholars are noticing the ideological

---

45. Ibid.

46. Benson Saler develops a detailed defense of the family resemblance methodology. See Saler, *Conceptualising Religion*.

47. Fitzgerald, "Religion, Philosophy and Family Resemblances," 226–27.

roots of religion and questioning whether religion is a universal category at all.

Many credit Wilfred Cantwell Smith for drawing attention to the connection between western ideology and religion. Smith asserts that our understanding of religion is like a window to the world and that it needs replacing.[48] Smith so strongly emphasizes the inextricable relationship between the West and religion that, for a better understanding of non-Western people and their faith, Smith suggests that the word religion be abandoned: "the term 'religion' is confusing, unnecessary, and distorting . . . the vitality of personal faith, on the one hand, and, on the other hand (quite separately) progress of understanding—even at the academic level—of the traditions of other people throughout history and throughout the world, are both seriously blocked by our attempt to conceptualize what is involved in each case in terms of (a) religion."[49]

Evidently Smith prioritizes "interiority and mystery of religion" over the phenomena that can be assessed by nonreligious data.[50] He urges that the focus of religion must change from the externals to the internals, our "cumulative traditions," namely faith.[51] One can critique Smith today by showing that his "cumulative traditions" and ideas of "faith" are categories still dependent on universal conceptions of religion. However, historically, his critique of religion has raised important questions about how our understanding of religion impacts our understanding of the "other," and the significance of his path-breaking work in this regard cannot be minimized.

Out of this legacy have emerged others scholars who draw attention to the connection between religion and the West more forcefully. The reason why the ideology of religion becomes problematic is because the study of religion has traditionally valued objectivity, especially in its observation of and relation to the phenomena categorized as religion. Yet, many scholars are not only showing that the entire religious studies project is a Western construct, but also that there are hidden theological motivations governing them.

Balagangadhara, an Indian scholar, is critical of the concept of universal religion and strongly asserts that religion does not exist in all cultures. He is critical of the claim that religion is universal by noting how anthropologists (not just missionaries) came to cultures like those in India looking for religion because they believed that all cultures had it. As a result, when

---

48. Smith, *Meaning and End of Religion*, 193.
49. Ibid., 50.
50. McCutcheon, "The Category 'Religion' in Recent Publications," 286.
51. Smith, *Meaning and End of Religion*, 168–69.

these scholars found something that did not look like religion, they adapted their definitions of religion to include these cultures because of the *belief* that religion had to be universal.[52]

Similarly, Harrison connects western thinkers to the concept of religion. He states, "'Religions' existed first in the minds of Western thinkers who thought that the lives of other peoples were governed by the kinds of concerns which were really only characteristic of one episode of Western history. The 'world religions' were thus generated largely through the projection of Christian disunity onto the world. It follows that much of the perceived conflict between the so-called world religions can be attributed to the grammar of the term 'religions,' rather than to substantive differences in matters of faith."[53]

Furthermore, Fitzgerald argues that the "persistent appearance" of religion despite the obvious problems facing the concept "can be explained by its theological and more generally ideological function."[54] As an example, Fitzgerald shows the link between many current theories of religion and the "modern myth of religion" that propounds an ultimate (or transcendent) reality that gives "meaning and purpose" to human history; where despite the diversity that is evident, the goal of humanity is viewed as, ultimately, the same.[55] Richard King also points to the "Christian theological and Enlightenment roots of 'religious studies'" and, further, links the ideology of religion with Colonialism.[56]

Dubuisson asserts that the West has in fact *constructed* religion and been constructed by it.[57] Dubuisson's central concept is that religion does not simply emerge from the West, but it is also the defining concept of the West itself: "religion not only appears as one of the typical creations of the West, among the most prestigious of them, but also becomes the West's fundamental creation and central reference point, the reference point around

---

52. For instance, Balagangadhara observes that "the belief about the existence of religion in all cultures is not a result of empirical research. Not merely that. It is theoretically so certain that no empirical enquiry appears necessary." Balagangadhara, *The Heathen in His Blindness*, 6.

53. Harrison, *'Religion' and the Religions in the English Enlightenment*, 174.

54. Fitzgerald, *The Ideology of Religious Studies*, 27.

55. Apart from "the modern myth of religion," Fitzgerald proposes that our ideas of religion are dependent on Christian and post-Christian concepts of privatization, deism, capitalism, imperialism and missionary propaganda. Fitzgerald, *The Ideology of Religious Studies*, 27–32.

56. King, *Orientalism and Religion*, 2.

57. Dubuisson, *The Western Construction of Religion*. The book was first published as *L'Occident et la Religion: Mythes, Science et Ideaologie* in 1998.

which it constructed, organized, and developed itself by erecting its own system of beliefs and representations ... it is that point of reference by which it has become, in and of itself, its own world—the referential center from which it has conceptualized the others—all the others, both those that it has dominated or conquered and those it has influenced."[58]

Dubuisson rejects the notion that there is a linguistic equivalent in other cultures by showing that the concept of dharma is not the same as religion. Dharma, unlike the religion of the West, "protects (*dharanat*) everything; dharma maintains all that is created ... dharma is indeed the principle that is capable of sustaining the universe."[59] Neither does dharma impose itself "on anthropological thought as an absolute system of reference."[60] Not surprisingly, dharma is not equivalent to religion: "We must take care not to confuse dharma and religion, as do so many superficial observations. Dharma is not the equivalent, and still less the Sanskrit translation, of the word 'religion.' The idea of an impersonal, uncreated, and unchanging cosmic order to which everything from plants to supernatural beings is subject is not in itself religious."[61]

Religion and dharma are then likened to two separate cultures sets—A and B—and Dubuisson points to the obvious danger of finding similarities between A and B by using A as the reference point: "To think religion(s) with words invented by religion. This variant on the hermeneutical circle, where the 'before' can never be analyzed except from an 'after' that is fashioned and conditioned by this 'before,' the perception of which is dependent on the after, which in turn depends... this complicates our task a bit more."[62]

For Dubuisson, that *after,* through which all that has gone *before* is measured, is the Christian frame of reference.

The Hindu scholar Badrinath also attempts to distance the word/concept of *dharma* from religion. Rejecting *dharma* as a religious concept, he categorically states that "In India, invading foreigners created for their own understanding, which turned out to be wrong, a set of words to describe a people and a world view that was alien and incomprehensible to them. Adopted carelessly in course of time by the native people, too, they allowed those words to give them an identity that was very opposite of the identity their own traditions had given them."[63]

58. Dubuisson, *The Western Construction of Religion*, 11.
59. Ibid., 100.
60. Ibid., 101.
61. Ibid.
62. Ibid., 102.
63. Badrinath, *Dharma, India and the World Order*, 19.

What Is Religion?

Historian Geoffrey Oddie observes that, in the nineteenth century, Hinduism was remolded to fit within the parameters of Christian thinking so that readers could use familiar language and concepts to critique or appreciate Hinduism.[64] Similarly, eminent and influential Indian historian, Romila Thapar, addresses the falsification of religious identity in *Early India*.[65] She notes for instance that European scholars prioritized textual sources for understanding religion, which led them (naturally) to Sanskrit works.[66] Many of these texts were "biases in favor of those in authority, generally adhering to Brahmanical theories of society irrespective of whether or not they had widespread historical applicability."[67] A case in point is when the *Dharma-shastras* were thought to be the foundation for a structured *varna* (caste) system, while the actual stratification of the common people was more complex and fluid than the upper-caste oriented *Dharma-shastras* suggested.[68]

Regardless of this Westernized-religion rhetoric, Lash is correct in stating that religion as a whole is becoming problematic because while it is commonplace to assert that the "modern Western concepts of religion are ill-fitted to describe the traditions of the 'East'" this concept has also proved disastrous for the "so-called traditions of the 'West.'"[69]

Thus, as religion is seen as a localized phenomena arising from the West, and used by the West to view others, it is difficult to argue that religion is a universal across cultures. Clearly, any identification of what is truly religion has been historically fraught with problems and it is not clear whether the field of religious studies has already overcome any of these limitations.

---

64. Interestingly, Oddie refuses to blame the missionaries alone and, in fact, states that the missionary experience of the people helped shape and correct ideas as well. Oddie, *Imagined Hinduism*, 342–43.

65. See particularly her assessment of Colonial imposition of religious identity through use of selective historical sources. Thapar, *The Penguin History of Early India*, 1–36.

66. Thapar, *Early India*, 9–10.

67. Ibid.

68. Ibid.

69. He goes on to offer that we understand the "great traditions, not as 'religions' in the modern sense, but as *schools* whose pedagogy has . . . the common twofold purpose of weaning us from our idolatry and purifying our desire." Lash, *Beginning and the End of 'Religion,'* ix–x.

Some Responses to the Problem of Religion

In such a quagmire, it is not unexpected that there are equally diverse responses to the problem. To understand religion, some scholars like Ninian Smart argue that the problem with the definition of religion is not that it cannot be defined, but that oftentimes, the wrong kind of definition (for instance, essentialist) is proposed. Smart therefore states that "a religion (or the religion of a group) is a set of institutionalized ritual activities expressing and evoking sacral sentiments."[70]

Other scholars, sensing the problems in Smart's definition, take refuge in the philosophy of language. For instance, Flood is critical of what he calls "quasi-theological" theories and "scientific reductionist" theories, both of which tend "towards universalizing claims about religion."[71] Flood argues that "there can be no essentialist understanding of religion" nor can there be a "discourse of religion outside of particular cultures."[72] In turn, Flood sees religion as "binding narratives and behaviors within cultures."[73]

Then there are voices which argue vehemently against the negation of religion and instead propose an alternative that is inclusive. Masih, for instance, critiques the attempts to show Buddhism and Jainism as nonreligious. He urges a movement away from theistic definitions of religions to encompass other religious traditions: "Westerners ... define religion as to exclude the claims of Jainism, Hinayana form of Buddhism ... [which also] cannot be regarded as ethical since both of them renounce the world as essentially illusory ... We regard Jainism and non-theistic Buddhism as religion because they emphasize the spiritual goal as the real end of life and its activities. They are to be called religion because of their commitment to a life of spiritual culture, issuing into an all-pervasive pattern of behavior."[74]

Or then there is Damayanthi Niles, representing another type of Asian voice in this debate. She critiques scholars like Dubuisson by saying that they use Western concepts to argue that religion is a Western construct and in turn shape the way particular religious traditions are understood. Niles' main concern is with their "method of thinking about religion" that "tries to explain religion as a comprehensive system under which all the so-called 'religious phenomenon' should be categorized and explained." She then goes

---

70. Smart, "Meaning in Religion and the Meaning of Religion."
71. Flood, *Beyond Phenomenology*, 43.
72. Ibid.
73. Ibid., 63–64.
74. Masih, *Introduction to Religious Philosophy*, 4.

on to use the terms "Buddhism" and "Hinduism" uncritically, within the frame of "popular religion."[75]

Another response is by scholars who parallel the problem of definitions in religious studies with the lack of definitional clarity in other terms such as culture, politics, literature and art, suggesting that theoretical clarity is not going to be arrived at in a hurry.[76] Thus Alves celebrates the mystery of religion and proposes that "Religion ... is an invisible presence, subtle, disguised, that constitutes one of the threads with which is woven the happenings of our daily existence. Religion is closer to our personal experience than we wish to admit."[77]

Other scholars are resigned to the diversity and avoid definitions or consensus of definitions altogether. For instance, Roger O'Toole suggests that social scientists "should abandon the search for the real meaning or essence of religion" because "the appropriate pursuit for a social scientist is to identify the most useful definition available for purposes of social research and analysis ... the social scientist's concern is with utility rather than reality."[78]

Despite O'Toole's assertions, there is an urgent need for clarity concerning religious issues. A case in point: Puniyani repeats the often-heard narrative that relates religion to violence.[79] In contrast, Indian Nobel Laureate Amartya Sen argues that the category of religion is reductionist, it has been falsely linked to the category of violence. Sen argues, "In partitioning the population of the world into those belonging to 'the Islamic world,' 'the Western world,' 'the Hindu world,' ... the divisive power of classificatory priority is implicitly used to place people firmly inside a unique set of rigid boxes. Other divisions (say, between rich and the poor, between members of different classes and occupations, ... between distinct nationalities and residential locations, between language groups, etc) are all submerged by this allegedly primal way of seeing the differences between people."[80]

Without clarity about definitions of religion, it is hard to see how anyone can determine which of these two is right.

The need for legal clarity regarding the definition of religion is also urgent. The Faculty of Religious Studies at McGill University hosted a symposium titled "What is Religion?" to address a problematic Canadian Supreme

---

75. Niles, "The Study of Popular Religions and Our Theological Task," 213–14.
76. Wilson and Slavens, *Research Guide to Religious Studies*, 7–8.
77. Alves, *What is Religion?*, 5.
78. O'Toole, *Religion*, 39–40.
79. Puniyani, "Religion," 27–43.
80. Sen, *Identity and Violence*, 11.

Court definition of religion.[81] After two days of discussion between the Faculty of Law and the Faculty of Religious Studies at McGill, there was no consensus about the definition of religion. One participant even pointed out that a two-day seminar was not enough to answer the question![82]

Another response to the problem of religion comes from those who recognize the problem and continue to work provisionally within it. Thus, some scholars argue that religion is not a thing in itself but is simply an academic category, a second-order activity, useful for academic purposes. Jonathan Z. Smith famously says, "while there is a staggering amount of data, of phenomena, of human experiences and expressions that might be characterized in one culture or another, by one criterion or another, as religious—there is no data for religion. Religion is solely the creation of the scholar's study. It is created for the scholar's analytic purposes by his imaginative acts of comparison and generalization. Religion has no independent existence apart from the academy."[83]

The force of this argument must not be minimized since the recognition of religion as a constructed category for academic purposes allows scholars like McCutcheon to continue to operate within the religious studies sphere, albeit in a qualified sense. For McCutcheon, the categories of religion can now be seen as "tools developed over time, tools with a history that come with theoretical, even political, baggage, tools that are used to classify, sort, and analyze human behavior."[84] Nevertheless, this view is not commonly adopted and has its own critics.[85]

It is not surprising, then, that there are also those scholars who are frustrated with all these questions and simply suggest a common sense meaning of religion. In Strenski's approach of "ordinary usage," he argues that just as "everyone knows" what art, politics, language and economics is, the idea of religion "lies in its reflecting a deep feature of the world in which we live."[86] He suggests that "we need no experts to tell us" what these concepts are; we only "need to introspect."[87] Strenski asserts that religion is

---

81. The Religious Studies Department of McGill University hosted the "What Is Religion?" symposium in honor of former Dean, Prof. B. Barry Levy, on November 6–7, 2008.

82. The definition that came closest to addressing the issue at hand was Francis Young's, namely that of "religion as world-view."

83. Smith, *Imagining Religion*, xi.

84. McCutcheon, "Redescribing 'Religion' as Social Formation," 52.

85. Strenski, "Why 'Theology' Won't Work," 31–44.

86. Strenski, "On 'Religion' and Its Despisers," 116.

87. Ibid.

a "cultural *a priori*"[88] and any definition of religion leads only to frustration among the masses since the word is already beyond "intellectual control."[89] Strenski strongly criticizes scholars like Fitzgerald who urge that the concept of religion be abandoned, calling this "an exercise in naïveté, bad faith, or ignorant mischief, or indeed all of the above."[90] In contrast, Strenski urges "getting on with the job" [of the study of religion][91] and offers that religion is an important way by which humanity interacts with the diversity of human experience.[92] Using examples from culture that demonstrate his point, he offers that religion is a shared complex cluster that includes ethnic, economic, political, spiritual and historical identities, and yet transcends each individually.[93] His project extends to using the concept of religion to "make sense of the world,"[94] and also contends that it is important in human culture. Thus Strenski states:

> the world today seems to be making it impossible and undesirable for us to ignore *religion* any longer. Who else but students of religion should take up the challenge of understanding *religion* and its place in explaining the way the world is?
> ... We have only just begun to show both how and that taking *religion* seriously makes a difference. Theology and religious studies need to speak with a single voice about the importance of religion in the world if we are to speak with voices loud enough to make a difference.[95]

Strenski's method, while appealing and popular, is problematic if used exclusively. First, it needs a concept of religion to begin with. Second, it fails to recognize the conflicting or even political *uses* of the concept of religion. The concept of religion is assumed to be universal, without any thought given to people who think otherwise. Adopting a democratic approach to theory, while sensible, still fails to address the issues raised by people who either disagree with one theory or feel oppressed by another.

Perhaps, then, Mark Taylor is correct in suggesting that the field of religious studies is in crisis. It should be clear that the field of religious studies

---

88. Ibid., 117.
89. Ibid., 118.
90. Ibid.
91. Ibid., 126.
92. Ibid., 117.
93. Ibid., 127.
94. Ibid., 132.
95. Strenski, "Why 'Theology' Won't Work," 32.

The Dubuisson/Balagangadhara Challenge

The definitional struggle in religious studies is not without consequence for Christianity. There is an influential voice that equates the category of religion with Christianity, and certainly not in flattering terms. This approach to religion is to see religion as a Western (read Christian) construction. Whatever meaning we have of religion today, some would argue, comes from (or is deeply associated with) Christianity. It is important to note that these scholars are not critiquing Christianity, though oftentimes they do not hold Christianity in high esteem either. Rather they critique secular academicians who continue to use the category of religion without recognizing its theological and ideological roots.

Dubuisson draws attention to how Christianity developed in the context of being uprooted and in exile, suggesting that it inevitably had to develop universal claims that transcended ethnic and cultural differences. Thus, even as it began to adapt to alien cultures and philosophies, it developed as the "sole true religion"—which Dubuisson finds "in a certain ironic sense is quite true."[96] This is to say, religion was so closely associated with Christianity that it was always its best example.[97]

Dubuisson highlights the key traits of Christianity and religion, the most important being opposition. Dubuisson states that, "The Christian religion, as much through its acts as in its spirit, rests on a system of antithetical categories or principles" such as true and false religions, God and humanity, knowledge and faith, soul and body, clergy and laity, and the like.[98] He shows that the Christian religion prefers "division and controversy as dominant modes of operation" even as Christianity itself is "reduced to radical alternatives."[99] A polarity that is particularly successful in shaping the character of religion is interiorization and universalization, which emphasizes subjective faith along with universally accessible experience across all humanity.[100] Another polarity is that of autonomy and imperialism,

---

96. Dubuisson, *The Western Construction of Religion*, 104.
97. Ibid., 105.
98. Ibid.
99. Ibid.
100. Ibid., 106–12.

which emphasize both the inward and outward movement of Christian holiness and mission.[101]

Noting the dominance and prevalence of these concepts in all aspects of Western life, Dubuisson asserts that "the intellectual equipment of the West was constructed and, above all, shaped in the very particular context of the Christian religion and its theology."[102] Religion emerged as the "cosmographical schema"[103] of the West and, thus, was too unique and specialized to be applied to all cultures.[104] The cosmographical schema, Dubuisson explains, is the "global conception" that defines in its scheme every aspect of life.[105] In this capacity, religion influences the "totality of our ways of conceiving and thinking the world."[106] When this schema was linked to the colonial expansion of Europe, it imposed a way of looking at other cultures that quite naturally viewed them as subsets of their own way of functioning. Insofar as the other cultures did not correspond to the qualities of the dominating culture, they were labelled as deformed, inferior and primitive.[107] Dubuisson adds that "abandoning the idea of religion" would be equivalent in Western thought to "abdicating part of its intellectual hegemony over the world . . . A world bereft of this idea would no longer be a world that was thinkable and thus controllable by Western categories alone . . . Through the idea of religion, the West continuously speaks of itself to itself, even when it speaks of others. For when it does so, it is implicitly in relation to the perfected model that it thinks itself to be. This is narcissistic objectification."[108]

Balagangadhara's point is similar, though broader and thus warrants further attention. He asserts that religion is not universal, but is equated with Christianity. Which is to say, it is possible to talk about religion in referential terms, that 'religion' is a category that refers to something—and that something is Christianity.[109] To begin his theory of religion, Balagangadhara takes Christianity as a "prototypical example" of a religion.[110] In that sense,

---

101. Ibid., 112–15.
102. Ibid., 106.
103. Ibid., 94.
104. Ibid., 116.
105. Ibid., 38.
106. Ibid., 39.
107. Ibid., 112–14.
108. Ibid., 94–95.
109. The following section is adapted from an earlier article I wrote. See Kumar, "Ritual Is Not Religion," 237–46.
110. Balagangadhara, *The Heathen in His Blindness*, 316.

for Balagangadhara, religion "must at the least be seen as referring to Christianity—unless we have a theory capable of explaining why it is not so."[111]

Balagangadhara proposes that cultures are differentiated by "configurations of learning," tools the culture uses to go about in the world.[112] A configuration of learning can be seen as the "cultural answer to the biological problem of our survival,"—the way cultures make their environment habitable and how they adapt to their natural and social environment.[113] Similarly, a configuration of learning of a culture is not only identifiable but also replicable—it is passed on from generation to generation. He then goes on to identify religion as the root "configuration of learning" of the West: "Religion is also the root model of order. It generates an attitude and an orientation; it puts constraints on the intellectual and practical energies of a culture; it forms the sense and feeling of relevance and importance; and so forth. It is able to do this because it is the ultimate example of what it is for something to be an account ... it is the basic model which inspires the other explanations."[114]

Religion, therefore, is shown by Balagangadhara to be the way the West understands the cosmos and orders its understanding of the cosmos. Religion emphasizes the act of "knowing about," as wanting to know about and make sense of the world, the cosmos, and humanity's place within the larger scheme of things.[115] Religion is "an explanatorily intelligible account of the Cosmos and itself."[116]

For Balagangadhara, there are four aspects that characterize this religion (and its secular form "worldview")—these are dominant in Christianity (as well as in the other Semitic religions, Islam and Judaism) but are not predominant in Eastern cultures such as India.[117] First is the prioritizing of beliefs and doctrines, to the extent that to understand a religion it is important to know the beliefs. Second is the emphasis on texts, especially texts with the status of revelation or with some sort of sacred connection. Third is the stress on meaningfulness of all life, which is expressed through an overarching explanation of history with its emphasis on the origins of life as well as the *telos* of life, namely the end and purpose of existence. Fourth is an

111. Ibid., 317.
112. Ibid., 463.
113. Ibid., 459.
114. Ibid., 448.
115. Ibid., 384.
116. Ibid.
117. The four points are summarized from chapters 8–10 of Balagangadhara's *The Heathen in His Blindness*.

oppositional tendency, where a religion defines itself in opposition to other beliefs and meanings. Balagangadhara makes a direct connection between these four aspects of religion and Christianity, and argues that Christianity recognizes itself in this portrayal of religion.[118] Furthermore, religion's emphasis on belief, text, historical purpose and opposition differentiate it as a root model of culture from root models seen in other cultures, particularly from performative cultures of the East, especially India. By postulating a connection between belief and action, and emphasizing the meaning (and meaningfulness) of the cosmos, religion is the configuration of learning for the (Semitic) West. India (the East) emphasizes performative actions rather than meaning making—India does not have religion but ritual.[119] Ritual is defined as *meaningless* action: "We have enough now to take the crucial step towards *identifying* the entity that could structure another configuration of learning. It is a structured set of actions that is generic; it could be described as a-intentional, agent-less, and goal-less. Does such an entity exist? Yes. Where? In Asia. What is it? Ritual. Ritual, just like religion, brings about a culturally-specific way of going-about in the world. In a configuration of learning generated by it, performative learning dominates."[120]

Key also to Balagangadhara's argument is to show that Christianity grew alongside the concept of religion. As Christianity developed, it *shaped* the concept of religion to correspond with itself so that any other meaning of religion in ancient cultures was lost. One of the ways Balagangadhara goes about depicting this complex relationship is by showing how Christians used a modified concept of *religio* to their own apologetic advantage. Balagangadhara explains that the early Christian use of the Latin word *religio* was categorically different from the "pagan" *religio*, to the extent that any conversation between the two entities, whether through apologetics or polemics, never occurred on mutual grounds.[121] In particular, Balagangadhara notes that *religio* was a synonym of *traditio* and, only later, with Christian usage, adopted new belief-oriented meanings. The main preoccupation of Greek and subsequently Roman culture, Balagangadhara argues, was the preservation and practice of the people's tradition, which was passed down over generations.[122] It is an interesting phenomenon that the Romans valued *religio*, even though they differed immensely in their beliefs about the gods. Unlike a belief-oriented approach, where right belief determines right

118. Ibid., 317.
119. Ibid., 465.
120. Ibid.
121. Ibid., 42.
122. Ibid., 44–46.

action, the Romans were surprisingly pluralistic (regarding beliefs) and yet consistently practiced their traditions.[123] While "theoretical disquisitions" occurred about gods and *religio*, "the former were not the reasons for the latter."[124] Balagangadhara highlights that beliefs "require no legitimization" save their traditional origin, and that while "philosophical argumentation may establish or prove some opinion . . . it is irrelevant to traditional practice."[125] Religion (*religio*) is what tradition (*traditio*) was all about.[126]

When we see religion as tradition, "as a set of practices transmitted over generations,"[127] it becomes evident why Christians could not accept a self-description within the polytheistic *religio* category. Instead, to legitimize their use of *religio*, Christians emphasized right belief, a concept unheard of in those times.[128] Earlier the Jews had appealed for Jewish legitimacy within the Roman Empire on the basis that their *traditio* was handed over much earlier than the Greeks, under Moses.[129] While the Jews were strange to the Romans, their argument made sense to the Romans. The Christians, however, had no *traditio* of their own without appealing to Jewish *traditio*. The Christians were so odd to the Roman "pagans" that they were even accused of atheism, "lacking religion."[130] Yet how could Christians, without history, traditions, or language, be considered a religion? Balagangadhara shows that Christians "transformed the very question" as they "tried to prove that their doctrines were ancient and therefore true."[131] Arguing further that the doctrines of Moses and Socrates were true since they conformed to ancient Christian doctrines, Christians argued that true doctrines were essential to true practice. Subsequently, by being bearers of true doctrine, Christianity proved itself to be a *religio* precisely because it was not *traditio*.[132] Balagangadhara goes on to show how Christians eventually criticized pagan practices, something that was beyond question simply because it was *traditio*.[133] What Christianity did was to postulate a "link between practices and

---

123. See also Rüpke, "Roman Religion," 180–95.
124. Balagangadhara, *The Heathen in His Blindness*, 42.
125. Ibid.
126. Ibid., 43.
127. Ibid., 46.
128. Ibid., 51.
129. Ibid., 47–48.
130. Ibid., 48.
131. Ibid., 51.
132. Ibid., 55.
133. Ibid.

beliefs," which eventually made the Roman *religio* a subset of the Christian *religio* that could be assessed on the basis of the truth or falsehood of belief.[134]

Accepting the dangers of generalizations, Balagangadhara still asserts that Asian cultures are not belief-oriented and do not need meaning to justify action. Balagangadhara introduces "ritual" as an "a-intentional, agent-less, and goal-less" configuration of learning found in India (and some other Asian cultures).[135]

To respond to an argument that there are similarities between Hindu and Christian rituals, Balagangadhara notes that the meanings (or lack of meaning) associated with the acts make them entirely different entities: "Ritual is not seen as an agent-centered activity. The so-called religious 'rituals' like the Catholic mass—are considered important by those who participate in them because of the liturgy. Some actions are allowed because they are textually guided and interpreted. They are better called liturgical actions, not rituals."[136]

Rituals, for Balagangadhara, are meaningless actions because they are repetitive, without resorting to significance. That is not to say that ritual has no prior meaning or purpose. Balagangadhara points out that ritual is actually an ordering mechanism for culture; among other things it keeps a culture together by its practice. A ritualistic community, as seen in the Roman *religio* earlier, does not need consistent, authoritative or directed belief to give significance or legitimacy. Instead, ritual brings the community together simply because people do it rather than because people believe it.

Another helpful pointer to what Balagangadhara means by religion is to see how he explains the concepts of worship and worldview. Balagangadhara shows how worship is essential to faith in Christian discourse.[137] This connection is established by postulating a strong relation between human beings and God's will, where human actions gain meaning and purpose when determined/governed by God's meaningful and purposeful actions.[138] Religion not only speaks of God's purposes, why human beings exist and what their goal is, but also of how this goal is to be achieved. That is, to specify God's purposes involves giving the reason for the existence of humankind, the goal humankind ought to pursue and the means for achieving it. Worship, thus, is the "means through which [religion] continues to retain its character to the believers. Worship is how faith is sustained;

---

134. Ibid., 56.
135. Ibid., 465.
136. Ibid., 467.
137. Ibid., 369.
138. Ibid., 371.

worship expresses faith. True worship requires faith; worship strengthens faith. Without faith, one cannot truly worship. Without worship though, faith cannot be sustained. In worship, man expresses his faith in God; that is, affirms that he is using the means required to be a part of the purposes of God. In so doing, he is affirming himself as that kind of a creation who is capable of so doing."[139]

Balagangadhara thus shows "why doctrines are a crucial component of religion" because "the means through which God's purposes can be achieved is itself rooted in doctrines."[140] To this extent, worship is an integral concept for religious life and doctrines: "Worship involves seeing the Cosmos as explanatorily intelligible; and doing what is necessary—as the doctrine in question specifies it—in order to continue to experience the cosmos in this way. It is the means for the reproduction of religion because it links anthropology, eschatology, origin etc., to each other. Without such a link, each would fall apart from the other."[141]

Similarly, for Balagangadhara, a worldview is only the secularization of the concept of religion, but not a category different from it.[142] He argues that religion and "worldview" are almost synonyms: "the properties of religion are retained in the description of a world view."[143] Primarily, what makes religion a worldview is precisely what makes something a religion—a meaningful life within a cosmological framework that includes a sense of the beginning and end of history.

Balagangadhara is correct to point out that people came to the East (even India) with the assumption that religion existed, without checking for the possibility of whether religion was a universal category in the first place. By allowing for the possibility that religion may not be a universal, Balagangadhara offers his own alternative.

When Balagangadhara applies this to the theory of religion, his equating religion with Christianity is a helpful starting point because it begins with the common sense of what religion is. However, one of the problems of this view is that it can confine religion to a fixed relationship between Christianity and religion, without the ability to reject this relationship if determined to be untrue. Furthermore, it constructs Christianity into a monolithic type, as if to suggest that in all its multiplicity, Christianity is still

139. Ibid.
140. Ibid.
141. Ibid., 372.
142. See the full discussion of religion and worldview in chapter 10 of Balagangadhara's *The Heathen in His Blindness*.
143. Ibid., 392.

the true example of religion. For instance, to view Christianity as religion fails to recognize the diversity within Christian traditions, especially those that focus less on doctrines and more on praxis. Furthermore, to accept Christianity as religion—especially the kind of religion that Balagangadhara describes—does not answer whether it is consistent to Christianity's self-description. Nor does it clarify, for the Christian, whether religion is a subset of Christianity or whether Christianity is a subset of religion.

Thus, from Dubuisson and Balagangadhara, five ideas about religion and Christianity emerge that need to be addressed. Firstly, the assertion that religion is actually a Christian construction and both categories are aligned to each other. Secondly, religion is shown to be belief-oriented because Christianity is made out to be a predominantly belief-oriented religion. Thirdly, religion is linked to individual subjectivity, with an emphasis on experience and inner conviction. Fourthly, the universalistic tendencies of religion are an expression of Christianity's universalism which are expressed through a "cosmographical schema," the way religion orders the world. Fifthly, religion (and Christianity) is shown to be antagonistic of differences, seeing the world through dualities, where Christianity will always come across as the true religion.

While Christian theologians can draw from the positive implications of religion as providing cosmological meaning much like a worldview, Dubuisson and Balagangadhara's theories are insufficient for how Christians should operate with this category, as a self-description and as a description of others. Furthermore, their theories need to be contested, especially if Christian theologians believe that their assessment of Christianity is incorrect. This challenge calls Christians to reassess, or at least clarify, what they mean by religion, especially in relation to the category of religion. Similarly, if there is indeed a Christian schema that is being employed, Christian theologians must test it to see whether their schemas to construct religion are consistent within the larger theological schema approved by orthodoxy. A Christian theology of religion is urgently needed.

THE PROBLEM OF RELIGION IN THE THEOLOGICAL STUDY OF RELIGION

In view of the general and specific problems facing religion, it is ironic that so few theologians (who claim to interact regularly with religions) have found the concept of religion to be problematic at all. In fact, Christian theologians freely use the category of religion to describe themselves and others, without ever critically reflecting on the category itself. In recent Christian history, we have seen a vast array of literature emerging from theological engagement with religion. Yet there remains a lack of sufficient engagement regarding theoretical issues about religion.

While Christianity has been confronted by those outside itself from its early history,[144] the specific and recent engagement of Christian theologians with other religions has come to be called a theology of religions.[145] This multifaceted exploration of the relationship between the unique Gospel claims, and the equally unique and often persuasive assertions of other "religions," has led to a wide range of theological assertions.[146] These include, Christianity is the superior religion,[147] all religions are equal,[148] and even that "an encounter with religions . . . contributes to the growth of Christian self-identity."[149] Usually theologians understand and explain religion differently, but the category of religion in these theologies invariably applies to one or more of the major world religions.[150] Also, regardless of their denominational flavor, theologies of religions rarely dispute the theory concerning what constitutes a religion. Instead they focus largely upon the theological concepts, belief systems and ethical practices that emerge out of these Christian and non-Christian religions.

---

144. For instance, the early Church father Justin Martyr asserted that the preexistent *logos spermatikos*, the seed of reason, enabled thinkers like Socrates and even some atheists, to reflect the person of Jesus. *First Apology of Justin*, ch. 46, in Roberts and Donaldson, *The Ante-Nicene Fathers*, 324–25.

145. Griffiths suggests that there even exists a systematic theology of religions that features of host of issues related to religions. See Griffiths, "An Evangelical Theology of Religions," 163–64.

146. Dupuis provides an excellent historical survey of attitudes of Christians towards non-Christians. Dupuis, *Jesus Christ at the Encounter of World Religions*.

147. Jan van Lin notes that the Japanese delegation to the International Missionary Conference in Jerusalem, 1928, expressed that Christianity is superior to other religions in its understanding of God, scripture and ethics. Van Lin, *Shaking the Fundamentals*, 78.

148. Hick and Knitter, *The Myth of Christian Uniqueness*.

149. Karkkäinen, *An Introduction to a Theology of Religions*, 23. See also Griffiths, "An Evangelical Theology of Religions," 166, who says that "these approaches can yield the claim that Christians may have something to learn from the non-Christian that Christians do not yet know, something of importance, moreover, to their own understanding of the gospel."

150. The list of major religions include at least Christianity, Islam, Judaism, Hinduism, and Buddhism. For a critical study of the development and Christian use of the phrase "major world religions," see Masuzawa, *The Invention of World Religions*.

An early exponent in the field, Alan Race, refers to the Christian[151] theology of religions as "that area of Christian studies which aims to give some definition and shape to Christian reflection on the theological implications of living in a religiously plural world."[152] He explains that, "Christian theology of religions is the attempt, on the part of Christian theologians, to account theologically for the diversity of the world's religious quest and commitment, a diversity which shows all the signs of continuing to exist, in spite of Christian missions . . . [It] is the endeavor to adumbrate 'some doctrine of other religions,' to evaluate the relationship between the Christian faith and the faith of the other religions."[153]

Since Race, the theologies of religions have diversified by adopting various methodologies which include the ideological-theological, the comparative-dialogical and the ethical-praxis approaches.[154] The most common approach is the ideological-theological approach, which attempts to see religions from within Christian ideas (usually the doctrines of revelation and/or soteriology). The typical quest is to determine the extent (if any) of God's revelation in other religions, whether that revelation is salvific, and through what/whom/how any salvific revelation is mediated. This ideological-theological approach is further divided into other methodologies. Chief among them is the popular tripartite taxonomy—exclusivist, inclusivist and pluralist—that governs theologians' positions about salvation in other religions.[155] Of late, many other taxonomies have emerged which extend the popular taxonomy or completely rework it.[156] However, these theologies invariably

---

151. While Race talks about "Christian" theology of religions, in my own work I presuppose that because I am a Christian my theology of religions will be Christian. I do not undermine other efforts for a theology of religion, such as Hindu or Muslim; however, simply because my focus is upon a Christian theology of religions alone, I refer to it simply as theology of religions without the added adjective.

152. Race, *Christians and Religious Pluralism*, ix.

153. Race goes on to note that this is a "loose" working definition; Race, *Christian and Religious Pluralism*, 2–3,

154. This taxonomy is mine and I use it knowing full well that taxonomies cannot fully capture the complexities of the discipline. This categorization however is helpful to show how I understand the various theological efforts in this field of study and also help me point to the differences in their methods. Needless to say, this taxonomy is based on my readings of the field, and can thus be seen as methodological presuppositions I now bring to my further reading in this field.

155. Race structures his *Christian and Religious Pluralism* chapters along these lines, ultimately supporting the inclusivist approach.

156. For instance, Karkkäinen adapts Dupuis' taxonomy for a theology of religions to include Ecclesiocentrism, Christocentrism, Theocentrism, Realitycentrism. For a discussion on typologies see Karkkäinen, *Introduction to the Theology of Religions*,

focus upon issues of shared and contrasting beliefs and doctrines, many of which are first reflected in the Christian faith.[157] Oftentimes, the theology of religions has looked to establish the uniqueness of Christ.

More recently, Amos Yong, who is disenchanted with Christocentric methodologies, offers a Pneumacentric approach for his theology of religions. Needless to say, both Yong's Pneumacentricism and the other Christocentricisms are predominantly doctrinal in their interaction with religions. The assumptions made by these scholars are that religions exist, they are identifiable and knowable by their beliefs and texts, and that they are able to discourse across similar categories.

One interesting proposal for a theology of religions that recognizes the problem of discourse across various religions is from Mark Heim. Aware that unitary dialogue between religions is impossible because their categories are entirely different, Heim offers a theology of "religious ends." He prioritizes the end-goals of individual religions, where followers of each religion will arrive at their own religion's cosmic end.[158] Heim remains ideological in that he prioritizes the doctrines of eschatology and salvation, and applies it (in a modified manner) to the same ideas present in other religions. Furthermore, he also accepts the framework of religion discourse and only emphasizes how one religion's goal should not negate the others.

The comparative-dialogical approach attempts to bridge the gap, both conceptual and functional, between religions, by comparing and discussing the belief-systems and rituals of other religions with that of Christianity. This approach particularly critiques the one-way traffic of the doctrinal approach and attempts to see the relationship between doctrines. While Samartha has been one of the most prominent proponents of this methodology,[159] a more recent advocate of this method is Michael Barnes, whose stated goal is to *actually* engage in dialogue with people of other religions rather than talk about dialogue.[160] In his effort to be practical, Barnes is even opposed to theoretical reflection on religion and intends to leave "the intractable, yet relatively insignificant, question of the definition of religion to one side,"

165–73.

157. For instance, it's more common to find studies of 'salvation' in the Hindu faith, rather than find Christian studies that seek to find 'reincarnation' in the Christian faith.

158. Heim, *The Depth of the Riches*, 271–96.

159. Samartha, *Courage for Dialogue*.

160. Barnes, *Theology and the Dialogue of Religions*.

and choose the more "practical issue" of a "community of faith seriously committed to engagement with the other."[161]

The ethical-praxis approach critiques static ideological and dialogical approaches that lead nowhere. Instead, it attempts to *develop* a theology of religions for the *improved* understanding of all religions, even to the extent that it promotes *working together* with other religions for a better world/society.[162] The difference between the comparative-dialogical approach and the ethical-praxis approach is small but evident through the intentional constructive attempt of this approach. An early form of construction was evident in John Hick, who provided a theological paradigm shift away from the Christocentric/Trinitarian views of God to the theocentric view which, for Hick, presented a morally superior starting point for a new theology of religions on *equal* footing.[163] Another popular construction has been offered by Catholic theologian, Hans Küng, who calls for a "global ethical" that he believes is not contradictory to Christian claims.[164] Both Hick and Küng are shown to adopt this method because they attempt to build a better theology of religions with ethical and practical principles guiding them. A more recent instance of this constructionist tendency is evident in Pia Gyger who proposes that the "treasure of plurality can become fruitful" for "new humanity."[165] We also have a growing number of ecotheologians that *use* religion to highlight the need for an environmental ethic.

One could also group theologies of religions with antireligion tendencies, where religion is seen as oppressive and needs to be overcome.[166] This confrontationalist, even deconstructive, type of the ethical-praxis approach to a theology of religions is seen when a theology of religions is practiced in opposition to traditional/dominant religious spheres. This is most apparent in post-Christian feminist writings, especially of Mary Daly and Daphne Hampson.[167] Indian examples of this method are evident in Dalit theologies

---

161. Ibid., 10.

162. This was evident as early as the Jerusalem Missionary Conference in 1928, where the driving force was the need for religions to come together to fight against the challenges of secularism-atheism.

163. See for instance Hick, *God and the Universe of Faiths*, as well as Hick, *God Has Many Names*.

164. See Küng, *Global Responsibility*, 1.

165. Gyger, "The religions and the birth of a new humanity," 90–96. See also Ward, *Religion and Community*.

166. Usually the Feminist and Dalit theologies that use 'hermeneutics of suspicion' to challenge traditional readings of the biblical and other religious text to offer counter-religious alternatives.

167. See Daly, *Beyond God the Father*; and Hampson, *After Christianity*.

that strongly reject Brahmanical religion (and its Christian derivatives) and aim to recover/develop their own traditions in opposition to the dominant religion.[168] Also, some Dalit theologies have been known to use religion as a "revolutionary force."[169]

Another kind of theology of religions has also emerged, particularly focused (though not exclusively) upon the methodology itself. The focus has shifted onto metatheological issues such as the philosophy of language or hermeneutics. Thus, George Lindbeck is able to propose a "cultural-linguistic" outlook to religion, to the extent that religions "resemble languages"[170] and "are thought of primarily as different idioms of construing reality, expressing experience, and ordering life."[171] With such an approach, the new questions that emerge can include the impossibility of communication within linguistically diverse traditions or even the importance of "narrative" theologies in dealing with other narratives. George Sumner offers another methodological reorientation, by arguing for "final primacy" as the "pattern" for Christian discourse with other religions, especially with an emphasis on retrospective narratives.[172] From the Indian context, Narendra Singh proposes the use of "dialectical method" to engage with religious traditions.[173]

Naturally these approaches to theology of religions are often interrelated, can use common sources and often have similar goals. Nevertheless, they discover some form of essentialist, substantive or functional similarity between religions and the focus is evidently upon the theology that arises from the engagement. Rarely is there any theological engagement on what religion is, or whether 'religion' applies to what they think religion applies to. Nor is there sufficient thinking on how a theology of religions is a (Christian) religious act. In fact, it is more common for theologians of religions to do just as Barnes recommends: to leave the "insignificant" questions of religion in favor of more practical issues.[174]

Yet, are not the theoretical problems facing religion practical problems? Especially if Christian theological conceptions of religion are importing ideological presuppositions that either misunderstand other people or

---

168. See for instance, Mosse, "The Politics of Religious Synthesis," 85–107, which briefly touches upon this conflict.

169. Thumma, *Dalit Liberation Theology*, 12–38.

170. Lindbeck, *The Nature of Doctrine*, 18.

171. Ibid., 47–48.

172. Sumner, *The First and the Last*.

173. Singh, *A Christian Theology of Religions*.

174. Barnes, *Theology and the Dialogue of Religions*, 10.

impose frameworks that they are just not willing to accept?[175] It is perhaps safer to admit that Christian theological discourse needs both a method of praxis, in dealing directly with people, and a theory of the tools used to understand them.

Of course, it would also be naive to suggest that none of these theologians attempt definitions of religion. In fact, as we have seen, many offer definitions, and all theologians who use the category of religion are already operating with a theory of religion, whether stated or not. Out of the theologians who do attempt definitions, most attempt mainly a clarification of the nature of religion rather than treat the concept of religion itself as problematic. Most also fail to ask whether religion even exists universally, and hardly anyone questions whether theology warrants discourse over the nature of religion in the first place. In addition, it is rare to see theologians develop a *theological* definition of religion and it is more common to adopt a popular definition from the social sciences and apply it to theology. For instance, Aragon promisingly begins his theology of religions with the question, "What is religion?" However, instead of discussing it like a question to be answered, he straightaway adopts Roger Schmidt's definition of religion and explains why it is a good one.[176] Similarly, Brockman confesses, "I understand religion to be a set of beliefs, perspectives, practices, and/or ways of living by which participants orient themselves with respect to questions of ultimate significance (e.g., life/death, good/evil, reality/illusion). Brockman adds, "Insofar as all persons are concerned with such questions, all persons are religious, even if they do not self-identify as such."[177]

Brockman's definition is typical of definitions of religion today,[178] and notably assumes that religion exists universally, and is used for creative purposes across all cultures. Similarly, Carl Braaten unassumingly states: "What is religion? It is the human response to divine revelation. It may be distorted, it may be deficient, it may be idolatrous, but whatever and wherever it is, it is not nothing. It is certainly not nothing but lies and falsehood. There is truth, beauty, and goodness—as well as morality and civility—in all the religions

---

175. For deeper engagement with this idea, see Goodchild, *Difference in Philosophy of Religion*. This book contains many articles by western and non-western scholars who critique traditional notions of philosophy of religion, and are especially critical of the related concepts of 'religion' that bring with them problematic ideologies when viewing non-western cultures.

176. Aragon, "Toward an Asian Evangelical Theology of Religions," 25–26.

177. Brockman, "Turning to Religious Others," n. 5, 3.

178. See for instance Clayton Crockett who also defines religion as an 'orientation.' Crockett, "On the Disorientation of the Study of Religion," 1–14.

of humanity. But all of that, no matter how admirable and awesome, does not add up to the special revelation God has given in the Bible."[179]

Like many theologians before and after them, these theologians make theological claims about the cosmos but provide no theological justification for their definitions of religion, which in effect are either founded on the "evidence" provided by anthropologists and sociologists or are simply repetitions of popular and unsubstantiated *beliefs* about religion. Needless to add, these definitions lack credibility and are prone to criticism.

This is not to say that there has been no theological reflection on what religion is. From the Western perspective, Paul Tillich devotes his entire *What is Religion* to answer the question, where he prefers a philosophy of religion to a theology of religion, preferring scientific objectivity above theological subjectivity.[180] A popular idea emerging out of Tillich is that religion is an "ultimate concern."[181] While Tillich's view has allowed religion to be understood and used outside the framework of religious studies,[182] the theological nature of his inquiry is evident since Tillich's ultimate concern is a *special* concern. Smith rightly draws attention to the theological nature of this view of religion by stating that in Tillich's definition is also embedded the idea of "insufficient, inadequate, and false convictions of 'ultimacy.'"[183] Evidently, Tillich is operating with an ethical view of the world, which is influenced by his Christian heritage.

From the Indian context, Samartha urges an understanding of what religion is; he even recommends an interdisciplinary approach for the study of religion, admitting that "we have a long way to achieve healthy interaction between different disciplines of theological education."[184] He feels that the traditional missiological approach to religion has a "hidden agenda" that aims to show the "inadequacy of other religions."[185] He, therefore, recommends the balance of secular approaches to the study of religion, namely the phenomenological, sociological-anthropological and dialogical approaches.[186] These approaches are geared to inculcate objectivity primarily aiding the student of religion to appreciate the religion in its own context on its own terms. For instance using the sociological/anthropological approach

---

179. Braaten, "The Christian Faith in an Inter-Faith Context," 234–35.
180. Tillich, *What is Religion?*
181. Tillich, *Theology of Culture,* 7–8.
182. For instance see McBride, "Tillich in an Alice-in-wonderland World," 516–17.
183. Smith, *Relating Religion,* 193.
184. Samartha, "Dialogue in a Religiously Plural Society," 5.
185. Ibid.
186. Ibid., 5–6.

Samartha says, "The study of rituals and symbols in relation to the cultural pattern of a particular society or group of people has brought out salient features to appreciate certain practices of people which once were considered superstitious."[187]

Commendably, Samartha does not want to take the assumptions about religion for granted and even senses problems in prevailing (missionary) perceptions of religion. Nevertheless, Samartha has an agenda of his own. While critiquing the missionary method of negative judgments of other religions, he is proposing that our study of religion should avoid a "negative attitude to other religions but [have] a clear view of their potentials and positive values."[188] Furthermore, he states that, with religion, one "could profitably be mobilized for the present fight against injustice and oppression."[189] Samartha clearly has a bias towards the positive value of religion and, thus, his position is dangerously similar to those of the missionaries he critiques. While he does call for the study of religion, he has actually made up his mind about religion before he begins his study. In effect, this shows how deeply ingrained his preconceived notions about religion really are, and also draws attention to the theological categories that influence his supposed objective discovery of religion.

More recently, noted evangelical scholar Alister McGrath correctly identifies religion as a "false universal."[190] McGrath suggests that religion belongs to the "universals of classification" rather than the "universals of content," which is to say that religion does not share content across cultures as much as "common patterns."[191] However McGrath still functions within a theory of religion by stating that while a universal singular religion does not exist, "individual religions exist."[192] In addition, he distinguishes nonreligion from religion (Confucianism is not a religion but a "philosophy of life") and religion from worldview, without offering a (theological) definition of religion that would help us justify these categories.[193]

From the Christian theologians' point of view, there is little guidance on whether to agree or disagree with Tillich and Samartha. Also, while we may agree with McGrath, we are still left with the need for a theological justification for his "religion of classification." The fact remains that most

187. Ibid.
188. Ibid., 4.
189. Ibid.
190. McGrath, *The Passionate Intellect*, 151.
191. Ibid.
192. Ibid.
193. Ibid., 151–52.

theologians of religions simply accept that religions exist, or use uncritical assumptions to develop their own views of religion. These theologians go on to believe that they, along with their readers, understand what is being talked about, and spend most of their theological effort engaging with what they think is uncontested reality. These theologians shy away from defining religion and prefer *practical* interaction, allowing general meanings of religion to prevail.

As we have seen, however, theories of religion have multiple problems. Simply because many people believe them does not make these theories valid. Theologians are still left with the need to be clear about what they are talking about. While it is appealing to discuss religion in a common sense way, theologians need to rely on something more than just the democratic principle of meaning.

The Need to Clarify a Theology of "What"

Paul Griffiths is correct in pointing out the "surprising absence" in theologians of religions,[194] of an answer to a fundamental question of their discipline: "A theology of *what?*"[195] The paucity of biblical evidence has consequences for the field of study, as he remarks:

> The very category 'religion,' whether used as a singular label for a type, or in the plural for various tokens of that type, raises some difficult questions for Christian theologians. The fact that the category itself raises questions should be especially obvious for evangelicals, since it is a term of almost no importance in Scripture ... *Religion,* then, is a term of almost no scriptural importance, and where it is used it bears few or no similarities to standard modern usage. This should raise questions, and I would very much like to hear more about why these questions were not addressed explicitly...[196]

Furthermore, Griffiths suggests that the current concept of religion has roots, not in the Bible but in the Enlightenment, and was generated by scholars who had "no Christian interests and did not use a Christian vocabulary."[197] As a result, he suggests that Evangelicals studying religion or religions must "consider more deeply ... what it is they're theologizing

---

194. Particularly the ones writing in Stackhouse, *No Other Gods Before Me?*
195. Griffiths, "An Evangelical Theology of Religions," 163–64.
196. Ibid., 164.
197. Ibid., 164–65.

about" and discover authentic "Christian language" to discuss these things, because otherwise it is likely that "commitments problematic for Christians will be smuggled into the discussion."[198]

Griffiths further points to how many Christians find the association of Christianity with religion problematic, largely because it implies "that Christianity is a species of a genus" which is to say it is just another type of religion, like Islam or Buddhism.[199] Griffiths claims that Christians are rightly offended by this because it is "against Christianity's self-understanding as a sui generis phenomenon."[200] Griffiths asserts that Christians,

> count themselves as the community of those gathered in public worship of the triune God, responsive in their worship to the incarnation, death, and resurrection ... On this view what is significant about Christianity is not what it shares with the religions ... but precisely what it does not. One version of this point can be seen in John Wycliff's fourteenth-century objections to calling Christianity a religion ... A more sophisticated one is argued by Karl Barth ... who identifies religion ... with human piety. He opposes piety to God's revelatory action, which has picked out the Christian religion ... for transfiguration into truth...[201]

Griffiths thus goes on to propose that Christians should avoid the use of the term 'religion':

> Given all these difficulties, it may reasonably be doubted that a concept of religion usable for Christian thought can be salvaged. One is scarcely needed for biblical exegesis, and its introduction into Christian theological thought tends to create more problems than it solves. The usual premodern antonym of *religio* is *superstitio* ... On this understanding, there are not many religions: there is only (true) religion and its simulacra, which are all characterized by superstitious impieties of various kinds. This is likely to prove a more productive understanding for Christian thought than the problematic modern synthesis.[202]

Ironically Griffiths, in a separate article, suggests that Christians should "baptize the concept of religion and so make it available for proper

---

198. Ibid., 165.
199. Griffiths, "Religion," 674.
200. Ibid.
201. Ibid.
202. Ibid., 675.

Christian uses."²⁰³ He fails to follow through with his own proposal for a *theological* definition and instead offers a definition of religion which is intentionally abstracted from the Christian context. His definition of religion is largely descriptive in that he calls religion an "account of things" that embraces all other accounts and has central importance and is "not capable of being surpassed or subsumed by other accounts."²⁰⁴ One could argue that Griffiths' own account smuggles in Western objective-textual understandings of religion, for it is not hard to see how Griffiths' definition would fail to capture how a Hindu grasps his/her own culture.

Notwithstanding this, theologians should consider the weight of his overall suggestion that theologians of religions do need to investigate what *religion* actually is. Neither should this distract from Griffiths' warning that for theologians of religions to be blasé about what religion is, is to be naive about the nature of their own discipline.

METHODOLOGY FOR THIS STUDY

Keeping in mind the challenges arising from Dubuisson/Balagangadhara and Griffiths, there is an urgent need for theologians to think critically *and* theologically about what religion is. Evidently, theologians have brought in more than just their Christian sources in looking at religion, and naturally so. Yet, in adopting theories of religions from sources that are often contrary to other theological sources, or even potentially problematic, there is an obvious danger that the theologians' own operations with religion would be contradictory and ill-founded. Not only do theologians need clarity about the nature and use of religion, but they (we) are also in need of criteria to formulate views about religion.

In view of the above, a more drastic and theological response to understanding religion, especially in the context of the contemporary debate, is needed. The theology of religions is in need of a method to determine not only what religion is, but also how to determine what view is right or wrong. I propose that what we need is a *theology of religion*, which I suggest is a methodology that can help address these concerns.

Thus, the aim of my study is to arrive at a theological answer to the question, "What is religion?" To do this, I look at how religion was addressed by an Indian theologian, Chenchiah. In addition, in view of the biblical and theological perspectives (historical and contemporary) of religion, I propose a method by which Christian theologians can address religion today.

203. Griffiths, "An Evangelical Theology of Religions," 165.
204. Griffiths, "Religion," 31–44.

My hope is that this theology of religion will be consistent with theological sources and relevant to the lived reality of contemporary Christian society.

To achieve this aim, I have adopted certain methodological procedures. My study combines a historical and theological approach, where I look at Chenchiah's theology and the historical context within which his thought emerged. In addition, my critical engagement with the concept of religion is based on a combination of secular theories, biblical studies and theological perspectives. In terms of secular studies, I adopt only a few of the leading theorists of religion, mainly because they resonate with my work. In terms of biblical studies, I adopt a word study approach, mainly to highlight that the concept of religion is aligned with a concept of piety and worship. In particular, my biblical methodology is not primarily exegetical; it seeks to broaden the concept of religion by the retranslation of the Greek words that have been translated as religion in English. In terms of theology, I have used various scholars who align with the confessional approach to theology, particularly focusing upon Augustine.

Now, before proceeding, I must clarify what I mean by a theology of religion.

What Is Theology of Religion?

A theology of religion is seen as distinct from a theory of religion as well as from a theology of religions. It provides both a theological theory of religion as well as definitional clarity for a theology of religions.

A theory of religion emerges out of the philosophical discipline of reflecting on the nature of the word "religion," without religious language or norms necessarily informing that reflection. Thus, even though a theory of religion is aware of the God-talk of various people, the theory itself is not informed by that (or the philosopher's) God-talk.

In contrast, a theology of religion is a definition of religion that emerges out of God-talk, a theory that takes the religion's own formulation of what is important to draw out a meaning for religion. In other words, a theology of religion is a theological theory of religion. Furthermore, a Christian theology of religion is a view of religion that emerges out of an engagement with Christian sources and criteria.

We must also distinguish a theology of religion from a theology of religions. Evidently, this distinction is not always made clear in Christian literature, where most theologians use theology of religion and theology of religions interchangeably.

It is rather common in theological scholarship to view a *theology of religion* as synonymous with a theology of religions. K. P. Aleaz uses the term "theology of religion/s" in his table of contents, but goes on to talk about a theology of religions.[205] Paul Knitter uses the terms "theology of religion" and "theology of religions" interchangeably, though he prefers the plural.[206] Similarly, Dale Little defines "theology of religion" in the same way a theology of religions could be defined, as "A theology [which] develops a theological understanding and description of non-Christian religious issues."[207] Elsewhere, Bernhardt's "theology of religion" is a theological enterprise of dialogue and relations with religions which, as we have seen above, is the goal of a theology of religions.[208] Clearly, not making a distinction between a theology of religion and a theology of religions is unhelpful. For instance, if we were to accept Bernhardt's (as well as other scholars') singular usage to refer to all Christian discourse with/about religions, we are still left with questions pertaining to how these scholars arrive at their definitions of religion, that serve as the normative foundations for their theological discourse with other "religions."

Another group of theologians accept a unique place for a theology of religion but define it as a constructive exercise to develop a singular theology from the religions. Reflected in the works of Ernest Troeltsch and Wilfred Cantwell Smith, this view is systematized in Swidler's *Towards a Universal Theology of Religion*.[209] The essays in Swidler's compilation propose a singular theology to challenge the limited perspectivalism of religious pluralism, to the extent that a theology of religion is seen as distinct from a theology of religions, and perhaps even greater in its task. More recently, this kind of thinking has been expressed by Frank Whaling, who describes a theology of religion "as a global enterprise that is based on transcending particularities."[210] He states that a "theology of religion can be seen to be a more universal matter. It can involve the search for a theology of religion that is not preceded by a particular adjective . . . It attempts to express the reality of what it says, namely that it is a theology of religion as such, rather than a particular theology of religion."[211]

---

205. Aleaz, *Theology of Religions*.
206. Knitter, *Introducing Theology of Religions*, 3.
207. Little, "The Significance of Theology of the Holy Spirit," 6.
208. Bernhardt, "Religion: Theological Factors," 577–78.
209. Swidler, *Toward a Universal Theology of Religion*.
210. Whaling, "Theological Approaches," 261–62.
211. Ibid., 253.

It is easy to sympathize with Whaling's concern while also noting the similarity this method and the ethical-praxis approach of a theology of religions. Similar to Küng, who wanted to develop a global ethic, Whaling attempts a theology that derives from the various religions, to become a singular (united) enterprise. Such a theology of religion changes little if we change its name to a theology of religions. Whaling does not offer an understanding of what religion is and instead only wants to highlight a universal *theology* that is derived from religions. This method clearly fails to ask and answer *how* one is to define the object of this theology, namely religion.

There are a few theologians who recognize the importance of distinguishing a theology of religion from a theology of religions. In his seminal and influential study on theology of religious pluralism, Dupuis provides a unique (and helpful) distinction between a theology of religion and a theology of religions. He explains that the "theology of religion asks what religion is and seeks, in the light of Christian faith, to interpret the universal religious experience of humankind; it further studies the relationship between revelation and faith, faith and religion, and faith and salvation."[212]

In contrast, a theology of religions, particularly in its Christian form, "studies the various traditions in the context of the history of salvation and in their relationship to the mystery of Jesus Christ and the Christian Church."[213] For Dupuis, "The questions on hand then are: How do the circumstances in which people live their religious life fit into God's one plan of salvation for humankind? What meaning in God's eyes—insofar as we may claim to penetrate God's secrets—has the reality of religious pluralism in the world, of which humankind (and Christianity within it) has acquired today a new consciousness?"[214]

Furthermore, a theology of religions embraces all the religious traditions and "relates it to the Christian mystery; to the event of Jesus Christ which is at the heart of the Christian faith."[215]

While Dupuis asserts that a theology of religion and a theology of religions are related organically, even inseparable, he goes on to say that since spiritual experiences are "naturally embodied in a religious tradition—made up of creed, cult, and moral code—the theology of religion becomes in turn a theology of religions."[216] By this he means that a Christian theology of religion cannot remain in the theoretical field of concepts alone but must study

---

212. Dupuis, *Christian Theology of Religious Pluralism*, 7.
213. Ibid., 8.
214. Ibid.
215. Ibid., 9.
216. Ibid., 8.

the various traditions in the context of the history of salvation.[217] Dupuis is disenchanted with the "number of current definitions of religion and of religious experience" and states that his own work "does not intend to enter into such abstract discussions."[218] Dupuis wants to ask "concrete questions" that deal directly with the "religious experience actually lived by people in the context of their respective religious traditions" and "what matters is not definitions but people's living experience."[219] In effect, with this brief introduction, Dupuis devotes the remainder of his opus to issues pertaining to Christian interaction with other religions, specifically using the rubric of religious pluralism. Dupuis' explanation of difference is in the context of arguing for the need to go beyond a theology of religion toward a theology of religions, and even to a theology of religious pluralism.

Clearly, Dupuis has adopted the common-sense approach that relates to religions in a theological and dialogical manner. Nevertheless, his brief yet significant demarcation gives later theologians, such as Karkkäinen,[220] a way forward in theologically demarcating between definition and practice, even as they still follow the *practical* route.

Amos Yong defends his use of the plural theology of religions over the singular theology of religion.[221] He represents the theology of religion as the "futile search for a theological essence of religion" and opines that it is more appropriate for theologians to account for both the "personal experience of faith"[222] as well as the "concrete manifestations of communities in pursuit of faithful living."[223] Perhaps Yong misunderstands the scope of a theology of religion, which is better expressed by Dupuis. Yet both Dupuis and Yong rightly make a distinction between the two theological approaches to religion.

Even though Davies makes no distinction between a theology of religion and a theology of religions, he is still on the right track by observing two functions of a theology of religions: "the theology of religions helps theologians interpret religion in much the same way as sociological or psychological theories help social scientists understand religion. One difference, however, is that it also often serves to relate a theologian's own tradition to the many 'other' religions in the world. This dual purpose adds a

217. Ibid.
218. Ibid.
219. Ibid.
220. Karkkäinen, *An Introduction to a Theology of Religions*, 25–26.
221. Yong, *Discerning the Spirit(s)*, 23.
222. Yong terms this as the position of Wilfred Cantwell Smith.
223. Yong, *Discerning the Spirit(s)*, 23.

degree of complexity to the theology of religion precisely because it involves a kind of self-reflection or self-analysis within the overall task."[224]

Evidently, Christian theologians need to be clear about what they (we) mean by religion, especially in the context of the contemporary debate against definitions of religion. Not surprisingly, many theologians neither see the need for definitions, nor do they feel the need for a separate theological methodology for arriving at those definitions. Nevertheless, as we have seen above, the call for an understanding of what religion is, warrants special theological attention. I prefer Jacques Dupuis' distinction between a theology of religion and a theology of religions. This is why I propose that, in addition to a theology of religions, a theology of religion is also needed. I suggest that a theology of religion is a methodology to understand religion theologically. The awareness that there is indeed a place for theological engagement with definitions is crucial in gaining clarity about what a theology of religion is and what it does.

In effect, a theology of religion is a theological theory of religion that uses theological norms while also being mindful of its impact on a theology of religions. A theology of religion thus attempts three things. First, it seeks to determine, using theological sources, whether religion is a valid category. Second, assuming that the first is answered in the affirmative, a theology of religion seeks to define religion by understanding the theological view of religion. This implies an exploration into how Christian theology would define the category of religion and, relatedly, what kind of theological assertions would influence the category of religion. Third, a theology of religion seeks to determine the extent to which the category 'religion' helps in Christian self-understanding and in the understanding of others. With this in view, we are now ready to see how I develop a theology of religion in this study.

Approaches to Chenchiah

To help me answer the question, "What is religion," I use the work of Pandipeddi Chenchiah. Chenchiah was a Hindu convert and a lawyer who was the epitome of an Indian lay theologian in the early twentieth century. He wrote several important articles that challenged his generation to "rethink" its Christianity in the pre-Independence era. Chenchiah was also one of the earliest Indian theologians to make a theological assertion about what religion was. Of course, he did not consciously write a theology of religion or a theology of religions, because its formal discourse did not exist back in

224. Davies, "The Theology of Religion," 7.

his day. Furthermore, Chenchiah's concerns were primarily theological; his effort was to seek and understand Christ and what he means to humanity, rather than provide a framework for discourse between multiple religions. Nevertheless, I find that Chenchiah was not only interested in theology, but was acutely aware of the religious context within which theology existed. Chenchiah used his theology of religion as a stepping stone towards his Christological formulations, and his views of religion provide a unique access to theological discourse about religion.

There is not much research done on Chenchiah, and even less on Chenchiah's theology of religion/s. Usually Chenchiah research focuses upon his Christology.[225] While I will be interacting with a larger list of theologians who addressed Chenchiah in my later chapters, a few notable Chenchiah scholars are listed below.

Robin Boyd's popular text book *Introduction to Christian Theology* may be introductory, but it is most helpful and perceptive in providing a broad overview of Chenchiah's theology.[226] However, while Boyd rightly identifies that Chenchiah's work is not systematic,[227] Boyd still finds that Chenchiah's "whole theology is oriented towards *new* creation, towards what man becomes in Christ."[228] His chapter on Chenchiah features Chenchiah's understanding of *major* Christian doctrines, which include Christology, sin, the church and so forth, seen through the dominant "new creation" motif. However, Boyd fails to mention anything of Chenchiah's view of religion, though he does mention Chenchiah's use of Hinduism in his theology[229] as well as his views about Hinduism *vis-á-vis* Christianity.[230] Of course, during Boyd's time, the theological study of religion was not so prominent or seemingly pertinent. Yet it remains to be asked whether Chenchiah's view of "what is religion" is important for Chenchiah's theology, especially his

---

225. For instance see, Jathanna, *The Decisiveness of the Christ-Event*; Varughese, "Christology in the Writings of Pandipeddi Chenchiah and Raimundo Panikkar"; Boyd, *Introduction to Indian Christian Theology*; and Boyd, "The Philosophical Context of Indian Christian Theology with Special Reference to P. Chenchiah," 47–69.

226. In conjunction with his lesser known article on Chenchiah, Boyd is an important reference point to understand Chenchiah, even today. Boyd, "The Philosophical Context of Indian Christian Theology with Special Reference to P. Chenchiah," 47–69.

227. Ibid., 147.

228. Ibid., 151. Note also the title of his chapter, "The Theology of New Creation: P. Chenchiah."

229. Ibid., 158–59.

230. Ibid., 163.

What Is Religion?

theology of religions. If it is so, as I argue,[231] then Boyd certainly misses an important part of Chenchiah's own theological framework.

The other Chenchiah textbook of sorts is Thangasamy's compilation of Chenchiah's articles.[232] Thangasamy has collected excerpts from Chenchiah's work, making them accessible to modern readers.[233] Thangasamy's book begins with a detailed study of Chenchiah's theology and, unlike Boyd, he focuses on more than just his theological (doctrinal) assertions. It is here that we gain a glimpse not only of Chenchiah's wide range of writing, but also of the importance of religion in Chenchiah's thinking. For instance, Thangasamy notes that even though Chenchiah's "writings cover a wide range of subjects," his "main interest . . . was religious."[234] In fact, Thangasamy is correct in stating: "Chenchiah's approach to the Christian religion . . . is based on his conviction that Jesus and the New Creation in Him form the only essence of Christianity . . . Christianity as religion . . . [is] relative and [has] to be evaluated in terms of [its] power to point to . . . that essence."[235]

Furthermore, Thangasamy draws attention to how, for Chenchiah, "Christianity is no better and no worse than other religions."[236] While these and other such remarks do not directly inform us about Chenchiah's theology of religion, still Thangasamy clearly draws our attention to the significance of the category of religion in Chenchiah's theological discourse.

Varughese, who opts to study Chenchiah's Christology, draws attention to how Chenchiah "clearly attempts to communicate the uniqueness of Christ to the Hindu mind."[237] Similarly, he states that Christological reflection in India "must take into account the church of Jesus Christ around the world and the long history of religious life in India."[238] Yet, unlike Thangasamy before him, Varughese does not make a connection between Chenchiah's view of religion and his Christology. I note this because Chenchiah's Christological formulations like the "raw fact of Christ" and even incarnation, two themes that Varughese pays special attention to, are referenced heavily in and through Chenchiah's view of religion. While it is difficult to

---

231. While currently it remains a presupposition, I intend to argue that Chenchiah's theology of religion is indeed important for his overall theological framework.

232. Thangasamy, *The Theology of Chenchiah*.

233. All of Chenchiah's full-text articles are available through Microfilms available at SAIACS and UTC libraries.

234. Thangasamy, *Theology of Chenchiah*, xvii.

235. Ibid., 24.

236. Ibid., 25.

237. Varughese, "Christology in the Writings," ii.

238. Ibid., 1.

say which comes first, whether Chenchiah's view of religion or his Christology, it is safe to assert that they are both related.

In contrast to Varughese, K.C. Abraham at least attempts to link Chenchiah's ethics with Chenchiah's view of religion. Abraham shows how Chenchiah relates the "good news of Jesus Christ and the new life which the people in India seek through their religion and culture."[239] Abraham also notes how the idea of new life is extended through Chenchiah's concept of "new creation" and subsequently shows how "religion primarily seeks to understand the purpose of creation."[240] Abraham's interest in Chenchiah's theology of religion is minimal, but sufficient to draw attention to a possible connection between the concept of religion with Chenchiah's overall theological enterprise.

Another Chenchiah scholar, O.V. Jathanna, offers some of the most insightful descriptions and assessments of Chenchiah's Christology. His extensive work featuring four scholars, is unparalleled in terms of depth and scholarship. Even though Chenchiah forms only one part of his opus, Jathanna is still extremely thorough in reporting Chenchiah's thought, to the extent that Jathanna extensively deals with Chenchiah's theology of religion (though he does not call it that). Before he gets to Chenchiah's Christology, Jathanna looks at Chenchiah's proposed relationship between Christianity and other religions (which as we have seen, falls under a theology of religions),[241] Chenchiah's concept of religion,[242] and Chenchiah's idea of Christianity.[243]

Regardless of the merits of Jathanna's work, a problem that emerges is that Jathanna offers limited critique of Chenchiah's view of religion, and when Jathanna does critique Chenchiah, there are no substantiated criteria by which to judge whether Chenchiah's view of religion was right or wrong. This is evident, for instance when Jathanna critiques Chenchiah's view of religion for "its emphasis on techniques and realization" which "makes religion a parallel enterprise to the physical sciences."[244] Jathanna goes on to say that this is wrong because "the religious sphere lies in the supra-natural level," suggesting that the religious sphere requires a perhaps transscientific methodology.[245] Obviously one could ask Jathanna where he got his theory

239. Abraham, "Interpreting Christian Social Ethics," 38.
240. Ibid., 44.
241. Jathanna, *The Decisiveness of the Christ-Event*, 359–70.
242. Ibid., 370–76.
243. Ibid., 376–83.
244. Ibid., 414.
245. Ibid.

44 What Is Religion?

that the religious sphere lies in the "supra-natural level," especially since Jathanna's work does not establish any criteria or theological grounding to make this claim. Without substantiating his own theory of religion, Jathanna has imposed his subconscious belief about religion onto Chenchiah.

Devasahayam provides a helpful look at Chenchiah's use of the Bible. Devasahayam is clued in to the importance of religion for Chenchiah and extensively treats Chenchiah's theology of religions (especially focusing upon the issue of salvation outside Christianity), though there is also a discussion on his theology of religion. Like Jathanna, he too makes a mistake in viewing Chenchiah's theology of religion as a dichotomy between pure religion and temple religion, even though there is no evidence of the phrase "pure religion" in the cited text.[246] Neither does Devasahayam offer any critique of Chenchiah's theology of religion; he aims to be primarily descriptive, and thus offers us no way of gauging whether Chenchiah is helpful or unhelpful.

Through my study of Chenchiah, particularly in Chapter 3, I will show that Chenchiah's discourse on religion is an important part of Chenchiah's theology. There is also a need to develop a critical framework to apply to Chenchiah's theology of religion, as the basis for judging whether his view of religion is right or not. This I do in Chapters 4 and 5. I arrive at the view that while Chenchiah's theology is fraught with inconsistencies, his theology of religion offers valuable methodological insights for the formulation of a theology of religion today.

How Does This Study Differ from Other Similar Projects

We have already seen how my work will differ from various other studies of Chenchiah. However, in the overall scheme of attempting a theological answer to the question of religion, at least four PhD dissertations have attempted to gain theological clarity about the category of religion in recent years.

First, Heung-Gyu Kim's concerns resonate with my own.[247] Kim rightly notes that "Many contemporary theologians are employing the nomenclature 'theology of religions' loosely without making any substantial definition or clarification of its prolegomenon issues."[248] Furthermore, Kim is also correct in pointing to the primal need for clarity regarding the

---

246. Devasahayam, "Role of the Bible," 241.
247. Kim, "Prolegomena to a Christian Theology of Religions," 20–48.
248. Ibid., 3.

concepts of religion and religions.[249] However, in his chapter two, while he acknowledges the "construction" of religion during the Enlightenment,[250] he ironically adopts a scientific definition of religion. While the first part of his chapter denies the essence of religion, even pointing to the dangers of "covert Christianizing" that the concept of religion can have,[251] in the next part he goes on to offer "family resemblance" as a definition of religion using Geertz' definition of religion as a controlling genus.[252] If Kim had attempted a *theological* definition of religion, then he would have been on the right track. However, in providing no theological foundation or engagement with his definition for a theology of religion, Kim makes a fundamental error in his own prolegomena. By offering a theological foundation for the definition of religion in my work, this is one error I hope to avoid.

I find much affinity with Joshua Braley's study, especially in his methodological use of Jonathan Smith's definition of religion. His key proposal, in terms of a theory of religion, is that religion is not about presence but about representation, implying that it is better to conceive of religion as a human cultural construction of how things are viewed rather than the actual presence of God and his activity.[253] However, Braley's work has a purpose that is different from my own. His intention is to see how *theology* can be changed by adopting religious studies, particularly Jonathan Smith's view of religion.[254] In contrast, I seek how theologians can look at, even transform the concept *religion*. The inverse attention naturally means that our paths diverge.

Nongbri's study on the problematic use of the concept of religion in studying the Bible also shares similar concerns. Much of Nongbri's dissertation details how the category of religion has been constructed,[255] and he shows how it has been falsely applied to understand Pauline discourses, especially in creating a contrast between Paul's religion and Judaism.[256] His final goal is to do away with the concept of religion entirely, by providing "a picture of what Paul without religion might look like."[257] I agree with

---

249. Ibid., 15.

250. Ibid., 18.

251. Ibid., 34.

252. Ibid., 35–48.

253. Braley, "Bringing God to Mind," 263–64.

254. Ibid., 3–4.

255. Including looking at the classical term *religio* as well as the emergence of the concept.

256. Nongbri, "Paul Without Religion," 258–59.

257. Ibid., 5.

Nongbri when he calls for a separation of our more recent concept of religion when looking at ancient and biblical texts. This separation is crucial for a better understanding of biblical literature. However, where I differ from Nongbri is in my emphasis on the possibility of gaining a better theological understanding of the category of religion and to see how it can be applied for use *today*. In effect, I do not seek to abandon the concept of religion but rather I investigate how theology shapes the concept.

The study closest to my own research is by Richard Hivner, who investigates the construction of religion particularly in the nineteenth and twentieth centuries. In fact, he also studies Chenchiah, along with Indian theologians R. C. Das and Appasamy, to see how they engaged with religions. Hivner's focus however is on the theology of religions. He investigates how his chosen theologians dealt as Christians with the plurality of Hinduism, especially as expressed through the work of the Christian Society for the Study of Hinduism (CSSH) and its journal *The Pilgrim*. Hivner spends little time investigating Chenchiah's (or other Christian) theories or theologies of religion, though he makes an interesting point that theologians like Chenchiah struggled with the conceptual categories of religion even as they tried to change them. Hivner rightly observes that "Chenchiah was deeply creative in his interreligious constructs and actions."[258] However, Hivner adds that Chenchiah "found no way to transcend the world religions paradigm and communitarian expressions of religious identity."[259] It is here that we diverge. I argue that Chenchiah offered a way to transcend the world religions paradigm by his dual theory of religion. Thus, my own work looks to spend more time on Chenchiah and see how he interacted with the category of religion. Additionally, while a shared concern for a theology of religions exists, my focus is primarily on how a theologian can construct a definition of religion, using Chenchiah as a point of reference.

Focal Theory and Outline

My definition of religion in this study will not be the perfect (or universal) definition of religion.[260] Rather, agreeing that there exists a problem of defining religion, I offer a particularly theological answer to the question "What is religion?"

---

258. Hivner, "The Christian Society for the Study of Hinduism," 275.

259. Ibid., 276.

260. Or what Strenski calls, the "Prince Charming" of definitions. Strenski, *Thinking About Religion*, 4.

My focal theory is expressed in three ways by responding in part to the Dubuisson/Balagangadhara challenge expressed earlier in this introductory chapter, and to which I will regularly return to in my subsequent chapters.

First, I agree and show that the growth of the concept of religion is linked historically with the growth of Christianity. However, I also show that since the contemporary view of religion is not entirely consistent with the Christian view of itself, a reassessment of what constitutes a Christian religion is in order. I argue that Chenchiah's construction of his own theory of religion, using the sources available to him as well as with an insider bias, is one such example of a Christian construction. Then, using McCutcheon's classification theory of religion, I offer that theologians today can and must construct the meaning of religion within the Christian theological framework.

Second, I agree with Dubuisson/Balagangadhara that a theory of religion is based on a cosmographical schema, but show, especially through Chenchiah and other theological interactions, that the cosmographical schema of Christianity, while universal, is not necessarily belief-oriented, individualistic or antagonistic.

Third, to answer the title question "What is religion?" I show that when theologically conceived, the category of religion works on two levels. On the more common-sense level, religion exists as a part of social *discourse* and theologians can and must use religion as they would use similarly problematic concepts such as culture, art or faith. At this level, religion would apply to certain religions and could also be phenomenologically identified and examined. Here, the need for a plurality of definitions could come into play as it is quite possible that our common-sense definitions of religion would either be shared with or be in opposition to what others believe about religion. At the second level, religion is a redescriptive category. It is a theologically constructed frame of reference to understand human existence in the light of God. In this sense, a Christian theology of religion would see religion as encompassing all the actions of humanity—whether conscious or subconscious, real or imagined, communal or individual, good or evil, that are in response to the true and good Trinitarian God. This is to say that a theology of religion would see religion as the worship of God and true religion as the true worship of the true God.

I finally assert that theologians of religions must also operate on both these levels—allowing common-sense references and objective interaction with religion to exist alongside an overarching theological view of religion. The former operates as an outsider discourse (etic), especially with those who profess other religions, while the latter informs insider discourse (emic) while also becoming the true motivation for the outsider discourse.

I develop my argument over six chapters. In this introductory chapter, I have shown that there is indeed a problem facing the concept of religion, and it needs theological attention. Chapter 2 provides the historical, philosophical and theological trajectory of the concept of religion, looking at the key theories and theologies that emerged from early Christianity to those that were dominant during Chenchiah's lifetime. Furthermore, in this chapter we also see the context of religious revival/reform and Indian nationalism, looking at the dominant theories of religion that emerged from the Indian context that set the local stage for Chenchiah's theology of religion.

Chapter 3 considers Chenchiah's theology of religion extensively. It draws from a large portion of his books and articles, to cull out what he said about religion, the theological foundation of those assertions, and how this view of religion related or contrasted with dominant theories of religion.

Next, in Chapter 4, I offer a preliminary critique and appreciation of Chenchiah, particularly focusing on aspects of his theory of religion that are useful for a contemporary Christian formulation.

In Chapter 5, I draw attention to secular and theological sources that are useful for a redescription of what religion is. In particular, I look at the methodology of classification, the theory of religion as practical engagement with supernatural beings/things, integrated religion and religion as worship.

In the concluding chapter, I draw together the lessons learned from the previous chapters to formulate a theological answer to the question, "What is religion?" In addition, I summarize the results of this dissertation and project how the theology of religion could affect a theology of religions within the contemporary interreligious context.

2

The Context of Chenchiah's Theology of Religion

INTRODUCTION

This chapter delineates the history and context of discussions about religion, so that we can better understand both the history of the concept of religion as well as Chenchiah's theology of religion. The argument of this chapter is threefold. First, I show the development of the theory of religion, from the early Christian era to the mid-twentieth century. In particular, I draw attention to those Western views of religion that were influential for classical Indian theology.

Second, I survey the socioreligious and political scenario that was prevalent when Chenchiah developed his theology. Chenchiah's primary writings were between the 1930s and 1950s, often referred to as the Independence era. However, the larger context of Chenchiah's theology was the nineteenth and early twentieth centuries. A time of Hindu renaissance and Indian nationalism, this period was marked by fluid conceptions of identity, especially concerning the concepts of "Hinduism" and "India." This proved to be influential not only for the identity construction of Indian Christians, but also for the building of Chenchiah's theological method. Particular mention is made of how the different theories of religion played out in development of the Indian theories of religion, especially in those promulgated by Sri Aurobindo, Swami Vivekananda, M. K. Gandhi and B. R. Ambedkar.

Third, I look at the theological views of religion that would have influenced Chenchiah's theology of religion. While being aware of the theological development of the category of religion, my focus remains on three responses to religion in the early twentieth century: 1) the World Missionary Conferences in Edinburgh (1910), Jerusalem (1928) and Tambaram (1938); 2) Karl Barth's early theology of religion; and 3) views on religion in the context of nationalism and the struggle for religious identity by a few Indian theologians.

All of this together forms the immediate context of Chenchiah's work, and will lead up to our discussion of his theology of religion in the next chapter.

DEVELOPMENT OF WESTERN THEORIES OF RELIGION

In the Introduction, I pointed out the existing lack of clarity about what religion is. However, this is not to say that there was no reflection on what religion meant. From ancient Greek to contemporary times, the concept of religion has undergone much critical study and seen several changes.

Antecedents to 'religion'

The ancient category of *religio* (the Latin root for 'religion')[1] did not specifically refer to religion in the modern sense of the word—which is to say that religion did not exist as something isolated from other cultural activities. Schott correctly notes that the Greek and Latin terms translated as religion in modern English, were essentially "markers of ethnic and civic belonging."[2] In the Roman era, religious identity did not exist as distinct from ethnocultural or civic identities: "many practices and discourses that stand out to moderns as 'religious' were not readily distinguished from other marks of belonging in the ancient world."[3] Schott adds that to be a Jew, Egyptian or Greek meant to "practice traditional rites of one's ancestors."[4]

However, confusion prevailed over the meaning of *religio*, a word that "was used in a great variety of senses, even by a single writer, without

---

1. Some studies of *religio* are to be found in Smith, *Meaning and End of Religion*, 23–31; and King, *Orientalism and Religion*, 33–41.
2. Schott, *Christianity, Empire and the Making of Religion*, 7–8.
3. Ibid., 7.
4. Ibid., 8.

precision."[5] From the 2nd century onwards, Christian writers used *religio* in ways that often differed from that of their contemporaries. Schott notes, for instance, how early Christians began to identify themselves as transcending ethnic identity, a concept quite uncommon at that time.[6] Thus, with the growth of Christianity, there was also a development of the sense of what *religio* and, subsequently, religion would mean.

Two important changes were evident. Firstly, with Christian influence, the category of religion came to be associated with truth, particularly the truth of God. Religion in that sense referred not simply to what one did or the traditions that one followed. Instead, it was related strongly to the one for whom one did those actions (namely, the only true God). Relatedly, the meaning of religion developed additional meanings of true and false religions.

Cicero, a pre-Christian Greek writer, was one of the early commentators who tried to make sense of *religio*. He distinguished religion (*religione*) from superstition (*superstitio*) by calling those who tried to get something out of the gods through prayer and sacrifices as superstitious (*superstitiosi*).[7] In contrast, the religious had the "best and also the purest, holiest and most pious way of worshipping [*cultus*] the gods . . . [they] venerate them with purity, sincerity and innocence both of thought and speech."[8] Cicero went on to associate *religio* with *relegere* to mean "retrace" or "reread," *relegendo* "choosing again," *leger* "picking out," *eligere* "elegant" or "select," and *diligere* "to care for," and even *intellegere* "to understand"—all the words provided a positive descriptor of people who acted rightly.[9]

Writing two and a half centuries after Christ, Christian apologist Lactantius offered another view of *religio*, emphasizing not the role of the worshipper to determine the good of religion, but the truth of God. *Religio* was thus associated with another Latin word *religare*, which meant "to bind" and Lactantius wanted to emphasize that, as *religare*, religion was "a chain of piety" that tied and bound us to God.[10] Lactantius noted the "ineptitude" of Cicero's definition, because regardless of the motives of the individual, the gods remained false: "religion is of course worship of what is true, and superstition is worship of what is false. And what you worship is absolutely important, more so than how you worship or what you should pray. But

5. Smith, *Meaning and End of Religion*, 19.
6. Schott, *Christianity, Empire and the Making of Religion*, 9.
7. Cicero, *De Natura Deorum* II: 71–72, 192–93.
8. Ibid., 71–72, 192–93.
9. Ibid., 71–72, 193.
10. Lactantius, *Divine Institutes*, 275.

because worshippers of gods think they are religious when in fact they are superstitious, so they cannot distinguish religion from superstition or explain the meaning of the words."[11]

Lactantius went on to explain that "the word religion comes from the bond of piety because God has bound man to him and tied him with piety: we simply have to serve him as master and obey him as father."[12]

Schott and Balagangadhara both note that Lactantius was moving the definition of *religio* away from one rooted in culture (and tradition), towards an acultural and transcendent category.[13] Schott in particular asserts that Lactantius defined true *religio* as a "set of theological propositions" that were authentic because they transcended culture.[14] With Lactantius' view of *religio*, we have a glimpse of how religion was emerging as a universal category with a "normative paradigm" for distinguishing true from false religion.[15]

In the fifth century, Augustine noted a problem facing the translation from the Greek θρεσκια to the Latin *religio*. Expressing how Latin translations do not always do justice to the Greek text, and attempting to persevere the true meaning of religion as worship of God, Augustine remarked:

> The word 'religion' might seem to signify more specifically not any worship whatsoever, but the worship of God; and our translators have therefore used this word to render the Greek term *threskeia*. In ordinary Latin speech, however—and not only of the ignorant, but even of the most learned also—we say that *religio* is to be observed in human relationships, affinities and friendships of every kind. The term therefore does not escape ambiguity when used in discussing the worship of the deity; for we cannot strictly speaking say that *religio* means nothing other than the worship of God, since we should then be unjustifiably disregarding the sense in which the word applies to the observance of duties in human relationships.[16]

Augustine, like Lactantius, interpreted *religio* to mean the "religion which binds us to God alone."[17] Augustine also conceived of religion pri-

---

11. Ibid., 276–77.

12. Ibid., 277.

13. See Schott, *Christianity, Empire, and the Making of Religion*, 105; and Balagangadhara, *Heathen in His Blindness*, 222–23.

14. Schott, *Christianity, Empire, and the Making of Religion*, 106.

15. Ibid.

16. Augustine, *The City of God*, X/1, 392.

17. Ibid., 393.

marily as an *activity* that was invariably positive to the extent of saying that the "Christian religion" was the "one saving and true religion." This meant that the Christian religion was the one true way of worshipping the true God.[18] In effect, while other people had "their religion,"[19] for Christians "our religion" referred to the Christian worship of God.[20]

A second major change in the concept of religion occurred with the use of the category of religion to describe the Christian religion, even as its best example. In 1474, when Italian thinker Marsilio Ficino wrote *De Christiana Religione* (Christian Religion), the phrase was "relatively new at the time."[21] Ficino believed that religion was a universal trait in humanity, which had diverse expressions (*ritus adorationis*).[22] The Christian religion was the religion of Jesus, and imitation of Christ is the Christian religion.[23] To this extent, any religion could qualify as Christian religion: "Every religion has something good in it; as long as it is directed towards God, the creator of all things, it is a true Christian religion."[24] This change was significant because religion was gaining an essential character of its own, by which Christianity and other religions were to be measured.

By the time John Calvin wrote in the sixteenth century, there was a clearer sense of what religion was and also of the Christian Religion. Calvin viewed religion as an essential human capacity, where a person expressed a fundamental religiousness.[25] Thus, in his *Institutes of the Christian Religion*, Calvin stated,

> is within the human mind, and indeed by natural instinct, an awareness of divinity [*Divinitatis sensum*] ... God himself has implanted in all men a certain understanding of his divine majesty ... there is ... no nation so barbarous, no people so savage, that they have not a deep-seated conviction that there is a God. And they who in other aspects of life seem least to differ from brutes still continue to retain some seed of religion [*semen*

---

18. Ibid., IV/1, 143.

19. Ibid., IV/7, 151.

20. Ibid., I/36, 49. We will look at Augustine's view of religion in greater detail in chapter 5.

21. Smith, *The Meaning and End of Religion*, 33.

22. Harrison, *Religion and the Religions in the Enlightenment*, 13.

23. Ibid.

24. "Omnis religio boni habet nonnihil, modo ad deum ipsum creatorem omnium dirigatur Christiana sycera est," Ficino, *Opera* 1.4, cited in Harrison, *Religion and the Religions in the Enlightenment*, 13. See also Smith, *The Meaning and End of Religion*, 33–34.

25. Preus, "Zwingli, Calvin and the Origin of Religion," 190.

religionis]. So deeply does the common conception occupy the minds of all, so tenaciously does it inhere in the hearts of all! Therefore, since from the beginning of the world there has been no region, no city, in short, no household, that could do without religion, there lies in this a tacit confession of a sense of deity inscribed in the hearts of all.[26]

Calvin also used religion to imply the true Christian message or doctrine. This included prescriptions of worship, attitudes, laws and traditions: the "duties of religion."[27] Therefore, to express his concern for genuine religion, Calvin said: "here indeed is pure and real religion: faith so joined with an earnest fear of God that this fear also embraces willing reverence, and carries with it such legitimate worship as is prescribed in the law."[28]

For Calvin, this religious capacity did not in any way draw people closer to the knowledge of God; even the prerequisite of "piety" to know God was shown to be an impossible task through man's own initiative.[29] However, even though Calvin described the Christian religion in terms of worship of God, and even though the truth of religion was based not on human actions but on God Himself, there was still a distinction made between religion and Christianity. Christianity was fast emerging as a subset to the larger category of religion. It was now more possible to talk about 'religion' outside the parameters of just the worship of God or even Christianity.[30]

In the post-Reformation world, there emerged a sharper distinction between revealed and natural religion. Harrison clarifies that that revealed religion referred to the religion of faith, expressed particularly through the doctrines and practices of the Church, while natural religion was that which was commonly available to humanity.[31] Harrison shows how some scholars at this time followed Calvin and emphasized *revealed* (genuine) religion being in opposition to or at least superior to *natural* religion.[32] Others, following Ficino, argued that revealed religion was consistent with natural religion.[33] Many of these thinkers were looking to establish not only how

---

26. Calvin, *Institutes of the Christian Religion*, I, 3.1, 43–44.
27. Ibid., II, 7.11, 376.
28. Ibid., I, 2.2, 43.
29. Ibid., 3.2– 4.4, 44–51.
30. For more on this see, Capetz, *A Seed of Religion*.
31. Harrison, *'Religion' and the Religions in the English Enlightenment*, 19.
32. Ibid., 5–6. Later I will be using a category of "dual theology," drawn for Chenchiah. However, this natural and revealed religion was not an early example of dual theory because invariably, the scholars adopted one method over the other.
33. Ibid., 27–28.

natural religion helped in their understanding of Christian religion, but also how Christian religion fulfilled the high standards of reason.[34] However, much stronger opposition against revealed religion emerged through the Deists, whose aim was to subject revealed religion to natural religion—religion had to be rationally scrutinised to the extent that the "laws of heaven" were subject to the same scrutiny as the laws of the "physical universe."[35] This, in turn, led to stronger attacks against the Deistic view of religion and, for some, to a retreat from rationalism. In effect, the shape of religion was influenced along these lines.

The Emergence of Modern Theories of Religion

In the centuries after the Reformation, especially in and from the era known as the Enlightenment (1700 onwards), religion rapidly took on a meaning closer to its modern day understanding. While a thorough study of this period has been sufficiently dealt with elsewhere,[36] there were at least three ideas from the theory of religion that had special implications for the Indian context.

First, in the conflict between revealed and natural religion, there emerged two approaches to religion, namely the rational and the nonrational. Second, there was an emphasis on the essence of true religion, where an essential body of teaching was emphasized, along with the detraditionalization of religion. In both cases, religion was moving away from being an activity to being belief-oriented (with predominantly doctrinal categories) or experiential (predominantly emphasizing religious feeling). Third was the emergence of the history of religions movement, with emphasis on evolutionary religion. Here religion was perceived not so much in theological or experiential terms as in historical and cultural categories.

The Conflict between Natural Religion and Revealed Religion

Rudolf Otto observed that much of the debate between revealed and natural religion occurred within the rationalist and nonrationalist approaches to religion.[37] The rationalist approach sought to explain the essence of religion

---

34. Pelikan, *Christian Doctrine and Modern Culture*, 5:104–5.
35. Harrison, *'Religion' and the Religions in the English Enlightenment*, 7.
36. Most notably, in relation to religion, in ibid.
37. Otto explains his division in the first chapter of his book, *The Idea of the Holy*, 1–5.

in terms of its reasonableness, while, almost in reaction, the nonrationalist approach aimed to preserve the spiritual and mysterious quality of religion in human experience. The rational view of religion emphasized the cognitive nature or function of religion, especially in view of reason as embedded in humanity. The aim of reason was to understand the world and thus religion too was best understood through reason. The nonrational view (not to be confused with "irrational"), emphasized the mysterious part of religion while also considering religion as an indispensable part of humanity that was usually positive in its power.[38] Here it must be added that while there were both essentialist and substantive theories of religion during this time, it was the essentialist views of religion that dominated. For the rationalist, the essential commonality was the mind. For the nonrationalist, the essential commonality lay in religious feeling.

While Immanuel Kant was not a pure rationalist,[39] he still attempted to negotiate the concept of religion within rationality. For Kant, there was no distinction between a natural religion and a revealed religion, since the truth of revelation could be understood within natural religion.[40] In effect, Kant famously stated how religion must follow the rules of reason to be taken seriously: "Our age is properly the age of critique, and to critique everything must submit. Religion and legislation commonly seek to exempt themselves from critique, religion through its sanctity and legislation through its majesty. But in doing so they arouse well-deserved suspicion and cannot lay claim to unfeigned respect; such respect is accorded by reason only to what has been able to withstand reason's free and open examination."[41]

Ironically, even deeply committed Christian scholars opted for a rational framework of religion, to either justify or defend the Christian religion or to use it to attack opponents. For example, Calvinist scholar Halyburton defended "rational arguments" because they were useful, so that the truth of the Christian religion would be "evinced and demonstrated against Atheists."[42] Halyburton stated that all Christians were called to believe in the Scriptures wholeheartedly through faith that was rational: "moral and rational considerations are, and may be in many ways useful to stop the mouths of enemies, to beget in them, who yet are unacquainted with the true intrin-

---

38. The non-rational view can also been linked with Romanticism and Pietism, two movements that attempt to preserve an appreciation of the mysterious and not-overtly evident essential truths.

39. Especially since Kant was well aware of the need for *a priori* reasoning for fundamental questions about *noumena*.

40. Seung, "Kant, Immanuel," 5079.

41. Kant, *Critique of Pure Reason*, 8.

42. Halyburton, *Natural Religion Insufficient*, 377–78.

sic worth of the word, some value for it, and engage them to consider it; to relieve them that do believe against objections, and strengthen their faith."[43]

A more direct challenge to the rationalist view of religion came from the non-rationalists. The nonrationalists, in response to the rationalist preoccupation with beliefs, proposed that authentic religion went beyond rationality, sensibility and moral behavior. They maintained the distinction between revealed religion and natural religion, but they also identified religion with feelings, emotions and attitudes that were devoid of (or had limited) cognitive content.

For Schleiermacher, religion was grounded in the feeling of absolute dependence and was an essential part of human experience. Schleiermacher offered that religion was essentially an experience—true religion was not found in the dogmas or institutions but in the actual contact with God. In fact, Boyer suggests that it was Schleiermacher who first brought the "what is religion" question into public consciousness.[44] Thus Schleiermacher stated, "The sum total of religion is to feel that, in its highest unity, all that moves us in feeling is one; to feel that aught single and particular is only possible by means of this unity; to feel, that is to say, that our being and living is a being and living in and through God."[45]

Unlike Kant, Schleiermacher viewed religion within the realm of experience. He critiqued the rationalists by pointing out that, "their zeal for the sciences, for the wisdom of life, and for holy freedom, is merely an empty sham battle . . . they seek knowledge; their wisdom is only directed toward a lamentable empiricism, and thus religion can be nothing else for them than a dead letter, a holy article in the constitution in which nothing is real."[46]

Schleiermacher urged instead for an experiential religion: "I fear that religion can be understood only through itself and that its special manner of construction and its characteristic distinction will not become clear to you until you yourselves belong to some one or other of them."[47] Arguing against the need for a religion that descends from heaven (revealed religion), Schleiermacher also stated that religion "springs necessarily and by itself from the interior of every better soul, it has its own province in the mind in which it reigns sovereign, and it is worthy of moving the noblest

---

43. Ibid., 378.

44. Boyer "What Is Religion?" 2–3. Of course Boyer is not suggesting that the question may not have occurred in the mind or work of anyone in the past, but that Schleiermacher's question brought into public light a question that fundamentally altered not only theology but religion.

45. Schleiermacher, *On Religion*, 49–50.

46. Ibid., 9.

47. Ibid., 113.

and the most excellent by means of its innermost power and by having its innermost essence known by them."[48]

Rudolf Otto was also a strong critic of a purely rational view of religion. He began his book with a critique of the "one-sidedly intellectualistic and rationalistic" interpretation of the idea of God.[49] Otto emphasized the non-rationalist nature of religion by asserting that experience can be understood through phenomena but not explained through objective rationality.[50] For Otto, there existed a realm of mental activity that was outside the scope of pure reason, and must, therefore, be represented through "nonrational feelings and intuitions."[51] Like Schleiermacher before him, Otto highlighted the existence of a legitimate religious sphere in humanity, to which Otto added a valid cognitive process which opened the possibility for "religious cognition" or even religious feeling (*numinous*).[52] By *numinous*, Otto meant a cognitive-experiential concept of the holy without its moral and rational aspects.[53] Thus, Otto claimed, religious cognition involved experiences of the Holy (sacred) that were not subject to correction or explanation by theoretical (material) reason:[54] "in the case of the non-rational elements of our category of the Holy we are referred back to something still deeper than the 'pure reason,' at least as this is usually understood, namely, to that which mysticism has rightly named the *fundus animae*, the 'bottom' or 'ground of the soul.' . ."[55]

In addition, Otto asserted that in order to study this experience of religion, a scholar must have the ability to experience the Holy to be able to relate his experiences of the Holy with those of others.[56]

Evidently, Otto was not trying to prioritize nonrational religion. Instead he argued for the legitimacy of religious feeling that was logically outside the purview of material observation and needed religious cognition for observance. Ironically, though his ideas were an attempt to defend Christianity from attacks of nineteenth century historians and natural scientists, he was less influential with theologians and more foundational

---

48. Ibid., 17.
49. Otto, *The Idea of the Holy*, 3.
50. Bellah, *Beyond Belief*, 6.
51. Alles, "Otto, Rudolf," 6929.
52. Ibid.
53. Allen, "Phenomenology of Religion," 7090.
54. Alles, "Otto, Rudolf," 6929.
55. Otto, *The Idea of the Holy*, 112.
56. To the extent that Otto requests those who have no access to their "deep-felt religious experience" to stop reading his book. Otto, *The Idea of the Holy*, 8.

for future phenomenological and scientific theories of religion.[57] However, Otto's impact in India was in his emphasis on experience as the point of contact. Especially through his participatory experiential emphasis, where he studied the Gita and other Hindu scriptures for himself, he proposed that in *bhakti* there was a deep connection between Christianity and Hinduism.[58] Such an emphasis on experience would later resonate with the Indian use of experience for both an understanding of their own religions as well as, when so inclined, the religions of others.

The debates over religion in the following centuries moved largely along these lines. Some scholars attempted making religion subject to scientific rational discourse, while others attempted legitimizing religion as a religious sphere outside rational discourse. The consequence of these approaches however was that religion became more commonly perceived as being about propositional content or common experience.[59] Religion came to refer to a "system of ideas" or as "observable product" of the faith of people.[60] There was both a secularization of the concept of religion for objectification and subsequent study[61] or the inverse subjectivist approach that looked to bypass the priority of the cognitive.[62] Either way, the "study" of religion as a phenomena grew in prominence during this era.

The Essence of Religion

The other feature of the Enlightenment era, Pelikan points out, was the emphasis on an essence of religion.[63] Keeping in mind that religion was taking the shape of beliefs, the attempt was to find the core teachings of Jesus that were essential and universal. For instance, Thomas Watson, writing in the early 1800s, asserted that Christian religion "has all the marks of an universal religion."[64] This was not just because Christianity was meant for all

---

57. Alles, "Otto, Rudolf," 6929.

58. See Röhr, "Bhakti and Christian Faith—According to Rudolf Otto (1869–1937)," 1–10.

59. Harrison, *'Religion' and the Religions in the English Enlightenment*, 24–26.

60. Smith, *The Meaning and End of Religion*, 37–38.

61. Harrison, *'Religion' and the Religions in the English Enlightenment*, 14.

62. Thus Otto states, "in the case of the non-rational elements of our category of the Holy we are referred back to something still deeper than the 'pure reason,' at least as this is usually understood, namely, to that which mysticism has rightly named the *fundus animae*, the 'bottom' or 'ground of the soul.'" *The Idea of the Holy*, 112.

63. Pelikan, *Christian Doctrine and Modern Culture*, 101–17.

64. Watson, *Popular Evidences of Natural Religion and Christianity*, 309.

people, but that its universal principles, which transcended the daily rituals, were universally influential.[65] Thus Watson argued, "The principles of the Christian religion prove it to have been designed for all mankind. All are interested in its general doctrines ... these principles wherever properly received, will have the most commanding influence ... The duties of the gospel are therefore addressed to all without distinction."[66]

While the focus was on the principles, there was also a rejection of the outward institution of Christianity. Watson added that even though it was a "holy religion," Christian "has been disgraced by numerous positive and unmeaning observances ... they are all the works of men ... contrary to the genius of this religion."[67]

There was also the growing voice of those who expressed the nonrational aspect of religion. For instance, Robertson Smith acknowledged that Christianity, along with Judaism and Islam, were "positive religions" that originated from "the teaching of great religious innovators, who spoke as the organs of a divine revelation."[68] However, Smith contrasted this kind of religion with an older "unconscious religious tradition."[69] Of this older system, Smith said, "A new scheme of faith can find a hearing only by appealing to religious instincts and susceptibilities that already exist in its audience, and it cannot reach these without taking account of the traditional forms in which all religious feeling is embodied, and without speaking a language which men accustomed to these old forms can understand."[70]

Either way, in both the emphases on religious principles and religious feeling, religion was now clearly a generic universal—all cultures were believed to possess it. Religion was also thought to be essential to humanity, either through a core belief that resonated across cultures or shared across humanity. The core belief or experience became the interpretive key of religion.

Related to the search for essentials was the detraditionalization of religion. There was a movement away from the authority of religious structures, like the Church and other dogmatic assertions. Detraditionalization, or "the internalization of authority" as Bellah would call it,[71] is when the authority in religion shifts from traditional systems to the self.

65. Ibid., 312–13.
66. Ibid., 313–14.
67. Watson, *Popular Evidences of Natural Religion and Christianity*, 317.
68. Smith, *Religion of the Semites*, 1.
69. Ibid.
70. Ibid., 2.
71. Bellah, *Beyond Belief*, 223.

As an example of this trend, Auguste Sabatier, writing in the early 1900s, contrasted the authority paradigm in the religion of law and the religion of nature, to that in the religion of the Spirit as heralded by Jesus:

> ... the religion of law no more than the religion of nature can save the man—that is, establish his union with the principle of his own being, and realize his harmony both with God and the world. These experiences having been made and repeated wherever the religion of law succeeded the religion of nature, the time was fulfilled. In Jesus of Nazareth appeared a third form of the human religious consciousness, the supreme form everywhere announced and prepared for by the spirit of reformers and prophets as well as by the plaints and hopes of pious souls, and which since Jesus has become a living Christian consciousness in the bosom of humanity. In the religious consciousness and personal piety of Christ the religious relation was once again transformed. It no longer rests upon power nor upon law and the resulting covenant, but upon a new sentiment, love . . . The religious evolution which took place in him took place in the very bosom and for the profit of all humanity.[72]

Troeltsch finds Schleiermacher's influence in this "new romanticism," and links the disappearance of the duality between flesh and spirit with the appearance of a "fully developed religious 'inwardness.'"[73] Troeltsch goes on to identify the sociological consequences of this fundamental position: "The religious community—both the Church and the conventicle—had lost all significance. Public worship had become entirely unnecessary, and without any meaning for religion. The historical element had simply become a symbol, a means of stimulus, while some went farther and regarded it with great suspicion. This historical element had almost entirely lost any connection with public worship; instead it had become a theme for scientific treatment, a subject for the free play of the imagination, or a means of stimulating certain moods according to one's own private fancies.[74]

Troeltsch was critical of this shift, but clearly, a shift had occurred where it was possible to think about religion as existing outside the expression of religion to a universal acultural realm. This was also an important factor in allowing for comparative studies of religion, where the category could be studied across the board.

---

72. Sabatier, *Religions of Authority and the Religion of the Spirit*, 373–74.
73. Troeltsch, *The Social Teaching of the Christian Church*, 793–94.
74. Ibid., 795.

What Is Religion?

The Evolutionary View of Religion

Distinct from the above ahistorical emphasis was the history of religions approach to religion that emphasized the historical conditioning and context of religion. A key influence to this kind of thinking about religion was evolutionism. Evolution in the late 1800s, referred primarily to the development of life on this planet, particularly from one species to another. The Darwinian notion of evolution was certainly the most popular. Darwin suggested that all species evolved through a process of natural selection where the goal of all species was to change biologically in order to survive in changing environments. Those species that adapted biologically were shown to have survived, and those that did not adapt biologically became extinct. Yet Darwin's theory of evolution was not the only theory of evolution. One of the alternatives proposed by James Baldwin, which would later be known as the Baldwin Effect, proposed that learned behaviors could affect the direction and rate of evolutionary change.[75] Importantly, Baldwin challenged the singular emphasis on natural processes. He highlighted the capacity of a species to learn new skills rather than be limited by its fixed genetic code. Thus, Baldwin emphasized that the (learned) behavior of a species could shape its biological nature within the evolutionary scheme.[76]

Evolution, however, was not just a scientific theory of biological life; it also became a philosophical principle known as evolutionism which impacted almost all areas of human thought, particularly religious thought. Thus we see that by the nineteenth century, many scholars of religion brought developmental evolutionary ideas to bear on religion, with a particular reference to the Christian form as the highest or at least the clearest example of that development.[77] This view gained further potency with the addition of evolutionary logic to describe and assess religious development.

Waller and others term "evolutionism" as the dominant theoretical framework in the nineteenth century that attempted to "account for the genesis and development of religion."[78] A key theory binding this approach was the presupposition that all human societies had similar developmental patterns, to the extent that one could determine the origin of religion by

---

75. Depew, "Baldwin and his Many Effects," in Weber and Depew (eds.), *Evolution and Learning*, 3.

76. Baldwin, "A New Factor in Evolution," 441–51.

77. Some of those scholars would belong to the History of Religions school. See Bianchi, "History of Religions," 4060–68.

78. Waller et al., "Evolution: Evolutionism," 2913.

studying the "primitive" people groups who most naturally represented the earliest form of religious behavior.[79]

At least two types of evolutionary methodologies in religion were prominent during the nineteenth and early twentieth centuries. One was the use of evolution within the scientific/naturalist method that focused upon the biological development of the cosmos and saw religion within it. The other method was to look at evolution as a philosophical principle that governed human phenomena.

Jesuit biologist Teilhard de Chardin is an example of the naturalist evolutionary religious discourse. de Chardin offered an extensively scientific (naturalist) understanding of the evolutionary process as affecting the cosmos, particularly humanity.[80] For most of his book, de Chardin developed a view of man well within the evolutionary biological framework. He conceived of evolution as both a diversification as well as an ultimate convergence (an involution) culminating for humanity in an Omega Point, a concept that includes the idea of an end and perfection.[81] He accepted the evolutionary premise of ascent of humanity, suggesting that this ascent was naturally towards a "supreme consciousness."[82] Nevertheless de Chardin supposed that the supreme consciousness would not be impersonal but hyperpersonal and an "involution of the being upon itself," the Omega Point.[83] de Chardin went on to integrate his Christian beliefs with this evolutionary standpoint, by perceiving that the evolutionary convergence is related to a state close to the Divine.[84] In particular, de Chardin saw that the Omega Point was already in existence, operative in this world and particularly seen in Christianity. In effect, de Chardin was a neonaturalist, in that he conceived of the evolving world within its natural structure while also seeing some (spiritual) direction and purpose behind its movement.

The other type of evolutionary methodology was to emphasize the simpler logic of process to religion. Waller and others define this *evolutionism* as the "account for the genesis and development of religion."[85] A

---

79. Ibid.

80. The key text is Teilhard de Chardin, *The Phenomenon of Man*. Julian Huxley's "Introduction" in the same volume offers a helpful inroad into de Chardin's complex thought.

81. The final chapters of de Chardin's book, particularly 283–99, deal with the integration of personality and the Omega Point.

82. De Chardin, *The Phenomenon of Man*, 284.

83. Ibid., 284–86.

84. See particularly ibid., 319–27.

85. Waller et al., "Evolution: Evolutionism," 2913.

key theory binding this approach was the presupposition that all human societies had similar developmental patterns, to the extent that one could determine the origin of religion by studying the "primitive" people groups, who most naturally represented the earliest form of religious behavior.[86] More directly, Waller and others note that evolutionary thought was impacted by the work of Herbet Spencer, who argued that evolution was the principle for all change, whether organic or inorganic.[87] The other famous theorist of evolutionary religion, James Frazer, argued that "general laws... regulated human history" and those laws would most probably regulate the future.[88]

Two further divisions in this approach are evident: i) to view the development *of* religion, and ii) to view the development *in* religion. An example of the development *of* religion is seen through E. B. Tylor. He proposed that since religion is "belief in Spiritual Beings," the primitive religions were identified by primitive beliefs, such as anthropomorphic (naturalized) deities.[89] Tylor also used the simple linear view of evolution, suggesting that there was a direct relation between primitive beliefs such as animism and the higher forms of thoughts that included myth making.[90] An example of the development *in* religion was seen through William James, where he identified the (negative) development of religion:

> A survey of history shows us that, as a rule, religious geniuses attract disciples, and produce groups of sympathizers. When these groups get strong enough to "organize" themselves, they become ecclesiastical institutions with corporate ambitions of their own. The spirit of politics and the lust of dogmatic rule are then apt to enter and to contaminate the originally innocent thing; so that when we hear the word 'religion' nowadays, we think inevitably of some "church" or other; and to some persons the word "church" suggests so much hypocrisy and tyranny and meanness and tenacity of superstition that in a wholesale undiscerning way they glory in saying that they are "down" on religion altogether.[91]

---

86. Ibid.
87. Ibid.
88. Frazer, *Psyche's Task*, 160.
89. Tylor, *Primitive Cultures*, 424.
90. See Kunin, "Edward Tylor," 99. For further discussion of Tylor's use of evolution, see Strenski, *Thinking about Religion*, 91–116.
91. James, *The Varieties of Religious Experience*, 261.

A more positive development *in* religion was envisaged by Abbott who proposed an integration of evolution with Christianity, to actually improve an understanding of Christianity. Abbott stated, "I have not abandoned the historic faith of Christendom to become an evolutionist, but have endeavored to show that the historic faith of Christendom, when stated in the terms of an evolutionary philosophy, is not only preserved, but is so cleansed of pagan thought and feeling, as to be presented in a purer and more powerful form."[92]

Abbott began with the assumption that all life proceeded in a orderly sequence "from simple and lower forms to more complex and higher forms" and went on to argue that "the Christian religion is itself an evolution; this life of God in humanity is one of continuous progressive change, according to certain divine laws, and by means of forces, or a force, resident in humanity."[93]

Simple evolutionary theories of linear progression were later replaced by more complex models as well as by many with phenomenological models that emphasized objective observation of societies. In terms of the Indian context, we will see that evolutionary models were significant, especially to the revivalist school of Hinduism. Chenchiah himself, as we will see in the next chapter, used evolutionary views for his own theological construction.

The Functional View of Religion

In contrast to the essentialist or historical views of religions was the functional view. Rather than focus on the beliefs or ideas that emerged out of religion, or even its historical origins and antecedents, the functional view of religion focused on the effect of religion in society. In an insightful article, Krech shows the rise of functional approaches out of historical approaches of religion, in the nineteenth and twentieth centuries.[94] Krech reveals the shift from histories of religions, which emphasized how religion originated, towards a more functional approach, to how religion and community were interrelated, and religion was particularly useful for society.

Marx, for instance, famously depicted religion as fulfilling a certain, albeit negative, function in society as an "opium."[95] Similarly, Marx stated that the "abolition of religion" would lead to the "real happiness" of people.[96]

92. Abbott, *The Evolution of Christianity*, iv.
93. Ibid., 1–2.
94. Krech, "From Historicism to Functionalism," 244–65.
95. Marx, "A Contribution to the Critique of Hegel," 243.
96. Ibid.

While this idea can be easily misunderstood, Marx's point was that the *need* that religion fulfilled had to be abolished. His belief was that religion was created by people to help cope with the struggles caused by the oppression in the world. Religion was the "opium" which helped people cope with their suffering, thus revealing a functional view of religion.

Like Marx, Emile Durkheim too offered a view of how society created its gods. However, this view was developed within a theory of religion that showed how both religion and community were dependent on each other. Durkheim offered the following definition of religion: "A religion is a unified system of beliefs and practices relative to sacred things, that is to say things set apart and forbidden—beliefs and practice which unite into a single moral community called a Church, all those who adhere to them."[97] To the traditional notions of religion, namely beliefs and rites, Durkheim added a constructive function. Religion was a collective thing, where religion belonged to a group and also imposed beliefs on the group in an obligatory manner.[98] Durkheim thus highlighted the value of the belief in god for the benefit of society, "A god is not only an authority to which we are subject but also a force that buttresses our own."[99]

Max Weber did not particularly emphasize the construction of gods, but chose instead to focus on the integration of religion and society. Weber's main work, on the relationship between Protestant religion and capitalism, was one such example of an integrated vision of religion. For instance, Weber highlighted that "the religious forces which express themselves through such channels are the decisive influences in the formation of national character."[100] Thus the focus of enquiry was religion within society. He sought to interpret the relationship between the various religious traditions and the cultural environment within which they emerged.[101]

As we will see later, a functional view of religion was also quite influential in the Indian context, to which we now turn.

DEVELOPING INDIAN THEORIES OF RELIGION

In the previous section, we saw how the category of religion developed in the West. We now look at some of the significant Indian theories of religion that were influential during Chenchiah's time. In the Introduction, I briefly

---

97. Durkheim, *The Elementary Forms of Religious Life*, 44.
98. Ibid.
99. Ibid., 211.
100. Weber, *The Protestant Ethic*, 102.
101. Capps, *Religious Studies*, 168.

mentioned arguments concerning the invention of Hinduism in the nineteenth century. Represented by scholars such as Geoffrey Oddie,[102] Robert Frykenberg[103] and others, the reasoning is that while a sense of who a Hindu was may have existed prior to the British colonial period, it was only after the colonial era that Hinduism was conceived in religious and cohesive terms. The researchers use varied data, and Oberoi's work is representative of some of these arguments:

> It is most striking that people we now call Hindus never used this term to describe themselves. The Vedas, the Ramayana and the Bhagavad Gita, which today are seen by many as the religious texts of the Hindus, do not employ the word Hindu ... at one stage the word Hindu as an ethnogeographic category came to englobe all those who lived in India, without ethnic distinction. It was only under the Muslim rulers of India that the term began to gain a religious connotation. But it was not until colonial times that the term 'Hinduism' was coined and acquired wide currency as referring collectively to a wide variety of religious communities, some of them with distinct traditions and opposed practices.[104]

On the other hand, there are those like Lorenzen[105] and Pennington[106] who discount that Hinduism was a category created by the British, and instead provide ample historical evidence of its existence prior to the 1800s. Lorenzen unequivocally states that "the claim that Hinduism was invented or constructed by European colonisers, mostly British, sometime after 1800 is false."[107] The proposals on what constitutes Hinduism, however, were varied and by the 1870s, Heehs notes multiple and even contradictory proposals such as "reform-minded modernism, conservative innovation, moderate conservatism, and outright reaction ... competing for the attention of people in an emerging 'public space.'"[108]

One must admit to an imposition of the categories of 'religion' and "Hindu" on the psyche of the Indian people. The category of religion, which helped distinguish Hindu from Christian and "Indian Christian" from "Indian Hindu," was equally in flux. For instance, Cox mentions, that as late as

102. Oddie, *Imagined Hinduism*.
103. Frykenberg, "The Emergence of Modern 'Hinduism,'" 82–107.
104. Oberoi, *The Construction of Religious Boundaries*, 16.
105. Lorenzen, *Who Invented Hinduism?*
106. Pennington, *Was Hinduism Invented?*
107. Lorenzen, *Who Invented Hinduism?*, 2.
108. Heehs, "Nationalism," 266.

the 1931 census in India, "The extent to which categories of religion were being imposed upon a population in ways that were baffling and in many cases tyrannical is obvious from the census reports, where the mocking and humorous tone adopted by census officials about public confusion over religious categories implies that it is all the fault of the enumerated rather than the enumerators. In many localities self-ascription was a matter of political and economic pressure."[109]

In such a context, the concept of religion was fluid and still up-for-grabs in terms of how it was used and to what it referred to.

However, Heehs states that, by the latter half of the nineteenth century, the English-speaking people in the urban centers "had a pretty good idea of what they meant when they said 'India' and 'Hinduism.'"[110] Heehs says that while Hinduism was a concept with a history that preceded the British conquest, Hinduism assumed its "modern form in response to pressure from British missionaries, scholars, and government officials."[111] Thus, the concern at this time was not to determine whether religion or Hinduism existed, but to discover what it essentially was: "The nineteenth-century discussion was not about whether Hinduism existed—everyone took this for granted—but what Hinduism was or ought to be. The central problem was to find the essence or distinguishing characteristics of the diverse though related practices subsumed under the English term."[112]

Aurobindo seemed to confirm this when discussing the problem of the imposition of religion. Aurobindo affirmed that if religion was viewed in an English linguistic sense, then the word was an imposition. However, if viewed spiritually, then it was useful to remind people of their spiritual goal:

> Perhaps there was too much of religion in one sense; the word is English, smacks too much of things external such as creeds, rites, and external piety; there is no one Indian equivalent. But if we give rather to religion the sense of the following of the spiritual impulse in its fullness and define spirituality as the attempt to know and live in the highest self, the divine, the all-embracing unity and to raise life in all its parts to the divinest possible values, then it is evident that there was not too much of religion, but rather too little of it—and in what there was, a too one-sided and therefore insufficiently ample tendency.[113]

---

109. Cox, *Imperial Fault Lines*, 268.
110. Heehs, "Nationalism," 265.
111. Ibid., 266.
112. Ibid.
113. Aurobindo, *The Renaissance in India*, 75.

Affirming Heeh's insight, it is important to ascertain the flux of the meanings of "religion," "Hindu" and even "Indian Christian," over the several decades leading up to the time of Chenchiah. To do this, we first turn our attention to the socioreligious Hindu reform movement of the nineteenth century, especially towards those who accepted a general view of Hinduism and religion and, in that process, shaped it to suit their own cultural needs.

The Hindu Renaissance: Revival and Reform

A significant context for Chenchiah was the resurgence of Hindu identity. The popular story, retold in numerous history texts, is of a Hindu renaissance which originated around the middle of the nineteenth century and played an integral role in the Independence struggle.[114] This multifaceted movement is usually associated with the establishment of organizations such as the Brahmo Samaj and the Arya Samaj, but also refers to the rising global profile of Hinduism through icons such as Swami Vivekananda and Sri Aurobindo.[115] Aurobindo himself wrote about the renaissance and believed it to be a timely rejection of foreign ideology and a transformation of the nation alongside an age-old tradition: "the first period of the superficial assimilation and aping of European political ideas and methods is over. Another political spirit has awakened in the people under the shock of the movement of the last decade which, vehemently national in its motive, proclaimed a religion of Indian patriotism, applied the notions of the ancient religion and philosophy to politics, expressed the cult of the country as Mother and *Shakti* and attempted to base the idea of democracy firmly on the spiritual thought and impulses native to the Indian mind."[116]

Various scholars have offered different reasons for the rise of Hindu reform movements in the nineteenth century. Madan asserts that it was the

---

114. The view that the nineteenth century was the period of Hindu reform was popular, even as early as the 1920s. For instance, see Kohn, *A History of Nationalism in the East*, 55–75. In his book, Kohn comments, "It was a period when men's outlook was immeasurably broadened and enriched. They became aware of ancient civilisations and wholly new conditions of life. Man was discovered anew, and man, as he emerged, was a social creature." Kohn, *A History of Nationalism in the East*, 75. A more recent and critical introduction to the beginnings of Hindu reform can be found in Salmond, *Hindu Iconoclasts*.

115. Chandra and others list several other reform movements, even those associated with Sikhism and Islam, that were "remarkably similar" and were "regional and religious manifestations of a common consciousness." Chandra et al., *India's Struggle of Independence*, 83.

116. Aurobindo, *The Renaissance in India*, 57.

impact of proselytizing Christianity and the "often crude and ill-informed" descriptions of Hinduism and Hindu culture, that provoked the two faces of the Hindu renaissance, namely the reformist and the revivalist movements.[117] Oddie draws attention to the more positive role of Christian missionaries in the formation of Hindu self-understanding.[118] Basu gives credit to modernism, where the desire to retain a "primal state of the Hindu dharma" was "first made by the rationalists who wanted to reform in order to restore the former glory of true Hinduism."[119] Krüger notes that the concept of Hinduism was dependent on its colonial context.[120] While Chandra and others assert that the reform movement arose out of a genuine struggle between a preservation of the past from colonial aggression and embracing the new society evolving in India.[121] For Chandra and others, the reaction against colonialism played an important role "in the formation of national consciousness" that was "instrumental in bringing about the initial intellectual and cultural break" from colonialism and "which made a new vision of the future [India] possible."[122]

While the reasons are many, not many scholars doubt that there were indeed Hindu reform/revival movements in the nineteenth century. Heehs' caution that the label "Hindu revivalism" need not apply to all Hindu activity of this era[123] is well taken, but need not stop us from accepting that reform/revival movements did exist and were formative not only for Hinduism but also for the Indian national identity.

For the remaining part of this section, we use Madan's distinction between reform movements and revival movements to help clarify some of the events that shaped nineteenth-century socioreligious identity of Hindus.

---

117. It must be noted that a distinction between reform and revival is generally not made by historians and I accept this polarity simply to highlight, as Madan does, the different approaches to the changes in Hinduism in the nineteenth Century. Madan, *Modern Myths, Locked Minds*, 204. See also Madan, "Hinduism: An Introductory Essay," in Chaudhuri et al., *The Hinduism Omnibus*, xxii.

118. Oddie, "Constructing 'Hinduism,'" 155–82.

119. Basu, *Religious Revivalism as Nationalist Discourse*, 5.

120. Krüger, *Indian Nationalists and the World Proletariat*, 87.

121. Chandra, et al., *India's Struggle for Independence*, 89.

122. Ibid., 90.

123. Heehs, "Nationalism," 267.

Reform Movements

For Madan, reform movements were those that engaged positively with their context and were willing to accept new ways of being Hindus. A vivid example of a reform movement is the founding of the Brahmo Sabha in 1828 (renamed Brahmo Samaj in 1843), in Calcutta, by Ram Mohan Roy "with a view to synthesizing the most valuable elements of vedic religion and Protestant Christianity."[124] It was seen as a means to "eradicate erroneous religious beliefs and social practices among Hindus"[125] such as child marriage, caste taboos, restriction on the remarriage of widows and the practice of *sati*.[126]

Furthermore, Roy propounded a monistic theism that affirmed the value of scriptures and rejected idolatry, ritualism and the authority of Brahmans.[127] Madan notes that Roy clearly had the European Renaissance in mind, even as Roy wanted Hindus to recover the "original purity of their religious thought and knowledge by subjecting it to a rational critique and by returning to its sources for inspiration."[128] Roy went on to promote a "universal religion" that comprised of a "theological consensus among the followers of major world religions."[129]

After Roy the social reform impetus continued through the work of Debendranath Tagore and Keshub Chandra Sen. However the movement eventually waned, partly because both Tagore and Sen themselves made significant concessions to Hindu orthodoxy later in their lives.[130] More importantly, as Jones comments, the Brahmo reform movement declined in influence because it was perceived as being in direct opposition to orthodox Hinduism.[131] In addition, the Brahmo movement depended too heavily on certain key leaders, upon whose death the Brahmo ideology was easily replaced by newer and more attractive religious and secular ideologies of the

---

124. Madan, "Hinduism: An Introductory Essay," xxiii.

125. Madan, *Modern Myths, Locked Minds*, 205.

126. Madan, "Hinduism: An Introductory Essay," xxiii.

127. Ibid., xxiii. Chandra and others note that these reform movements were not exclusively religious in character, and instead had a strong humanist inspiration. Furthermore, they judged social reform by an intellectual rationalist critique. Chandra et al., *India's Struggle of Independence*, 83–85.

128. Madan, *Modern Myths, Locked Minds*, 205.

129. Ibid. Chandra and others note that Roy's "universalist perspective . . . strongly influenced by the political and social outlook of the time." Chandra et al., *India's Struggle of Independence*, 86.

130. Madan, *Modern Myths, Locked Minds*, 206–8.

131. Jones, *Socio-Religious Reform Movements*, 167.

twentieth century, not the least being the ideology of nationalism itself.[132] However, Basu notes that the Brahmo movement helped institutionalize Hinduism, by including congregational worship, reading of texts and singing of hymns.[133]

Revival Movements

In contrast to the reform movements, revival movements were those which reacted sharply against the interreligious context and looked to Hinduism's own resources to recover a pure Hindu identity.[134] A predominant example of the revivalists was the Arya Samaj which was established by Dayanand Saraswati in Bombay in 1875. While the key concerns for Hindu social reform were upheld—the rejection of idolatry, child marriage, elaborate rituals and Brahmin priests.[135] However, there was an insistence on "Vedic truth" and the "infallibility of the Vedas."[136] In addition, Saraswati also supported *shuddi* (purification), the reconversion "of Hindus who had been seduced by the missionaries, but were willing to return to their own religion."[137] Madan notes that while arguing for the significance of the Vedas gave the Arya Samaj a distinct identity, it was *shuddi* that made them popular. This was true particularly in regions like Punjab which faced multiple threats from Christianity, Islam, Sikhism and even Brahmo Hindus who were tolerant towards other religions particularly Christianity.[138] In emphasizing essential truth of Hinduism, the Arya Samaj was clearly borrowing from the forms and techniques of Christianity, Islam and Sikhism, and yet was using it to make inroads in the Hindu community.[139]

A true form of revivalism, however, came through the direct defence of Hindu traditions. Even as Hinduism became more respectable as a global religion, as well as a legitimate field of study for scholars, various Hindu intellectuals began to highlight the superiority of Hindu philosophy over other world systems. The greatest success of Hindu revival came through

---

132. Ibid., 37–39, 167.
133. Basu, *Religious Revivalism as Nationalist Discourse*, 2.
134. Madan, *Modern Myths, Locked Minds*, 208, 211–12.
135. Jones, *Socio-Religious Reform Movements*, 97.
136. Ibid.
137. Madan, *Modern Myths, Locked Minds*, 213.
138. Ibid.
139. Jones, *Socio-Religious Reform Movements*, 100.

the "appeal to emotions rather than intellect," through the lives and works of Ramakrishna, Aurobindo and Vivekananda.[140] These Hindu saints, also referred to as neo-Hindus, adopted the path of spiritualism, proposing a Hindu revival from within. Through a predominantly Vedantic approach, the emphasis on the oneness of all things under Brahman, these spiritual thinkers were able to propose a cultural change in Hinduism with the use of deep spiritual resources within Hinduism itself, especially Advaitic Vedanta. In doing so, they not only argued for Hinduism's ability to generate moral and cultural change, but also for its being better equipped than Christianity and other western religions to accomplish the change.[141]

Basu states that even as the Brahmo reform was weakened by severe resistance from conservative (orthodox) Hindus, Hindu revivalism was strengthened when Vivekananda brought together conservative and popular elements of Hinduism through a nationalist discourse.[142] Basu argues that Vivekananda's assertion of an "abstract core was a neo-Hindu invention of the Hindu religion"[143] and yet it had sufficient roots in the "essential Hindu dharma" to become more readily acceptable.[144]

The success of the neo-Hindu position lay in its integration of Hindu revivalist concerns with nationalist concerns. Sharpe notes how this was partly achieved through the integration of national symbols with religious symbols, where "nationalism was being proclaimed as an *avatara*" and "India was being revered as a *shakti* of the Eternal."[145] Sarkar similarly states that Vivekananda's mixture of patriotism with Hindu glory added to the appeal, especially in the upcoming *Swadeshi* period.[146]

It can thus be accepted that, during the nineteenth century, Hindu identity was in a state of flux. No one group had a full hold on what it meant to be a Hindu. The reform and revivalist movements however successfully served to align Hindu discourse with Christianity and Islam—especially in terms of cohesion of thought—and also sought to relate Hinduism to the burning issue of the time: nationalism.

---

140. Sarkar, *Modern India*, 72.
141. For more on this idea, see Jones, *Socio-Religious Reform Movements*, 41–46.
142. Basu, *Religious Revivalism as Nationalist Discourse*, 3.
143. Ibid., 5.
144. Ibid., 6.
145. Sharpe, *Faith Meets Faith*, 38.
146. Sarkar, *Modern India*, 73.

Indian Struggle for Independence: The Rise of Nationalism and Communalism

The Indian struggle for independence forms the other important context of Chenchiah's early theology. While there are a plethora of sources on the twentieth-century Indian independence struggle, it is possible to divide the independence movement into at least three distinct phases.[147] The first includes the years of moderate nationalism, emphasized by the quest for home-rule, where the intention of the dominant Indian voices was to strengthen local governance in India by Indians.[148] Roughly spanning the late nineteenth century to the early twentieth century, this period in Indian history featured increased administrative responsibility for Indians coupled with scepticism from the British government and some educated Indians on whether India was even capable of handling government.[149] Madden reveals that apart from a few "romantic nationalists," in the early 1900s, many western educated Indians generally regarded British rule as a "providential release from Mughal despotism and were ambivalent towards rapid attainment of Indian self-rule."[150] Madden may be overstating the case for Indian loyalists since there were many calls for independence and a growing unrest and dissatisfaction with British government policy.[151] However, there was no unified call for Indian independence nor was there a common understanding of how that could be achieved.[152] The Indian nationalist fight for *swaraj* (self-rule) was limited to a call for autonomy for Indians in

---

147. I use phases not to suggest a linear historiography, as if to suggest that the Indian Nationalist Movement began with the Congress and ended at 1947. I am aware of alternative historiographies, particularly Marxist readings of nationalism, that see nationalism not as a linear (and thus teleological) phenomena but rather a social phenomena that involved a vast array of people and ideologies. My usage is more to highlight three movements, certainly related, but distinct nevertheless. For more discussion on multiple historiographies dealing with Indian nationalism see Seth, "Rewriting Histories of Nationalism," 95–116.

148. Seth reports that in this period, "nationalism sought reform of the bureaucracy that ruled India, the key elements in such reform being Indianization of the Indian civil service and the introduction of some measure of responsible government." Seth, "Rewriting Histories of Nationalism," 100.

149. Madden, *The Dominions and India Since 1900*, 655.

150. Ibid.

151. For instance see Ramnath, "Two Revolutions," 7–30, Brown, "The Hindu Conspiracy," 299–310 and Gupta, "Defying Death," 3–27.

152. For more on the Home Rule movement and its fallout see Chandra, et al., *India's Struggle for Independence*, 159–69.

governance.¹⁵³ Zimand, writing in the 1920s, captures the general mood for self-government as follows: "Indians want to be free. The tradition which moved a Washington, an Adams, and a Franklin animates the best of India's manhood, who feel, rightly or wrongly, that India should be governed by its own people. They demand a home rule by which they will control the internal affairs of the land. And they refuse to listen to those who assure them that good British rule is at least as good—or even better—than to be governed ill by one's own people. They want Swaraj, which in plain English means self-government."¹⁵⁴

The shift, and thus the second phase in the modern Indian independence movement, is associated with the emergence of Gandhi.¹⁵⁵ Roughly between 1920 and 1940, Gandhi not only garnered Muslim support for the freedom struggle, he also inspired the masses towards his reinterpreted idea of *swaraj*, social reform and moral upliftment.¹⁵⁶ Gandhi redefined *swaraj* to mean more than autonomous governance, to include the idea of inner freedom.¹⁵⁷ The departure of the British was to be only a partial fulfillment of *swaraj*; the true effect was a change in the lives of the masses and the disadvantaged.¹⁵⁸ This change included political independence (freedom from the British), economic independence through *swadeshi* practices (the support of indigenous and simple living) and socioreligious reform through the rejection of untouchability and the use of *satyagraha* (the fight for truth using nonviolence). Chatterjee notes that with Gandhi's ideology, for the first time Indian politics had an "ideological basis for including the *whole people* within the political nation."¹⁵⁹ In addition, "there was also a determinate political structure and process, specific and historically given, within which the task had to be accomplished. And here it was the 'experimental' conception of truth, combining the absolute moral legitimacy of *satyagraha*

---

153. Chakrabarty, *Social and Political Thought of Mahatma Gandhi*, 54.

154. Savel Zimand, *Living India*, 245.

155. Gandhi in fact wrote a tract called "Indian Home Rule" which become hugely popular, and thus subsequently banned by the British government. The main thrust of that booklet was a discussion between Home Rule from moderate and extreme perspectives. The extremists interpreted Home Rule as driving the British out by force. The moderates interpreted it as conceding that British presence was needed for the time being. Gandhi disagreed with both, though said he was willing to serve both, by proposing a declaration of non-violent resistance of British rule, to encourage a truly Indian way to reestablish Indian society. Gandhi, *Hind Swaraj or Indian Home Rule*.

156. Madden, *The Dominions and India Since 1900*, 657.

157. Chakrabarty, *Social and Political Thought of Mahatma Gandhi*, 54–55.

158. Ibid., 55.

159. Chatterjee, *Nationalist Thought and the Colonial World*, 110.

with the tactical considerations of *ahimsa,* which made the Gandhian ideology into a powerful instrument in the historical task of constructing the new Indian state."[160]

Therefore, in this phase of India's struggle for independence, there emerged a semblance of a united nationalist movement, as well as a clarion call for freedom; where the call for *swaraj* became a call for *Purna Swaraj,* or complete independence.[161] Gandhi's key contribution to the nationalist movement was his emphasis on the link between *swaraj* and *swadeshi,* as well as his use of *satyagraha* (through *ahimsa*) to reach out to the masses.

In the third phase, roughly in the 1940s, India's independence was seen as inevitable, with the focus shifting towards the how and when. Despite this, the road to independence during this third phase was far from smooth. It was here that communal rifts, especially between Hindus and Muslims, surfaced with greatest intensity.[162] Aloysius points out that the class and minority divide within the nationalist movement was exposed as a central problem for the unity of the independence movement.[163]

Heehs points out that the goals of early Indian nationalism were both cultural and spiritual.[164] Pandey paints a more detailed picture of pre-independent India, where both communalism and nationalism "arose together" since they "were part of the same discourse."[165] He notes that prior to the 1920s, Hindu and Muslim political involvement was both necessary and inevitable.[166] Gandhi, for instance, saw no contradiction in the Muslim love for their country even as they were "Mussulmans first and everything else afterwards."[167] However, by the mid-1920s, "communitarian mobilization" began to be termed by nationalists as distorted and unnecessary.[168] Pandey notes the emergence of a secular nationalist rhetoric that strongly urged the people to work for the interest of the nation outside community interests. The same Gandhi went on to say that "Nationalism is greater than sectari-

---

160. Ibid.,110–111.

161. Chakrabarty, *Social and Political Thought of Mahatma Gandhi* 49–50. See also, Chandra et al., *India's Struggle for Independence,* 264.

162. Madden writes that by 1945 "the real question was not whether India should become independent ... [but] whether the Muslim League, insistent that it alone spoke for all Indian Muslims ... would accept any formula for a united independent India." Madden, *The Dominions and India Since 1900,* 659.

163. Aloysius, *Nationalism without a Nation,* 218.

164. Heehs, "Bengali Religious Nationalism and Communalism," 132.

165. Pandey, *The Construction of Communalism,* 236.

166. Ibid., 235.

167. Gandhi, "To The Mussulmans of India," 192.

168. Pandey, *The Construction of Communalism,* 235.

anism... we are Indians first and Hindus, Mussulmans, Parsis, Christians after."[169] Eventually "pure nationalists" aimed to suppress and even discredit community voices, offering that secular nationalism was the only way for unity and progress in India.[170] Nationalism was presented as rational, relevant to real issues and progressive, while communalism was projected as premodern, irrelevant and regressive.[171]

Religious and lower caste communities, understandably, reacted fiercely against the notion of a secular nation as defined by a "Hindu elite."[172] The strongest reaction came from Muslims and other caste and religious minorities, who refused to follow the Congress desire for national integration unless their interests were met. Heehs notes that even the Hindu religious nationalism that emerged after the 1920s, with Savarkar and Golwalkar, was a form of extreme communalism rather than the spiritual cultural nationalism of just a few decades before it.[173]

Since there was no fundamental commonality of interest in the nationalist movement,[174] beyond the desire for independence from the British, it was inevitable that there would be a struggle as even minorities asserted what they perceived to be their rights.[175] It is also here that Gandhi's influence in Indian politics diminished,[176] while other leaders like Nehru and Ambedkar began to shape the destiny of the future "secular" Indian nation.[177] Moraes notes the changing mood towards secularity through Nehru, who adopted a strongly functional view of religion that attributed a positive value

169. Gandhi, "Hindus and Moplahs," 268. Pandey draws attention to this change in Gandhi, in Pandey, *The Construction of Communalism*, 238.

170. Pandey, *The Construction of Communalism*, 239–42.

171. Ibid., 241.

172. For instance, see Low, *Eclipse of Empire*, 86.

173. Heehs, "Bengali Religious Nationalism and Communalism," 136.

174 Aloysius argues that nationalism represented by Gandhi "blunt the thrust of the popular militancy." It diffused "the mass struggle against the old Brahminic social order in particular" and alienated or subdued others "to serve its own agenda... devoid of any serious social change." Aloysius, *Nationalism without a Nation*, 220.

175 Aloysius goes on to point to how Gandhi's "rhetoric of moral reform, search for truth, critique of Western civilization and restitution of our own traditional way of life... drove away a substantial portion of the Muslim masses along with their leaders, caused embitterment and thus antagonized a vast number of depressed classes and their representatives." Aloysius, *Nationalism without a Nation*, 220–21.

176. For instance, Chatterjee shows that by 1945–46, Gandhi was less than enthusiastic about his *khadi* workers joining politics. Similarly, *khadi* was seen as resistance even to the soon-to-be formed Indian Government. Chatterjee, *Nationalist Thought and the Colonial World*, 113–21.

177. See Rajagopalan, "Secularism in India," 241.

to religion only if it worked for the good of the nation.[178] In his *Discovery of India*, Nehru captured the changing mood towards religion by a section of the nonreligious pro-development Indians;

> ... even if God exists, it may be desirable not to look up to Him or to rely upon Him. Too much dependence on supernatural factors may lead, and has often led, to a loss of self-reliance in man and to a blunting of his capacity and creative ability ... Whether we believe in God or not, it is impossible not to believe in something, whether we call it a creative life-giving force or vital energy inherent in matter which gives it its capacity for self-movement and change and growth ... Whether we are conscious of it or not most of us worship at the invisible altar of some unknown god and offer sacrifices to it—some ideal, personal, national or international; some distant objective that draws us on, though reason itself may find little substance in it; some vague conception of a perfect man and a better world. Perfection may be impossible of attainment, but the demon in us, some vital force, urges us on and we tread that path from generation to generation.[179]

The nineteenth and early twentieth centuries were not just times of reform, revival and nationalism, but also times during which the concept of religion was being constructed in ways that were relevant to the people.

Indian Theories of Religion

Evidently, in the late nineteenth and early twentieth century, the nonrational, detraditionalized and the evolutionary views of religion—arising from Western discussions—influenced Indian ideas about religion.[180] Key Hindu thinkers, however, also significantly shaped how religion was understood by Indian Christians.

---

178. According to Moraes, Nehru believed that "Religion clouds men's minds because it rests on doctrine and dogma, and thereby discourages clear thinking." It is not surprising therefore that "religion in its formal sense, with its worshipping, temple-going and prayer-saying, had no appeal for him." Moraes, *Jawaharlal Nehru: A Biography*, 225.

179. Nehru, *The Discovery of India*, 513–14.

180. The rational view of religion was largely unpersuasive to Indian thinkers who, as religious practitioners, saw it as a limited understanding of religion.

Sri Aurobindo

Aurobindo's is a good example of a nonrationalist theory of religion that emerged during this time. Aurobindo began his political life as a nationalist revolutionary, but ended as a spiritual guru outside politics. Yet, in both senses, Aurobindo was in the mode of the revivalists because he did not accept the traditional views of Hinduism as they stood but looked to transform them for the context in which Hindus existed. One of the important contributions that Aurobindo would make to the religious understanding of Hinduism was the clarification of yoga,[181] especially "integral yoga."[182] Sen identifies Aurobindo's yoga as a "new vision and possibility of advance in spiritual life."[183] Expounding the value of each of the yogas, Aurobindo went on to offer a synthesis of yogas, where new possibilities could be discovered.[184] Key to Aurobindo's synthesis was to mobilize all the yogas, including Tantra, to achieve "revolutionary change and transformation" so that the soul was converted from a natural life to a "divine being."[185] In an extended quote from Aurobindo's work, it is evident that key themes of evolution, transformation, power and Divine, were part of his system:

> The passage from the lower to the higher is the aim of Yoga; and this passage may affect itself by the rejection of the lower and escape into the higher,—the ordinary viewpoint, —or by the transformation of the lower and its elevation to the higher Nature. It is this, rather, that must be the aim of an integral Yoga. But in either case it is always through something in the lower that we must rise into the higher existence, and the schools of Yoga each select their own point of departure or their own gate of escape . . . If indeed our aim be only an escape from the world to God, synthesis is unnecessary and a waste of time; for then our sole practical aim must be to find out one path out of the thousand that lead to God, one shortest possible of short cuts, and not to linger exploring different paths that end in the same goal. But if our aim be a transformation of our integral being into the terms of God-existence, it is then that a synthesis becomes necessary.[186]

181. A theme that Chenchiah accepts and wholeheartedly applies in his own work.
182. Sen, *Sri Aurobindo on Yoga*, 9–10.
183. Ibid., 9.
184. Aurobindo's work on integral yoga is found in Aurobindo, *The Synthesis of Yoga*.
185. Aurobindo, *The Synthesis of Yoga*, xxvii.
186. Aurobindo, *The Synthesis of Yoga*, 39–40.

One can also see Aurobindo's synthesis in *Superman*, where the ideal of religion is seen in the context of evolutionism: "The gospel of true supermanhood gives us a generous ideal for the progressive human race and should not be turned into an arrogant claim for a class or individuals. It is a call to man to do what no species has yet done or aspired to do in terrestrial history, evolve itself consciously into the next superior type already half foreseen by the continual cyclic development of the world-idea in Nature's fruitful musings."[187]

In addition, nonrationalism and evolutionism were combined through the emphasis on the goal of union with the Infinite: "For what is supermanhood but a certain divine and harmonious absolute of all that is essential in man? He is made in God's image, but there is this difference between the divine Reality and its human representative that every thing which in the one is unlimited, spontaneous, absolute, harmonious, self-possessed becomes in the other limited, relative, laboured, discordant, deformed . . . But in this constant imperfection there is always a craving and an aspiration towards perfection. Man, limited, yearns to the Infinite."[188]

Finally, similar to Advaitic Hindu thinking, Aurobindo linked evolution[189] with *moksha* by portraying "the ultimate goal" of human evolution to be "liberation out of a state of bondage."[190] Thus Aurobindo stated:

> we move from a state of bondage to an original liberty. This is what our own religion teaches. This is what our own philosophy suggests as the goal towards which we move, *mukti* or *moksha*. We are bound in the beginning by a lapse from pre-existent freedom, we strive to shake off the bonds, we move forward and forward until we have achieved the ultimate emancipation, that utter freedom of the soul, of the body or the whole man, that utter freedom from all bondage towards which humanity is always aspiring.[191]

As a result, we see that Aurobindo was nonrationalist primarily because his focus was on the nonmaterial aspect of life, like spiritual/divine essence and the power to harness that essence. Similarly, his theory of religion

---

187. Sri Aurobindo, *The Superman*, 2.

188. Ibid.,8–9.

189. For more on Aurobindo's view of evolution see Srivastava, "The Integralist Theory of Evolution," 133–42.

190. Aurobindo, *Speeches*, 104–5.

191. Ibid.,105.

was founded on his own cosmographical scheme of the existence of a divine nature, which a person could evolve towards through yoga.[192]

Swami Vivekananda

Like Aurobindo, Swami Vivekananda was revolutionary and arguably more influential. Having an accessible writing and speaking style, he not only gave many Indian Hindus reasons for self-respect but also helped carve a positive space for Hinduism in global consciousness. Key to Vivekananda's view of religion was the integration of Western evolutionism with Advaitic Hinduism. In fact, Vivekananda was of the view that Hinduism was "the only religion with a strong philosophical content,"[193] to the extent that it took religious evolution more seriously than in the West: "The theory of evolution, which is the foundation of almost all the Indian schools of thought, has not made its way into the physical science of Europe."[194]

For Vivekananda, the soul of the Indian nation was in Hinduism,[195] and it had unity despite its diversity because it bypassed rational discourse and preferred religious actualization:

> The Hindu religion does not consist in struggles and attempts to believe a certain doctrine or dogma, but in realizing not in believing, but in being and becoming . . . the whole object of their system is by constant struggle to become perfect, to become divine to reach God, and see God; and this reaching God, seeing God, becoming perfect 'even as the Father in Heaven is perfect,' constitutes the religion of the Hindus. And what becomes of a man when he attains perfection? He lives a life of bliss infinite . . . enjoys that bliss with God . . . This is the common religion of all the sects of India.[196]

Furthermore, Vivekananda would hold that the evolution of religion was linked with biology, in that if we look at humanity as a "vast organism," then all processes of religion, including doctrines, mythologies and rituals, are part of the process of "slowly coming towards light—a wonderful plant, slowly unfolding itself to that wonderful truth which is called God."[197]

192. An idea that Chenchiah would adapt for his own theory of religion.
193. Basu, *Religious Revivalism as Nationalist Discourse*, 178.
194. Vivekananda, *The East and the West*, 79.
195. Ibid., 19.
196. Vivekananda, *The Chicago Addresses*, 11.
197. Vivekananda, *The Complete Works*, 40–41.

Within evolutionism, Vivekananda also offered a view of the ultimate goal, the ideal of universal religion being transformation: "true religion never changes. Religion is realization; not talk, nor doctrine, nor theories, however beautiful they may be. It is being and becoming, not hearing or acknowledging; it is the whole soul becoming changed into what it believes. That is religion."[198]

A related concept for Vivekananda was the idea that man in the body was imperfect, changeable, but the unchangeable man was the man of spirit who was perfect; the "perfect man" was "God-man."[199]

Evidently, Aurobindo and Vivekananda emphasized a nonmaterial spirituality, where not just the human body but also the rituals of religion were of less importance than the divine essence (and true religion) within.

Mahatma Gandhi

Along with these theories of religion, there emerged others which were more integrated with the life and culture of India—the theories of Gandhi and Ambedkar.

The popular story about Gandhi's religion, derived primarily from his autobiography,[200] paints a picture of a man who had no real sensibility about religion until he went to a foreign land, both England and South Africa. Gandhi tells of how the Bhagavad Gita, along with his encounters with Hindu and Christians thinkers, as well as his readings of Western literature, sparked his religious consciousness and his subsequent religio-political philosophy. Without being too critical of these claims, it can be assumed that Gandhi's religion developed as an eclectic encounter with other religions, though grounded fundamentally in his own Hindu faith. Ultimately, Gandhi's religious philosophy developed along the lines of the nineteenth century reformers. He sought to reshape Hindu thinking by being critical of many religious traditions,[201] while remaining deeply loyal to the religion of his heritage.

It would be natural to link Gandhi with the nonrational view of religion, especially since he broadly defined religion as "self-realization or

---

198. Vivekananda, *Complete Works*, Vol 2, 396.

199. Ibid., 40. I state this here, because Chenchiah will adapt the idea of God–man to mean Jesus Christ.

200. Gandhi, *An Autobiography*.

201. For instance, animal sacrifice and dedication of *devadasis*. cf. Jordens, *Gandhi's Religion*, 87.

knowledge of self."[202] However, Gandhi also had much in common with the rational view of religion. Gandhi tended to emphasize religious and ethical principles over devotion to God, even as he prioritized the *karma marga* (morality) over the *bhakti marga* (devotion).[203] In addition, Gandhi's de-traditionalization was represented through his emphasis on truth above all else. "Truth is superior to everything, and I reject what conflicts with it . . . that which is in conflict with nonviolence should be rejected . . . on matters which can be reasoned out, that which conflicted with Reason must also be rejected."[204]

Gandhi was no mystic, though his lack of interest in the historicity of religion and his individual judgment to prioritize nonviolence as the core of all religions suggests he was nonrationalist.[205] However, Gandhi would go on to emphasize truth that was not the kind that focused on rationalism, but an inner truth of *ahimsa* and moral transformation. As a result, Gandhi leaned towards an ethical view of religion, one that aimed at moral transformation in life and work. His prioritizing of individualistic readings of the text was evident when even though others read the Gita as a text of violence, he chose to see it as nonviolent.[206] In addition, "if the worst came to the worst and if I came to the conclusion that the Koran teaches violence, I would still reject violence, but I would not therefore say that the Bible is superior to the Koran or that Mohammed is inferior to Jesus. It is not my function to judge Mohammed and Jesus. It is enough that my non-violence is independent of the sanction of scriptures."[207]

Nanda rightly draws attention to how Gandhi's conception of religion was different from what was generally believed to be religion—the dogmas, rituals and institutions.[208] Nanda goes to the extent of saying that Gandhi's religion was an "ethical framework for the conduct of daily life."[209]

Furthermore, Gandhi had a strong belief in the unity of religion. However, this was not in the sense of the flattening of differences but through an essential oneness that transcended differences. This belief was supplemented with a strong belief in being loyal to one's own religion; it was a

---

202. Gandhi, *An Autobiography*, 27.

203. Gorringe, "Gandhi and the Christian Community," 163.

204. Gandhi, "Interview to Dr. Crane," 398.

205. See also, Minz, *Mahatma Gandhi and Hindu-Christian Dialogue*, 28. Minz here highlights how Gandhi valued his personal experience more than scriptures.

206. Gandhi, "Interview to Dr. Crane," 399.

207. Ibid.

208. Nanda, *In Search of Gandhi*, 24.

209. Ibid.

self-respect derived from Gandhi's *swadeshi* philosophy, where one was to stay faithful to the religion one was born into. Gandhi did also conceive of true religion as transcending Hinduism. "Let me explain what I mean by religion. It is not the Hindu religion, which I certainly prise above all other religions, but the religion which transcends Hinduism which changes one's very nature, which binds one indissolubly to the truth within and whichever purifies. It is the permanent element in human nature which . . . leaves the soul restless until it has found itself."[210]

Evidently, while religion transcended the particularities of Hinduism, religion was still common to all people, inherent in human nature as a "religious spirit," thus implying a universal religious essence in human nature.[211] This also formed the basis of Gandhi's pluralism and a view of religion as something that bound all religions.[212] Jordens points out that much of what Gandhi said about religion was similar to what he said about other religions as well, especially as Gandhi believed that the fundamentals of every great religion were the same.[213] His view of idol worship affirmed that it was the right for believers to worship God in the form they were comfortable with, to the extent that even the belief that God was revealed only in the Koran or the Bible was a form of idol worship.[214]

However, this should not be taken to mean that Gandhi operated outside the Hindu framework. In fact, there were times when he strongly expressed his views using Hindu categories, though it must also be noted that scholars like Nanda opine that he did not believe in those categories.[215]

While Gandhi's use of Hinduism was selective, he remained to the core a Hindu. In his famous retort to Moonje, the Hindu Mahasabha leader who argued that untouchability was a part of Hinduism, Gandhi stated that his Hinduism does not bind him "to every verse because it is written in Sanskrit."[216] Despite Moonje's "literal knowledge of the *shastras*," which Gandhi stated was "a distorted kind of Hinduism," Gandhi affirmed, "I claim in all humility to have lived Hinduism all my life."[217]

---

210. Gandhi, "Neither A Saint Nor a Politician," 406.
211. Ibid.
212. Nanda, *In Search of Gandhi*, 24.
213. Jordens, *Gandhi's Religion*, 84.
214. Ibid., 89.
215. Nanda, *In Search of Gandhi*, 28.
216. Gandhi, "Letter to Dr. B. S. Moonje," 322.
217. Ibid., 323.

Similarly, even as he reinterpreted *ahimsa* as the central theme of the Gita, over against orthodox Hindu interpretations, Gandhi believed that Hinduism was the best example of tolerance and respect for life:

> I have found [Hinduism] to be the most tolerant of all religions ... Its freedom from dogma ... gives the votary the largest scope for self-expression. Not being an exclusive religion, it enables the followers of that faith not merely to respect all the other religions, but ... to admire and assimilate whatever may be good in the other faiths. Non-violence is common to all religions, but it has found the highest expression and application in Hinduism ... Hinduism believes in the oneness not of merely all human life but in the oneness of all that lives.[218]

However, it was his doctrine of *swadeshi* that would explain how Gandhi was so pluralistic as well as so strongly against conversion, even forcefully promoting the indigenous religions of India above Christianity.[219] Gandhi stated, "Certainly the great faiths held by the people of India are adequate for her people. India is in no need of conversion from one faith to another."[220] However Gandhi clarified that there was a need for conversion, but that conversion was of a spiritual kind, "a conversion in the sense of self-purification" and "self-realization:" "Faith is not imparted like secular subjects. It is given through the language of the heart. If a man has a living faith in him, it spreads its aroma like the rose its scent. Because of its invisibility, the extent of its influence is far wider than that of the visible beauty of the colour of the petals."[221]

Another of Gandhi's significant contribution was to offer an integrated view of religion for all facets of life. Jordens is correct in pointing out that Gandhi drew from the revival of Advaitic Vedanta philosophy,[222] combined it with the down-to-earth practices of *bhakti*,[223] and presented a religion that "penetrated all aspects of his private, public, and political activity."[224]

Along the lines of the reformers, it is not surprising that Gandhi related religion to social reform. In fact, there are natural parallels between Vivekananda and Gandhi, especially as both rejected ceremonial religion for inner transformation, appealed to a divine spark in all people, and

218. Gandhi, *Hindu Dharma*, 8.
219. Gorringe, "Gandhi and the Christian Community," 162.
220. Gandhi, "Foreign Missionaries," 28.
221. Ibid., 28–29.
222. Jordens, *Gandhi's Religion*, 69.
223. Ibid., 9.
224. Ibid., 3.

integrated belief with social action.[225] However the key difference, and thus the unique contribution of Gandhi, was in how Gandhi integrated his religion with politics,[226] to the extent that spirituality could not be conceived outside nationalism—inner and outer freedom were related. In the concluding pages of his autobiography, Gandhi summarized his integrated view of religion: "To see the universal and all-pervading Spirit of Truth face to face one must be able to love the meanest of creation as oneself. And a man who aspires after that cannot afford to keep out of any field of life. That is why my devotion to Truth has drawn me into the field of politics; and I can say without the slightest hesitation, and yet in all humility, that those who say that religion has nothing to do with politics do not know what religion means."[227]

The way that Gandhi integrated religion with politics was through *satyagraha*. Almost in line with the Christian view of the cross, Gandhi's *satyagraha* was predominantly portrayed as a moral struggle to conquer the enemy within and the enemy outside—by excluding hatred, deceit and violence, and embracing self-sacrifice and love.[228]

Of course, Gandhi has numerous critics. For instance, Aloysius points out that Gandhi's political mobilization was strongly based on religion, such as his emphasis on removal of untouchability and affirming moral reformation.[229] This marginalized the economic and social concerns of the Muslim and lower caste masses, whose desire was for education, shared power and social mobility.[230] As we will see in the next chapter, it was Gandhi's vision to integrate religion with life that largely influenced Chenchiah's own theology of religion.

Babasaheb Ambedkar

In contrast to Gandhi was Ambedkar. If Gandhi offered an integrated vision of religion that was spiritual, Ambedkar's integrated religion was functional. In the post-Marxian context, Ambedkar's voice rose strongly on behalf of the masses, especially the untouchables, and his work displays little patience for the spiritual interpretations of religion. To get a visceral distinction, one

---

225. Nanda, *In Search of Gandhi*, 68–70.
226. Ibid., 70.
227. Gandhi, *An Autobiography*, 420.
228. Nanda, *In Search of Gandhi*, 24.
229. Aloysius, *Nationalism without a Nation*, 223.
230. Ibid.

The Context of Chenchiah's Theology of Religion 87

needs to see these two figures from the point of view of the Dalits who hail Ambedkar as their hero and oftentimes Gandhi as the villain.[231]

Fitzgerald is correct in pointing out that in the study of Hinduism, preference is given to the "high caste view of the ecumenical construct Hinduism," to Gandhi and others, while the voice of untouchables and the critique of ideological religion, as represented by Ambedkar, is ignored.[232] In the process of his critique of the elite and his desire for the liberation of the untouchable masses, Fitzgerald finds that Ambedkar went beyond the traditional conceptions of religion.[233]

Ambedkar's key text against caste is *Annihilation of Caste*,[234] which was a speech to be delivered in front of the Jat-Pat-Todak Mandal, a Hindu reform group, but which was cancelled because it was considered too controversial.[235] Its main argument is that social reform cannot succeed without the eradication of untouchability, and this eradication can only be achieved by a complete rejection of the wrong beliefs of Hinduism:

> Caste may be bad. Caste may lead to conduct so gross as to be called man's inhumanity to man. All the same, it must be recognized that the Hindus observe Caste not because they are inhuman or wrong headed. They observe Caste because they are deeply religious. People are not wrong in observing Caste. In my view, what is wrong is their religion, which has inculcated this notion of Caste. If this is correct, then obviously the enemy you must grapple with is not the people who observe Caste but the *Shastras* which teach them this religion of Caste . . . The real remedy is to destroy the belief in the sanctity of the *Shastras*.[236]

This attack on the Hindu religion is ultimately reflected in Ambedkar's theory of religion. In the same speech, Ambedkar called for the destruction of the religion of the Hindu texts,[237] which Ambedkar stated was the

231. See Rajshekar et al., *The verdict of history*. Importantly, Rajshekar also depicts "Dalits" as separate from "Hindus."

232. Fitzgerald, *Ideology of Religious Studies*, 122.

233. Ibid., 123. One must note that while Fitzgerald's study here seeks to demonstrate that Ambedkar moved beyond the concept of religion, I use Fitzgerald here to simply show that Ambedkar had an alternative view of religion. My rationale is Ambedkar's own use of the term in his writings, which, while certainly non-traditional, nevertheless still opted for the use of the word and thus allowing for an alternative understanding of that word.

234 Ambedkar, *Annihilation of Caste*.

235. Fitzgerald, *Ideology of Religious Studies*, 124.

236. Ambedkar, *Annihilation of Caste*, XX.

237. "You must destroy the Religion of the *Shrutis* and the *Smritis*. Nothing else

destruction of a type of religion. His premise was that there was a difference between rules and principles, and thus there existed a religion of rules and a religion of principles. For Ambedkar, a religion of rules was not a religion and only a religion of principles upheld the responsibility of religion: "To permit of this responsibility, Religion must mainly be a matter of principles only. It cannot be a matter of rules. The moment it degenerates into rules it ceases to be Religion, as it kills responsibility which is the essence of a truly religious act."[238] For Ambedkar, the Hindu religion, as represented through its Vedas, was "nothing but a mass of sacrificial, social, political and sanitary rules and regulations . . . a multitude of commands and prohibitions."[239] In effect, the Hindu religion of rules was not religion but Law, and thus open and even encouraged to being abolished/changed:

> I have, therefore, no hesitation in saying that such a religion must be destroyed and I say, there is nothing irreligious in working for the destruction of such a religion. Indeed I hold that it is your bounden duty to tear the mask, to remove the misrepresentation that is caused by misnaming this Law as Religion. This is an essential step for you. Once you clear the minds of the people of this misconception and enable them to realize that what they are told as Religion is not Religion but that it is really law, you will be in a position to urge for its amendment or abolition. So long as people look upon it as Religion they will not be ready for a change, because the idea of Religion is generally speaking not associated with the idea of change. But the idea of law is associated with the idea of change and when people come to know that what is called Religion is really Law, old and archaic, they will be ready for a change, for people know and accept that law can be changed.[240]

For Ambedkar, true religion had the power to guide responsible thinking[241] and so he asserted that the religion of principles was the "foundation of society."[242] Thus Ambedkar clarified, "when I urge that these ancient rules of life be annulled, I am anxious that its place shall be taken by a Religion of Principles, which alone can lay claim to being a true Religion."[243]

---

will avail." Ambedkar, *Annihilation of Caste*, XXII.
238. Ambedkar, *Annihilation of Caste*, XXIII.
239. Ibid.
240. Ibid.
241. Ibid.
242. Ambedkar, *Annihilation of Caste*, XXIV.
243. Ibid.

Where Ambedkar really differed from Gandhi was in his almost exclusive reference to the utility of religion for society, devoid of the need for personal/spiritual transformation. Ambedkar scholar Larbeer reports that Ambedkar did not acknowledge the transcendental grounds of religion such as divine revelation, nor did Ambedkar recognize the mysteries of religion such as *avatar* or *moksa*.[244]

Gandhi, as we saw, offered a religiopolitical philosophy that began with a battle in the human soul. Ambedkar, on the other hand, emphasized structural changes wrought due to religion. Ambedkar's own conversion to Buddhism shows this; it was a move that was made less because of spiritual goals akin to Gandhi and more to make a strong sociopolitical statement. The popular belief about why Ambedkar chose Buddhism is because of its anticaste stance. However, in the autobiographical preface to his book on Buddhism, Ambedkar explained that he opted for Buddhism not for what it offered a believer, but a thinker. He regarded Buddha's Dhamma to be the best religion: "No religion can be compared to it. If a modern man who knows science must have a religion, the only religion he can have is the religion of the Buddha. This conviction has grown in me after thirty-five years of close study of all religions."[245] The attraction, to a large part, was attributed to the scientific relevance of Buddhism: "Buddha's Religion was the only religion which a society awakened by science could accept, and without which it would perish. I also pointed out that for the modern world Buddhism was the only religion which it must have to save itself."[246] In the conclusion of his book, Ambedkar extolled once again the rational aspects of Buddhism: "In no other religion are the values of knowledge and evil of ignorance so much insisted upon ... No other religion lays so much stress upon keeping one's eyes open ... No other religion has formulated such deep laid plans for mental culture."[247]

Evidently, Ambedkar adopted a scientific-rational view of religion that promised genuine social reform. Nevertheless, while Ambedkar preferred rationality over spiritualism, his theory of religion still belonged within a detraditionalist tradition.

---

244. Larbeer, *Ambedkar on Religion*, 203.
245. Ambedkar, *The Buddha and His Dhamma*, 2.
246. Ibid., 3.
247. Ibid., 344.

EARLY TWENTIETH-CENTURY THEOLOGIES OF RELIGION

With an awareness of the theories of religions in the West and the East, we are now ready to move into the theological constructions of religion, particularly in the early 1900s. Sharpe documents Christian attitudes through the nineteenth and twentieth century concerning other religions, especially Hinduism, showing a range of Christian attitudes, from general antagonism to respect.[248] Sharpe draws attention to the difference between rationalist and Pietist approaches to religion in the nineteenth century which, despite their differences in methods and purposes, were still similar in their rejection of non-Christian religions.[249] Basu correctly notes that at this time, Hinduism was characterized by binaries, whereby Christian missionaries "held the heathen Hindus as separate from the religious, the enlightened, and the ethical . . . infantile, the lower, the darker," drawing these conclusions from the Christian position that was supposedly rational, philosophical and mature.[250]

With the rise of Orientalists like Max Müller, attitudes towards non-Christian religions began to change rapidly. Müller attempted to look at Hinduism on its own terms, without judgment. More specifically, Müller challenged the dominant negative views of Hinduism by arguing for both the intellectual coherence and the moral value of the Hindu way of life.[251]

The impact of Orientalists on the Christian views of non-Christian religions, Sharpe notes, was to at least blunt the force of their traditional moral critique[252] and even allow for the belief that there were many more similarities between religions than had been previously conceived.[253]

Fulfillment Theory

One important change in Christian perceptions of the other religions took place when the religions of the world were seen to be in direct continuity with Christianity. The fulfillment theory was clearly influenced by evolutionism and though it was employed by several scholars, it has been

---

248. Sharpe, *Faith Meets Faith*.

249. Ibid., 7–10.

250. Basu, *Religious Revivalism as Nationalist Discourse*, 13.

251. See especially Lecture II on the "Truthful character of Hindus," in Müller, *India: What Can It Teach Us?*, 34–75.

252. Sharpe, *Faith Meets Faith*, 16.

253. Ibid., 17.

popularly associated with Farquhar. The main argument of the fulfillment theory, as Farquhar put it, was that Christ was the apex or even completion of the aspirations of other religions: "Jesus Christ in His person and in His life fulfils those cravings which gathered about the names of Krishna and of Rama, and which labored to idealize these not altogether ideal figures."[254] The fulfillment position was hardly a liberal compromise since it arose in a strongly evangelical context. Farquhar, for instance, strongly believed in the ultimacy of Christ when he states:

> Christ provides the fulfillment of each of the highest aspirations and aims of Hinduism . . . every line of light which is visible in the grossest parts of the religion reappears in Him set in healthy institutions and spiritual worship. Every true motive which in Hinduism has found expression in unclean, debasing, or unworthy practices finds in Him fullest exercise in work for the downtrodden, the ignorant, the sick, and the sinful. In Him is focused every ray of light that shines in Hinduism. He is the Crown of the faith of India.[255]

Farquhar did not always distinguish between Christ and religions, though when he stated "Christianity is the Crown of Hinduism,"[256] there was an appeal to the superiority of the Christian religion: "Every thinking man sees clearly the superiority of the great religions over the lowest faiths. The Christian sees as distinctly the superiority of Christianity to the rest of the great religions; and he believes the evidence can be set forth with overwhelming force."[257]

Others like Newton Scott also did not strive to make a distinction between Christ and Christianity. Scott proposed that the "more spiritually advanced" a religion is, the closer it would be towards the doctrines of Trinity, Incarnation, and the Atonement, so that even "the Incarnation was delayed until, 'in the fulness of the time,' the religious education of the most progressive races of mankind was sufficiently advanced for them to appreciate and welcome the Atonement,—until 'the fields' were 'white already to harvest.'"[258]

Nicol Macnicol felt that Hinduism represented "a sincere attempt to find God, and learn His will" and was still "capable of being so used by an earnest spirit."[259] Many who were unwilling to make such a pronouncement

---

254. Macnicol, *Indian Theism*, 259.
255. Farquhar, *The Crown of Hinduism*, 457–58.
256. Ibid., 55.
257. Ibid., 31.
258. Scott, *The Religions of Antiquity*, 183.
259. From Nicol Macnicol's original manuscripts now housed in Missionary

about Hinduism would at least believe that the "highest points of Hinduism were to be used mainly as points of contact and departure of the Christian message."[260]

Mallampalli makes an interesting point about the "fulfillment theory" in India, where Christian missionaries felt that the Hindu renaissance, despite its anti-Christian nature, was part of the natural progression of Hinduism toward Christian belief.[261] Many missionaries, Mallampalli believes, defended their efforts of working with the educated class by "portraying Hindu nationalism as a movement toward Christian ends,"[262] and by especially emphasizing that reformed Hinduism was a religion in the "image of Christianity."[263]

Edinburgh, 1910

To this extent the World Missionary Conference in Edinburgh, in 1910, best represented the attitude that Christianity was the highest religion.[264] Edinburgh (1910) was the first of the mission conferences that addressed the urgency of world evangelism. Gairdner indicates that the participants were aware of the "vastness of the task,"[265] where the Church needed to act like never before to meet the urgent needs of the "unoccupied fields of the world."[266] To Kraemer, "It seemed as if the non-Christian world was spread out before the eye as a world to be conquered."[267] For D. T. Niles, the chief emphases of Edinburgh 1910 were missionary cooperation and missionary occupation, and in both senses the goals were remarkably achieved.[268]

In terms of religion, the general sense of Edinburgh was to urge missionaries to have "a sympathetic attitude towards India's most ancient

---

Research Library, New York, cited in Sharpe, *Faith Meets Faith*, 35.

260. Sharpe, *Faith Meets Faith*, 35.

261. Mallampalli, *Christians and Public Life*, 99.

262. Ibid.

263. Ibid.

264. Here one must note Sharpe's warning about overemphasizing the importance of the Conferences as representational of universal understanding of religion. While I accept Sharpe's warning, my use of the conferences here is to draw attention to some dominant thinking about religion that would influence Chenchiah. See Sharpe, *Faith Meets Faith*, 33–34.

265. Gairdner, *Edinburgh 1910*, 70.

266. Ibid., 78–81.

267. Kraemer, *The Christian Message in a Non-Christian World*, 36.

268. Niles, *From Edinburgh to Tambaram*, 2.

religion."²⁶⁹ There was the missiologically practical emphasis on "points of contact" and *praeparatio evangelica* within Hinduism.²⁷⁰ Furthermore, there was even the suggestion that non-Christian religions help to highlight "the latent riches of the absolute religion," namely Christianity.²⁷¹ Evidently, in extension to the fulfillment theory, the sympathetic approach towards religion strengthened the belief that religion was common across cultures, though Christianity was its best example.

Jerusalem, 1928

A decade since Edinburgh, it was clear that Christianity could not be considered as sufficient in itself and there were doubts about single-minded Christian optimism. Sharpe notes that this was largely because Christian optimism was shaken after the First World War: "The Christian world was by now much less sure of itself than it had been as recently as at the time of the 1910 Edinburgh conference. The war to end all wars had shattered many dreams. The simple categories of evolution, of inevitable Western-assisted moral and ethical progress . . . now convinced fewer people."²⁷²

Niles makes a similar point by showing that the Jerusalem conference in 1928 was the Church's response to the postwar challenges that faced Christianity and the world: "[The] rising tide of secularism not only constituted a problem in itself but was also inadequate to meet the problems of a war-shattered world. As a reaction it was understandable, as a permanent mood it was tragic. Those in East and West who sensed the need of the day immediately called for a new alignment of forces to meet this situation. The Jerusalem conference of 1928 was the endeavour of the churches to discover what their task should be."²⁷³

Furthermore, in contrast to the confidence about Christianity at Edinburgh, there was a growing recognition of the power of non-Christian religions, which had grown more confident. Sharpe notes that the rise of Gandhi in Western consciousness led many Christians to believe that, perhaps, being a Hindu was not such a bad thing after all.²⁷⁴ According to

---

269. Cairns, *World Missionary Conference*, 171.
270. Ibid., 177–87.
271. Ibid., 278.
272. Sharpe, *Faith Meets Faith*, 46.
273. Niles, *From Edinburgh to Tambaram*, 4.
274. Sharpe, *Faith Meets Faith*, 47.

Kraemer, the mood of Jerusalem was introspective and observant, urging towards responsibility.[275]

This is not to say that presumptions about Christian superiority had ended. Macnicol, for instance, clarified Christian views on religion and Hinduism by saying:

> Christianity is not a rival religion [to Hinduism]; it is, we believe, in its essentials the expression of that which Hinduism, 'with stammering lips and another tongue,' has been striving to utter, the realisation of its incoherent dreams. For the Gospel of Christ ... is not a religion, but religion itself in its most universal and deepest significance ... Hinduism is a great museum of human needs and searchings, and for that reason it must discover to us many places of desire where it reaches towards and so confirms the Christian revelation.[276]

However, Macnicol went on to speak of how Christian attitudes towards Hinduism and vice versa were changing, especially after the reform movement within Hinduism. From enmity, there was now a "new sympathy and desire to understand."[277] There was also a general mood for "Hindu-Christian synthesis," for social reform as well as the attempt to bridge the gulf between the two religions.[278]

Hence in Jerusalem (1928), there was openness to and a healthy respect for the vitality of religion, while reaffirming the priority and necessity of the Christian gospel. The Jerusalem approach to religion can thus be seen as an attempt to combat the antireligious forces of materialism and secularism, with non-Christian religions as allies. This was a clear development post-Edinburgh because people had already begun to suggest that in religions there were many more commonalities than differences.

The cooperation perspective was reflected in discussions by Ernest Hocking, Rufus Jones and several others. Hocking emphasized religious cooperation for social good, stating that modern mission needs to make a "positive effort" not only to "know and understand the religions," but also to "recognize and associate itself with whatever kindred elements there are."[279] Hocking specified that the "variety of religious experience" must not be allowed "to perish until it has yielded up to the rest of its own ingredient of

---

275. Kraemer, *The Christian Message*, 36.
276. Macnicol, "Hinduism and Christianity," 324.
277. Ibid.
278. Ibid.
279. Hocking, *Re-thinking Missions*, 326.

truth."²⁸⁰ The Christian was thus urged to "regard himself as a co-worker with the forces within each such religious system which are making for righteousness."²⁸¹

Jones, for his part, argued that the greatest enemy of Christianity was not any of the non-Christian religions but "a worldwide secular way of life and interpretation of the nature of things."²⁸² Jones identified dangers in humanism, nationalism, scientism and industrialization, chiefly in how they fail to take into account the spiritual picture and, in fact, suppress it. Jones did admit that there was a "kind of religion" in some aspects of "socialists, communists and reformers of society" as they had a "passion for a new world, a better civilisation."²⁸³ However, Jones urged Christians to look at non-Christian religions with more sympathy since "other religions are not so much 'false' as they are inadequate and hampered by their limits."²⁸⁴ Jones concluded that in Christian mission, "we go as those who find in the other religions which secularism attacks, as it attacks Christianity, witnesses of man's need of God and allies in our quest of perfection. Gladly recognising the good they contain, we bring the best that our religion has brought to us, that they may test it for themselves."²⁸⁵

Furthermore, in a memorandum presented by the Swedish Missionary Council, another positive view of religion, particularly in substantive terms, was affirmed: "All religion . . . claims to establish real life-fellowship, life unity between the Eternal and man, to infuse in man divine life . . . All true religion aims at permeating the whole of human life with the Divine. God living in the soul, the soul united with God. This is the goal of religion."²⁸⁶

The final statement by the Jerusalem Council, regarding the Christian message, strongly emphasized that Jesus Christ was sufficient for salvation, and the Church was bound to proclaim Christ's salvation to all people. Yet it also added: "To non-Christians also we make our call. We rejoice to think that just because in Jesus Christ the light . . . shone forth . . . we find rays of that same light where He is unknown or even is rejected. We welcome every noble quality in non-Christian persons or systems as further proof that the Father . . . has nowhere left Himself without witness."²⁸⁷

280. Ibid., 326–27.
281. Ibid., 327.
282. Jones, "Secular Civilisation and the Christian task," 284.
283. Ibid., 320.
284. Ibid., 334.
285. Ibid., 338.
286. Speer, "What is the Value," 425.
287. Speer, "The Council Statement," 490–91.

Furthermore, the cooperation was recommended, even if it was to study Jesus:

> We call on the followers of non-Christian religions to join with us in the study of Jesus Christ as He stands before us in the Scriptures, His place in the life of the world, and His power to satisfy the human heart; to hold fast to faith in the unseen and eternal in face of the growing materialism of the world; to co-operate with us against all the evils of secularism . . . to discern that all the good of which men have conceived is fulfilled and secured in Christ.[288]

The result of the Jerusalem Conference was mixed. Sharpe notes that there was no genuine consensus concerning a Christian approach to other religions after Jerusalem.[289] Sharpe also points out that many in the Conference took exception to the accommodation of non-Christian religions as it compromised traditional Christianity.[290] Similarly, Sharpe states that many, like Chenchiah and K. T. Paul, were frustrated by the attempts to preserve Christianity above non-Christian religions, when in fact they should have acknowledged Christ above all religions.[291] Niles adds that Jerusalem prefigured the growing participation of the "younger churches" in the global debate.[292]

In terms of theories of religion, it was evident that there was a growing view that non-Christian religions were not only of the same type but also had potential value. Hallencreutz remarks that while the primary emphasis of the conference still remained—distinguishing between Christ's revelation and the "values" in non-Christian religions—"this line of thought presupposed that 'religion' was a positive concept."[293] In effect, Jerusalem's assessment of other religions was more positive than would be the case a decade later in Tambaram, which would produce a more negative assessment.

---

288. Speer, "The Council Statement," 491–92.
289. Sharpe, *Faith Meets Faith*, 73.
290. For instance, see Speer, *"Re-thinking Missions" Examined*.
291. Sharpe, *Faith Meets Faith*, 72.
292. Niles, *From Edinburgh to Tambaram*, 6.
293. Hallencreutz, *Kraemer Towards Tambaram*, 197.

In between Jerusalem and Tambaram: Karl Barth's Early Theology of Religion

Between Jerusalem and Tambaram stood Karl Barth and his revolutionary theology of religion. Barth was to develop his theology of religion through his entire writing career. However, for the purposes of this study, our review of Barth's theology of religion is sourced primarily from his little-known article in the *Student World*, asserting the danger of a wrong view of religion[294] and from his commentary on *Romans*, which was written in 1919, but revised in 1921.[295] In both *Romans* and the *Student World* article, we see a younger Barth and a clear statement of why he believed that religion was problematic.

Student World: Christianity and Religion Are Different

In the article, "Questions which 'Christianity' must face," Barth differentiated between philosophy and religion. Barth stated that a "scientific, political, moral or aesthetic philosophy of life" was chosen or invented; it left a person "essentially independent" because his real anchor was elsewhere.[296] A religion, by contrast, Barth stated, "takes hold of a man with a power which overcomes all personal choices and desires and which forces him to obey without knowing, or wishing to know why he does so. A 'religion' is a message which claims the right and power to lay hands on his real existence . . . to take captive his whole being, and make of him a new messenger and soldier."[297]

Subsequently, Barth depicted three kinds of religions. These were: a) the traditional religions of the world; b) the new religion of genuine communism and fascism, which claimed "supreme sacrifice" and excluded "all other claims";[298] and c) what Barth called "Americanism," with its emphasis on "health and comfort" and "which imposes its standard of uniformity upon every section of the globe."[299]

---

294. Karl Barth, "Questions which 'Christianity' must face," 93–100.

295. I focus primarily on the early work because they are closest to Chenchiah's context. A deeper study of Barth's theology of religion is found in my MTh thesis. Kumar, "Karl Barth on Religion."

296. Barth, "Questions which 'Christianity' must face," 93.

297. Ibid.

298. Ibid., 93–94.

299. Ibid., 94.

Barth went on to state how all these religions along with philosophies could work together, without contradiction. Yet, when confronted with Christianity, they bitterly opposed it.[300] Barth asserted, "What "Christianity" ought to realize today is that it has antagonism, and nothing but antagonism, to expect from all "religions," whatever their name or policy. The reason for this antagonism being, that "Christianity" is their natural opponent, because it attacks them by its very existence, and calls them all—as no 'religion' does to another—to make an unconditional surrender . . ."[301]

Stating that this antagonism was natural, Barth warned against Christian attempts to compromise with religion, as seen in the Jerusalem conference:[302]

> How easy it is to adapt Christianity . . . How easy it is to leave unsaid, or render harmless, certain things in 'Christianity' which represent its aggressive attitude to all 'religions.' Three years ago we saw an international Christian missionary conference (in Jerusalem!) devoting weeks not so much to the understanding of the Gospel as to the 'values' of the non-Christian religions . . . Ought and can Christianity's answer to the 'religions' be anything but: mission? Not propaganda which deals with human 'needs' and adapts itself to them, but mission which tells man to his face, that he misunderstands his own deep 'needs,' if he seeks to satisfy them in those 'religions.'[303]

Barth went on to emphasize that Christianity was "something different, something more than all the philosophies *and* 'religions.'"[304] Barth urged that Christianity must understand itself as a Church "to be the one place when man listens and God speaks in the midst of a world of . . . brilliant "religions.'"[305] If there was solidarity with other religions, it was in being "united in a common need which contains . . . only one hope, and united in the same questioning, to which the "religions"—the curse of mankind—reply with their sinister and false answers."[306] Furthermore, the Church was differentiated from religion insofar as it "hears the word of God" and says "what must be heard."[307] Thus, the Church was differentiated from religion

300. Ibid., 94–95.
301. Ibid., 96.
302. Ibid., 98.
303. Ibid.
304. Ibid.
305. Ibid.
306. Ibid., 99.
307. Ibid.

not by the value of the revelation (its reasonableness), but by the fact of revelation (obviously believed through faith) and its mission to communicate it.

Romans: Religion as the Final Frontier

Barth went on to present a much richer exposition of his view of religion in his commentary to the Epistle of Romans. In *Romans*, Barth depicted religion as a human capacity, even the pinnacle of human achievement.[308] According to Barth, religion was an entirely human effort to access the "Wholly Other." To show this, Barth made an important hermeneutical jump in *Romans* by equating law with religion.[309] He used law synonymously with "religion," and thus law/religion stood in contradiction to grace and faith.[310] Religion became the desire to justify oneself, to work for one's own salvation. The limits of religion meant that man could not escape this world. Yet, according to Barth, religion was the effort to do just that. In effect, religion was an attempt to access the infinite through the finite, which was doomed to failure.[311]

However, religion did not stop at the effort to gain the inaccessible. In its effort to cross over, religion, to Barth, became idolatry, which was ungodliness and unrighteousness.[312] This was exhibited when men became restless with the invisibility of God, since "the invisibility of God seems to us less tolerable than the questionable visibility of what we like to call 'God.'"[313] Doomed to a this-worldly limitation at every stage, religion not only existed in distinction from the "Wholly Other"[314] but insofar as religion claimed to

308. Barth, *Romans*, 229–30.

309. This is especially evident in Chapter 7 of *Romans*, and is visible for instance when Barth says "The dominion of the law over a man means that men are wholly entangled in the uncertainty which exists within the realm of the possibility of religion." Barth, *Romans*, 231.

310. For instance, "In this final balance sheet, in which religion and grace confront one another as death and life, our pardon is assured and we are enabled to recognize the freedom of God." Barth, *Romans*, 234.

311. According to Barth, hope is found only in Grace and not in any other human possibility. Grace is the impossibility achieved by God, Barth, *Romans*, 231.

312. Barth says, "when the law claims to possess in itself ultimate reality and to be like God, it becomes ungodliness and unrighteousness." Barth, *Romans*, 135. Further, more specifically, "Whenever men suppose themselves conscious of the emotion of nearness to God, whenever sermon-making and temple-building are thought of as an ultimate human occupation, whenever men are aware of divine appointment of being entrusted with a divine mission, sin veritably abounds." Barth, *Romans*, 136.

313. Barth, *Romans*, 47.

314. Ibid., 49.

contain or know God, it changed from being a signpost to being idolatry,[315] exchanging the truth for a lie.[316] This idolatry was the naming of anything "God" which is not God. For Barth, there could be no such naming except through revelation, through what revelation revealed itself to be.

What this amounted to was that, any claim to finding God was not only impossible but in contradiction to God and hence not-God. This would include anything institutionalized to suggest that God existed within a system. The irony of religion was that when we had "dared, offered, sacrificed everything, [we] stand with nothing in [our] hands, mere dust and ashes, separated further than ever from the One."[317]

Finally, and most destructively, religion was shown to be the illusion of fulfilling the impossible which results in turning people away from revelation.[318] Religion provided the illusion of security and fulfillment. In religion, man became secure, especially in the eyes of himself and others.[319] Echoing Marx, regarding people who were assured within religion, Barth asserted that religion "acts upon them like a drug which has been skilfully administered . . . Instead of counteracting human illusions, it does no more than introduce an alternative condition of pleasurable emotion."[320]

Religion to Barth was not a heroic effort to reach the unreachable, but an evil where people give name to that which is not, and which dulls them into believing that what they have is sufficient. Thus, "religion is the adversary, the adversary of man, of the Greek and the barbarian, disguised as the truest friend; it is the *krisis* of civilization and uncivilization."[321] Yet, attempts to elude religion only led to a further frustrated entanglement.[322]

---

315. Ibid., 50.

316. Ibid., 51.

317. Ibid., 256.

318. For instance in his later work Barth says, "In religion man bolts and bars himself against revelation by providing a substitute, by taking away in advance the very thing which has to be given by God." Barth, *Church Dogmatics*, 303.

319. Barth, *Romans*, 236.

320. Ibid.

321. Green's translation of Barth, *Der Römerbrief*, 273 in Green, "Barth's Theory of Religion," 476. Barth adds that religion is "the most dangerous adversary that man has this side of death (apart from God). For it is the human possibility of recalling that we must die, the possibility of recalling God." In this idea there is hidden a positive aspect of Barth's view of religion. However, the subtlety of the positive argument cannot hide the force of the negative judgment of religion in the context of the Jerusalem affirmation.

322. Barth, *Romans*, 240–42.

The pinnacle of religion, for Barth, could be seen through the prophets.[323] For Barth, the prophets functioned in the truest sense of how religion at its best should function. When religion failed, it was the prophets who spoke out against it fulfilling its primary task: "prophets see what men in fact are: they see them, confronted by the ambiguity of the world, bringing forth the possibility of religion; they see them arrogant and illegitimately daring the impossible and raising themselves to equality with God."[324]

Barth's view of religion was influential in a negative sense, where for a long time scholars disapproved of his reference to "religion as unbelief" as well as his call for the "abolition of religion."[325] Only recently is it emerging that Barth was attempting not a theory of what religion was but a "theology of religion."[326] Barth's view of religion was the final human possibility, almost an opposition to God's revelation.[327] In this sense, religion was no longer about the "right" way of life as Calvin suggested, nor even an inner disposition, as Schleiermacher suggested. Perhaps Barth was closest to Augustine in viewing religion as an "activity," but even here Barth differed when he considered religion as a human activity in contradistinction from God's activity.

Tambaram (1938)

The impact of Barth was keenly felt in Tambaram. If Jerusalem recommended cooperation with other religions to meet the challenges of secularism, the World Missionary Conference in Tambaram (1938) featured a growing sense that the Christians had compromised too much religion and culture.[328] Hendrik Kraemer was commissioned to write a book on Christian relations with other religions, to clarify what the position of the missionary must be.

323. Ibid., 243.

324. Ibid., 244.

325. For instance, most Indian scholars are critical of Barth after knowing that Barth's harsh words about religion were made without knowing anything about Hinduism or other religions, as he seems to have admitted to D. T. Niles. For this discussion see, Niles, "Karl Barth—A Personal Memory," 10–11.

326. For instance see, Di Noia, "Religion and the religions," 251–52.

327. Barth describes the frontier as "the line of death which separates flesh from spirit, time from eternity, human possibility from the possibility of God." Barth, *Romans*, 229–30.

328. By this time it was becoming clear that the secular forces against which Jerusalem was striving also had religious overtones. As a result, nationalism, communism, scientific scepticism were termed as neopagan movements. cf. Jathanna, *The Decisiveness of the Christ-Event*, 493–94, 497.

The book, *The Christian Message in a Non-Christian World*, served as the controlling document for the Tambaram conference, and became for some an important reference while for others it became a point of departure.[329] In his book, Kraemer aligned himself with Barth and stood over and against not simply religions but ways of understanding religion. He rejected the treatment of the Bible and Christianity as an "embodiment of universal and sublime truths and ideals."[330] Neither did Christianity entirely suit the cravings of man for "rational coherence."[331] He even rejected the quest for making Christianity the universal religion.[332]

Partly due to Kraemer's influence,[333] the concern at Tambaram shifted from the earlier concern for cooperation with non-Christian religions, towards God's response to non-Christian religions. More specifically, the question asked was whether God was involved *in* non-Christian religions.[334] Kraemer asserted that there were two options with regard to religion. Firstly, one could take "the essence of religion and take that as our standard of reference," or secondly, and more preferably, one could "derive our idea of what religion really is or ought to be from the revelation in Christ, and consistently stick to this as the sole standard of reference."[335] Thus, according to Kraemer, God was involved in non-Christian religions but there was and continued to be a "fundamental discontinuity" between God and religion.[336] Christ was not the perfection of things before, but the "radical recasting of values."[337] Kraemer stated,

> ... even when we recognise that Christ may *in a certain sense* be called the fulfillment of some deep and persistent longings and apprehensions ... In this fulfillment is contained a radical recasting of values, because these longings and apprehensions when exposed to the searching and revolutionary light of Christ, appear to be blind and misdirected ... in Christ all things become new, because He is the crisis of all religions ...

---

329. Kraemer, *The Christian Message*, 36.
330. Ibid., 64.
331. Ibid.
332. Ibid., 109.
333. Sharpe rightly points out, Kraemer's was not the only position yet Tambaram conference studies focus unfairly on only Kraemer's point of view. cf. Sharpe, *Faith Meets Faith*, 98.
334. Jathanna, *Decisiveness of the Christ-Event*, 499.
335. Kraemer, "The Authority of the Faith: Continuity and Discontinuity," 23.
336. Kraemer, "The Authority of the Faith," 4.
337. Ibid., 3.

> This fundamental discontinuity of the world of spiritual reality, embodied in the revelation in Christ, to the whole range of human religion, *excludes* the possibility and legitimacy of a *theologia naturalis* . . . This rejection . . . does not, however, *include* denying that God has been working in the minds of men outside the sphere of the Christian revelation . . . Yet to represent the religions of the world as *somehow* . . . be, a παιδαγωγός, a schoolmaster to Christ, is a distorted presentation of these religions and their fundamental structure . . .[338]

Kraemer tried to preserve some value for religion, especially when he suggested that religion had "natural vitality and tenacious strength."[339] Furthermore, "human possibilities and realities in the field of religion manifested many analogies to the possibilities and realities of divine revelation."[340] This, for Kraemer, was evidenced because "everywhere man is conscious of being related to an Ultimate" and "is speaking of the same things as Christianity does; of sin, of salvation, of revelation."[341] Kraemer took pains to say that the judgment of religion was in relation to Christ and not Christianity, so that all human responses to God, including Christianity, were unbelief.[342]

However, despite Kraemer's essentially negative view of religion—particularly when viewed in contrast to the Edinburgh view of religion—there was a preference for Christianity. By virtue of the revelation of Christ, all religions are "judged from the standpoint of the Christian revelation, not the reverse."[343]

This latter point still suggested Christian superiority over non-Christian religions and there were those who argued against him.[344] Hogg for instance responded to Kraemer by rejecting the dichotomy between God and religion, by asserting a more positive view of religion because "without the revealing initiative of God there would be *no* religions."[345] Hogg famously worked with the distinction between *faith* and *faiths*, asserting that there was a difference between the religious life of the non-Christians (their faith) and their religions (their faiths).[346] It is not hard to see the precursor of "anony-

---

338. Ibid., 3–5.
339. Kraemer, *The Christian Message*, 284.
340. Kraemer, "The Authority of the Faith," 19.
341. Ibid.
342. Kraemer, "The Authority of the Faith," 21.
343. Ibid., 19.
344. Horton, "Between Hocking & Kraemer," 148–62.
345. Hogg, "The Christian Attitude to Non-Christian Faith," 125.
346. Ibid., 102.

mous Christian" theology here, though in view of a theology of religion, Hogg was differentiating between the content of religion from the experience of religion. Hogg admitted that it was the "content of the revelation" that differentiated Christianity from other religions.[347] Nevertheless, Hogg also suggested that missionaries should expect to find "genuine adherents of other religions, men of God for whose non-Christian faith one should feel not mere respect . . . but religious reverence."[348]

Clearly, there was no consensus and Tambaram represented a fork in the road of understanding religion, where some chose to keep exploring the shared experiences among various religions while others highlighted discontinuity.

INDIAN CHRISTIAN VIEWS OF RELIGION

To understand Indian Christian views of religion, particularly those most like Chenchiah's, it is important to see them within the context of the nationalist movement.[349] With the rise of nationalism arose a view of a universal India. Alongside, however, there also arose communal voices that fought hard against universalization of what it meant to be an Indian. Many of the English-educated protestant Indian Christians chose to align themselves with the nationalist movement at the cost of their religious privileges, arguing that they saw no contradiction between their religion and their nationality. On the other hand, the same Christians also maintained a strong sense of dissimilarity between Christianity and other religions, rejecting views that all religions were the same, or even that salvation was available in all religions. The Christians negotiated between this universalization and particularization through their theory of religion that emphasized the core of religion, namely Christ himself.

Abraham Thomas offers a negative assessment of Indian Christian involvement in the freedom struggle. In reviewing Christian participation in the nationalist movement, he says that Indian Christians had nothing much to be proud of as "large sections of the community . . . were lukewarm to the prospect of Indian independence."[350] He gives a few reasons for this, including the isolation of the Christian community from the local communities and the close association of the Indian Christian community with foreign

347. Ibid., 125.

348. Ibid., 102-3.

349. Parts of this section are adapted in Kumar, "Communalism and Nationalism," 155-73.

350. Thomas, *Christians in Secular India*, 105.

missionaries and churches.[351] Moreover, "There was also the widespread feeling, especially among the uneducated, ordinary members of the community that the future of Christians would be bleak under a government in which the Hindus would be in the majority. They looked to the British government as the protector of their religious freedom."[352]

In addition, George Thomas highlights the sociological factors that limited Indian Christian participation in the nationalist movements: unlike Sikh and Muslim communities, they were neither a homogenous group with a social or cultural ethnicity, nor were they concentrated in particular areas.[353] Christianity was also largely dominated by lower and backward castes, many of whom were naturally looking for cultural and social liberation as a source for new life, and the concerns of national freedom were secondary.[354]

Of course, the educated Christians were the exception,[355] many of whom supported the nationalist movement and took an active part in the freedom struggle at both national and local levels.[356] Nevertheless, the educated Indian Christian responses were neither unanimous nor concerted. There were certainly educated Indian Christians who supported the British Raj, others who wholeheartedly joined the nationalist programme, and still some who were hesitant about the directions that the national leadership was headed towards.

For instance, George Thomas points out that, during the Quit India Movement in the 1940s, Bishop Azariah rejected the call for civil disobedience and instead "upheld obedience to the Civil authority as absolute and which could not justify disobedience to the ruler."[357] Azariah asserted that obedience to state was a theological demand; "The Indian Christian's religion has taught him to 'render unto Caesar the things that are Caesar's.' Scriptures tell him that 'He that resisteth the power withstandeth the ordinance of God.' 'The ruler is a minister of God; wherefore ye must needs be in subjection.'"[358]

---

351. Ibid., 101.
352. Ibid.
353. Thomas, *Christian Indians and Indian Nationalism*, 249.
354. Ibid., See also, Cox, *Imperial Fault Lines*, 269.
355. The Indian Christians who were most often trained in England and returned for a lucrative practice in law or civil administration.
356. Thomas, *Christians in Secular India*, 101–3.
357. Thomas, *Christian Indians and Indian Nationalism*, 225.
358. Dornakal, "The Bishop's Letter," 2.

Moreover, while Azariah believed in freedom for India, he asserted that an Indian Christian could not agree to the "civil disobedience," "non-cooperation "and "rebellion": "When therefore his countrymen wish to wrest swaraj by these methods, he feels his hands are tied by his religion."[359]

Other moderate Indian Christians disapproved of the "civil disobedience movement" because it could cause communal violence.[360] Even the Jesuit publication *The Examiner* regularly featured articles calling for loyalty to the government, going to the extent of saying that "they that resist the powers that be, purchase to themselves damnation."[361]

George Thomas notes that these lines of reasoning were strongly rejected by some other Indian Christians, who argued that "disobedience to a Government that was not recognized by the people and that did not serve their interest, was valid for Christians."[362] In this vein, H.G. Thomas stated: "Our community is inter-related to the rest of India. It is impossible for us to take up any other attitude than the attitude which the purest and noblest patriotism demands . . . I may even go to the extent that Indian Christians cannot reconcile themselves to a blind submission to the repressive policy that is now going on in India. Nationalism has many faults for which it must atone, but Indian nationalism is today the least guilty of all the nationalisms of the world."[363]

There was also strong and almost universal support from Indian Christian students for the freedom struggle, in particular for the Quit India Movement. Many students left their colleges and/or joined Christian student movements, while urging their leaders who rejected Gandhi's method to reconsider. These students made loud and passionate appeals to their leaders to reject differences and focus on the goal of full independence for India.[364]

Evidently, a conflict existed between absolute loyalty to country and absolute loyalty to religion. This was resolved by some Indian Christians in the political and theological sphere, by a theory of religion that viewed religion as a subset of something deeper than the visible markers.

---

359. Ibid.

360. Thomas, *Christian Indians and Indian Nationalism*, 226–27.

361. [na], "Editorial" 24 May, 1930.

362. Thomas, *Christian Indians and Indian Nationalism*, 226. See also Chetsingh, "The State and Conscience," 46–49.

363. Thomas, "Christian Leaders of Madras and the Crisis," 414.

364. Thomas, *Christian Indians and Indian Nationalism*, 228–29.

Religious and Political Identity

During the early part of the 1900s, new communal identities and aspirations were in continual conflict with national identity and aspirations, especially when it came to protecting the interests of minority communities.[365] The British government affirmed the communalisation of the political sphere by accepting the Muslim demand for separate electorates in the Legislative Assembly through the Indian Councils Act of 1909, also known as the Morley–Minto Reforms. Chandra and others say that the Indian Councils Act offered no real power to Indian legislators but functioned to divide the nationalist movement by encouraging Muslim communalism: "the Reforms introduced the system of separate electorates under which Muslims could only vote for Muslim candidates in constituencies specially reserved for them. This was done to encourage the notion that the political, economic and cultural interests of Hindus and Muslims were separate and not common."[366]

In 1932, the Morley–Minto Reforms were extended through the Communal Award, to include Sikhs, Christians and Depressed classes so that "Muslims, Christians, and Sikhs could only vote for candidates of their own community."[367] While Congress nationalists and others were apprehensive of this move, most conceded to allowing communal electorates for at least the Muslims.[368] However, almost all Congress nationalists, led by Gandhi himself, opposed communal electorates for the Scheduled Castes.[369]

Indian Christians reacted differently to the offer of separate electorates, though many of the reactions were colored by another event around that time. In 1931, Gandhi came out strongly against conversion. Influenced largely by his own *swadeshi* ideology of self-reliance, and motivated by an opposition to mass conversions, Gandhi stated, "Certainly the great faiths held by the people of India are adequate for her people. India is in no need of conversion from one faith to another."[370] Gandhi went on to challenge the key institutions of Christianity, by rejecting the use of Christian hospitals and Christian schools as a platform for conversion: "why should I change my religion because a doctor who professes Christianity as his religion has cured me . . . why should the doctor expect or suggest a change whilst

---

365. Chandra et al., *India's Struggle for Independence*, 402, 404.
366. Ibid., 142.
367. Weiner, "The struggle for Equality," 200.
368. Ibid.
369. Ibid.
370. Gandhi, "Foreign Missionaries," 28.

I am under his influence?"³⁷¹ In fact, Gandhi suggested that he opposed conversion to the extent that if missionaries used humanitarian work as a means for proselytizing, he would ask them to withdraw from India.³⁷²

Albuquerque reveals that Gandhi's views against conversion came as a "bolt-from-the-blue" for Indian Christians who had till then largely supported Gandhi.³⁷³ The rise of anticolonial attitudes had already led to fear concerning their safety after the British left. Gandhi's statements made matters worse. Furthermore, negative views of conversions dominated the national psyche after the British government supported separate electorates for Christians, the accusation being that the Christian community was attempting to gain political clout by increasing their numbers through conversions of backward classes.³⁷⁴

Subsequently, in response to the general antagonism against Indian Christians, many Christians believed that "safeguards for religious rights" was a fundamental issue for them.³⁷⁵ Many also asserted that communal representation through separate electorates was the "only possible safeguard for the community."³⁷⁶

Mallampalli notes that Christians, for the first time, could "pursue their interests through political mobilization, based on their strength in numbers within any given electorate."³⁷⁷ The Catholic Church, in particular, "stridently advocated communal electorates in order to secure 'Catholic interests.'"³⁷⁸ Catholic spokesmen provided the further rationale that since "communal identities constituted the very fabric of Indian society," there was "the need to retain strong communal boundaries" because, by so doing, Catholics were participating in the true fabric and culture of India.³⁷⁹

However, there was a competing position, voiced particularly by the "Protestant elites" (as Mallampalli calls them). Protestant leaders joined the Congress in their opposition to separate electorates, or at least tempering it

371. Ibid.

372. Gandhi, "Interview to the Press," 320.

373. Albuquerque, "The Role of the Christians in the National Struggle for Freedom," 202.

374. Beaglehole, "The Indian Christians—A Study of a Minority," 63.

375. Albuquerque, "The Role of the Christians in the National Struggle for Freedom," 202–3.

376. Beaglehold, "The Indian Christians," 65.

377. Mallampalli, *Christians and Public Life*, 121.

378. Ibid., 3.

379. Ibid. Mallampalli actually presents this view positively by arguing in his book that Catholics were therefore less marginalized from the national discourse as opposed to the protestants.

with demands for reserved seats in joint electorates.[380] Christian nationalists like K.T. Paul and S. K. Datta opposed separate electorates for Christians. In fact, speaking as the Indian Christian delegate in the Round Table Conference, S. K. Datta stated, "There are some of us in India who have been brought up with a fierce belief in voluntarism in religion . . . I believe that there is an infringement of my rights when the State says, 'you shall vote in a particular constituency.' What if I say I have got no religion? Does that mean I am going to be disfranchised? I shall have no vote."[381]

Many Protestant Christians objected to the consequent political alienation that Christians would face if the Award was put in place. An editorial in the *National Christian Council Review* gave this strong critique of the communal approach and advocated political participation:

> [T]he communal electorates . . . means that an Indian the moment he enters into public life ceases to be an Indian and becomes either a Hindu or a Muslim or a Christian . . . For the growth of the political life of the country, it is clear that the present policy of grouping the followers of each religion as distinct political units should be given up and Indians of all religions, or of no religion . . . should be classified together as one unit for the exercise of their common civic and public rights. Religion should come in as helping and inspiring all to do the right thing.[382]

Other Protestants advocated a spiritual approach—Christians were to see themselves as non-political communities, the "salt of the earth," where Christians could be dissolved in the service of the nation. Azariah, for instance, offered a theological reason for rejecting the Award: "The Award stamps the followers of Jesus Christ as a communal entity, with distinct political interests of their own, like Moslems or Sikhs or Europeans . . . [but] the religion of Christ is one of the most dynamic factors in the world. It always bursts its boundaries, however strong and rigid those boundaries may be laid. It refuses to be confined to any one race, class or caste . . . The inclusion of Christians in 'a communal award' is a direct blow to the nature of the Church of Christ."[383]

Related to this, Azariah stated that Christians were not a singular sociopolitical unit defined by their religion. Azariah remarked that Christians, despite their religion, often had social and political opinions that

380. Mallampalli, Christians and Public Life, 123.
381. Editorial, "Indian Christians and the Communal Award," 349.
382. [na], "Editorial Notes," 580.
383. Azariah, "The Communal Award," 368.

were identical to their non-Christian neighbors. Was it right to force these Christians to vote in a Christian constituency, despite having opinions that were similar to the general constituency?[384] Notice how Azariah attempted to maintain unique Christian identity (in Christ) while also urging for the flattening of identity across political grounds.

Another article in the *Guardian* attempted to draw attention to the theological problems: "The Award stamps the followers of Jesus Christ as a communal entity, with distinct political interests of their own. But it is of the essence of our whole conception of the Church of Christ that it transcends all differences of community or race or caste in one all-embracive Brotherhood."[385]

Furthermore, there was an awareness of the political realities alongside the need to bring to bear spiritual principles:

> By the present Award, Christians are cut off from the rest of the country. We are prevented from throwing in our lot with the whole nation and are ranked as a particular sect, seeking for its own position. Now, even if the matter be viewed from the point of view of self-interest, it is surely evident that the interests of Christians would be better preserved by their winning the sympathy and support of the country through a truly national outlook and spirit than by maintaining a very small body of special representation in the Councils, chosen by themselves. But, in fact, we are bound by the principles of our religion to take a higher line than that of self-interest and to set an example of losing our own life to find it.[386]

The principle of religion to take the "higher line" included self-sacrifice, which was an important religious principle for Indian Christians like D. S. Ramachandra Rao. Rao reiterated, "No sacrifice is too great for the achievement of national unity . . . Leadership comes to those who deny themselves and serve unselfishly. The Christian Indians will never regret throwing their lot with the country. But will they rise to the occasion? Something tells me—'they will.'"[387]

Chakkarai made another point by saying that "there is no such entity as the Christian community nor do we desire to have one."[388] Chakkarai stated that since Christianity was based on the principle of voluntarism, the

---

384. Azariah, "The Communal Award," 386.
385. [na], "Christian and the Communal Award," 434.
386. Ibid.
387. Rao, "Indian Christians and the Communal Award," 422.
388. Chakkarai, "Indian Christians and Communal Award," 356.

bond among Christians was religious.[389] In a provocative essay, Chakkarai asked rhetorically, "Should the Indian Christian Community Continue?"[390] Citing the example of K. T. Paul, who had asked Indian Christians to be like salt—useful only when dissolved—he sided with those who favored Christianity "extinguishing itself *qua* community."[391] Chakkarai recognized that this was idealistic and for a while India would continue to see "strongly nationalistic and non-communal" Christians alongside "strongly conservative and communal" Christians.[392] However Chakkarai urged that Christians "should renounce separatist claims and take its place within the body politic."[393] This would naturally lead to a "weakening" and even a "wholesale withdrawal of many . . . hall marks [sic] of Christianity," and Christianity, "as ordinarily understood," would be "relegated to the sphere of the forum of the individual conscience."[394] The strengthening of Christianity, Chakkarai hinted, would be in the "highest sense" outside the traditional forms of Christian institutionalism.[395]

A pragmatic solution was offered by J. J. M. Nichols Roy, who combined spiritual and political concerns. Roy suggested that Christians must not negatively condemn the Award and, instead, look at it as a challenge. Roy accepted the spiritual directive:

> Turning to ourselves as Indian Christians we should work for the ideal that there should be no communalism, that the whole of India should be like one nation. Though we are a small community we are willing to lose our individuality in the flow of the national tide, in order to work for the ultimate good of India as a whole. We do not like to see India divided into various communities and form themselves into water-tight compartments. Universalism against Radicalism, and Nationalism against Communalism, are our ideals. Equality in political and social life is our ideal which we have imbibed from our holy universal religion.[396]

---

389. Ibid.
390. Chakkarai, "Should the Indian Christian Community Continue?–I," 100–101.
391. Ibid.
392. Ibid., 101.
393. Chakkarai, "Should the Indian Christian Community Continue?–II," 116.
394. Chakkarai, "Should the Indian Christian Community Continue?–II," 116.
395. Ibid.
396. Roy, "Indian Christians and the Award," 428.

Nevertheless, Roy also stated that the ideal can be "adapted to circumstances for the sake of gaining its object."[397] Roy argued that while communalism is rooted in "evil practices, habits and desires," it was possible for Christians with a mind for noncommunal thinking to enter the communal political scene with the purpose of changing the country. Roy believed that if the Christian community sent members to the Councils who kept "the noble object of fostering the spirit of peace, justice and goodwill and nationalism against communalism," these Christian representatives would "rise above communalism" and have "a very healthy influence in the Councils for the good of our land."[398] The theological basis: "Our Lord was born among the Jews but He rose above all races and communities."[399] Thus, for Roy, the Communal Award was not such a bad thing for the present moment. The key factor was that if good Christians were to take high positions, they would make a positive impact by their ethical behavior. A similar sentiment was reflected by D. A. Chowdhry who urged "leaders of our community [Indian Christians] who can rise above communal aspects of things" to join the general elections to "win the love and confidence of the people by their life and service" and gain popular mandate.[400] This type of Christian humanism, the belief in the goodness of a Christian, was yet another example of how theological reasoning was used within sociopolitical discussions in a volatile time.

Clearly, in all this, a unique theory of religion was at play—one that allowed the erasure of the outward markers of religion, while emphasizing a combination of internal (spiritualist) expression with ethical (political) engagement. Similarly, there was a strong emphasis on the ethical function of religion, related to both high moral conduct and pro-nationalist involvement. The Indian Christians, struggling to identify with the radical claims of a new Indian nation, saw their religion as the power that influenced their political involvement and thus saw no contradiction between the two concepts. Religion was promoted in terms of its effectiveness rather than relegating it simply to its status of giving identity.

Detraditionalization of Religion in an Anti-Western Context

The theological identity of Indian Christians was developed in a context of suspicion, taunts and violence. For instance, many Indian Christians did

---

397. Ibid.
398. Ibid., 429.
399. Ibid., 428.
400. Chowdhry, "Communal Award," 392.

well to distance themselves from the missionary apathy to the Jallianwalla Bagh massacre, in 1919.[401] Yet, despite the fact that most Indian Christians decried the event, it did not stop Indian Christians from becoming victims of retaliatory violence where "the forces of communalism became even stronger than those of nationalism."[402] At another time, when the Prince of Wales visited India on 17 November, 1921, riots broke out for three days with Christians, Parsis and Anglo-Indians being the "special targets of attack" since they were easily identifiable as loyalists.[403]

Indian Christians found themselves having to oppose not only British aggression but also foreign missionary perspectives—the need for grappling with both Indian nationalism and religious identity was all the more urgent for Indian Christians. Eventually, and unsurprisingly, many Indian Christians veered towards an increasingly anti-Western and anti-institutional stance.

George Thomas rightly points out that the Indian Christian movement was "in part the result of the confrontation between Western Christianity and classical Hinduism in the Colonial setting."[404] Indian Christians struggled with the duality that while Independence was a dire need for the nation, only Christ could fulfil the true potential of India.[405] George Thomas writes, "The Indian Christianity movement rejected the view that India's modernity consists in the extension of Western values and religion into India. But they represent a regeneration which India experienced as a result of the confluence of the West and the East, of Christianity and Hinduism."[406]

The Indian Christians were acutely aware that the West was not the source of a pure Christianity, and thus not absolute and binding.[407] This in turn "helped them to relativise the denominational Christianities introduced by Western Christian missions" and become more "aware of the need to reconstruct Christianity in the Indian religious and cultural traditions."[408] Thus, the Indian Christian community, through the interaction between

---

401. Thomas, *Christian Indians and Indian Nationalism*, 163–64.

402. Albuquerque, "The Role of the Christians in the National Struggle for Freedom," 199.

403. Chandra et al., *India's Struggle for Independence*, 189.

404. Thomas, *Christian Indians and Indian Nationalism*, 246.

405. Ibid.

406. Ibid.

407. Thomas, *Christian Indians and Indian Nationalism*, 247.

408. Ibid.

nationalism and its own theology, "discovered its own self-image in integral relation to indigenous religious and cultural life."[409]

Many Indian Christians went on to attack the "spiritual bondage of the church" to Western mission which, they felt, was bound by "creeds and doctrines" that "refused to allow for the effort to Indianize Christianity."[410] Cox mentions that, despite progress towards multiracial egalitarian goals of missionary Christianity, "missionaries and Indian Christians remained divided by permanent disputes over control of the mission institutions they had built together."[411] Many Christians even opposed foreign clergy and alleged that the Indian church was only Indian in name unless the leadership changed.[412]

Within this was a reiteration of the essential nature of the Christian faith. For instance, Subba Rao rejected institutionalized religion, while favoring an experiential faith. In a pamphlet called *Retreat Padri*, Subba Rao criticized the priests and missionaries for throwing innocent converts into a pit. In that text, Rao writes to the Padri: "You have made religion a fashionable thing. Change of names, taking of oaths, daily prayers, Sunday gatherings, putting on attractive garb, observing festivals and several such things you do, except what the Lord preached and practised. What the Lord said and did is made into a religion and transformed into a department. Decrying other religions is your religion."[413]

Similarly, Sadhu Sundar Singh, in "Reality and Religion" was typically noninstitutional when he stated, "Christ did not write anything. Nor did He ask His apostles to write down His teaching. This is because, in the first place, His words are spirit and life. He knows that life can be infused only into life, not into the pages of a book. In the second place, other Teachers left behind books, which took the place of their living voice. Our Lord, on the other hand, has never left His followers. He is with us always and His living Voice and Presence ever give us counsel."[414]

Chakkarai referred to religion as a this-worldly region, in which God was involved.[415] Religion was equated to law and remained in the "flesh" realm.[416] In this sense, religion was imperfect and even a corruption. Hence,

409. Thomas, *Christian Indians and Indian Nationalism*, 252.
410. Sudarisanam, "Editorial: Imperialism in Religion." 17.
411. Cox, *Imperial Fault Lines*, 269.
412. Thomas, *Christian Indians and Indian Nationalism*, 234.
413. Rao, *Retreat Padri*, 16–17.
414. Singh, *Reality and Religion*, 18–19.
415. Chakkarai, "Karl Barth on Religion–I," 213.
416. Chakkarai, "Karl Barth on Religion–II," 228.

Chakkarai stated, "It is in this world that religion functions; to this world it belongs. By the works of the law no man can be saved. Salvation cannot come by means of religions, as it belongs to the vitality of death. Within this sin-controlled world, religion can manage, manipulate, and perform its magical feats. It cannot take you beyond death to life, for life comes from the unknown God."[417]

Echoing Barth, Chakkarai identified religion as the final frontier of human possibility and aligned religion to human effort, that is consequently *maya*, idolatry and sin.[418] Nevertheless, God's involvement in religion suggested a hope for religion. Jesus stood separate from religion as the living power, and in relation to Him all religions fell short.[419] Chakkarai described Christianity as a western "system of truths, or ideas, rites, ceremonies and institutions" that are the human testimony of the revelation of God in Jesus.[420] In that sense, Christianity was not much different from other human testimonies like Hinduism.[421] What differentiated Christianity from other religions was its centrality—Christ, especially Christ crucified.[422] In relation to other religions, there was something unique in Christianity and that is the scandal of the cross,[423] which provided the strongest feelings of sin and repentance.[424]

It is not surprising, therefore, that a strongly anti-institutional theory of religion took root in Indian theories of religion. Like the internal markers of religion in the political sphere, there was an emphasis on a core of religion that surpassed the external expression of religion. As a result, Indian Christians were able to distance themselves from the Western religion while still claiming some consistency with its "faith." Insofar as those theories were made theologies, they looked at that internal essence of religion as Christ or the power of the Holy Spirit above all else.

---

417. Ibid., 228–29.

418. Chakkarai, "Karl Barth on Religion–II," 185–86. Also, "The law instead of being a guide and revelation of the supreme mind for man became the revealer of his sin and the active agent, provocateur, of it." Chakkarai, *The Cross in Indian Thought*, 231.

419. Chakkarai, "Christianity and Non-Christian Faith," 201.

420. Chakkarai, "Rethinking Missions–II," 150–51.

421. Ibid., 151.

422. According to Chakkarai, "In Christian experience the most central thing is Christ Himself, and it is hardly possible to think of historic Christianity without Christ Jesus." Chakkarai, *Jesus the Avatara*, 49.

423. Chakkarai, "Rethinking Missions–II," 151.

424. Thomas, *Chakkarai 1*, 28.

SUMMARY OF THE CHAPTER

Through this chapter we are able to make the following observations. First, it is clear that, while religion as a concept emerged in a Greco-Roman context and was utilized by the early Christians, it was nevertheless quite different from how religion came to be understood in the modern era. Early Christian views of religion identified it as a life directed to the true God, even a life of worship. The modern view of religion emphasized doctrines, spiritual experience and ethical conduct.

Second, Indian thinkers—influenced by the reformist and revivalist trajectory—redefined Hinduism to suit the modern times. The Indian theories of religion, as propounded by Aurobindo, Vivekananda, Gandhi and Ambedkar, focused on different ways to relate their context with the ancient Hindu religion. Their view of religion was particularly nonrational, evolutionary and detraditionalist. They also promoted their own cosmographical schema, but one that usually emphasized the goal of religion as inner spiritual achievement.

Third, the theological methods of dealing with religion tended to oscillate between the positive and the negative. Some Christians, adopting primarily substantive evolutionary logic, believed that Hinduism was the same form of religion like Christianity. Others like Barth reinterpreted religion as a theological category, and viewed it as something opposed to God.

Fourth, Indian Christians agreed that religion must be superseded by Christ. However, in their theological context, Indian Christians were attempting to reject the dominance of their ancient religion (Hinduism) and Western colonial powers.

Thus, Indian theologians like Chenchiah lived in a volatile time, when social reformations of Hinduism and nationalism were vying for ideological and political space in the Indian landscape. For the most part, there was a critique of traditional religion, and a desire to make a positive social impact. They were naturally inclined to share similar concerns. Indian theological reflection in this context reflected nationalist concerns as well as anti-Western tendencies. The key methodology Indian theologians adopted at this time was to accede neither to the Western line of thinking nor to persuasions of their own religious contexts. Instead, the endeavor was to hold on to Christ, who was the essence of their "religion."

3

Chenchiah's Theology of Religion

INTRODUCTION

Having looked at the general development of the concept of religion, we now move towards building a theological answer to the question, "What is religion?" This I do by looking at Chenchiah's theological definition of religion. This chapter first provides a methodological introduction to Chenchiah, which includes a brief look at his biography and his overall theological emphasis. The focus then shifts to an extensive summary of Chenchiah's theology of religion, where we look at 'religion' in some key articles, his general theory of religion, and a particular theology of religion that is developed. Within the theology of religion, we will be mindful of how theological categories influenced his theology of religion, namely the definition, purpose (function) and value (judgment) of religion. The chapter ends with a summary of Chenchiah's theory and theology of religion, arguing that his theory is actually influenced by his theology of religion, which in effect allows him to engage with religion as both an outsider and an insider. In the next chapter, I provide a critical appraisal of his theology of religion.

THE SHAPE OF CHENCHIAH'S THEOLOGY

Pandipeddi Chenchiah was born into a Telugu Hindu Brahmin family in 1886, in Nellore, Andhra Pradesh.[1] Chenchiah was the eldest of twelve

---

1. Devasahayam, "Role of the Bible," 12. Devasahayam offers the most extensive

children, who grew up together in a joint family.² In 1901, at the age of fifteen, Chenchiah converted to Christianity, along with his family.³ He was baptized by Scottish missionary, William Miller.⁴ After marrying Matilda Raghaviah, the daughter of the pastor of the Anderson Memorial Church, Chenchiah stayed home to take on the responsibility of running his father's home.⁵ He had five children—one son and four daughters.⁶

Chenchiah was affiliated to the United Free Church of Scotland and attended the Anderson Memorial Church in George Town, at the Madras Christian College, George Town.⁷ Despite his strong critique of the church, he regularly attended church services and preached occasionally.⁸

Chenchiah graduated from the Madras Christian College in 1906, where he earned the Samuel Sathianathan Gold Medal for "proficiency in Philosophy."⁹ He obtained a B.L. degree in 1908 and an M.L. degree in 1913, both from Madras Law College, wherein he also received the Mckenzie Gold Medal, becoming one of the earliest Masters in Law of the Madras courts.¹⁰

While Chenchiah was involved in some teaching and practice, his legal career featured no significant highlights, except perhaps his two visits to London.¹¹ In 1928, he became the judge of a small district of Pudukottah, in Tamil Nadu, and remained in that position for about 10 years.¹² Devasahayam reveals that Chenchiah voluntarily retired from that position after refusing to yield to the Government's pressure to pass a verdict in their favor.¹³ He rejoined the Madras High Court, but focused more attention

report on Chenchiah's biography. Other useful sources to understand Chenchiah's life include Wagner, Thangasamy, Boyd and Jathanna.

2. Devasahayam adds that most of his brothers became prominent in their respective fields. Devasahayam, "Role of the Bible," 12.

3. Devasahayam, "Role of the Bible," 12.

4. Ibid., 36.

5. Ibid., 13.

6. Ibid.

7. Thangasamy, *Theology of Chenchiah*, viii.

8. Ibid.

9. Devasahayam, "Role of the Bible," 14.

10. Ibid., 14.

11. Thangasamy, *Theology of Chenchiah*, vii.

12. Devasahayam, "Role of the Bible," 15. Wagner's date for Chenchiah becoming a judge is 1935, which may be correct since he was referred to as the "Chief Judge, Pudukottah" in the book *Rethinking Christianity in India*. See Wagner, *Erstgestalten einer einheimischen Theologie*, 13. However, the only difference this would make is the recognition that Chenchiah was doing his most significant writing while being a judge.

13. Devasahayam, "Role of the Bible," 15.

on academics by becoming the Chief Examiner of the Law exams for the Madras and Andhra Universities, as well as becoming a thesis examiner for the theological students of Serampore College.[14] His career trajectory suggests that Chenchiah did not gain much wealth.[15]

Thangasamy notes that Chenchiah was a voracious reader, gaining proficiency in Eastern and Western philosophy, and Western literature.[16] It was through this interest in philosophy and ethics that Chenchiah grew in prominence in Christian circles. Wagner observes that Chenchiah became one of the theological and spiritual leaders of the small, but influential, circle of modern, Western-educated, nationalistic Indian Christians who would discuss Christian theology in the context of India and Hinduism.[17] According to Jathanna, Chenchiah had "penetrating insight into the religious currents in India."[18] This led him to pursue active friendships with people of other faiths, and he was involved in many interfaith discussions.[19] Chenchiah's literary skills were put to use in the many articles he wrote for two prominent Christian journals, *Guardian* and *The Pilgrim*. He was even the editor of *The Pilgrim* from March 1949 to June 1952.

While not directly involved in politics, like his brother-in-law Chakkarai, Chenchiah remained politically engaged, joining many formal and informal discussions on nationalism and improving Christianity in the volatile context of pre-independent India.[20] He represented the South Indian Union Church[21] at the International Missionary Conferences at Jerusalem (1928)[22] and Tambaram (1938).[23] His most famous association was with the "Madras Rethinking Group," that urged the rethinking of Christianity in Indian terms. The results of the Group were eventually published as

14. Ibid.
15. Thangasamy, *Theology of Chenchiah*, vii.
16. Ibid., viii–ix.
17. Wagner, *Erstgestalten einer einheimischen Theologie*, 14.
18. Jathanna, *Decisiveness of the Christ-Event*, 353.
19. See for instance, Chenchiah, "Indian Christians and Co-operation with Non-Christians," 175–77.
20. Jathanna, *Decisiveness of the Christ-Event*, 354.
21. Wagner, *Erstgestalten einer einheimischen Theologie*, 14.
22. According to the Jerusalem Meeting report, Chenchiah represented the Jerusalem conference as Member of the Executive Council of the South India United Church and of the National Missionary Society. [na], *Addresses and Other Records*, 208.
23. According to the Tambaram Meeting report, Chenchiah represented Tambaram simply as Chief Judge of Pudukkottai State. [na], *Addresses and Other Records*, 185.

Rethinking Christianity in India, just before the World Missionary Conference in Tambaram, 1938.[24]

In terms of positions towards the independence movement, Chenchiah was clearly a nationalist. Not once did Chenchiah join the other Indian Christians who asked for Christian minority rights,[25] nor did he align with the "secularists" who looked to distance themselves from religion. Chenchiah remained critical of the two extremes of identity politics or secular politics and, instead, aligned himself with the Gandhian nationalist movement, that appealed for an India that integrated a religious vision with nationalism: "it should be remembered that Mahatmaji embodies in his life and outlook some of the features of the unique religious situation and thus was able to create a unique political instrument."[26] Chenchiah was critical of the demand for minority privileges, clearing siding with the integration of Christian and national identity, and calling for a full association with Gandhi, even to the extent of rejecting the traditional notion of conversion.

All through his life he contributed to Indian Christianity as a layperson. Appasamy, a contemporary theologian, felt that Chenchiah's lay perspective gave Chenchiah a theological edge and yet Appasamy was critical of Chenchiah's deficiency in biblical exegetical study.[27] Appasamy also critiqued Chenchiah's lack of knowledge of "original" biblical languages.[28] Chenchiah's response, while not immediate or direct, was to critique the obsession with "original" languages, when in fact the "original" words of Jesus had been lost to translation.[29]

Believed to be a "pious rebel,"[30] Chenchiah remained controversial as well as respected right up to his death due to a short illness on April 19, 1959, in Madras.[31]

---

24. For more on the impact of the Rethinking Group, see Jathanna, "The Rethinking Group and Its Contributions," 74–97.

25. See Chenchiah's article, "Indian Christian Politics," 315–17. In this article, Chenchiah critiques the Indian Christian tendency to align themselves with Muslim and other minorities to secure its interest and protection while failing to deal with the fundamental inequality still evident in class and caste struggles within Christianity.

26. Chenchiah, "Christian Youth," 452.

27. Appasamy, "Who Is Jesus?" 461–63, 474–75.

28. Ibid. 461.

29. Chenchiah, "Indian Christian Theological Task," 99–100.

30. Adinarayan, "Sri P. Chenchiah," 197.

31. Wagner, *Erstgestalten einer einheimischen Theologie,* 15.

How to Read Chenchiah

Chenchiah's main theological writings are found in coauthored books *Rethinking Christianity in India* and *Asramas: Past and Present*, as well as in several articles written in *Guardian*, *The Pilgrim* and a number of other journals. The *Guardian* and *The Pilgrim* were two Christian journals that aimed to engage with the political and religious landscape of India. Chenchiah's articles were primarily socioreligious and theological comments, directed to Indian Christians. While his articles do not provide a systematic treatise on theology, they do reveal Chenchiah's diverse theological concerns. Predominantly, his articles were fragmentary explorations of a variety of themes—culture, religion, science, politics and the arts.[32]

Devasahayam is right to note that neither the Church nor academia are the context of Chenchiah's writings, but rather fellow Christians—as gleaned from conferences and conversations.[33] In this sense, even though there was a lot of engagement with people of other faiths, the primary context and audience of Chenchiah's writings were Christians in India. Chenchiah was not a systematic thinker: he did not develop a theological system, but rather his theology was expressed as Chenchiah reflected on contextual issues their theological implication. More positively, he explored many topics and addressed issues as they arose. Wagner remarks that while Chenchiah's writings featured pointed formulations and fierce polemics that were a bold synthesis of Indian, occidental and Christian thinking, they lacked unity and systematic presentation.[34] Jathanna opines that Chenchiah was more of a prophet than a theologian,[35] an overstatement that at least expresses his style of writing. Devasahayam notes that, while Chenchiah was capable of writing a book on his own, the coauthorship was part of his belief that theological exploration in India must be a joint effort.[36]

Chenchiah's writings were concerned with Indian independence, the nature of Christian religion, interreligious cooperation, the importance of Jesus and the Holy Spirit. In his early years, Chenchiah's writings were quite naturally largely concerned with Christian identity in the midst of the national struggle for independence.[37] The concern for independence, from simmering hope to eminent reality, dominated most of Chenchiah's writ-

32. For instance see Chenchiah, "Notes by the way—Praises," 283–84.
33. Devasahayam, "Role of the Bible," 20.
34. Wagner, *Erstgestalten einer einheimischen Theologie*, 107.
35. Jathanna, *Decisiveness of the Christ-Event*, 358.
36. Devasahayam, "Role of the Bible," 23.
37. See Chenchiah, "Aspects of Nationalism," 580–86.

ings. In fact, it is out of this concern that Chenchiah said: "The struggle for independence overtops all other issues in its urgency and value" so that "compared to it all else is subsidiary and secondary."[38]

Yet Chenchiah was clearly writing in two Indian contexts—the pre-independent India (prior to 1947) and the post-independent India. Interestingly, while his theology remained largely consistent, there was a change in focus after Indian independence. In his later writings Chenchiah was keenly aware that the lack of a British government meant that Indian Christians must learn to rely more on the Holy Spirit.[39] His articles in the 1950s show Chenchiah's theological and political concerns for a post-independent India, and religion is no longer in the forefront of his discussion. The fact of religion was assumed, and Chenchiah positioned Indian Christianity vis-à-vis the ideologies and politics of the Indian state. For instance, Chenchiah warned, "religion of the state and religion of science have joined the company of ancient religions. All these have common aims and seek to establish prosperous and healthy conditions for men. The Christian has to fight old and new religions. The new are difficult to fight because they are more an atmosphere than a concerted code. The state dominates the Christian and non-Christian—science converts the priest and laymen."[40]

It would, however, be an error to call the later Chenchiah more mature. Instead of a change in theological position, we see that, after Indian independence, Chenchiah attempted to move beyond the philosophical-theological frameworks that concerned him early in his career to the practical concerns of building the newly independent Christian Indian community. Thus, to understand his theology and religion, one must rely primarily on his writings prior to Indian independence.

It is also worth listening to Wagner that Chenchiah was not formally trying to construct Indian Christian theology, but rather, for Chenchiah, Indian theology stood as everything different from Western theology.[41] Furthermore, Chenchiah's entire theological effort was a contribution to indigenous Christian theology in India.[42]

---

38. Chenchiah, "Indian Christian Politics: The Communal Way, and the Way of the Ideal," 315.

39. Chenchiah reminded Christians that while the British were not avid supporters of Christianity during the Raj, still now more than ever Christianity stood "powerless" in India and thus needed to rely more on the power of the Holy Spirit. Chenchiah, "Christian message in a Hindu environment," 84–85, 100–101.

40. Chenchiah, "Christian message in a Hindu Environment," 100.

41. Wagner, *Erstgestalten einer einheimischen Theologie*, 108.

42. Ibid.

Chenchiah's Theological Method

There were two contexts to Chenchiah's discussions on theological method. The first context was Marcus Ward's *Our Theological Task,* in which Ward drew out a prolegomena for theology in India.[43] Ward followed the popular notion that there were fundamental unchanging truths (dogmas) of the gospel that needed to be preserved, while the expressions of those truths (doctrines) varied from culture to culture, even as they were communicated in different ways.[44] Ward went on to offer that the primary source of dogma was the Bible, while the secondary source was the "three-fold witness" of the people of God, namely, "Preaching, Creed and Experience."[45]

For Chenchiah, Ward's theology allowed only a pre-packaged gospel to the Indian Christian, with no room to explore the true meaning of Christ for themselves. Chenchiah thus launched a series of counter articles in response to Ward's book, titled "Indian Christian Theological Task: Review and Restatement," that dealt primarily with issues of theological method for the Indian Church—mostly rejecting the notion that there is a core truth that the Indian Church must simply translate and communicate in their own language. Similarly, he rejected the primacy of the Bible and the Church, and offering instead that the direct experience of Jesus was the primary source for any theology. This in turn made him more open to the idea of development in theology and development through cultures. Chenchiah was also wary of employing words such as "norm" or "standards" for theology.[46] If the word "norm" was to be used, then it would apply to the only norm for theology in India—the living Jesus Christ himself. He famously stated: "Let it be clearly understood that we accept nothing as obligatory save Christ. Church doctrine and dogma, whether from the West or from the past, whether from Apostles or from modern critics, are to be tested before they are accepted. We do not see any reason why Aristotle and Plato, Kant and Hegel, should be regarded as safer guides for Christian theology than the Indian philosophers, Sankara and Ramanuja."[47]

The other context to Chenchiah's methodological discussions was Appasamy, who proposed that in India the norms of theological thought

---

43. Ward, *Our Theological Task.*

44. Ibid., 3.

45. Ibid., 22.

46. "We distrust profoundly all this talk of norms standards, tests, legislation, authority in spiritual sphere, all agencies that ask us not merely to believe but to believe in the particular manner fixed for us." Chenchiah, "Indian Christian Theological Task," 58.

47. Chenchiah, "The Christian Message," 8.

(*pramanas*) ought to be *shabda* (scripture), *anumana* (reason), *prathyaksha* (perception/experience) and *sabha* (community/Church).[48] For Appasamy, these sources were epistemological categories through which God's revelation occurred, and through which Christian doctrine was formed.[49] Appasamy also believed that this system was foundational for all theological discussion in India.[50]

Chenchiah did not directly counter Appasamy, though Appasamy's theological norms were known to Chenchiah. Appasamy had in fact quoted Chenchiah extensively to explain his understanding of the *pramana* of *prathyaksha*.[51] Nevertheless, while Appasamy found Chenchiah's method problematic, especially in its insistence that a direct experience of Christ was the only norm for the Indian Christian theologian, Chenchiah never changed his stance. Instead, he vociferously stood his ground that a direct experience of Christ, through the Holy Spirit, remained the fundamental starting point of any Christian theological exploration.

This is not to say that Chenchiah was naive about the other sources of theological reasoning. In fact, other theological sources functioned like filters to help shape Chenchiah's theological thinking. Keeping the primacy of Jesus in mind, Chenchiah favored local/Hindu cultures over the church, offered a qualified use of the scriptures, and promoted the value of experience. To these sources, we now turn.

Culture, not Church, as Source

While Chenchiah was a nationalist theologian who preferred indigenous thinking, he was still influenced by Western thought. Devasahayam believes that Chenchiah was influenced by William Miller, who was a strong proponent of the reality of revelation in other religions, and believed that Christianity meets the aspirations of other religions even as other religions

---

48. Appasamy, "The Christian Pramanas," 56–69. Parallels can be made with his method and the Wesleyan Quadrilateral: Scripture, Church, Reason and Experience.

49. See particularly, Appasamy, "The Christian Pramanas," 58.

50. That Appasamy's *Pramanas* are a creative Christian reconstruction of Hindu philosphical thinking, and not representational of it, is evident when we read Mohanty's study of *Pramanas*. Mohanty argues that the Western concepts of reason and experience have no parallels in Hindu thought, and thus even disagrees with the use of *anumana* for reason and *prathyaksha* as experience Mohanty states, "In Sanskrit philosophical vocabulary, the words 'reason' and 'experience' have no exact synonyms, and the epistemological issue was never formulated in such general terms." Mohanty, *Reason and Tradition in Indian Thought*, 227–28.

51. Appasamy, "The Christian Pramanas," 60–61

meet the aspirations of Christianity.[52] Jathanna finds traces of French vitalist philosopher Henri Bergson.[53] Thangasamy finds parallels between Chenchiah and Tielhard de Chardin.[54] Wagner links Chenchiah to speculative and neonaturalist philosophies, especially in the tendency to move freely beyond sacred text while also looking to subject evolutionary thinking to a sacred perspective.[55]

However, because Chenchiah's writings were so "original,"[56] it is difficult to determine the exact extent of Western influence in Chenchiah's writings. Perhaps it is adequate to recognize some amount of Western debt, while also noting that Chenchiah never fully reproduced the views of any Western counterpart. Chenchiah's theology differed vastly from Western thinkers largely because he was similarly influenced by Indian thinkers and philosophy, not the least being neo-Hindu thinkers like Vivekananda and Aurobindo, and the religiopolitical philosophy of Gandhi.

In terms of the Church, however, Chenchiah was less gracious. Chenchiah rejected the essential value of the Church, and was especially critical of the turn towards the institutionalized Church since Constantine's conversion in the 4th century. He argued that as soon as the Christian movement "conquered Rome" in the early centuries, the community was "conquered by Rome" by becoming an institution much like the Roman empire.[57] As a result, Chenchiah urged the recovery of an Indian theology not simply to reject Western theology but to recover something fundamental that he believed was lost through the Western Church tradition.

Chenchiah was thus more open to the use of culture, and in his case, Hindu religious culture, as an important source for his theology. Chenchiah's belief in the value of Indian culture stemmed from the argument that local traditions, like Hinduism, could lead a person to Jesus and also inform a person how to live a more relevant faith in Jesus:

> In pressing towards the heart of Hindu heritage, [an Indian Christian] is forging near the heart of Christ himself. A recovery of the Hindu heritage may give back to the Church that wealth of emotion, that depth of sincerity which is essential for higher Christian life. Reliving all that is purest in Hinduism may be the

---

52. Devasahayam, "Role of the Bible," 36–37
53. Jathanna, *Decisiveness of the Christ-Event*, 353.
54. Thangasamy, *The Theology of Chenchiah*, 20–23.
55. In particular, Wagner contends that Chenchiah's theology is "speculative naturalism." See Wagner, *Erstgestalten einer einheimischen Theologie*, 117–26.
56. "Original" is a descriptor that Boyd and many other scholars use for Chenchiah.
57. Chenchiah, "Problems of the Indian Christian Community," 28.

very condition of that understanding of Christ which is to be India's contribution to the spiritual experience of Christendom. It might set the Indian Christian on the new venture of discovering some hidden aspects of our Lord's life of great value to the world.[58]

The idea that Hinduism could help Christian theology was expressed especially in the essay "The Church and the Indian Christian mind," where Chenchiah argued that the Hindu view of community, particularly the idea of religion without formal institution, was a corrective to the Western idea of the Church.[59] In effect, insofar as it conformed to the wisdom of Jesus, Hinduism was seen as "worthy of the highest respect."[60]

Chenchiah was not dismissive of the history of Christianity. In fact, Chenchiah urged that Church history be read with the awareness that not all that the Church did was valid:

> I endorse the recommendation [to read Church history]. For I know of no means better calculated to open our eyes to reality and see things as they were. The habit of throwing a shining robe over the deformities of the past and making institutions idealistic is one of the ways theologians seek to reconcile us with the irreconcilable. An Indian cannot read Church history without feeling profoundly disturbed as to the competency of the church to guide in high spiritual matters so long as it claims authority after the manner of the State. Creeds were as much measuring rods and summations of faith as *lathies* freely used in *lathi* charges against those who disturb the peace and order of the Church.[61]

It must be added that Chenchiah was not uncritical of his Hindu heritage, nor did he accept Hinduism wholesale. He knew that Jesus was different from Hinduism and felt compelled to do theology with the missional aim of being intelligible and appealing to the Hindu. Yet more than simply contextualize the message, the concern was also to learn from Hinduism. Thus, in his inaugural note as Editor of *The Pilgrim*, Chenchiah wrote, "The Indian Christian by virtue of his heritage and profession, has qualifications for building a living bridge between Hinduism and Christianity . . . we shall encourage every attempt calculated to bring about a true fellowship and

---

58. Chenchiah, "Christianity and Hinduism," 120.
59. Chenchiah, "The Church and the Indian Christian," 81–100.
60. Ibid., 89.
61. Chenchiah, "Indian Christian Theological Task," 58.

understanding between Christianity and Hinduism. It will be our constant endeavour to present Christ to the Hindu and Hinduism to the Christian."[62]

Note that a categorical differentiation exists between presenting Christ *to the* Hindus and the Christian learning *from* Hinduism. This differentiation, often ignored when looking at Chenchiah, is the key point that makes his theology of religions primarily Christian and Christological.

Jathanna further points out that Chenchiah strongly rejected some Hindu philosophical traditions, especially Shankara's Advaita.[63] Furthermore, even as far as Chenchiah admired the yogic techniques of Aurobindo and C.V.V. (Master Kanchupati Venkataswami Rao), Chenchiah promoted a new Christ-centerd, spirit-enabled yoga called "Amrita Yoga."[64]

Chenchiah, as a result, came across as a theologian who moved inside and outside his Hindu framework, exploring how his culture impacted his view of God and how his view of God impacted his culture, all the while attempting to move beyond the intellectual and theological grip of the Western church.

The Qualified Use of Scripture as a Source of Theology

Another source of Chenchiah's theology was scripture, but neither the entire scripture nor even exclusively the Christian scriptures. The Gospels, which Chenchiah believed were closest in depicting the words and works of Jesus, took priority, while everything else was secondary: "Indian Christian theology should be based on the life and teachings of Jesus as recorded in the Gospels and not on the reactions of disciples as recorded in the epistles. As guides, St. Paul, St. John and St. Peter are valuable but they are not final interpreters of Jesus."[65]

It was not as if the other parts of scripture were not important; it was just that they did not get the same priority. Similarly, Christ was given priority above the scriptures:

> We are not so anxious to be scrupulously faithful to Greek and Latin originals but to the Hebrew and Christian original—the original being the words which Christ spoke and not what was rendered into Greek by the disciples. Of course we cannot do this for teachings in the New Testament other than the Gospels,

---

62. Chenchiah, "Editorial," 1.
63. Jathanna, *Decisiveness of the Christ-Event*, 356.
64. See Chenchiah, "Christians and Yoga," 136–37.
65. Chenchiah, "Indian Christian Theological Task," 111.

for they are cast in Greek, not translated into Greek. But we can proceed by recovering the ideas, actions behind the life and teachings of Jesus to the extent that these could be detached from their first wrappings in Greek.[66]

Using the same principle, Chenchiah rejected the necessity of the Old Testament, arguing that just as the Jewish scriptures were helpful in leading the Jews to Christ, in a qualified sense, so also the Hindu scriptures functioned for the Hindu convert: "Old Testament contains revelation of God. So does Hinduism. In the measure they reveal God and truth they are useful to understand Jesus. While useful, they are not however integral to Christianity. We can understand Jesus without accepting Jewish or Hindu scriptures."[67]

Chenchiah was aware that it was the Christian vision that enabled the early Christians to make connections between the Old Testament and Jesus. It was that same vision that informed the connections between Jesus and Hinduism:

> In truth, the Jew does not walk forward from the Old Testament to the New. What was done was the Christian walked backwards from New Testament to the Old. The Jewish Messianic proof text did not point to Jesus. Matthew unearthed texts in Old Testament to suit Jesus. Jesus did not fulfill prophecy. [Prophecies] are picked up after Jesus to form a sort of background for Jesus. This sort of trick effect can be produced if you turn Jesus towards Hinduism. Those who advanced the fulfillment theory of the relation between Jesus and Hinduism, seek to build the same sort of bridge as the disciples built. It was a bridge not built by Jews from the Old Testament side but by Christians from the side of Jesus. I can pick up material for an Old Testament in Hinduism making selections in the light of what Jesus said and did. That was exactly what early Christians did and later Hindu converts ought to do.[68]

More importantly, Chenchiah emphasized that understanding other scriptures in the light of Christ could be a bridge to help improve relations with the people of the ancient faiths: "Neither Judaism nor Hinduism lead to Christ. Christ abrogates Judaism and Hinduism much more than he fulfills

---

66. Ibid., 99.
67. Ibid., 112.
68. Chenchiah, "Indian Christian Theological Task," 88.

them. Indian Christian theology builds bridges from Jesus to Judaism and Hinduism and not bridges from Judaism and Hinduism to Jesus."[69]

Devasahayam correctly observes that, for Chenchiah, scripture was not authoritative but was a guide and the lessons of scripture were not binding but illuminating.[70] Yet Devasahayam notes that Chenchiah was not averse to the Bible and used it extensively to help explain or even support his views.[71] For instance, Chenchiah's rejection of the Church in favor of the Kingdom of God was based on the hermeneutical principle that, in the Gospels, Jesus never talked about the Church but rather the Kingdom.[72]

Interestingly, Chenchiah avoided using Hindu scriptures to explain Christian doctrine, except when explaining Hinduism itself. Thus, despite his positive view of Hindu scriptures, never in actuality did it replace the Christian scriptures. It can be argued that Chenchiah used both the Hindu and the Christian scriptures in a qualified manner. In terms of Christian scriptures, his controlling hermeneutic was the desire to meet Jesus directly, and the attempt to search the scriptures was "to know the mind of the Lord."[73]

Experience, and not Reason, as a Source of Theology

Chenchiah disagreed with Ward that there were three absolutes—an unchangeable core, unalterable faith and an essential deposit—that needed only to be translated in the Indian context.[74] In contrast, Chenchiah offered that "the only fixed immovable absolute center in Christianity [was] the fact of Christ."[75] Consequently, Chenchiah proposed that the "Christian experience and faith" were in the "relative sphere" which set "theology the task of renewing direct experience of Jesus."[76] This meant that the "fresh and firsthand contact with Christ, God and Holy Spirit" enabled a "new-creation theology," whose aim was to formulate a "biological lifeline Christianity in contrast to ideological or credal Christianity."[77]

---

69. Ibid., 112.
70. Devasahayam, "Role of the Bible," 116.
71. Ibid., 131.
72. Chenchiah, "The Church and the Indian Christian," 81–100.
73. Ibid., 89.
74. Chenchiah, "Indian Christian Theological Task," 206.
75. Ibid.
76. Chenchiah, "Indian Christian Theological Task," 206.
77. Chenchiah, "The Religious Situation in India," 314.

This led Chenchiah to defend the direct experience of Jesus in three ways. Firstly, he argued that direct experience was both possible and also necessary for salvation. In fact, he opined that a direct experience of Jesus led (and not followed) salvation, and that only then could discussions or theologies emerge. Chenchiah used the example of Paul, John and Peter, all of whom had direct experiences of Jesus. Chenchiah then pointed out that the Church assumed that direct experience could not exist and made the people dependent on the systems of the Church, like communion and the Bible:

> If he appeared to St Paul, why not to you and me? Why do Churches and books intervene and bring Him to us like water from a distant fountain head? Is it because nobody wants to meet Him and we are all satisfied with the Bible and the Church? . . .
>
> The Church mechanism assumes that direct knowledge of Jesus is not possible. The central importance given to Mass among Catholics and the equally central place given to the Bible among Protestants confirms the view. If there could be direct contact with Jesus, why should we seek it through bread and wine? If God speaks to us today, why hear His words through a book written about 20 centuries ago?[78]

Elsewhere Chenchiah stated that theology emerged out of the direct experience of Christ:

> The broader view taken by a group of Indian thinkers holds that except for the fact of Jesus, all the rest—experience, interpretation, translation—[are] relative and within the province of theology. While Jesus does not change, our experience of Jesus progressively expands and varies, our discovery of spiritual riches in Him belongs to time. Theology is based on experience. Faith arises out of experience. Experience issues out of contact with Jesus. Indian Christian theology had for its province the whole range of experience that arises out of contact with Jesus. Indian Christian experience of Jesus may vary from that of the west, for the experience of Christ depends on the training of the contacting mind with Jesus. New experiments of Christians, new techniques of contacting with Jesus, new interpretations of Jesus, are all within the province of Indian Christian theology.[79]

This direct experience was justified by the truth of the experience itself, and eventually became the measure through which other things were

78. Chenchiah, "Indian Christian Theological Task," 78.
79. Ibid., 7.

to be evaluated. "Direct experience requires no verification—being self-authenticative. Perceptions are the direct material of experience and, in spite of possibilities of false perception, impress themselves with their reality. We do not verify experience. We verify something not within experience by experience."[80]

Chenchiah's second defence of direct experience came through the idea of transformation of the individual. While Christ remained absolute, the interpreter of Christ would undergo a change in character, which would improve the vision of and understanding of Christ. Chenchiah strongly urged the need for the transformation of the one who claimed to experience Jesus:

> If I am in any way a representative of the Indian Christian—not Indian Christian community—if I to any extent sum up the heritage of Hinduism and the experience of Jesus, I feel the two great urges of the Indian Christians are a desire for direct contact with Jesus (*pratyaksha*) and an aspiration for rebirth—to be born a Son of God in the image of Jesus (*punarjanma*). It is not so much a desire to be a Christian, i.e. a follower of Christ, as to be identified with Christ—for *sayojiya* with Jesus—a longing that made St. Paul to say, "I no longer live but Christ in me." Whether these longings are legitimate or not, there they are and theology that neglects them has no title for being called Indian Christian.[81]

It is interesting that while Appasamy did not agree with Chenchiah's "direct access to Jesus" he still used Chenchiah as an example of *prathyaksha* (perception/experience), the vision of God, and seeing God with clarity and certainty, as a valid source of theology.[82]

The third defence of direct experience lay in the experiments of Christian living that helped the (Indian) Christian to know Jesus better, which for the Indian Christian was a mystical union through yoga. It was the ultimate act of transformation, through the Holy Spirit, that enabled the individual to become like Jesus even as it was Jesus, the living guru, who showed the way.[83] It was a dual cycle—where Jesus was a guru to us, and we were sent as gurus to others.[84] Yet this transmission occurred through the Holy Spirit. In effect, Chenchiah held that the true Christian yoga was Amrita Yoga; "the

80. Ibid., 78.
81. Ibid., 67.
82. Appasamy, "Pramanas," 52.
83. Chenchiah, "Christians and Yoga," 136.
84. Ibid.

yoga of everlasting life, the yoga which abolished death," and the yoga for the reception of the Holy Spirit.[85]

In each case, the controlling factor was the use of experience as an important source of theology where Chenchiah did not found his thinking on the Bible or Church tradition but on his own experience of Christ. The experience was the actual experience of being made a new creation and the path of this was through a modified yoga. The closer one got to the experience of the true Jesus through the Holy Spirit, the better one was able to become like Christ and help others do the same. It was this experience that lifted humanity, gave perspective and governed thinking.

Chenchiah as Post-Hindu Christian Theologian

In view of the above discussion, it is possible to assert that Chenchiah was a post-Hindu.[86] He never fully repeated Hinduism as the correct framework nor did he look to return to it. Rather, from his Christian vision, he saw his Hindu heritage in a positive light to aid what he considered the future of Christian thinking in India. So strong was Chenchiah's Christocentric vision that, even though he used community, scriptures and experience, the ultimate norm for theology in India remained a direct experience of Jesus Christ: "The fear behind all protest at departure from norms is that we may lose something invaluable in Jesus by our non-conformist action. The fear however is not justified. So long as it is Jesus we interpret, so long as our experience comes from direct and renewed contact with Him certain deep profound affinities will exist. Indeed for a common faith the only guarantee is common life and experience of a common Lord. All creeds and experience have to be tested by their fidelity to Jesus."[87]

Not only did Chenchiah believe that the reinterpretation of the past from the point of view of Christ was a normal biblical principle, it was also what Hindu converts "ought to do."[88]

One way of seeing this is to use George Sumner's term, "retrospective narratives."[89] Sumner adapts his principle of "final primacy" to the retrospective narratives of Indian theologians like Upadhaya and Chenchiah,

---

85. Ibid., 137.

86. Post-Hindu is a category I adapt from the "post-Christian" category of feminists like Daphne Hampson who argue that they cannot fully reject their Christian heritage, yet look to move beyond it.

87. Chenchiah, "Indian Christian Theological Task," 58.

88. Ibid., 88.

89. Sumner, *The First & the Last*, 166.

who use Hindu terms for a "deeply Christian end."[90] Thus, "truths ultimately cohere around Jesus who is the *prima veritas*."[91] With this in mind, we now turn to Chenchiah's theological system.

The Theological System Undergirding Chenchiah: Synthesis

There are currently few but excellent summaries of Chenchiah's theology, especially those that highlight the full range of his thinking that include Christology, the Holy Spirit, new creation, Kingdom of God, role of the Church and relations with non-Christian religions.[92] Rather than reiterate these summaries, I highlight Chenchiah's system of thought, which holds these various theological explorations together. For this, Wagner's little-known chapter on Chenchiah in his study of Indian Christian theology points the way.

Wagner rightly warns against the risk of doing violence to the author's intention by attempting to present a system of Chenchiah's theology.[93] Nevertheless, Wagner is also optimistic that Chenchiah's thought moves within certain theological and philosophical limits and so allows for a "tentative systematization of the otherwise amorphous-appearing thoughts."[94] Wagner asserts that Chenchiah's is a theology of "double synthesis" (*doppelsynthese*)—Chenchiah tries to balance the identities of Indian and Christian, but also negotiate between Indian Christian theology and Western neonaturalistic philosophies.[95] Wagner thus states that Chenchiah boldly attempts to unify not only religionaturalism within the theological framework, but also the Western scientific worldview with the spirit of Indian philosophy.[96] Wagner concludes that the final distinctive of Chenchiah's theology is that he always keeps Christ at the center of the discussion, never allowing him to slip into the periphery.[97]

---

90. Ibid.

91. Ibid., 174.

92. After all these years, Robin Boyd's chapter on Chenchiah in his *Introduction to Christian Theology* is still one of the best introductions to Chenchiah. However, Boyd does not do justice to the significance of the Holy Spirit in Chenchiah's theology, nor does he adequately highlight the idea of religion.

93. Wagner, *Erstgestalten einer einheimischen Theologie*, 107.

94. Ibid.

95. Ibid., 195.

96. Ibid., 195–96.

97. Ibid., 197.

Drawing from Wagner, yet also in contrast to him, I assert that Chenchiah's theology is in fact a single synthesis. The point of double synthesis—"Christian theology with naturalist philosophy" as one synthesis and "Indian with Christian" as another synthesis—is well taken. However, Chenchiah's theology has a more straightforward view of Christ as center. Christ's incarnation is shown to be the single synthesis that governs all things. Chenchiah's philosophical assertions arise out of this theology. From such a framework, one can look at all Chenchiah's theological explorations as a synthesis between God and man, as well as the possible synthesis between man and God, through the Holy Spirit. It is this synthesis that binds all of Chenchiah's other theologies, even his theology of religion.[98]

Who Is Jesus? A Synthesis of God and Man

In his article review of Kraemer's book, Chenchiah strongly rejected what he considered the Barthian distance between God and man.[99] Chenchiah argued that this paradigm failed to clarify who Jesus was for us today. Chenchiah's main assertion was that Jesus was "the vertical descent of spirit into the horizontal stream of creation which . . . comes from on high . . . Man is not the last and highest term of creation. The process of creation finds its crown and culmination in Jesus. Jesus is a new Man—the dream of mankind come into life. He is more than a Redeemer, Messiah, Teacher. He is the prototype of a new creation, the first of a new race of children of God. He is the latest term of the creative process and may be the last."[100]

Jesus is visualized as a synthesis, not pure God who leaves humanity untouched, nor pure human, that is trapped by its own limitations.[101] A theological implication that Jesus could be *less* than God is not important for Chenchiah, who prefers to focus on the idea that Jesus is that act of God which not only brings God down, but also helps raise humanity to a new level. This is seen as a synthesis between Hegel's sense of horizontal development in history and Barth's sense of vertical development through the

---

98 It must be said that "synthesis" is not Chenchiah's word for himself, but Wagner's. However, it is still a useful category to help understand Chenchiah's theology. Chenchiah himself clarifies that his synthesis is not a synthesis of a mathematical balance like Hegel's thesis–antithesis, but the creation of a new center and thus a new circumference.

99. See particularly Chenchiah, "Appendix," 10–19.

100. Chenchiah "Who Is Jesus," 378.

101. See Gurukul Group, *A Christian Theological Approach to Hinduism*, 63. The Gurukul Group argue that the biological process of new creation should not deter us from seeing its spiritual character.

revelation. Chenchiah finds that while "Barthians have the advantage over Hegelians" in their "interpretation of the development of creative process," the Hegelians provide "deeper insight" into the "understanding of the actual mechanism of development."[102] Yet both visions—of Hegel and Barth—are inadequate for Chenchiah, who sees the need for a combination of horizontal and vertical visions. Thus, evolutionary logic (horizontal) is combined with incarnational logic (vertical) are combined to emerge as new creation in Christ.

Chenchiah attempted to overcome the problems of Western and Eastern thought by not conceding entirely to either, but by providing a combination—a synthesis. He was able to do this because he was so focused on the incarnation of Christ as the ultimate synthesis:

> Jesus is not God and is not Man, but is the Son of God and the Son of Man. The word 'son' indicates the measure of unity—something less than complete identity with God but something more than difference in category—between God, Jesus, and the Christian. God is God. Man is Man. The twain have met in Jesus: not merely met, but fused and mingled into one. Hinduism always longed for a state in which we could say as Jesus did, 'I and my Father are one'—which was our Lord's affirmation of the Brahma Vakya *Aham Brahmasmi*. It may be, in the mouth of a mere man, the assertion is a travesty. In Jesus it was, for the first time in history, an accomplished reality, not an unrealised aspiration. India will not be afraid of claiming Jesus as belonging to our race as the head of humanity, as the Son of Man.[103]

It is for this reason that Chenchiah did not idealize Christ into a Christ principle; the history of Jesus was of crucial importance to him.[104] It is because Jesus was historical that the evolutionary process could take place *in* history. Jesus was thus ontologically from God and also from Man, and yet not identified with either but as someone new. Chenchiah noted that it was the fact of Jesus being the 'new creation' that made him savior and redeemer. Jesus' life, birth and operation were, "totally different from that of man. He was born differently from man and if in death he fulfilled the common destiny of man, in resurrection he transcended it. Virgin birth, miracles, cross, resurrection are not isolated incidents, indicating the divinity of Jesus but symbol of new destiny of man. What happened to Jesus will happen to hu-

---

102. Chenchiah, "Who Is Jesus," 365.

103. Chenchiah, "Appendix" 27.

104. Though, ironically, Jesus' Jewish history from the Old Testament was not as important.

manity. Since Jesus prefigured a new human destiny, he became its Saviour and Redeemer."[105]

One must note that Chenchiah's argument, especially in the earlier part, was not grounded on philosophical or scientific data. It is almost as if he stated things out of his own experience, expecting his readers to resonate with it or at least that its truth would become apparent. When discussing Hinduism, he did take recourse to research methodologies that looked at the *Vedas* or other scriptures and commentaries. Yet the force of his argument came alive when he used the incarnation as the synthesis principle. It is evident that, for Chenchiah, the fact of Jesus justified his previous argument. While such argumentation need not be accepted in today's modern critical scholarship, the point is that Jesus Christ functioned as the controlling principle, and thus Chenchiah offered a theological system even when looking at non-Christian (namely Hindu) systems.

The Role of the Holy Spirit: A Synthesis for Humanity

Continuing with the singular principle of synthesis, the role of the Holy Spirit must not be ignored in Chenchiah. Scholars have usually focused upon Chenchiah's Christology, yet both Christological and Pneumatological are important to Chenchiah. For instance, Joseph believes that Chenchiah's Christology was actually a "[C]hristology of the Spirit,"[106] which may not be entirely wrong, especially since Chenchiah said that "the Holy Spirit is the universal Jesus" and "Jesus as the Holy Spirit meets India's special needs and demands."[107] Nevertheless, one must guard against an overemphasis of this point. Joseph, for instance, states that according to Chenchiah "it is the Holy Spirit who makes Christianity different from other religions."[108] This is misleading because, for Chenchiah, the distinctive of the Christian religion lay not in the Holy Spirit transformation alone but also in the historical fact of Jesus as God-man. Thus, while it is true that Chenchiah's Christology is Pneumatological, it is equally correct to say that Chenchiah's Pneumatology is Christological. It is thus safer not to make too great a distinction between the Holy Spirit and Jesus and allow for mutual usage—when Chenchiah says "Christ," the Spirit is not far behind, and when Chenchiah says "Spirit," the Spirit is shown to be the Spirit of Jesus.

---

105. Chenchiah, "Essentials of Christianity," 378–79.
106. Joseph, *Indian Interpretation of the Holy Spirit*, 66.
107. Chenchiah, "Christianity and Hinduism," 136.
108. Joseph, *Indian Interpretation of the Holy Spirit*, 66.

The importance of the Holy Spirit was highlighted after the following problematic: the new life in Christ was attractive and desirable, yet the Church was unable to do anything about helping people become like him: "Christ attracts. He creates a desire to be like Him. But we do not know how to become like Him. The weakness of Christianity and missionary methods lies right here. The missionary and the pastor have no answer save hurling texts at humanity. India wants realisation and does not see in us Christ realised. We should like to be transformed into Christ. But nobody can tell us how this can be done. All pretend. The Church is the greatest pretender of all. None know. Hence the primacy of the experimenters in science and religion. How shall we reproduce God or Christ?"[109]

Chenchiah's answer to this problem of the inability to *reproduce* Christ was the Holy Spirit. In a series of articles entitled "The Holy Spirit: Meaning and Significance of Christianity," Chenchiah clearly expressed his view of the Spirit and the Spirit's role for Christian life.[110] Differing from traditional theology, Chenchiah suggested that the Holy Spirit dwelt in all people: "In every one of us—deep down beneath the foundations of our being—the Holy Spirit lies latent. As the Hindu has said, in every man lies coiled up and quiescent, the great creative energy—the *Kundalini*."[111] Yet, to counter the belief that the Holy Spirit existed as an inner potential in all human beings, Chenchiah asserted that the Holy Spirit entered as a result of Christ: "The Holy Spirit has entered Man in the person of the New Man, Our Lord."[112]

There were three aspects to the Holy Spirit. First, Chenchiah acknowledged the epistemological role of the Holy Spirit by stating that only the "possession of the spirit of Christ" yielded any meaning of "Christ word."[113] According to Chenchiah, no one could have taken to Christ in a "living way" without the "possession" of the Holy Spirit.[114]

The second role of the Spirit was to create an ontological change in human beings to become like Jesus. The Holy Spirit was also seen to be the "universal and universalizing power behind Jesus."[115] In terms of the Christian, the Holy Spirit was the *shakti*, the force, that changed us from within. The *shakti* was the "operative factor" of the evolution.[116] The Spirit transfor-

109. Chenchiah, "Religion in Contemporary India," 756.
110. Chenchiah, "The Holy Spirit."
111. Ibid., 323.
112. Ibid.
113. Chenchiah, "Indian Christian Theological Task," 100.
114. Ibid.
115. Chenchiah, "The Challenge of Modern Hinduism," 566.
116. Chenchiah, "The Holy Spirit," 323.

mation went beyond the purely spiritual realm. As the Holy Spirit became active in life, the Spirit integrated the whole being, including personality, thought and will:

> The Holy Spirit is preeminently an in-dweller (i.e.) dweller in you. God is in heaven, Christ sits at His Right Hand but the Holy Spirit dwells in you. He interpenetrates your personality, lives closest to you—as close as your life itself. The Holy Spirit has not to be sought out but sought in. The quest is in your inner domain. The eyes should be turned inside you, and in the realm of your personality—the world of thought and will—you search for this hidden Lord. There can be no pilgrimages to the Holy Spirit as to a distant shrine—no *dharsan* of Him as of a god outside. What you need is to see him as the opening of third eye, the eye of insight. You need not move about, you need only awaken.[117]

The third role of the Spirit was to link the Kingdom of God to human possibility.[118] While the Kingdom of God was the "main impulse" of Jesus' life, the Holy Spirit was the force that made the Kingdom of God possible.[119] While Jesus was the new creation, the new Adam, who heralded the new Kingdom, it was only through the Holy Spirit that humanity could evolve into the new creation and become like Jesus. Chenchiah went on to assert that "the Holy Spirit must descend into the profound depths of our being and therefrom recreate us anew."[120]

Thus, the synthesis of the Holy Spirit would be achieved when people would be made God-men just like Jesus was God-man, and also when humanity was enabled by the Holy Spirit to live the new life in the Kingdom of God: "The Holy Spirit descends on humanity and begets the sons of God, thus making an entry into human beings permanently as a new order in evolution . . . the Holy Spirit presides over the new creation and lives in the sons of God as their atman."[121]

In this sense, Chenchiah offered what he called the yoga of the Holy Spirit, the Amrita Yoga also referred to as *parisuddha atma yoga*. Yoga was defined as the "psychophysical discipline and technique for attaining the

---

117. Ibid., 324.
118. Chenchiah, "The Holy Spirit," 252.
119. Ibid. Chenchiah further develops the idea of ethics of the kingdom, stating that only through the Holy Spirit can the kingdom ethics be accomplished.
120. Chenchiah, "The Holy Spirit," 287.
121. Chenchiah, "Christians and Yoga," 136.

spiritual end of union or communion with God."[122] The yoga that Chenchiah talked about was the discipline to specifically receive the Holy Spirit, the "yoga will be a discipline for his reception."[123] Evidently, the Holy Spirit was not an afterthought but a fundamental idea that along with Christ held Chenchiah's theology together.

Christological Synthesis as the Fundamental Theological Assertion

Through the above discussion it is clear that Chenchiah used the incarnation of Jesus within the work of the Holy Spirit, as a singular synthesis. However, did Chenchiah use the synthesis of Jesus as the controlling system, or did he highlight the system because other Indian theologians did the same thing? Frank Whaling suggests that the tendency to synthesize is a common trait in Indian Christian theology.[124] Thus, for Whaling, Chenchiah's attempt at synthesis was symptomatic of his age.

While Chenchiah's actual theological formation is not so clear-cut—it is difficult to identify where Christianity began and Hinduism ended—there was certainly an intentional attempt to prioritize Jesus. One must not minimize Chenchiah's theological statement that Jesus was and must be the norm and source of all theological thinking. Similarly, there was no attempt in Chenchiah to ground the logic of synthesis in anything other than Christ.

Another way of looking at this synthesis is through Chenchiah's discussions of *asramas*.[125] Chenchiah depicted the Asrama system, especially the *vanaprastha asrama*, as emerging as a synthesis between the *vedas* and *tapas*; the vedic religion of mantras and the quest for personal transformation through austerity.[126] This synthesis was shown to be the synthesis of Brahman which was right detachment and right attachment. Here, certainly, a synthetical principle existed in Hinduism prefiguring Christ.

However, through the argument, and certainly by its end, Chenchiah pointed to Jesus as the true synthesis. Chenchiah explained synthesis not simply as a philosophical concept but as a radical life-giving center; rather than being shaped by the reality around it, it shaped reality around it. In talking of the synthesis it is easy to see that Chenchiah saw Jesus as the center of the new creation:

122. Ibid.
123. Ibid.
124. Whaling, "Indian Christian Theology," 319–33.
125. Chenchiah et al., *Asramas: Past and Present*.
126. See especially, Chenchiah, "Rebirth of Asrama—Search after Brahman," 23–29.

> The Indian simile of water on the lotus—which does not attach itself to the leaf, yet like a diamond drop, moves on the surface—is one way of describing it. 'In the world' and 'not of the world' is another way of putting it. It is a middle and a mean. It is not, however, a mathematical middle point which we reach by measuring equal distances from the ends . . . It is not an artist's neutral colour composed on the palette by careful mixture of colours, strong and mild. It is not a synthesis of thesis and antithesis . . . It is a living centre that creates the circumference—the primeval twilight out of which day and night, light and darkness emerge—primal stuff of which sun and moon, day and night are produced. It is the middle that throws off the ends. Though we start from this life, we reach a level wherefrom we look at it as from a distance yet without losing the sense of vividness and reality.[127]

Similarly, Chenchiah was unwavering in his approach to bring the attention to Christ. He argued that the incarnation of Jesus served as the ultimate principle of the detachment quest of Hindu yoga:

> Incarnation in the true sense represents the creative mean between man and God. It creates a balance between natural life and the new life that detaches us from the old. If incarnation means a temporary descent of God into life, the new life does not create. If it involves absolute identity with life, then incarnation does not mark any progress. Incarnation is the creative expression of a life which though it enters into this life yet acts with puissant power from its own centre. Jesus is neither God nor man. He is the Son of God and the Son of Man—the son representing alike the identity and the difference. The son is the detached reproduction of the Father. Incarnation signifies the emergence of a new man, partaking of divinity yet possessing humanity, detached and attached to both God and man. The reproduction of incarnation lifts the Christian above the world yet operating on it. In Christ, the Christian is between God and Man, desire and action, attachment and renunciation.[128]

In addition, it was in meeting with the "spirit of Jesus" that the traditions, valuable as they were in Chenchiah's eyes, were given new meaning and possibilities:

---

127. Chenchiah, "Vanaprastha Asrama: Assessment," 138–39.
128. Chenchiah, "Vanaprastha Asrama: Assessment," 135–36.

> The mind of our Lord draws in sympathy to the deepest spiritual longings of India and by infusing them with a new passion of love sanctifies them with spiritual power. In the public life of India, innumerable currents from the East and West, from the past and the present, meet. But of these conjunctions none are so charged with power for good as the meeting of the spirit of Jesus with the spiritual streams that the asramas of the past have set in Hinduism. Whoever misses this conjunction loses the key to read the soul of India aright.[129]

Thus we are able to see that for Chenchiah, synthesis was not based on a philosophical idea but was founded in Christ. This idea of synthesis must be seen in the context of Chenchiah's own belief that Christians must look to Christ and then look back at Hinduism; for the Hindu scriptures did not by themselves point to Christ, but it was only in retrospect that Christians could see these connections.[130] It was a post-Hindu vision of yoga that arose after the Hindu met Christ, not before.[131] Christ was the union between God and man and thus he was the destination, through the Holy Spirit, for humanity's union with God as well. With this theological assertion in mind, we are now ready to face Chenchiah's theology of religion.

A SURVEY OF CHENCHIAH'S VIEWS OF RELIGION

The following section describes Chenchiah's views on religion from key texts on religion. After a survey of these articles, we will then be able to look at his theory of religion and his theology of religions.

A Survey of Religion in Contemporary India

One key text on Chenchiah's view of religion is "Religion in Contemporary India," published in both *Guardian*[132] as well as in *Rethinking Christianity in India*, in 1938.[133]

129. Chenchiah, "Introductioni," in *Asramas*, xiv.
130. Chenchiah, "Indian Christian Theological Task" 88.
131. Of course Chenchiah notes that Aurobindo and Master C.V.V. got very close to it. Yet never were they shown to be the answers of Christian Yoga, or even the Yoga of the new creation. It was only the new Spirit yoga that could reproduce Christ, and only the reproduction of Christ was the true goal of humanity and the Kingdom of God.
132. Chenchiah, "Religion in Contemporary India," 740, 756.
133. Ibid., 201–14.

In the article, Chenchiah surveyed the many religious movements in contemporary Indian culture. However his particular focus was on the revolutions that were occurring in the religious world of India, especially within Hinduism. Chenchiah drew attention to the changing expectations of religion. Chenchiah revealed that there was currently a revolution in place, one that was challenging conventional religion. It began with the desire for Indian independence, where people were no longer concerned with a religion of the future (afterlife), but with a religion for now. The desire of the people was no longer for a religion that guaranteed the unseen of life, but for one that was practical and useful for today. The older religion of ritual and philosophy had centerd around either the question of "how to be saved"[134] or on the desire to ensure a good future after death.[135] However, now there was a revolution where the people were asking, "What shall we do to save the country and nation?"[136] Describing the changing moods, Chenchiah stated,

> We are no longer troubled with personal salvation and individual future. It has been replaced by the quest for national salvation and concern for its future ... The quest for national salvation though associated with our political leaders, is nevertheless a religious pursuit. We are seeking it in the same spirit as we sought personal salvation—only instead of 'my soul' the 'soul of the nation' has become substituted ... Life in the past was under the jurisdiction of religion. But today religion comes under the jurisdiction of life. We refuse to accept a 'credit religion' to be cashed in future: we want a religion negotiable now. It is no longer, am I worthy of my religion, but is religion worthy of the nation? The writ is against religion and it has to justify its existence by its contribution to life. Can religion unite us? Can it give us strength to fight the evils of life? Can it so enrich our life as to make us contribute to the world life?—are the questions we put to religion.[137]

Furthermore, Chenchiah was impressed by the example of Gandhi who integrated politics with religion so that "religious power" was used "to build up free states and societies and individuals"—for example, Gandhi's

---

134. For Hindus from *samsara*, the "endless wheel of births and rebirths." Chenchiah, "Religion in Contemporary India," 201.

135. Chenchiah, "Religion in Contemporary India," 202.

136. Ibid.

137. Ibid.

use of the Sermon on the Mount as well as *ahimsa*.[138] Gandhi's religion was seen as the paradigm of what Chenchiah wanted to convey. Chenchiah went on to offer an integrated view of religion, one that did not seek to cut off religion from politics, but saw religion as the life-force of politics, especially of the pre-independence movement. Chenchiah thus stated that true religion would give the power to live.[139]

In the article, Chenchiah went on to show that religion was not simple in contemporary India and there were many struggles between various revolutions, reactions and reconstructions. Chenchiah categorized these into four kinds of religious movements/ currents. First was the religion of no-religion that looked to fulfill the function of religion outside religion. A soft-example was Jawaharlal Nehru, whose socialist leanings were expressed through a general agnosticism towards religion. According to Chenchiah, Nehru remained religious because his "religion [was] not always a conscious creed," and that religion was expressed even within those who renounced it.[140] This kind of religion applied also to the cult of patriotism, that worshipped the land, even Bharatha Matha as goddess.[141] Deeper still was the idea of those who had "turned into a war against religion itself" and sought "humanitarianism without pronounced religious bias."[142] Chenchiah, nevertheless, saw religious elements in all these.

Another kind of religious current was the religion of beauty, that expressed itself through the religion of the artiste. Examples of this were Rabrindranath Tagore, the religions of science in Theosophy, and the religions of Bhakti, seen through the Hari Nath and Marga Nath movements.[143]

A third kind of religious movement was the established tradition, examples ranged from the *Sanatana Dharma* orthodox Hindu tradition to the reforms within Advaitic tradition. The Sanatanists were shown to have their own internal movements through the workings of the Arya Samaj and the Hindu Mahasabha.[144] However, they were depicted negatively in the article since their chief concern was to stick to preserving their "eternal traditions."[145] The Advaitists, through the traditions of Ramana Mahrishi

---

138. Chenchiah, "Religion in Contemporary India," 203.
139. Ibid.
140. Ibid., 203–5.
141. Ibid., 205–6.
142. Ibid., 206.
143. Ibid., 208–11.
144. Ibid., 206–8.
145. For instance Chenchiah says, "They have not come into contact or collision with the real religious forces of other faiths." Also, their "constant opposition to the

and Ramdas, were commended for seeking to integrate social action with their religion of realisation.[146]

Finally, Chenchiah depicted the religion of experimentation, the religion of yoga. It is here Chenchiah's own affinities lay.[147] Chenchiah spoke highly of the "great experimenters," Sri Aurobindo and Master C.V.V., whose efforts had the potential to transform personality. They formed a climax of the revolution in Hinduism since both offered a way of becoming something new. Through a "new creative energy" it was possible to become and help others become a new humanity capable of living the ideals of religion.[148] This idea of new humanity was highly valued by Chenchiah, and was shown to be the turning point in Hinduism as well as in Christianity.

It is easy to see that Chenchiah had been influenced by Hindu renaissance rhetoric, especially the idea that Hinduism was growing more aware of itself. Yet there never was blind acceptance of all reform movements. Instead, there was a clear leaning towards a certain kind of religious reform that conformed to Chenchiah's own view of religion as experiment or adventure.

While Chenchiah never justified the criteria for determining which tradition was the more favored religious current, the implied criteria, knowing Chenchiah's theological concern, are easy to determine. Chenchiah viewed Christ as the one who was not only the "new creation," but one who heralded the new creation for all humanity. The closest representation of this fact in Hinduism, according to Chenchiah, came through Sri Aurobindo and Master C.V.V.

Medieval Versus Modern Religion: Practical Religion for Today

Making a similar point to the one in the previous article was "Religions and the World," written later in Chenchiah's career.[149] Chenchiah used the medieval/modern taxonomy to distinguish between traditional religion that provided the promise of future salvation, and modern religion that offered

---

newly awakened social consciousness which demands fair play and justice to women and depressed classes, has not added either to their prestige or strength." Chenchiah, "Religion in Contemporary India," 207–8.

146. Chenchiah, "Religion in Contemporary India," 210–11.

147. Elsewhere Chenchiah says, "Religion like science, has to live on observation and experimentation." Chenchiah, "Characteristics of Vanaprastha Asrama," 119.

148. Chenchiah, "Religion in Contemporary India," 211–13.

149. Chenchiah, "Religions and the World," 220.

a practical religion of the here and now—a shift from "world negation to world affirmation":

> the essential differences between modern and medieval religions relate to the direction of human effort, the attitude towards life, the conception of religious ends. Of these, four may be mentioned as determinative. The medieval religions, all of them, had the other-worldly outlook and regarded life as a discipline for a super-worldly goal, as a theatre where you qualified yourself to enter heaven or escape hell. In modern religions, whether Hinduism, Islam or Christianity, there is hardly a trace of interest in, and anxiety for the post-mortem destiny of man. The repented sinner does not ask "What shall I do to go to heaven?" but "How shall I live an ideal life on earth and be a child of God here and now?[150]

In effect, Chenchiah would say, religion no longer functions as redemption or escape, lifting man from the predicament of worldly life, but as a call summoning men to produce a new heaven and a new earth and people, the Kingdom of God on earth, than with a race of new men and women, children of God."[151]

Chenchiah also drew attention to three separate entities of modern religions—Church (institutions), State and Science. What bound them together was their function: "All of them have perceived the vision of the same goal—a perfect humanity saved from disease, destitution and from mental shackles and moral inhibitions and developing to the full its potentialities, in short, a new humanity."[152]

Chenchiah depicted the great saints of other religions like Ram Mohan Roy, Swami Vivekananda, Sri Aurobindo, Master C.V.V., and Swami Chinmayananda, as the "prophets of new India," who urged humanity towards courage, freedom, frustrations and victories, the religion of experimentation and adventure. Nevertheless Chenchiah still held to the view that the confluence of the revolutions, both in the East and the West, were "fertilized . . . by the stream of Christ's teaching of the Kingdom of God."[153]

Thus, the "future of religion" was envisaged through a rejection of tradition-bound churches and temples, and an alignment with the new task to which other religions were also aligned, namely to realize "the dream of Christ for mankind," that all religions may together sing: "'Thy Kingdom

---

150. Ibid.
151. Ibid.
152. Ibid. See also, Chenchiah, "Christian Message in a Hindu Environment," 100.
153. Chenchiah, "Religions and the World," 220.

come and Thy will be done on earth as it is in heaven' and feel that God has set for them, through Christ, a common task."[154]

Jesus and the Non-Christian Faiths: Christianity and the Concept of 'religion'

In "Jesus and the non-Christian faiths," another article in *Rethinking Christianity in India*,[155] Chenchiah described religion in largely negative terms, even showing how Christianity, as a religion, was no better or worse than other religions. However in the same article, an alternative version of Christianity was presented and there Christianity (in its best form) was said not to be a religion. Thus, the article has Chenchiah's strongest critiques of religion.

In terms of religion, Chenchiah discussed the tendency of religion to institutionalize, to make replications of their gods, and to believe in the possibility of religion being able to achieve its limitless goals. The tendency of religions to become institutional was evident through a series of steps that also revealed a substantive view of religion. Every religion started with a "radiant core"—a founder or a key thought.[156] The personality or central idea grabbed the attention of people and generated both positive and negative responses.[157] Eventually the community of followers interpreted the central person or idea through "doctrines and dogmas, worship and ritual" to the extent that the "bright nucleus" tended to get "enveloped by a huge globe of tradition and testimony."[158] The next step was when the outer traditions and rituals attached themselves to the central core to the extent that these rituals eventually became the "centre of influence" and slowly replaced the "original fact."[159]

The second phenomenon was the "duplication of gods and saviors" where humans created God in their own image.[160] Chenchiah strongly rejected the Christ of experience, an idea differentiated from the direct experience of Christ: the "Christ of experience" was the product of the person's imaging, where Christ was "made to fit in with the faith and order of the

154. Ibid.
155. Chenchiah, "Jesus and Non-Christian Faiths," 47–62.
156. Ibid., 49.
157. Ibid., 50.
158. Ibid.
159. Ibid.
160. Ibid., 52–53.

church."[161] Chenchiah agreed with Barth's critique of this human religion, and even equated Christianity with other religions like Barth.[162] Christianity was shown to be of the same category as and equal to other religions.[163]

The third phenomenon was the (false) belief in the "infinite potentialities of man."[164] This humanism, within the naturalist framework, was something that Chenchiah rejected, especially in religion: "Religion . . . has immense faith in the intellect and will of man . . . religions aim at the development of the inner potentialities of man or woman with the endowments of man that is intellect, will or emotion . . . Religion is *our* effort, *our* realisation of an end."[165]

Chenchiah was aware that, "Viewed as a human effort directed towards divine object, Christianity [was] a religion on par with other religions."[166] Nevertheless, Chenchiah asserted that the core of Christianity did not seek to make perfect men but was concerned with the new birth in Jesus Christ through the Holy Spirit.[167] True Christianity was not the reliance on human power but on the power of the Spirit.[168] In effect, "Christianity [was] not a religion."[169] Chenchiah thus created a distinction between the category of religion and new creation: "Christianity has been a failure because we made a new religion of it instead of a new creation."[170]

The way Chenchiah made the distinction, and thus justified that the category religion would not apply to Christian discourse about Jesus, Holy Spirit and Kingdom of God, was by defining religion in functional terms. Religion in a negative sense was ultimately a series of creeds, rituals and institutions, that controlled the people while hiding the core. Christianity as the new creation was a "birth process," where people would "reproduce Jesus" (through the Holy Spirit) and could "tell the world how."[171] Furthermore, while religion was a complete system, Christ exposed a limitation in religion but also had the efficacy to answer this limitation: "Other religions are answers to the questions, how shall I perfect myself, how shall I be saved

161. Ibid., 53.
162. Ibid., 52–53.
163. Ibid., 56.
164. Ibid., 53–54.
165. Ibid., 54.
166. Ibid.
167. Ibid., 54–55.
168. Chenchiah, "Jesus and the Non-Christian Faiths," 55.
169. Ibid.
170. Ibid.
171. Ibid., 59.

from the conflict of personality from divided self. Other religions answer the cry, what shall I do to be saved from my sins? Jesus is God's answer to man's ambition to become like God, to escape fate and destiny, to become master of life and death. This is an aspiration of all religions for which the answer can only be new creation."[172]

Through Jesus and the Holy Spirit: The New Possibilities of Religion

Another important idea about religion came across in the article, "Who Is Jesus?"[173] While the thrust of the entire article was to explore Jesus, the question was framed within a presupposition of what religion was: a concern for life and creation. In the article, Chenchiah stated that the question "Who is Jesus?" had been answered before the confluence of the world's great religions—a situation that would now (after the confluence) necessarily influence the answer to this fundamental question.[174] Now, with the new interreligious reality, Jesus could be understood anew.[175]

Chenchiah founded his understanding of Jesus on two prior assertions about religion. The first assertion had to do with the primary activity of religion, which was to understand creation and to lead us into the heart of the mystery of life.[176] Other activities like prayers, sacraments, moral and ethical guidance and rituals were some of the many secondary activities of religion and were not to take people away from the central focus on creation. In this sense, Chenchiah looked at religion and science as having the same goal, to understand creation and life:

> Our prayers and worship, our sacraments and *samskaras,* our rites and rituals, draw us away from creation, even as civilization with its innumerable allurements and seductions drag us away from this primary touch with man and nature. The scientist, the historian and the prophet have only one book to read—the book of creation. If religion is revelation, revelation is essentially creation. The 'given' in science and religion alike is the creation; the 'developed' is our manipulation of it. The failure to realise

---

172. Ibid., 60–61.

173. These are a series of four articles, the first of which was published on July 29, 1943. Chenchiah, "Who Is Jesus," 352–53.

174. Ibid., 352.

175. Elsewhere Chenchiah said, "The Christian in India . . . still feels he can never understand Jesus till he understands the drama of God's dealing with man in and through the other religions of the world." Chenchiah, "Appendix," 2.

176. Chenchiah, "Who Is Jesus," 352.

this primary objective of religion makes theology a secondary science easily liable to petrification and incapable of movement and progress"[177]

Chenchiah's second assertion about religion was about its relationship with evolution. For Chenchiah the evolutionary process meant that creation had been punctuated at "critical stages" with a series of revolutions.[178] These revolutions had in fact led to the previous evolutionary leaps in history.[179] These revolutions occurred when creation had reached its limit, its potential, when it could move no further.[180] While these revolutions occurred because creation was fundamentally geared to improve and grow, these revelations could not occur simply because of the nature of creation; something was needed beyond creation itself.[181] Thus, Chenchiah stated: "[t]he horizontal flow of creation receives new force and elements that descend on it vertically from above and break into it."[182]

This evolutionary process was related to religion through analogy. Like creation, religion too had reached its potential and needed a revolution to move beyond its limitations. Like creation, religion too needed Jesus: "The world situation at his advent shows that the potentialities of man had been worked out in every direction . . . In religion specially, all possible changes had been rung. Nature worship, all types of impersonal and super-personal conceptions of God, theisms had thrown in their contribution. Since the beginning of the Christian era, religion in India has been permutations and combinations of what had been discovered earlier. Even the idea of incarnation was anticipated and worked out."[183]

However, in view of this, new life could not emerge without the annihilation of the old.[184] Thus, Jesus was that "latest revolution of the creative process," the surge of God's activity in creation for new creation.[185] Chenchiah explained,

> Buddha was the perfect man, but Jesus was the new man . . . Buddha was the end of the old Man, Jesus was the beginning of

---

177. Ibid., 352.
178. Ibid., 364.
179. Ibid.
180. Ibid.
181. Ibid.
182. Ibid.
183. Ibid., 389.
184. Ibid.
185. Ibid.

> the new. In Him [Jesus] Man, perfected man faced with death obtains a new lease of life. Death is not only the wages of sin, but the reward of perfection. The sinner dies, the sage attains Nirvana ... The soul having been perfected as religions in China and India shows the spirit came in Jesus. This context is again a proof that Jesus is a new creation. Christianity, then, is the belief that in Jesus, creation mounts a step higher, that man is redeemed by the Son of God and that Jesus is the origin of the species of Sons of God. If you relinquish this belief, Jesus is no more than a religious leader like Buddha; ceases to be the power that saves you, in the largest sense.[186]

Chenchiah thus held the view that religions had limitations, even in their goal for perfection. However, these limitations were mitigated in Christ who was ultimately the one, even the first one, who could grant religions access to the new creation (through the Holy Spirit). It was Christ therefore who caused the ultimate revolution in life, in creation, and in religion.

Kingdom of God and Religion: Two Types of Religion

If the previous article had a hint of a positive view of religion, through the article "Kingdom of God and religion," Chenchiah clarified how religion could be both negative and positive by offering a dual theory of religion.[187]

In the article, Chenchiah drew attention to the fact that all religions presupposed two worlds: the physical world in which Man resided and the inaccessible spiritual world of God. Thus, the "whole effort of religion" was "either to force open the doors of the spiritual world from our side or to implore God to open it from his."[188] In addition, "all religious experience [was] founded on the sense that man [was] able to draw upon ultra mundane sources of strength and inspiration."[189] This, as we saw, was Chenchiah's view of true religion.[190]

The corruption of religion occurred, unsurprisingly for those who are aware of Chenchiah's writings, in the institutionalization of religion.

---

186. Ibid.
187. Chenchiah, "Kingdom of God in India," 260–61.
188. Ibid., 260.
189. Ibid.
190. While this article does not feature this terminology, Chenchiah still used "true religion" as a concept to mean the right kind of religion and not a right instance of religion. See Chenchiah, "Appendix," 17.

Chenchiah called this "another type of religion"[191] and elsewhere he even referred to it as a "new religion."[192] This new religion was "manufactured by men," where a temple "retained the memory of God," priests "reminded the people of God," and "mystic institutions like sacrifice" witnessed to "man's effort to get rid of sin."[193] This religion was the "religion of education,"[194] which was quite different from the earlier effort to either meet God directly or to be met by him directly.

The corruption of religion included the secularization of religion, where the State determined the shape of the Church rather than the other way round: "instead of carrying the principles of religion to dominate secular life, bring the principles of secular life to shape forces of spiritual life."[195] Similarly, even as religion existed with the distinction between the spiritual and material world, the new religion in particular further emphasized an illusionary dichotomy—where a Christian would think he was retreating from the secular world into the spiritual, not recognizing that both the secular state and the supposedly spiritual Church were from the same world.[196] For Chenchiah, the World Conference at Tambaram was an expression of the "utter helplessness of Christian leaders in the face of the world situation."[197]

So far, Chenchiah's critique of religion is familiar, and his solution of Jesus as the new creation and the Holy Spirit as the new creative *shakti* for the Kingdom of God, is expected. However, notably Chenchiah was operating with two views of religion. One type of religion was vibrant and original while the other type of religion was static and corrupted.[198] It was only the original religion that attempted to "open the doors between the temporal and the spiritual worlds."[199] Thus, when Jesus Christ himself opened the doors and created a new world order, there was no longer a gap between the two worlds—this original religion became the "meeting point of the eternal and the temporal order of things."[200]

---

191. Chenchiah, "Kingdom of God in India," 260.
192. Chenchiah, "Jesus and the Non-Christian Faiths," 55.
193. Chenchiah, "Kingdom of God in India," 260.
194. Ibid.
195. Ibid.
196. Ibid.
197. Ibid.
198. Chenchiah even calls the effort to seek God or to be found by him, the "fundamental aspect of religion." Chenchiah, "Kingdom of God in India," 261.
199. Ibid.
200. Ibid.

Thus, Chenchiah's proposal was for a transformed, even re-created, religion. He urged that people needed to approach Jesus as "scientists" who experimented and researched "to find out new things in him."[201] This was in tune with Chenchiah's identification of religion as "a fascinating and beautiful adventure, the calling of heroes and sons of God."[202] Similarly, this type of religion helped "the Indian mind" to "discover Christ" and to "discover the Holy Spirit," even as people came in "actual contact" with him. This type of religion would also help "develop the technique of new birth,"[203] an example of this technique of new birth being the Holy Spirit yoga (Amrita Yoga).

Therefore, regardless of Chenchiah's negative views of religion, he often used the word religion in two different senses with the positive view always on his mind.

In Response to Kraemer: The True Religion

An even more positive statement of religion emerged in Chenchiah's response to Hendrik Kraemer, featured as an "Appendix" in *Rethinking Christianity in India*.[204] The article on the whole has several ideas already represented in other writings of Chenchiah. However, this article helps clarify Chenchiah's view of true religion.

Chenchiah's concept of true religion did not refer to an instance of a religion, or even right or wrong religion, but to a right *kind* of religion. When Chenchiah referred to the "living forces" of religion,[205] he was talking in terms of the true religion. The true religion was a process, a living force that, when seen through Christ, caused Christian growth.[206] This true religion was the religion of adventure and experimentation, and was achievable by the common man,[207] and also by the priest if he was willing to stand along with the scientist as an experimenter.[208] The goal of the experimentation in religion was to gain a new understanding of Jesus, to become like Jesus, to know how to pass Jesus on.[209] This experimentation would discover

201. Ibid., 262.
202. See Chenchiah, "Appendix," 1–2.
203. Chenchiah, "Kingdom of God in India," 262.
204. Chenchiah, "Appendix," 1–50.
205. Ibid., 9.
206. Ibid.
207. Ibid.
208. Chenchiah, "Appendix," 17.
209. Ibid., 19–20.

a Jesus who was the "redemption of the social order," not one who drove us away from society.[210] Thus, this new kind of religion, also related in Christian terms to the Kingdom of God, would be realizable in this world and it could be attained.[211]

This religion would also lead to new avenues of cooperation with other religions, especially those non-Christian religions which were similarly on the path of discovery and experimentation of Christ.[212] This religion however was not like traditional Christianity and Hinduism, since both, and others like them, were limited. Chenchiah was under no illusion of the limitations of Hinduism and Christianity. While Hinduism and other non-Christian religions "not only register longings and aspirations but also satisfactions," Chenchiah would also say that "in all religions there [was] a residue of unfulfilled desire, partly arising out of the very satisfaction religion achieves and partly out of the failure of religion to satisfy the aspirations of man so far."[213] Chenchiah stressed that it was Jesus who "kindles new hopes not felt before and kills some of the deepest and persistent longings of man . . . Jesus stands in definite relation to the residuary problems of other religions rather than with the satisfied longings of man. In other words, the relationship of Christ to the non-Christian heart and hope lies in the unexplored regions of our Lord's life and not in the region already mapped out."[214]

Nevertheless, as in the heart of Christianity lay something other than what was typically seen, this true concept of religion had also been evident within the heart of Hinduism: true religion is "a conception of religion which means a widening, deepening or enlarging of human personality— a problem different from education— the working out of potentialities."[215] Gandhi's "experiments" with the Sermon of the Mount for a political and spiritual ethic—notice the experimental terminology—were commended even though Gandhi did "not accept dogmatic Christianity."[216]

The importance of Jesus and the Holy Spirit working together in the process to achieve this true religion cannot be overstated. At the heart of Christianity, Chenchiah would say, "is the genetic or creative aspects of Jesus—it is the Holy Spirit as a creative energy that takes the Indian into the

---

210. Ibid., 19.
211. Ibid., 30.
212. Ibid., 20.
213. Chenchiah, "Appendix," 42.
214. Ibid.
215. Ibid., 53.
216. Ibid., 29–30.

new 'given' — in Jesus."²¹⁷ Furthermore, "Christianity brings into evolution the new Sakti of the Holy Spirit."²¹⁸

Ultimately, true religion was the religion of the lived experience of new creation, not an arrival but a spiritual experiment:

> India awaits the fruition of this experiment. It is on the tiptoe of expectation. Already some of the mature souls of modern India have caught the fascination of the great experiment . . . we need to possess reality. India always searched for reality and yielded to reality. The future of Christianity lies in the spiritual laboratory. The Indian Christian must concern himself with 'rebirth.' God gave Jesus. True evangelism consists in reproducing Jesus. The process is Christianity. When we have discovered it, the Hindu will besiege you, instead of you begging for his attention . . . The Indian Christian who can see deeper should take to the prayer room and experiment on *rebirth*—harness the Holy Spirit to the creation of new life.²¹⁹

It is important to distinguish Chenchiah from A. G. Hogg at this point, simply because Hogg had critiqued Kraemer by arguing that religions were not purely a seeking, but also a finding.²²⁰ Hogg's point however was to affirm the genuine faith of the religious adherents, a meeting of the true God despite an untrue religion through a genuine religious experience. Chenchiah in contrast was asserting that a religion could find fulfillment within its own structures. However, this fulfillment was very different and not directly connected with the new-fulfillment that Christ offered. For Chenchiah, if the religion can fulfill its longings, it does so only within its own (non-Christian) goals; the longings that Christ fulfills can only be fulfilled by Christ.

Temple Religion, Ascetic Religion, and the Asramas

We now move to one of Chenchiah's most important descriptions of what religion must be, the religion of the Asramas. Through the concept of the Asramas, Chenchiah depicted the true synthesis of Indian Christianity with non-Christian religions, the spiritual discipline of yoga and social reform.

---

217. Ibid., 23.
218. Ibid., 43.
219. Ibid., 53–53.
220. Hogg, "The Christian Attitude to Non-Christian Faith," 103.

As we have already noted, Chenchiah operated with various taxonomies to describe religion and its development. In the collection of articles in *Asramas: Past and Present,* Chenchiah (who wrote the bulk of the historical material), represented the religion of the Asramas through the taxonomies of vedic (temple) religion and *tapas* (ascetic) religion.

Chenchiah painted a picture of the Hindu religion that was dynamic, filled with experiments, errors and growth. We are shown the struggle between vedic religion, where the gods were manipulated with rituals, and the religion of *tapas*, where the individual practised severe austerity and struggle, to purify the body. Both paradigms, according to Chenchiah, were flawed.[221]

The religion of the Vedas, Chenchiah wrote, had the altar as its center and sacrifice as its central activity.[222] The emphasis was so much on ritual that not only were the gods manipulated into granting favor, priests even claimed to be better than the gods because the gods needed sacrifices.[223] However this system led to many unanswered questions, such as the speculations of human destiny, mystery of life and creation, and so forth. Those with burning questions left for the forest to "think deep."[224]

Chenchiah then showed how the *sanyasi* emerged as those who felt the gods need not be manipulated by rituals; the power of prayer was not in rituals but in the "attitude of the mind . . . purity of heart, determination of will."[225] People went to the forest for *tapas*, "sustained and intense spiritual effort."[226] In contrast to the religion of ritual, the temple religion, the *tapas* religion was the religion of emotion and faith.[227] Thus *tapas* emerged as the "will to achieve, the determination to win power from gods by persistent austerities directed to the conquest of body and mind."[228]

Then emerged the philosophy of the Upanishads, the advent of Brahman philosophy, that heralded not the conquest of body and mind but the quest to be liberated from its desire. Influenced, both by Buddhism as well as the forest dwellers themselves, Chenchiah showed that in the subsequent

---

221. See especially Chenchiah, "Birth of the Asrama," 12–14.
222. Ibid., 12–13.
223. Ibid., 13.
224. Ibid.
225. Ibid., 14.
226. Chenchiah, "Characteristics of Vanaprastha Asrama," 119.
227. Ibid.
228. Chenchiah, "Birth of the Asrama," 14.

centuries, "the doctrine of Brahman and the discipline of yoga" created a new conception of religion, making the old way obsolete.[229]

The Asramas, particularly among those who dwelt in the forest, represented an ideal of "realization in religion."[230] The quest was not to win the favor of the divine, but to become one with the divine. Thus there emerged Brahman philosophy, especially expressed through yoga, to experiment with the oneness philosophy and the self. Neither through the ritualism of vedic ways nor by emphasizing the inward singular obsession of *tapas*, the vedantic forest dwellers became a paradigm of the true religion. Drawing from the *tapas* of the *sanyasi*, the pursuit of Brahman led to the serious work of yoga, the attempt to achieve the quest.[231] Their conception of religion was not merely a belief but a realization, even the "actualization of the ideal"—harmony with Brahman and all things—involving the need for experimentation and inner purity.[232]

The Asramas thus formed a "new brotherhood,"[233] a union with Brahman that was expressed as harmony with people, animals and nature.[234] Another social angle emerged, especially through the renunciation of caste and adoption of universality.[235] While attracting rebels against the oppression of the vedic rituals, Asramas became a haven for harmony: "a spiritual family, based not on blood as the natural family is, but on mutual love and regard, as slowly evolved as the result of religious discipline that purified the ego and its natural inclinations."[236]

Similarly, Chenchiah compared the Hindu Asramas of old, as a family: "Vanaprashta Asrama was the continuation of the family life. There were no rules and regulations, no vows or creeds. This Asrama was not only a life in the forest, but also a life of the forest."[237] Also, "The asrama was the extension of the family—a joint adventure with a wife—a spiritual excursion by the middle aged."[238]

---

229. Chenchiah, "Rebirth Asramas," 26–29.

230. Chenchiah, "Characteristics of Vanaprastha Asrama," 119.

231. Chenchiah, "Rebirth of Asrama," 26.

232. Ibid., 29.

233. Chenchiah, "Rebirth of Asrama, " 26–27. When Chenchiah talked about the *Asrama*, he often meant the historical *varnaprastha asrama*.

234. Chenchiah, "Rebirth of Asrama," 27–29.

235. Ibid.

236. Chenchiah, "Retrospect," 301.

237. Chenchiah, "Characteristics of Vanaprastha Asrama," 117.

238. Chenchiah, "Asramas: Comparisons and Contrasts," 123–24.

The *vanaprastha asrama* stood for basic principles. Those practising it were nonauthoritarian, nontraditional, nonritualistic, nonsectarian, nonsacerdotal (laymen oriented), and noninstitutional.[239] They encouraged, "free association for social and religious purposes. There was no law, no legislature, no binding custom in forest life. If vanaprasthas lived together, it was out of their free choice. The writ of the king and the priest did not run there. The features of the asrama life . . . grew spontaneously . . . Asrama in this sense was an experiment of great social value to the modern world and its ideology . . ."[240]

This was no renunciation. It was the religion of union, realization, experimentation, and social reconstruction. The method of yoga was heavily employed, especially to achieve detached interest (*asanga*):[241]

> This ideal of realisation stands in clear contrast to a religion of ritual on one side and a religion of emotion and faith on the other. Religion has to be lived, life has to be carved into the figure of the ideal . . . Religion like science, has to live on observation and experimentation. It was the primary feature of an asrama life that religion was thought of as . . . ideals to be embodied in flesh and blood . . . The religion of the vanaprastha was applied religion, not assertive and aggressive faith that seeks to expand by propaganda of doctrines. It demanded obedience to the divine urge. It was creative not expansionist, primarily.[242]

Furthermore, this true religion highlighted the doctrine of *asanga*: "In religion this detachment is attained not by tearing oneself from life but by placing oneself between the two great magnets—God and the world. Placed between them, man attains to the detachment necessary for fuller life . . . in religion by placing oneself between two powerful attractions, the bhakta attains and keeps to the mean. Religion does not under-value the need for detachment. It fortifies it and renders it easy by drawing on the great reserves of God."[243]

It must be noted that the value of *asanga* for the Christian was seen through the religion of Jesus:

> The religion of Jesus emphasizes the value and necessity of detachment. It does not use the language of Gita nor its method.

239. Chenchiah, "Characteristics of Vanaprastha Asrama," 114–17.
240. Ibid., 120.
241. Ibid., 121.
242. Chenchiah, "Characteristics of Vanaprastha Asrama," 119.
243. Ibid., 135–36.

> Yet the teachings of Jesus imply that his followers should attain detachment. Incarnation in the true sense represents the creative mean between man and God. It creates a balance between natural life and the new life that detaches us from the old. If incarnation means a temporary descent of God into life, the new life does not create ... In Christ, the Christian is between God and Man, desire and action, attachment and renunciation.[244]

Chenchiah related the diminishing of Asramas with the decline of Buddhism and the emergence of "new theism" and the "temple religion" of ritual.[245] Chenchiah remarked that Hinduism started becoming more "temple-centric" to the extent that the temple took over religion and the outmoded *Asrama*.[246] The alternatives to temple religion were the religions of theism and *bhakti*, which were as guilty as vedic rituals and *tapas* of attempting to manipulate God, only this time one could "chain God by your faith" and "God was the servant of the faithful servants."[247] In both cases, "all anxiety for the soul, all straining after the Absolute, introspection," ideals that Chenchiah held dearly, became unnecessary.[248]

The new revolutions in the contemporary scenario, the new yoga that promoted an engagement with life,[249] and the reemergence of the Asramas in the Indian political-religious context, were signs for Chenchiah that another revolution, similar to the revolution of the Upanishads, was taking place—the hope of the recovery of true religion. Yet Chenchiah's concern was not simply for Hinduism, but for Christianity.

For the Christian, the true religion was expressed through the "value of meditation and contemplation," the "pursuit of the Holy Spirit as the dynamic of Christian life," and the "desire to serve the poor and suffering."[250] While obviously critical of institutional (temple) Christianity, Chenchiah also rejected *bhakti* Christianity, promoting instead a practical religion:

> The Indian Christian does well to put obedience above confession, application of the teaching of Christ to life, above a mere

---

244. Ibid.
245. Chenchiah, "Retrospect and Prospect," 298.
246. Chenchiah, "The Passing Away of the Asrama and the Asrama Dharma," 98.
247. Ibid., 100.
248. Ibid., 99.
249. "Yoga has always been the child of applied religion. Doctrinal and creedal religions do not require Yoga on the intellectual level of their faith. The need for Yoga is felt in religion only when we try to embody the religious ideas and ideals in practice." Chenchiah, "Christians and Yoga," 136.
250. Chenchiah, "Retrospect and Prospect," 302.

self-expression in song and praise. Our Bhakti type of Christianity, mostly emotional, must be supplemented by ethical and will Christianity which shapes history by action and sacrifice. Above all the Christian must search and apply the power of Holy Spirit and not lose himself in adoration. The Hindu reaction is a call to us to go beyond the Church and dogma and face the vital issues of reproduction of Christ in the Christian. That we should become Christ's—is true to Christian ambition and while the service may be necessary discipline, sonship is the dream of Jesus for all men.[251]

Thus, as the Asramas represented the quest for "harmonized and integrated life," the kind of Christians who would take to the Asramas would be people of the true religion, "men who are dissatisfied with partial embodiment of the spirit of Christ in the individual and the social life and who have decided to devote themselves to a thorough reproduction of the Christian spirit in service and in social groupings and actions—in short men who follow the Master's path without compromise. . ."[252]

Through this article Chenchiah was doing two things. He was reading into Hinduism the concept of religion even as he was reconstructing Christianity within a Hindu mould. However, this was not a synthesis of Christianity and Hinduism, because the true religion was ultimately measured in Christ, the Holy Spirit and the Kingdom of God. Anything else, no matter how positive, remained incomplete.

The Words 'Religion' and 'Theology'

Finally, a brief description of how Chenchiah sought to translate the word 'religion' in the Indian context, and how he drew parallels between theology and religion, will give a picture of how Chenchiah viewed religion.

Chenchiah extended a discussion over the nature and translation of theology, to include one on the word "religion." He offered that several parallels for the word 'religion' in Sanskrit could be attempted. For instance, "religious" could be seen as *Mata*—a concept associated with opinion but also referring to the "intellectual aspect of dogma and doctrine."[253] This Chenchiah found unsatisfactory because religion "goes deeper."[254] Then, Chenchiah opined that *Marga*, associated with pathways, could apply to

251. Chenchiah, "Christ of Hinduism," 92.
252. Chenchiah, "Retrospect and Prospect," 301–2.
253. Chenchiah, "Samapada Chaturanga," 32.
254. Ibid.

religion as being "a way of life;" not simply as a means to an end, but also a "fundamental mode of self expression."[255] In addition was the concept of Yana, a word for the "way of life."[256]

Dharma was another good contender, yet not exclusively suitable.[257] Chenchiah was aware that Hinduism or even Buddhism were names that were "imposed by foreigners" and were often referred to by them as the Hindu or the Buddhist Dharma.[258] Chenchiah did not address whether Buddhism or Hinduism were rightly or wrongly called Dharma, however he opined that a better word was needed to express Christianity as religion. To do this, Chenchiah went to the etymological meaning of religion—religion as *legare* (to bind). To this Chenchiah explored the concept of yoga, which expressed uniting, "making one."[259] Chenchiah offered parallels between "binding" and "uniting," two aspects present in yoga: "both bind and unite represent different shades of meaning in the way many may be made into one."[260] As a result, Chenchiah offered that Christianity in India could be called Christu-yoga, which would best express Christianity's "realization aspects."[261]

Relatedly, Chenchiah provided a range of definitions for theology. Significantly, Chenchiah distinguished theology from philosophy by showing that theology was concerned with revelation.[262] More importantly, apart from the knowledge and the visionary aspect of theology, Chenchiah noted that spirituality or religiosity and theology were synonymous. He especially highlighted *Adhyatma Vidya* (theology with an emphasis on the spiritual) as an important component of how theology should be understood in the Indian context.[263]

Similarly, in a follow-up article, Chenchiah offered a reinterpretation of religion and theology as coexisting together:

> The theologian with his mind saturated with thought forms of the past is becoming ... more an anachronism ... More than the theologian, the theology has become anaemic, incapable of striking into new adventures, trying to save itself from the

255. Ibid.
256. Ibid.
257. Ibid., 32–33.
258. Ibid., 33.
259. Ibid.
260. Ibid.
261. Ibid.
262. Ibid., 31.
263. Ibid.

constant proddings with sharp weapons from science and state. If theology desired to get acclimatized to modern conditions, it has to draw closer to modern man and his religion. If religion is life, theology must strike roots into religion and popular religion at that, to draw its living energies. To the Indian Christian ... his task is not merely to bring together traditional Christian religion and a traditional Christian theology but to step out of both of them and try to grasp Christ with all his heart (religion) and with all his mind (theology).[264]

While mind/heart divisions for theology and religion may seem like a caricature, Chenchiah's point was to discover both the religious and theological foundations of Christianity. Chenchiah's view of theology was in fact his view of what religion should be: "theology must develop a new branch of experimental religion consisting of Christian Yoga."[265] This is to say, "'experimental religion' offers a new technique of approach for the integration of religion and theology."[266]

Thus, while Chenchiah did not get into controversies about using Dharma for religion, he certainly offered yoga as an adequate way to conceive of 'religion' theologically.

CHENCHIAH'S THEORY OF RELIGION

While there was no classical definition of religion in Chenchiah's writings, one can still get a sense of his theory of religion. Through the above writings, I now make some remarks about his theory and subsequently his theology of religion. As we have seen, it is possible to see Chenchiah's definition of religion in terms of a theory of religion and a theology of religion. Chenchiah did not differentiate between the two. However, it is helpful to see where and how Chenchiah used philosophical categories and ask what theological categories applied. I argue that Chenchiah was working with two types of definitions of religion, the religion of the outside and the religion of the insider. As an outsider, *what is religion* was depicted as religion was commonly understood. As an insider, religion was depicted in relation to Christianity and accepted as *what religion ought to be*. The former is his theory of religion, the focus of this section, while the latter indicates his theology of religion, the focus of the next section.

264. Chenchiah, "Theology and Religion," 2–3.
265. Ibid., 3.
266. Ibid.

What Is Religion?

Basic Fact of Religion: The Common Sense and Broad Sense of Religion

Chenchiah did not question the basic fact of religion as a category of human phenomena.[267] Chenchiah assumed that religion exists, if not in all, in most cultures. There was, in Chenchiah, the *common sense* belief that religion as a category was understandable and recognizable across cultures. In addition, there was an implicit assumption that Christianity, Islam, Hinduism, Buddhism, in their traditional senses, were all religions. These implications can be drawn from Chenchiah's uncritical use of the word 'religion' and "religions," with reference to the religions found in both Western and Eastern cultures.

This way of talking about religion is not surprising since Chenchiah's contemporaries tended to speak of religion in this way as well. For instance, Radhakrishnan referred to Christianity, Buddhism and Hinduism as religions.[268] Radhakrishnan's problem of religion was an internal problem facing religions, like the quest for meaning, rather than a problem with the category itself.[269] The same was true of Vivekananda, Gandhi and even Ambedkar.[270]

If there was one aspect that Chenchiah differed in, it was his adoption of the *broad sense* of religion, to include state, ideologies and science as religions.[271] For instance, Chenchiah stated Jawaharlal Nehru's movement towards secularizm had religious overtones.[272] Similarly, Chenchiah noted: "religion of the state and religion of science have joined the company of ancient religions. All these have common aims and seek to establish prosperous and healthy conditions for men. A Christian has to fight old and new religions. The new are difficult to fight because they are more an atmosphere than a concrete code. The state dominates the Christian and non-Christian—science converts the priest and laymen."[273]

Chenchiah was making these statements with an objective intention, thus speaking as an outsider. In this sense, religion remained a common phenomenon, controlled by the traditions, and yet was also more common

---

267. In fact, in view of Chenchiah's background, it would be quite anachronistic to even expect that the universality of religions would be questioned.

268. Radhakrishnan, *The Hindu View of Life*, 91.

269. Radhakrishnan, "The Indian Approach to the Problem of Religion," 36–38.

270. See previous chapter for discussion on Vivekananda, Gandhi and Ambedkar.

271. See, Chenchiah, "Christian Message in a Hindu Environment," 100.

272. Chenchiah, "Religion in Contemporary India," 741.

273. Chenchiah, "Christian Message in a Hindu Environment," 100.

than we perceived because it was a vibrant part of society outside the traditionally religious institutions.

This broad sense of religion was popular, particularly in Christian circles. For instance, at the Jerusalem conference, secular altruistic movements were referred to as a "kind of religion."[274] Even Barth highlighted how communism and "Americanism" were religions, in that they overcame all personal choices and desires of the individual.[275] This idea extended to Kraemer who called movements like Communism and Fascism "spiritual and social revolutions."[276] They were "pseudoreligions" demanding allegiances, much like traditional religion, and had their own philosophies, creeds and systems to master the chaos of the world.[277]

Note that these associations of broad sense were made by Chenchiah's attempt to speak objectively and as an outsider. In addition, he noted both a substantive and functional similarity between all religions, including his own. Chenchiah portrayed religion as having shared concepts and shared functions, a point to which we now turn.

Substantive-Functional Theory of Religion

For Chenchiah, that there was religion led to the idea that there was a unified concept of religion across cultures. Chenchiah indeed held to the conceptual unity of religion. However, this must be seen as different from the theological unity of religions, of all roads leading to the same goal, an idea already popular in Chenchiah's day and one that Chenchiah regularly opposed.[278] For Chenchiah, the common basis of religion was similar to how "all men must have a skeleton."[279]

Keeping Kunin's taxonomy in mind,[280] Chenchiah's conception of religion had some essentialism, especially through his idea that religion met the "longings of the heart," assuming that all people had an inherent spiritual longing.[281] However, there were primarily substantive and functional elements in Chenchiah's theory of religion.

---

274. Jones, "Secular Civilization and the Christian Task," 320.
275. Barth, "Questions which 'Christianity' Must Face," 93.
276. Kraemer, *The Christian Message in a Non-Christian World*, 15.
277. Ibid., 15–16.
278. Chenchiah, "Appendix," 41.
279. Ibid.
280. Discussed in the Introduction as essentialist, substantive and functional.
281. Chenchiah, "Appendix," 41–42.

Chenchiah's substantive theory of religion is seen through his reference of religion as being of a certain type, or of being expressed in certain ways. Even as Chenchiah pointed to diversity within religions, the common skeleton was seen, for instance, through how "every religion [was] a circle complete and perfect in itself," or even how religions "start[ed] with a quest which they more or less achieve[d]."[282] Chenchiah opined that the nature of all religion was to presuppose the existence of two worlds, to the extent that the "whole effort of religion has been either to force open the doors of the spiritual world from our side or to implore God to open it from his."[283] Elsewhere, Chenchiah stated how the primary activity of religion was to understand creation, and to lead us more deeply into the heart of the mystery of life.[284] Another popular image for Chenchiah was to view religion as an "adventure."[285] His ideas of temple religion, even though they pertained to the "secondary activities of religion,"— prayers, sacraments, moral and ethical guidance and rituals—were also signs that Chenchiah's theory of religion was substantive.[286]

Nevertheless, Chenchiah was also functional in his approach to religion because his larger emphasis of religion was on what religion did in society or what it should do. We saw this in his strongly worded assertion that religion had to "justify its existence by its contribution to life."[287] Functionalism was also evident through his emphasis on how religions, broadly understood as Church (institutions), State and Science, were bound together by the "same goal," namely "a perfect humanity saved from disease, destitution and from mental shackles and moral inhibitions and developing to the full its potentialities, in short, a new humanity.[288] Add to this, regardless of the evident essentialism in the idea of "human longings," Chenchiah saw that religion effectively *satisfied* the longings of individuals.[289]

The emphasis on functional religion brings us to two types of functionalism: that of Nehru/Ambedkar, who believed that religion had little usefulness; and that of Gandhi, who believed in the integration of spirituality and politics. Chenchiah was critical of Nehru and Ambedkar for failing

282. Chenchiah, "Appendix," 41.
283. Chenchiah, "Kingdom of God in India," 260.
284. Chenchiah "Who Is Jesus," 352.
285. Chenchiah, "Appendix," 1.
286. See previous section for a discussion of the concepts.
287. Chenchiah, "Religion in Contemporary India," 202.
288. Chenchiah, "Religions and the World," 220. See also, Chenchiah, "Christian message in a Hindu environment," 100.
289. Chenchiah, "Appendix," 42.

to recognize the role/potential of religion for social reform and, instead, replacing faith and God with humanism: "Nehru and Naicker, Ambedkar and Annadorai, are seeking asylum in a faith which does not obtrude God on them and yet kindles humanism in them."[290]

Chenchiah unsurprisingly preferred Gandhi, and resonated with four of his ideas: first, that religion was "intended to build up free states and societies and individuals;" second, that Jesus' teachings on the Sermon on the Mount and the Cross gave man a "new weapon of defence and offence, far more powerful than force and coercion and oppression," namely *ahimsa*; third, that religion must give the individual the power and spiritual temperament to practise the ideals of *ahimsa*; fourth, that this religion being sought after is its "living centre and not to its institutionalized petrifactions."[291]

Chenchiah's views of religion were also similar to Gandhi's, in that Chenchiah was not primarily concerned with spiritual upliftment alone, but with an ethical basis for nationalism and life. Like Gandhi's integration of spirituality and politics, the turn of religion to new creation was to transform creation.[292] Without the integration of spirituality, it was impossible to have renewed life. It is here that Chenchiah chose Gandhi over Ambedkar because, while Ambedkar had social concerns, he failed to emphasize the inner spirituality needed for people to address society. Chenchiah liked Gandhi's emphases on *swaraj* and on the integration of religion in normal political/social life. It is within this paradigm that Chenchiah would stress "new creation," or even "new man," because without a new insurgence, there was no hope for a better future.[293]

Evolutionary Religion

As we saw earlier, evolutionary thinking was quite common during the time of Chenchiah, influencing not just Western but also Indian thinkers. Chenchiah strongly adopted the evolutionary framework in his work, especially for his theory of religion. There were three ways Chenchiah used evolution in his theory of religion. Firstly, he depicted an evolutionary development of religion in a negative sense where "every historic religion" began with a "historic personality of outstanding significance or power" and then,

---

290. Chenchiah, "The Religious Situation in India," 315.

291. Ibid., 740.

292. For further discussion of this point, see Abraham, "Interpreting Christian Social Ethics," 247.

293. Chenchiah, "The Future of Christianity in India," 316–17.

through time, degenerated.²⁹⁴ Chenchiah noted with dismay that when a community was formed around that personality and associated teachings, the teachings would be codified into dogmas, passed on from generation to generation, with an entire superstructure developed to protect and control its communication: "in other words doctrines and dogmas, worship and ritual, mysteries and ceremonies, gather round till at last the bright nucleus gets enveloped by a huge globe of tradition and testimony."²⁹⁵

Chenchiah also used evolution in a more value-neutral sense, where he saw development *within* a religion. For instance, he depicted how religions, in this case Hinduism, passed through various stages of development. The earliest "primitive" stage was the worship of the sun. Religion proceeded next to when the sun dwelt with the people who worshipped fire. This movement carried on to when Surya (the Sun God) took on human flesh. The final stage was with yoga, where we could become like the gods.²⁹⁶ Chenchiah depicted a similar sense of movement in three stages of human relation with God: from worship (the most distance), to friendship (the familiar) to union (least differentiation).²⁹⁷ This usage of evolution, seen within Hinduism, was also within the "old creation" metaphor, where Hinduism has its own fulfillments.

The third way Chenchiah used evolution extended beyond the history of religions approach, where evolution was connected with revolution. Chenchiah critiqued science whose object was to "eliminate purpose in creation," to limit creation only to natural processes.²⁹⁸ The danger, Chenchiah felt, was that science limited the process of evolution to what had gone before and could not foresee the future. In effect, all of creation's development, including life, was seen to exist in simple matter. Chenchiah, for his part, argued instead that evolution needed an impetus from above to keep it moving forward: "the horizontal flow of creation receives new force and the elements that descend on it vertically from above and break into it."²⁹⁹ Thus, matter did not have in itself the potential to evolve, but in history, there were several revolutionary moments, propelled from outside, that pushed creation towards a new destiny.³⁰⁰

---

294. Chenchiah, "The Dilemma and Dialectic of Religions," 293.
295. Ibid.
296. Ibid., 294.
297. Ibid.
298. Chenchiah, "Who Is Jesus," 353.
299. Ibid., 364.
300. In the next section we will see how Chenchiah applied this theologically to show Jesus as that revolution.

Chenchiah applied this theory of evolution to his theory of religion, by referring to the stages of religious development as revolutions. We see this especially in his discussion of Hinduism, as having undergone a series of revolutions that helped in its evolution. Chenchiah likened the contemporary movements towards yoga within Hinduism as "revolutionary currents" that were "creating a spiritual commotion."[301] This revolution was likened to the "days of Upanishads" where "that revolution gave us Brahman."[302] Furthermore, "Gods no longer sit in heaven commanding and condemning us. They come to us, move with us—uplifting us. The Creator is portrayed as taking interest in creation."[303] This ideological/religious evolution in religion was perceived as the kind of thrust that moved creation, and religion, forward. In effect, religion was conceived as being in a constant state of evolution, moving the worshipper and worshiped to a state of greater union.

This was applied to Christ and the Spirit, where Jesus was portrayed as the ultimate revolution in the evolution of religion. He stated, "If evolution is going to be the crucial concept of Indian Christian theology, it is not pre-existence of Jesus but his entry as a new form and power into the cosmic process that demands attention."[304] Elsewhere, Jesus was referred to as the origin of the new species of the "Sons of God."[305] Furthermore, this evolutionary leap was achieved through the power of the Holy Spirit to create a new man, a new being, of a different kind from that of the old creation; an actual biological entity exactly along the lines of how Jesus was a new being: "Jesus is not man made perfect, but a new creation—the manifestation of a new cosmic energy. A Christian is a man born not of blood and will of man, but by the Holy Spirit overshadowing man. This new creation is like our Gospel and its demonstration. The Word Uncreate has become create in Jesus. Human history has turned a new revolutionary chapter in Jesus. Christianity is not primarily a doctrine of salvation but the announcement of the advent of a new creative order in Jesus."[306]

---

301. Chenchiah, "Religion in Contemporary India," 757.
302. Ibid.
303. Ibid.
304. Chenchiah, "Indian Christian Theological Task," 99.
305. Chenchiah, "Who Is Jesus," 389.
306. Chenchiah, "Jesus and Non-Christian Faiths," 58.

Dual Theory of Religion

The key distinctive in Chenchiah's theory of religion was that he operated with a dual theory of religion.

He accepted the traditional understandings of religion (even though he also accepted a broader definition of religion) that seemed to suggest that religions were systems made up of several beliefs, rituals and institutions which had a particular function in/for society. The typical observable qualities like temples, priests, texts, creeds, worship and fasting were all markers for the traditional category of religion, which was expressed in two ways—temple and ascetic. Certainly, Chenchiah neither doubted nor rejected that such religion existed and was cross-cultural. However, Chenchiah operated with a second view of religion, namely true religion. This view of religion allowed him to make value judgments on both traditional notions of religion, namely, temple and ascetic religion.

Temple religion aimed to control the gods through rituals, doctrines, and institution. The alternative, ascetic religion, was expressed through mysticism, austerity, and *bhakti*, fleeing the world (in a quest for purity from the world) to join with God. True religion, in contrast, was the religion that reduced the separation between God and humanity, transforming people and making them new. True religion, for Chenchiah, was religion that aimed to rightly grapple with the two worlds, of God and creation.[307] It placed the person "between the two great magnets—God and the world" rather than in opposition to either. Thus, rather than pure detachment, the person's life is fortified by "drawing on the great reserves of God."[308] Thus, for Chenchiah, true religion was "applied religion," that demanded obedience and practical living, not simply ritualistic or doctrinal adherence.[309] The balance lay in seeking union with God, something similar to the Brahman philosophy, but governed not by the negation of creation but through new creation.[310]

So what can we say about Chenchiah's definition of religion? There were two definitions. One was the traditional (to his day) definition of religion that looked at religion as emerging in history and moving forward. This definition was both substantive and functional, in that it looked at religion as having some commonality across cultures and also having a purpose for society. It was also seen from an evolutionary point of view, thus existing

---

307. Chenchiah, "Kingdom of God in India," 260–62.
308. Chenchiah, "Vanaprastha Asrama: Assessment," 135–36.
309. Chenchiah, "Characteristics of Vanaprastha Asrama," 119.
310. An idea we will explore further in his theology of religion.

as an ever-changing phenomenon. All these views of religion could have been held either by a Christian or a non-Christian.

However, there was another theological definition that shaped his view of religion, even provided a value judgment on traditional religion and attempted to move beyond it. The theological definition allowed Chenchiah to move beyond the traditional notions of religion, to something more unique. Here clearly Chenchiah was operating from within his Christian theological framework. It is to this theological religion that we now turn.

CHENCHIAH'S THEOLOGY OF RELIGION

We now look at Chenchiah's theology, to discover what aspects of his view of God and Christ influenced his views of religion.

Religion as an Insider: The Convert

First, concerning Chenchiah's theology of religion, we must note that he addressed religion as a convert, as an insider. Chenchiah distinguished his own methodology for understanding religion from those of both the scientist and the missionary.[311] The scientific scholar looked at religion through comparative eyes, though without making any assessment of value of one or the other.[312] Such scholars readily believed that religions were "perfect systems" that satisfied the felt need of their adherents.[313] The problem of the scientific scholar, for Chenchiah, was that they were noncommittal, even indifferent, to the claims of religion. In effect, "science justifie[d] the relativist view of religions, while admitting all of them [made] absolute claims."[314] The scientific scholar attempted objectivity and was "committed to no presuppositions."[315] Thus the scientist believed that all religions were simply different ways to respond to the mystery of life, and no religion could be seen as being the definitive answer.[316]

The missionary's methodology, in contrast, began with the conviction that "Christianity alone can be the true religion" and sought to prove Christian superiority either by extolling the virtues of the Christian religion or by

---

311. Chenchiah, "Jesus and Non-Christian Faiths," 47–49.
312. Ibid, 47–48.
313. Ibid., 48.
314. Ibid.
315. Ibid., 47.
316. Ibid., 48.

showing other religions in a negative light.[317] While this usually resulted in a condemnation of other religions, Chenchiah did note that, in his time, the awareness of the richness of non-Christian religions had been shaking the confidence of the missionary.[318]

The third approach, the one that Chenchiah adopted, was that of the convert. The convert neither hated Hinduism nor followed the West blindly. Instead, "he discovers the supreme value of Christ, not in spite of Hinduism but because Hinduism has taught him to discern spiritual greatness. For him, loyalty to Christ does not involve the surrender of a reverential attitude toward the Hindu heritage . . . (yet) he still believes that Jesus and his demands alone are obligatory."[319]

The convert had been attracted to Christ and knew him to be true, and yet he did not try to prove his spiritual past as folly but rather was grateful that his spiritual heritage as a "spiritual mother" had led him to Christ.[320] Chenchiah was therefore clearly not hiding from the subjectivity of his explorations.

Consequently, it must be reiterated that, as a Hindu convert, Chenchiah was a post-Hindu, one who naturally used Hindu categories but was not necessarily operating within the Hindu framework. Instead, the priority for Chenchiah was Christ, and all his dealings with Hinduism, along with the concept of religion, were controlled by his attempted faithfulness to Christ.

The Substance and Function of Religion Determined by Theological Categories

We saw in the previous section that Chenchiah's theory of religion was both substantive and functional. Here we see that there was a theological underpinning to that theory of religion. The idea that religion was concerned with a duality may have been common, but Chenchiah certainly would have been exposed to that particular aspect of it in relation to Jesus' synthesis, through the Jerusalem Conference in 1928. While Chenchiah never directly stated that his ideas came from the conference, it is not hard to see a few

---

317. Ibid.

318. Ibid.

319. Chenchiah, "Jesus and the Non-Christian Faiths," 49. Elsewhere he puts this more positively, where "The convert is not a double deserter from the culture and religion of his race. He has accepted Christ. He still accepts his obligations to his country. He remains the son of the land, a patriot anxious and willing with the rest to achieve his country's freedom and prosperity." Chenchiah, "Appendix," 8.

320. Chenchiah, "Jesus and Non-Christian Faiths," 48–49.

parallels. For instance, in the Memorandum presented by the Swedish Missionary Council, Chenchiah's own declarations about religion, concerning two worlds, as well as the stress upon the unity achieved through Christ, are prefigured: "All religion . . . claims to establish real life-fellowship, life unity between the Eternal and man, to infuse in man divine life. It is not sufficient that these two, the Divine and the human, stand in juxtaposition as two parties fundamentally different although reconciled to each other. The Eternal and man must not be contrasts. They must not be impenetrable to each other. All true religion aims at permeating the whole of human life with the Divine. God living in the soul, the soul united with God. This is the goal of religion."[321]

Similarly, some of Chenchiah's theology of religion resonated with the ideas of Rufus Jones, who was writing during the Jerusalem Conference. Jones, as we saw earlier, called for "the spirit of adventure" where Christianity was conceived, not as seeking safety in the "ark" but as a perilous journey full of "risk and danger."[322] Jones also identified Christianity with a "laboratory experiment," where "the transforming and creative power of Christianity can fully meet the condition of the world to-day."[323] Jones added:

> Too few have seen that a Christian is 'a new creation,' a person living in and by a new life-energy, and taking Christ's way of life seriously and sincerely. Too many have comfortably assumed that it was a religion of talk . . . In other words, the conviction has not filtered down into the heart of the common man who makes up the Church that Christianity is a religion of life, something we do, a daily walk, the practice of strenuous ideals, the building of a Kingdom of God here among men, an experiment of faith, a conquest of the world.[324]

The remarkable similarity of these ideas to Chenchiah's is self-evident for those who know Chenchiah's writings. Chenchiah too urged that Christians approach Jesus as scientists: "we turn to Christ not merely repeating what we know of him, but by experimenting and researching to find out new things in him."[325] Chenchiah called for the "the primacy of the experimenters in science and religion" where thinking and practice of the Christian religion developed through "analysis and discovery," much like in science.[326]

321. Speer, "Value of the Religious Values," 425.
322. Jones, "Secular Civilization and the Christian task," 309–10.
323. Ibid., 328–29.
324. Ibid., 329–30.
325. Chenchiah, "The Kingdom of God in India," 262.
326. Chenchiah, "Religion in Contemporary India," 756.

All this, of course, was with the view of the theological purpose of religion: "the actual achievement of the Kingdom of God."[327]

The point is that Chenchiah had allowed, consciously or subconsciously, Christian theologians to influence his thinking about the purpose of religion. This is not a critical comment, but a statement of the natural and appropriate method for theologians acting as insiders—Western and Indian Christianity was the theological context of Chenchiah's theology of religion.

More directly, Chenchiah's theory of religion is theological because it was formed in view of a theological category, namely the Christ event. Wagner helps draw attention to this by noting Chenchiah's taxonomy of religion that distinguished between invocatory religions and deification religions—those where the gods come to man and those where man becomes God.[328] Wagner correctly shows how Chenchiah abandoned this taxonomy when talking about Christianity and, instead, argued that the divide between the material and spiritual worlds, presupposed in the invocatory and deification religions, was bridged by Christ.[329] Clearly, the argument is already in favor of the Christian religion because, in Chenchiah's interpretation of Christ, Christ through the incarnation was the union of the two worlds. Thus, when defining true religion to be a union, Chenchiah kept the deck stacked towards Christianity and against other religions.

The Evolution of Religion Determined by Theology

Rather than side with Jathanna, who states that Chenchiah "tried to interpret the Christian faith in relation to . . . modern evolutionary thinking,"[330] I make the inverse point that Chenchiah reinterpreted contemporary evolutionary categories from a theological framework. This is not to say that he was not influenced by evolutionary thinking, but rather that Chenchiah did not assimilate evolutionary thinking entirely and sought instead to apply his Christo-theological principle to evolutionary religion. This can be seen in how Chenchiah distinguished himself from Hindu evolutionary thinkers like Aurobindo, the Christian neonaturalist de Chardin and the fulfillment theologian Farquhar.

---

327. Chenchiah, "Essentials of Christianity," 405.
328. Wagner, *Erstgestalten einer einheimischen Theologie*, 114.
329. Ibid., 115.
330. Jathanna, *The Decisiveness of Christ*, 52.

Differing from Darwin's Evolution

In his article "Who Is Jesus," Chenchiah briefly distinguished his theory of evolution from philosophical Darwinism. In particular, he disagreed with Darwin's theory of the survival of the fittest, arguing instead that creation has enough diversity, where the weak and the strong coexist and cooperate.[331] The other way that Chenchiah differed from Darwinian evolutionism was by asserting that the evolutionary process was "moving to a predestined end."[332] Chenchiah noted a purpose, a design behind evolution, with the human being at the apex of evolution. In particular, Chenchiah stated that the "march of life towards man can only be explained . . . that he is pre-determined type-form as the goal of evolution."[333] Chenchiah however, agreeing that there was an imperfect process of evolution, asserted that this process was experimental. For Chenchiah, the experimental method would be the basis of his theory of religion, and would be especially supportive of the theological notion that not only man, but a certain type of man, was the revolutionary destiny of creation: "Evolution does not disclose an omniscient mind behind it. It reveals an experiment in intellect which profits by failures. Nature resembles a painter who has a picture in his mind but succeeds in transferring it on the canvas only after several unsatisfactory attempts . . . Nature learnt after experimentation. This attempt and correction, this forward march and deliberate regression, are indications that evolution had not only a purpose but also a goal, the final type."[334]

Chenchiah added another theological dimension to the predestination of religion, namely the fullness of time—a concept that was "vaguely hinted in the major religions but firmly grasped as an aid to interpretation of history by the Jews."[335] Here Chenchiah noted that evolution was not only a destiny, but that there also existed a right time—a "fixed time"—when that destiny could be fulfilled.[336] Obviously for Chenchiah the fixed time was not only the coming of Jesus as the incarnation, but specific to religion, the meeting of the East and the West in India. Chenchiah suggested that Indian theology had a responsibility not only to be authentic to its heritage, but also to do theology with the hope to improve global theology, suggesting that

---

331. Chenchiah, "Who Is Jesus," 353.
332. Ibid.
333. Ibid.
334. Ibid.
335. Ibid.
336. Ibid.

now was the time where such experimentations within Christianity could bear the ultimate results.[337]

The theological differentiation from scientific evolution came with the revolution of Christ.[338] There was a revolution, a break in the process that led to an upward leap in evolution: "Science regards evolution as a mere drawing out of what exists in the earliest terms of the series. It suggests that all that creation has produced ... exist[s] potentially in the atom. Evolution, is the drawing out, is the all-sufficing explanation of the unfolding of creation."[339]

In contrast, Chenchiah offered that, "we have to picture creation as evolution punctuated at critical stages with revolution. The horizontal flow of creation receives new force and elements that descend on it vertically from above and break into it. Life, instinct, reason or soul (to use Pauline language) mark such descents of new creative energies into creation from beyond itself."[340]

That revolution, Chenchiah states, is Jesus, who is the "latest revolution in the creative process."[341] Unlike the scientific matter, or anything that exists, Jesus is "a new creative power, the potentiality of a new creative order."[342]

Differing from Aurobindo's Evolutionary Views of Religion

While many scholars point to the Aurobindo's influence on Chenchiah, there were still some significant differences, particularly in their views of evolution and religion. Aurobindo emphasized that the potential for evolution existed within humanity, and emphasized the *superman*. Importantly, for Aurobindo, the potential for evolution was within man: "supermanhood ... is a call to man to do what no species has yet done ... evolve itself consciously into the next superior type."[343] Chenchiah, in contrast, emphasized the radical event of Christ as that revolution that caused an evolutionary leap; he identified that evolution was not a continuation to something higher but to something new. Furthermore, unlike Aurobindo, who called

---

337. Chenchiah, "Who Is Jesus," 365.
338. Ibid., 378.
339. Chenchiah, "Who Is Jesus," 364.
340. Ibid.
341. Chenchiah, "Who Is Jesus," 377.
342. Ibid.
343. Aurobindo, *The Superman*, 2.

for knowledge as the path to evolution,[344] Chenchiah pointed to the need for a revolution of Christ through the power of the Holy Spirit, from outside creation, to take creation to the next level:

> Revolution occurs in creation and society when perfection threatens annihilation. It is God's way of prolonging the line of life. It is the only way out of frustration. For without revolution, evolution will lead us to stagnation. When perfection is reached God grants a new lease of life by sending out a new creative energy and he does so because evolution has led us to exhaustion and death and revolution is the only gateway of life.[345]

The fundamental difference hinged, unsurprisingly, on Christ. Chenchiah felt there was a "family resemblance" between traditional Christian theology and Aurobindo, both of whom had a view of a crisis in man, and pointed to the need of a new man: "Both systems hold that the new term of the evolution awaiting creative expression is the Son of God—a human being who embodies fullness of divine consciousness in flesh."[346] Aurobindo's view of evolution was thus associated with liberty: "the ultimate goal" of human evolution would be the "liberation out of a state of bondage."[347] Chenchiah emphasized Christ's new creation as the ultimate goal:

> One difference remains. The Christian sees in Christ the new destiny of man realised. Sir [sic] Aurobindo does not, at any rate in his writings. We say the new Man has arrived in evolution; Sri Aurobindo expects him. The interaction of these two schools has this curious and tangible result. To the Christian, Christianity assumes a new shape, gives a new meaning, sets a new task. It tell us what the Indian apprehension of Christ is likely to be and gives us a glimpse of future Indian Christian Theology. Christianity gives to Hinduism the image of the New Man, the fact that holds the power of the new creation.[348]

Astutely, Chenchiah felt this inability to reconcile with Christ was a bias within Hinduism that made it suspicious of *foreign* elements; a tendency facing not just Aurobindo, but also Ram Mohan Roy, Gandhi and Master C.V.V. They were impressed more by Christ's teachings than by Christ: "This method of approach to Jesus is largely due to the fact that an ethnic religion

344. See Aurobindo, *Essays: Ideals and Progress*, 4–5.
345. Chenchiah, "Who Is Jesus?" 378.
346. Chenchiah, "Aurobindo—His message," 437.
347. Aurobindo, *Speeches*, 104–5.
348. Chenchiah, "Aurobindo—His message," 438.

like Hinduism is by its very antecedents unable to receive a foreign personality into its Valhalla of Gods."[349]

Chenchiah, for his part, was fully convinced about the importance of Christ, who was more than the summit or crown of creation.[350] Similarly, it was the Holy Spirit who "has entered the Creation and is an operative factor in Evolution."[351] Furthermore, certainly in view of the tendency to differentiate between human potentialities and radical revolution, Chenchiah strongly asserted that the need for Indian Christian theology was *not* to emphasize the preexistence of Jesus but rather "his entry as a new form and power into the cosmic process."[352] Chenchiah is thus theological, in that he combines Christ and Spirit with religion, while also adapting and rejecting the prevalent Hindu humanist evolutionary thinking of his day.

In Contrast to de Chardin's Universal Omega Point

Many scholars find parallels between Chenchiah and de Chardin. For instance, Whaling believes that Chenchiah and de Chardin share a "structural similarity."[353] Similarly, Boyd points to the "interesting similarity" between Chenchiah and de Chardin, particularly that they both thought in biological terms and were both "influenced by Bergson's creative evolution."[354] In addition, Boyd believed that Chenchiah's thought resonated with de Chardin's Christification and Omega Point, "at which mankind and the cosmos become conformed to the image of Christ."[355]

In contrast to the above, I argue that Chenchiah was quite different from de Chardin both in the use of evolution as well as the Omega Point. While reading de Chardin and Chenchiah together, the stark difference in focus, style and method are apparent. de Chardin was a biologist who developed a theory of evolution in the cosmos, which was then seen to parallel the evolution of man. Chenchiah, as a lawyer, unsurprisingly used evolution in a limited sense without engaging with the scientific theories of evolution. This is evident primarily in his lack of any specific use of Darwinian or related theory of evolution, as well as through a general silence about

---

349. Chenchiah, "Christ of Hinduism," 92.
350. Chenchiah, "Who Is Jesus?" 377.
351. Chenchiah, "The Holy Spirit," 323.
352. Chenchiah, "Indian Christian Theological Task," 111.
353. Whaling, "Indian Christian Theology," 323.
354. Boyd, *Indian Christian Theology*, 156.
355. Ibid.

the principle of evolution in the cosmos, outside the human phenomenon. Chenchiah's use of evolution was simply (though not simplistically) as development and process. Thus, Chenchiah was not a naturalist nor even a neonaturalist, as Wagner believes. Instead he was a theologian with limited scientific expertise and who used science conceptually rather than actually. It is more correct then to say that Chenchiah used evolutionism in his theology of religion.

Another difference between de Chardin and Chenchiah was in the emphasis of discontinuity within evolution. Boyd, for instance, believes that Chenchiah and de Chardin were influenced by Bergson.[356] The Bergson influence in de Chardin is easier to identify, especially with the idea that, through the entire evolutionary process, a "vital impulse" continually developed and generated new forms.[357] However, Boyd does not distinguish Chenchiah from both Bergson and de Chardin enough. Chenchiah had a strong sense of discontinuity in creation. His emphasis on the new creation was not a symbolic expression of continuity, but an actual, historical, biological re-creation. Thus, Chenchiah's evolutionism was not a universal ever improving evolutionary process, but an imposition (revolution) from beyond—from Christ and the Spirit.

In effect, Chenchiah also differed from de Chardin's Omega Point, an idea that suggests that the whole world is destined or fated to achieve a central unity by the natural movement of the evolutionary process. Chenchiah, in contrast, had a strong theological focus that not only highlighted a radical discontinuity, but also emphasized the role of human participation in accessing new creation through Spirit Yoga. Chenchiah certainly urged that there be interreligious cooperation and union, but not outside Christ, certainly not as an automatic consequence and not outside the discipline of Spirit Yoga (that enabled the transformation from old to new creation). Chenchiah's new creation was thus not a universalism that de Chardin's Omega Point could suggest. Instead, it was a much more local and focused event that confronted people, whether they were Gandhi, Aurobindo or C.V.V., within and outside Christianity, to reckon directly with Christ and the Spirit.

Beyond Farquhar's Fulfillment Theology

As we have seen, evolution was a strong theme in Chenchiah's theory of religion. Thus, it would not be surprising if Chenchiah went along with

356. Boyd, *Indian Christian Theology*, 157.
357. Samson and Pitt, *The Biosphere and Noosphere Reader*, 57.

theologians like Farquhar who suggested that Christianity was the fulfillment of all the major religions. However, while Chenchiah sympathized with the concerns of fulfillment theology, he did not fully agree with them. Fulfillment theology implied both the superiority of Christianity,[358] and a belief in an "underlying unity in all religions."[359]

Chenchiah resisted notions of Christian superiority by pointing to the self-sufficiency of religions. Of religions like Hinduism and Buddhism he noted,

> ... [they] have fully developed and clearly formulated problems of religion, philosophies and theologies of life and a well planned out method of attaining the goal. Intellectually they are not inferior to Christianity and in some respects superior. They have their moral discipline no less earnest than in Christianity. They answer in their own manner all the questions which Christianity asks and answers. All the dogmas of Christianity—Sin, Salvation, Redemption, Incarnation—have their parallels in them. Each of them has an immense following greater in number in India than Christianity. These religions satisfy their followers as Christianity does its adherents. These followers live under the shadow of their inspirations and die in the consolations of a better world. Institutionally they have their temples and mosques, sacraments and priests, scriptures. Islam and Buddhism are missionary—Hinduism is contagious... The challenges of these faiths have begun.[360]

Chenchiah thus argued that a religion was a "circle complete and perfect in itself," capable of providing its own satisfaction within its own paradigm."[361]

Yet not perfection but new life was the ultimate goal for Chenchiah; new life prevented the stagnation that perfection implied. While Chenchiah accepted that Christianity was equal to the other religions, there was a need for religions to evolve. This Chenchiah asserted by making a distinction between Christ and religion: "The religion of Christ is not the same as Christ."[362] Jesus stood as a contradiction to perfect religion; he could "kindle

---

358. Farquhar, *The Crown of Hinduism*, 31.
359. Ibid., 26.
360. Chenchiah, "Christian Message in a Hindu Environment," 100.
361. Chenchiah, "Appendix," 41.
362. Chenchiah, "Jesus and the Non-Christian Faiths," 52. See also, "Jesus stands in definite relation to the residual problems of other religions rather than with the satisfied longings of man." Chenchiah, "Appendix," 42.

new hopes not felt before" in the religious man, or even "kill some of the deepest longings" felt by the religious man.[363] Thus, about Jesus, Chenchiah asserted,

> Jesus never regarded himself as the perfect man. That place he gave to John the Baptist. He affirmed that there is infinite qualitative difference between John and himself. This was so because His was a new order overtopping the old. Redemption was not redemption in the world but from the world. Jesus held that the righteous and the sinner alike require salvation . . .[364]

This radical discontinuity meant that Jesus was the revolution that moved a "perfect" religion towards an entirely new life.[365] Chenchiah would also stress that it was not just the religions, but all creation that was moving towards new life in Christ.[366]

Chenchiah was aware of the retrospective construction of his evolutionary logic. He was aware that where a Christian may see "linear progression, like steps in a staircase, where every development is a stage towards Christ," for a Hindu, in contrast, "each way is a complete alternative not necessarily dependent on the other."[367] Yet, as we saw earlier, Chenchiah urged that, for Christians, this was the way to go.

Christ and Religion: Judgment and Truth

Earlier we saw Chenchiah's implicit dual theory of religion, his second and preferred theory being true religion, which was also a theological category. Evident in this were two theological approaches towards religion—the negative judgment of religion, and the positive affirmation of religion. Chenchiah's ideas were related to and different from Barth's theology of religion.

Negative Religion (The Judgment of Religion)

A negative view of religion, as we have seen, was common in theological discussions of religion, particularly surrounding discussions at the Missionary

---

363. Chenchiah, "Appendix," 42.
364. Chenchiah, "Who Is Jesus," 389.
365. Ibid., 378.
366. Chenchiah, "Christian Youth, Non-Christian Faiths," 453.
367. Chenchiah, "Christ of Hinduism," 91.

Conference at Tambaram. Chenchiah for his part offers a twofold judgment of religion.

The first critique of religion was the rejection of traditional religion and it drew from his dual theory of religion, where the popular temple and ascetic religions are contrasted with true religion. Without reiterating too much the ground we have already covered, Chenchiah showed how religion naturally degenerated into a self-propagating and self-perpetuating institution. Chenchiah was also especially critical about the claim that religion emphasized the "infinite potentialities of man."[368] Barth too had identified religion with human capacity, where religion was human effort while revelation, in contrast, was God's initiative.[369] Barth described religion as a frontier that separated "flesh from spirit . . . human possibility from the possibility of God."[370] Chenchiah seemed to agree with Barth's negative judgment of religion: "the signal contribution of Karl Barth to the theological thinking of the day is the merciless cutting of the globe of religion into the original core and the accumulated tradition called by him religion."[371] However, Chenchiah certainly did not accept the full force of Barth's critique, that included equating religion with idolatry and sin.[372]

Interestingly, while Chenchiah used the language of "true religion," he avoided the language of "false religion." What he did do was dichotomize between true religion and traditional religion. Chenchiah's critique of religion was actually a critique of temple and ascetic religion. In one place, Chenchiah called religion "the religion of the aged," which expressed itself in "cautious circumspection" that suggested "waning energies" and promoted "a safe religion—built of the solid foundation of dogma and doctrine."[373] In contrast of course, Chenchiah promoted the religion of adventure, of life in Christ and the Spirit.

Chenchiah's negative critique of this type of religion stemmed from the difference between religion and Christ: "The religion of Christ is not the same as Christ. To belong to the religion of Christ is not necessarily to come into contact with Jesus and to be dominated by Him."[374] Chenchiah also differentiated religion from Christianity, famously stating that "Christianity

---

368. Chenchiah, "Jesus and the Non-Christian Faiths," 54.
369. Barth, *Romans*, 229–30.
370. Ibid., 236.
371. Chenchiah, "Jesus and the Non-Christian Faiths," 52.
372. Barth, *Romans*, 43, 50–51.
373. Chenchiah, "Christian Youth, Non-Christian Faiths," 468.
374. Chenchiah, "Jesus and the Non-Christian Faiths," 52.

[was] not a religion."³⁷⁵ However, rather than being a contradiction (because Chenchiah did also refer to Christianity as a religion), this type of reasoning was an example of Chenchiah's dual theory of religion. Chenchiah was not saying that 'Christianity is not a religion,' but that Christianity was not meant to be a religion of human effort. Traditional religion was shown to be the effort of man (using his infinite potential) to become perfect. The goal of Christianity, as a true religion, was to share the goal of Christ, which was new life. Unlike Barth, whose focus on Christianity as true religion was based on its elected purpose to bear the word of God,³⁷⁶ Chenchiah's concept of true religion was a shared function that even other religions could share. This true function of religion could only be seen and achieved through Christ and his Spirit. Chenchiah thus used his theological framework to critique traditional religion, and related what he perceived as the function of Christ, as the defining factor of true religion.

Chenchiah's second critique of religion was to show how religion was sufficient and yet also limited. At one level, Chenchiah clearly stated that religion was able to fulfill its own longings and that it was a perfect/complete system:

> Non-Christian religions not only register longings and aspirations but also satisfactions. The facile presumption that in Hinduism we have searched for salvation without satisfaction and that Christianity satisfies the longing is untrue to fact. The same persons who reveal the longing testify to the satisfaction. Unless we disbelieve their testimony, we cannot reject their experience.³⁷⁷

Yet on another level Chenchiah said that, in religion, there was also a residue of unfulfilled longing, or even a new unfelt longing, that only Christ could fulfill. For instance, Chenchiah stated that, in Hinduism, there was an "unrealized longing" for a life that transcended karma³⁷⁸ and also that, in contrast to the satisfactions of the religions, "Jesus kindles new hopes not felt before and kills some of the deepest and persistent longings of man."³⁷⁹ Of all religion, Chenchiah would go on to say,

> In all religions there is a residue of unfulfilled desire, partly arising out of the very satisfaction religion achieves and partly out of the failure of religion to satisfy the aspirations of man so far.

375. Ibid., 54.
376. See Barth, *Church Dogmatics*, I/2, 326.
377. Chenchiah, "Appendix," 42.
378. Chenchiah, "Appendix," 53.
379. Ibid., 42.

> Jesus stands in definite relation to the residual problems of other religions rather than with the satisfied longings of man. In other words, the relationship of Christ to the non-Christian heart and hope lies in the unexplored regions of our Lord's life and not in the region already mapped out.[380]

In this negative critique lay the positive hope that Jesus could indeed fill these longings. Nevertheless, the negative critique existed especially from a theological point of view—that to get the life of Christ, the only way was through Christ and his Spirit.

To this limitation of religion, Chenchiah added the idea of discontinuity between Christ and the religions, a point made all the more important in view of the prevalent fulfillment theologies: "Neither Judaism nor Hinduism lead to Christ. Christ abrogates Judaism and Hinduism much more than he fulfills them. Indian Christian theology builds bridges from Jesus to Judaism and Hinduism and not bridges from Judaism and Hinduism to Jesus."[381]

In this sense, the traditional religions were the "final fruits of the old creation," while Jesus was the "first fruits of a new creation."[382]

Positive Religion

Even as Chenchiah had a dual theory of religion, it is not surprising that his negative judgment of religion was accompanied by a positive view of religion. This positive view of religion did not arise out of a balance or synthesis of two types of religion—true religion stood in opposition to the newer and false religions.[383] However, if Chenchiah's theology of religion arose out of a synthesis, it was a synthesis that drew from the incarnation, Jesus. In effect, not only did (true) religion help people come close to Christ, true religion was also *like* Christ.

For Chenchiah, the basis of positive religion was linked to Christ. Chenchiah thus talks about how "the distinctive features of Christ ... advance[d] the religious movement as a whole."[384] As Jesus Christ himself opened the doors and created a new world order where there was no longer the distinction between the temporal and spiritual worlds, true religion became the meeting point between the eternal and the temporal order:

---

380. Ibid.
381. Chenchiah, "The Indian Christian Theological Task," 112.
382. Chenchiah, "Appendix," 43.
383. Chenchiah, "Kingdom of God in India," 261.
384. Chenchiah, "Christ on Hinduism," 91.

> We have to open the doors between the temporal and the spiritual worlds. We must find Christ. Jesus, according to Christian tradition, is not now a spirit. He has a resurrection body and it is with a body that he has gone to heaven and therefore actual contact with him must be far more easy than with God who is a spirit. And the very purpose of incarnation is to make it easy for the transition from one world to the other . . . He is in the world, but we have turned [him] into a doctrine: instead of opening our hearts to him, we are merely worshipping and praising Him. The first task therefore is to make religion really the meeting point of the eternal and the temporal order of things.[385]

We had earlier seen how the Asramas were the model for true religion. This was because the forest dwellers did not choose either the polarities of ritualism (domesticating the gods) or asceticism (running away from the world). The direction of true religion lay in the practical religion of unity, brotherhood and common effort, towards spiritual union with God. The Asramas represented a religion of true detachment and also encouraged transformed living in context.

Chenchiah would thus state that, in the religion of Jesus one did not tear oneself away from the world but one was placed in between God and the world:

> The religion of Jesus emphasizes the value and necessity of detachment . . . Incarnation in the true sense represents the creative mean between man and God. It creates a balance between natural life and the new life that detaches us from the old. If incarnation means a temporary descent of God into life, the new life does not create. If it involves absolute identity with life, then incarnation does not mark any progress. Incarnation is the creative expression of a life which though it enters into this life yet acts with puissant power from its own centre. Jesus is neither God nor man. He is the Son of God and the Son of Man—the son representing alike the identity and the difference. The son is the detached reproduction of the Father. Incarnation signifies the emergence of a new man, partaking of divinity yet possessing humanity, detached and attached to both God and man. The reproduction of incarnation lifts the Christian above the world yet operating on it. In Christ, the Christian is between God and Man, desire and action, attachment and renunciation.[386]

---

385. Chenchiah, "Kingdom of God in India," 261.
386. Chenchiah, "Vanaprastha Asrama: Assessment," 135–36.

The religion of Jesus was thus to live in right balance between God and man.[387] Furthermore, religion was about living a new life in this world, with God:

> Religion has to be lived, life has to be carved into the figure of the ideal . . . Religion like science, has to live on observation and experimentation. It was the primary feature of an asrama life that religion was thought of as ideas, ideals to be embodied in flesh and blood.[388]

Chenchiah thus talked about "Jesus' outlook on religion" as the "the actual achievement of the Kingdom of God" or even "the conception of religion as the creation of a world of power and relations, not merely as a scheme of conduct."[389] This suggested that Chenchiah's view of religion was not simply drawing from the principles of Christ, or even improving religion through Christ, but rather a more dramatic transformation that related the work of Christ with the work of religion.[390]

Chenchiah noted the importance of Emmanuel, "God with us," where Christ truly became a "significant cosmic event" that affects all things.[391] Jesus as the new creation, the new man, was now reflected onto religion as a new creation. It was not enough for Chenchiah to view Jesus as a God-man union. Chenchiah was equally concerned about humanity rising to Jesus and achieving, through the Spirit, the same new creation. Jesus as new creation permeated through true religion. It was the logic of the incarnation that enabled religion to take on new meaning. Religion was thus the actuality of the Kingdom of God. Without the creative energy of Christ through the Holy Spirit, all religion, like the temple religion and ascetic religion (including examples found in Hinduism and Christianity), was limited to the old world of institutions, rituals and beliefs. However, true religion was neither about beliefs in the new creation nor beliefs about Jesus, but the space in which individuals could become new like Christ.

---

387. Ibid.

388. Chenchiah, "Characteristics of Vanaprastha Asrama," 119.

389. Chenchiah, "Essentials of Christianity," 405.

390. Chenchiah stated three methodologies, and preferred the third: "First that Christ becomes universal by drawing out the likeness of himself in other religions; second by other religions developing in their own religions features of Christianity or third, by Christ reproducing himself in the children of God. The Hindu suggests the second answer and I hold the third." Chenchiah, "Professor Kraemer and Syncretism," 200.

391. Chenchiah, "Retrospect and Prospect," 308.

CHENCHIAH'S THEOLOGY OF RELIGIONS

Coming to the close of this chapter, we are now ready to make some remarks about Chenchiah's theology of religions, the effort to see how religions relate (or ought to relate) to each other.

Chenchiah stated that the future of Indian Christianity lay in the interrelations of religions: "To us in India the interrelations of religions have become a matter of life and death. We can have no peace here or hereafter and our nation can have no future till we find the key to the mystery."[392] According to Devasahayam, Chenchiah unceasingly sought to relate with his neighbors from other religious traditions.[393] His interactions included centers for dialogues, multireligious prayer groups that advocated "common worship," and he actively participated in yoga at home.[394] Chenchiah's interreligious activities however made him controversial. He confessed that threats of the withdrawal of financial support for *The Pilgrim* ultimately led to his resignation as editor.[395] In particular, Chenchiah stated that the offence was caused by his advocacy of the "fellowship of religions," expressed through common prayer and philanthropic work along with Hindus and Muslims for drought victims.[396]

Chenchiah based his logic of interreligious activity on his theology of religion. He argued that the major religions in India were bound together by their "interrelation in the evolution of human history," and their common function, to cooperate together for "the welfare of the world" and the "regeneration of India."[397] Chenchiah moved away from the traditional model of interreligious cooperation that focused either on ethnic or creedal similarities, a move that invariably led to isolation or conflict.[398] Instead, a newfound unity—a "spirit of brotherhood and enquiry," particularly in the nationalist context—was discovered with "new visions and hopes of cooperation and fellowship."[399] The unity also made people aware of the sharp differences, which Chenchiah did not gloss over. He noted the

---

392. Chenchiah, "Appendix," 2.

393. Devasahayam, "Role of the Bible," 18.

394. Ibid.

395. Chenchiah, "Editorial Notes: I have resigned," 2.

396. Chenchiah, "Editorial Notes," *The Pilgrim* 11 (2 June 1952), 1–2. The original article can be found in Chenchiah, "Editorial," *The Pilgrim* 9 (2 June 1950) 1–11, under the sub-section "God, Science and Rain."

397. Chenchiah, "Editorial Notes," 1.

398. Ibid., 2.

399. Ibid.

transmissible value of differences since they could be "absorbed by one religion from another."[400] In line with the reformist and revivalist thinking of his age, Chenchiah recommended,

> The cry for reform and regeneration, for healing and consoling, for enlightenment, has been so great that pooling of resources has been purposive. It leads them to go out together in common redemptive effort . . .
>
> 1. To stress the importance of the study of comparative religion—for the formation of universal faith.
> 2. To point out in what common practical efforts religions have tried to draw together and co-operate.[401]

Thus, Chenchiah pointed to several substantive similarities between adherents of the "new" religion (as opposed to traditional religion), which provided the above-listed avenues—for instance, the longing for "mutual understanding," common joy through festivals, and even the fact that every religion people have the "instinct and desire for prayer."[402] However, being largely functional in his definition of religion, Chenchiah's theology of religions was conceived in participatory terms. Hence, Chenchiah proposed common Prayer Halls, common celebration of festivals, even a common congregational worship service.[403] Importantly, the goal was to "mobilize dormant religious forces in the country for national reconstruction."[404] One such proposal was that "all religious . . . rally together and courageously stand by the truth and endeavor to form the national backbone by laying down in precept and practice the National Dharma."[405]

That said, an important point about Chenchiah's theology of religion was that while he advocated interreligious activity, it was never an objective space outside his own faith. He was distinctly Christian, even when trying to create a common platform for interaction. In his article against communalism in the Indian context, Chenchiah revealed that religious cooperation in India has a future. He argued that Hindus, Muslims and Christians can achieve a "union" because Hindus are ready to let go of their idolatry and mythologies without any detriment to their religion.[406] Clearly using the

400. Chenchiah, "Editorial Notes," 2.
401. Ibid.
402. Ibid., 2–3.
403. Ibid., 2–8.
404. Ibid., 9
405. Ibid., 3.
406. Chenchiah, "The Indian Situation," 197.

detraditionalized theory of religion, and appealing to the reform movements within Hinduism, Chenchiah promoted a "monotheistic, non-idolatrous, non-mythological religion as our national faith for all public functions—whatever might be our individual faith."[407]

Chenchiah also emphasized that other religions could help Christians understand Christ's new creation better. The focus was not on a general interreligious dialogue, but on understanding Christ and new life: "The Christian in India . . . still feels he can never understand Jesus till he understands the drama of God's dealing with man in and through the other religions of the world."[408]

Chenchiah clearly did not subscribe to the view that all religions were the same. In one instance, Chenchiah stated that "any religion" will have a "form and feature" that differentiated it from others: for Christianity, this difference was Christ.[409] Chenchiah rejected what he called "spineless and nerveless syncretism" and, instead, maintained a pragmatic concern for "definite action" to face the "realities of life."[410] In that respect, Chenchiah offered a positive relationship between religions: "Our theory of relation of religions should be that God has been revealing and incorporating something new through each religion. This new should be absorbed by all—should be made common property of all. Instead of pretending that each has, what the other has, it is wisdom to pool together the various revelations—to focus various rays into a central flame warming us all. This means co-operation in religions, the hardest lesson we have to learn."[411]

More specifically, Chenchiah found that once both Hindus and Christians left behind their temple religions, there was much they could share with each other: "Hinduism is imprinting on Christianity forms of thought which are its distinctive contribution to spiritual vision, and here Christianity is drawing out of Hinduism the forms of the new creation, of which Jesus is the proto-type . . . the supreme reasons why we should study and study diligently these two movements lies just here that they are influencing and are being influenced by each other towards a common direction."[412]

In addition, there was also a missional aspect to Chenchiah's theology, which was expressed in preaching the Christ of the Spirit: Christians

---

407. Ibid.
408. Chenchiah, "Appendix," 2.
409. Chenchiah, "Indian Christian Theological Task," 44.
410. Chenchiah, "Reviews: Professor Radhakrishnan," 20.
411. Chenchiah, "Problems of Conversion in New India," 12.
412. Chenchiah, "Sri Aurobindo—His Message," 424.

should present the Gospel as "life and power, and not as an institution."[413] Chenchiah urged that Christian missions must "emphasize the formation and growth of the Lord in the human heart," with full reliance on the Holy Spirit, who "alone can lead" a person to Jesus.[414]

There was also an emphasis on contextual preaching to Hindus in view of the complexity of interreligious understanding. He opined that modern Christian preaching had been "largely ineffective" since it neglected the psychology of the Hindu.[415] He noted, "We preach to the Hindu, Muslim, South Sea Islander, the same stereotyped theological religion without taking into account their respective psychologies and mental backgrounds. Much of Christian preaching does not enter the Hindu mind either because it is alien to its ways of thought or because it fails to evoke memory of association on which the mean and appeal of words and ideas depend. The Hindu does not reject Christianity. Often he simply does not understand it."[416]

Furthermore, showing the misunderstanding that arises from confused terminology, Chenchiah explained:

> Words which mean much to a Christian signify very little to [the Hindu]. For ages he was taught that life is a burden and salvation redeems him from rebirth. A Saviour who gives re–birth does not appeal to the Hindu as a desirable saviour for he and his forbears sought to be saved from the cycle of lives and death. The same word 'salvation' may be used but it conveys different meanings . . . Their outlook on life differs. Salvation of the Jew looks to the Hindu like a bondage—like riveting the chains he tried to break.[417]

To supplement this, Chenchiah urged that Christians should attempt to "construct a picture of the Hindu mind" so that they could reckon with the Hindu's "religious psychology."[418]

Relatedly, Chenchiah emphasized evangelism by example. Chenchiah was critical of evangelism that emphasized doctrinal communication or even number games. Instead he urged Christians to focus more upon becoming like Jesus through the Spirit and learn how to pass the Holy Spirit onto the others, so that people of other religions could also be transformed like Jesus: "To evangelize is to cast people into the mould of Christ—to make

---

413. Chenchiah, "Christianity and Hinduism," 137.
414. Ibid.
415. Chenchiah, "The Psychology of the Hindu Mind," 11.
416. Ibid.
417. Chenchiah, "The Psychology of the Hindu Mind," 12.
418. Ibid., 13.

people adopt his pattern and life."[419] Chenchiah preferred that Christians participate in the lives of non-Christians through friendship, to influence by example: "live with non-Christian[s] ... in utter friendship and fellowship and so transmit Christ to others by contagion ... [J]oin them in common adventure as to make them catch the Christ in you ... [You] should live a joyous, infectious Christian life. Then Evangelism will take care of itself."[420]

Yet Chenchiah was aware that Christians were not always the best examples of the transformation they preach: "The greatest obstacle to the spread of Christianity in India does not come from ... the Hindu ... The real obstacle comes from failure to make good the claims we make for Jesus and his religion. We claim that Jesus saves us from sins and sin has no longer power over us. The Hindu does not feel we are sinless and nor do we. We may try to save the position by saying that Christ forgives our sins, though He does redeem us from sin completely. This looks more like a subterfuge than an honest argument."[421]

Keeping in mind that the Hindu faced the same limitations as a traditional Christian, Chenchiah's theology of religions stressed upon mutual cooperation towards Christ. He urged that should Christians engage with Hindu friends with humility, as co-workers and as equals, in their search to understand Christ:

> This common misfortune [of mutual sin] makes us bedfellows but cannot give us the right to adopt a superior tone. It must be confessed frankly and honestly that the Christian in practical life does not make good the claim he makes about Jesus on the basis of which he invites the Hindu to become a Christian. This situation demands three radical changes in the preacher's attitude. He cannot afford to stand against the Hindu and preach at him and to him. He can only stand beside him and point out Christ in the humility of men who have not realized Him. The message should be—Jesus I feel has the key of life, the power to unify us with God. Let us search for it, for we both have not yet realized him. We need each other's help to translate him into life terms.[422]

Chenchiah thus pointed to the need for a "common effort" by the Hindu, the Muslim and the Christian towards Christ: "We should not ask the Hindu 'lend me your ears' but 'take my eyes' and 'give me yours' that

---

419. Chenchiah, "Christian Youth, Non-Christian Faiths," 453.
420. Chenchiah, "Christian Youth, Non-Christian Faiths," 470.
421. Chenchiah, "Christian Message in a Hindu Environment," 100.
422. Ibid.

we both together may see him [Jesus Christ] aright."[423] This kind of pluralism would certainly be offensive in today's world because it assumes the centrality of Christ, which adherents of other religions would not agree to. Similarly, one must be careful not to equate Chenchiah with the later pluralisms that followed in India, which asserted that there were many ways to understand God, and Jesus Christ was only one of them. Chenchiah had no doubt that it was Christ who was central for all people, regardless of their religious background. This quotation rightly summarizes the Christian optimism with which Chenchiah envisioned his theology of religions:

> Since the change cannot come from custom-bound, creed-shackled, tradition-ridden churches and temples, the challenge has to be picked up by laymen, with whom the future of religion lies. In aligning with other religions in this task, the Indian Christian disobeys no command of Christ, but awakens, for the first time, to the urgency of realising the dream of Christ for mankind—the children of God and the Kingdom of heaven! All religions may sing together—"Thy Kingdom come and Thy will be done on earth as it is in heaven" and feel that God has set for them, through Christ, a common task.[424]

SUMMARY OF THE CHAPTER

A few points can now be made by way of summary. Chenchiah's theology of religion can be seen as a dual theory of religion. The first type of religion was the traditional view of religion, viewed objectively. Here religion was *what it is,* as it was commonly understood, with the typical associations of institutions, doctrines, priests and rituals. Even the reform movements against institutionalization, such as the religion of suffering and *bhakti*, tended to be typically religions. Both expressions of typical religion either domesticated God (temple) or led to escapism (ascetic).

The other type of religion Chenchiah identified was *religion as it ought to be,* a theological religion that was seen through his concept of "true religion." True religion was an adventure towards a unity with God. Hence, it was an activity and not a belief. From a Christian theological standpoint, it was best understood as the quest for new life in Christ through the power of the Holy Spirit. Jesus Christ, for Chenchiah, was the prototype of new creation and also of true religion.

423. Ibid.
424. Chenchiah, "Religions and the World," 220.

What we eventually see is that Chenchiah prioritized Christian theology so that his assessment was based on Christian presuppositions, particularly the concept of incarnation. Traditional religion was judged, not simply because it fell away from its ideals, but because it could not, by its own effort, attain the ideal God–human unity, that could come through Jesus and the Spirit. Similarly, his theological priority influenced even his use of evolution and his engagement with other religions.

With this in view, we are ready to move now to a critical appreciation of Chenchiah, particularly to assess how much of what he said about religion is valid for a contemporary theological understanding of religion.

4

Evaluation of Chenchiah's Theology of Religion

INTRODUCTION

Having looked at Chenchiah's theology of religion, we are now ready to evaluate it. In particular, we analyze Chenchiah from the perspective of the dominant Chenchiah scholars whom I mentioned in the Introduction. As it turns out, most of the critiques of Chenchiah's concept of religion emerge from a faulty view of his theology of religion. However, while there is much to affirm in Chenchiah's theology of religion, certain weaknesses are also evident—particularly in his theology—emphasizing that Chenchiah need only be an entry point for a theology of religion and not the end. In the next two chapters, I will construct my own theology of religion—my proposal for the question "what is religion"—using aspects of Chenchiah's theology of religion alongside contemporary theories of religion, biblical bases and theological traditions.

DEFENDING CHENCHIAH FROM HIS CRITICS

Much of the critique of Chenchiah's view of religion is based on a misunderstanding of his theory/theology of religion. Varughese, for instance, says that Chenchiah believed that Christ was the ultimate goal of all religion.[1] Yet

---

1. Varughese, "Christology in the Writings," 219.

Chenchiah said something quite different by emphasizing that religions had their own longings and satisfactions and had no continuity with what Christ had to offer, since Christ through the Spirit brought new longings never felt earlier by religion.

The Gurukul Group finds fault with Chenchiah's rejection of the authority of scripture and the Church.[2] They are critical of Chenchiah's theology—which they think is a syncretic philosophy—and argue that Chenchiah was offering a theology of "interfusion,"[3] to the extent that "Christianity as preached by the Church has nothing unique in comparison with Hinduism or other non-Christian religions."[4] In terms of religion, they specifically take exception with Chenchiah for wanting to "build bridges between the ancestral religion and Christianity" or more specifically, for wanting to fuse Hinduism and Christianity and "thereby to create a new religion."[5] However, this critique arises out of a misunderstanding of Chenchiah and his theology of religion. Chenchiah neither believed that all religions were the same, nor did he intend to create a new religion out of a Hindu-Christian union. His use of Hinduism was more a methodological approach to engage with Christ, much like the use of philosophy to understand the Bible. The Gurukul Group fail to appreciate that Chenchiah insisted that Jesus, through the power of the Spirit, offered something unique to all religions, past and future. It was the radically new event of incarnation that allowed Chenchiah to differ from Vivekananda, Aurobindo, C.V.V. and Gandhi, none of whom, Chenchiah noted, took Jesus as seriously as they could have done. Thus Chenchiah's formulation of "true religion" was not the construction of a new religion out of an *interfusion* with Hinduism. Rather, it was an appreciation of religion being active in certain strands of Hinduism, particularly in the experiments of Aurobindo and C.V.V. In contradiction to what the Gurukul Group believes about Chenchiah, this was not a re-creation of, but a reconnection with, the past, without compromising the norms of Jesus and the Spirit. The recognition was of a religion that existed of old, though often hidden to those who adhered to the institutional forms of religion or even to the ascetic practices of religion. The goal of "true religion" was the union with God, and was made possible, according to Chenchiah, only through the coming of Jesus and the Holy Spirit, the revolution in our evolution.

---

2. Gurukul Theological Research Group, *A Christian Theological Approach to Hinduism*, 61.

3. Ibid., 54.

4. Ibid., 60.

5. Ibid., 49.

O. V. Jathanna is another scholar whose exceptional study of Chenchiah is marred in part by a misunderstanding of Chenchiah's concept of religion. Jathanna is convinced that Chenchiah had a largely negative view of religion to the extent that a dichotomy existed between Chenchiah's trump concept "Kingdom of God" and religion.[6] Jathanna also opines that Chenchiah's theology of religion was excessively humanistic, especially in focussing on humanity as well as in the human effort to realise its end.[7]

Jathanna is correct when he says that Chenchiah particularly emphasizes human effort. However, Jathanna wrongly views Chenchiah's theology of religion as negative. In one instance, Jathanna asserts that Chenchiah projected a "pure religion" in contrast to "temple religion."[8] Interestingly, the concept of "pure religion" is absent from the article which Jathanna cites and Jathanna misses the point that Chenchiah was critical of both pure religion (of the ascetics) and temple religion (institutions). Further, Jathanna fails to reckon with Chenchiah's concept of true religion, which depicts religion positively as the religion of the adventure to become a new creation, or even how the religion of the incarnation actually provides a way to achieve new creation.

Similarly, Jathanna's classification of Chenchiah's humanism is not entirely correct since Chenchiah offered both a negative and positive view of human effort towards upliftment— negative human action was the institutionalization of religion, while positive human action was the adventurous seeking of religion. In both cases, the upliftment of humanity (creation) was sought, yet the upliftment was not a universal lifting up of humanity but a struggle for new creation in the manner of Christ.[9]

Jathanna misreads the issue of religion at another point. He is critical of Wagner, saying that Wagner wrongly interpreted Chenchiah's concept of religion as "timeless metaphysical truth" and that "Chenchiah subsumes Christianity under the concept of religion."[10] Jathanna does not offer an adequate alternative understanding of Chenchiah at this point, and simply says that Chenchiah had much more "dynamic thinking."[11] Ironically, the text which Jathanna is referring to is the same one Wagner uses to show that Chenchiah was doing something entirely different—by differentiating

---

6. Jathanna, *The Decisiveness of the Christ–Event*, 375.

7. Ibid., 374.

8. Ibid., 372.

9. I do agree with Jathanna's critique that there is an overemphasis of human effort in Chenchiah's soteriology, a point to be discussed later in this section.

10. Jathanna, *The Decisiveness of the Christ–Event*, 376, n.1.

11. Ibid.

Christianity from the religions of invocation and propitiation.[12] Jathanna for his part simply accepts Chenchiah's invocation/propitiation taxonomy without emphasizing, as Wagner rightly does, that Chenchiah bypassed the taxonomy by arguing that Christianity was a religion of incarnation that met the needs of both types of religion.

However, Wagner too misses the point of Chenchiah's view of religion when he contends that Chenchiah expressed Western neonaturalist thinking along the lines of Aurobindo.[13] It is not valid to put a neonaturalist label on Chenchiah, especially along the lines of Aurobindo, because Chenchiah did more than bring an awareness of a religious perspective into the evolutionary process. As we have consistently seen in Chenchiah, it was specifically the power of God, as displayed in Christ and the Spirit, which not only provided a religious framework to the evolutionary system, but also directed it. Chenchiah never applied an evolutionary system to Christ but saw Christ (and the Spirit) as above the evolutionary process and also as the key force fuelling it.

All this is to suggest that Chenchiah's theory of religion, understood in its own terms, provides a corrective to many general critiques of his work. However, we now turn to specific aspects of his theology of religion.

CHENCHIAH'S THEOLOGY OF RELIGION

Earlier I used the terminology "theory of religion" to denote those aspects of Chenchiah which attempted to define religion outside the bounds of theology. However, evidently Chenchiah's theory of religion and theology of religion were so intertwined that it is impossible to separate one from the other. Thus, my intention here is to highlight and interact with an integrated view of Chenchiah's theology of religion, which includes both his theory and theology. Later, I will highlight his theology of religions, showing how his theology of religion affects his interaction with religions.

Theology of Religion as Dual Theory of Religion

Wagner is the only Chenchiah scholar to draw attention to Chenchiah's multiple use of the concept of religion. Wagner notes that Chenchiah proposed a view of religion in a historical sense rather than in a dogmatic/doctrinal sense. Christianity was not a dogmatic belief but a process in

12. Wagner, *Erstgestalten einer einheimischen Theologie*, 114–15.
13. Ibid., 196.

history.[14] Wagner notes that Chenchiah also attributed a metaphysical meaning to religion when he identified the Christian religion as the solution to the problem of all religion, namely the problem of the two worlds of God and humanity.[15] Christianity, here, was not simply a historical movement, but a metaphysical solution of new creation.[16] Christianity in Chenchiah was shown to be concerned not simply with the deification of man or the humanization of God, but with both simultaneously. Jesus was shown to be that new man who represented not only the coming down of God but also the raising up of humanity through his Spirit. Thus, Wagner notes, "From its eschatological starting point, Chenchiah refuses the term religion for Christianity. Yet he applies the term religion from his metaphysical starting point as an overall term in the sense of a problem which a religion works out . . . Without doubt, Chenchiah puts the Christian religion at the top of all religions because the Christian religion in its Christology is able to solve the religious metaphysical problem at its best."[17]

Wagner even identifies a third diversification of the meaning of religion, where religion is identified as an activity with regard to the spiritual world: religion is meditation, realization, yoga, experience of the eternal and spiritual.[18] Wagner adds that at this point Chenchiah is open even to mystical thoughts and experiences as part of religious discipline, which he had earlier rejected.[19] Wagner notes that a contradiction exists in Chenchiah's theory, where the historical aspect of religion (expressed in eschatological and evolutionistic terms) is mixed with a separate category of metaphysics. In effect, the metaphysical understanding of religion, which is understood as a "timeless eternal truth . . . always needs to be done again and again."[20]

Chenchiah's dual theory is not a contradiction. As we have seen earlier, Chenchiah operated with two theories of religion, one that viewed religion in a normal traditional sense and the other in a theological sense. Religions traditionally had founders, institutions and histories. However, Chenchiah's judgment against this type of religion was that, within the evolutionary framework, the religions degenerated and did not naturally (by their own merit) evolve upwards. This kind of religion (and traditional Christianity fell within this schemata as well) was prone to the specific degeneration

---

14. Wagner, *Erstgestalten einer einheimischen Theologie*, 115.
15. Ibid.
16. Ibid.
17. Ibid.
18. Ibid., 116.
19. Ibid.
20. Ibid., 115.

of the temple or ascetic types of religion. Chenchiah thus stated that the Church had made Christianity into a new religion, instead of what it was originally meant to be, a new creation.

The other part of Chenchiah's theory of religion was to bring in theological categories. This kind of religion, referred to as "true religion," was entirely different in that it promoted a new creation, where metaphysics and eschatology combined. For Chenchiah, true religion aimed at union between God and man, and only in Christ and through the Spirit could this union be achieved. The new creation occurred within the evolutionary (historical) scheme, yet Jesus was shown to be the revolution that prevented the descent of religion (into temple or ascetic religion) and led to an entirely new ascent. This religion was also a call to transformation and a new life. It was neo-essentialist. This type of religion was not a static metaphysical event, which Wagner seems to suggest, but a religious activity that worked, in the context of time and in community (*asrama*), towards the new creation. Jesus was a historical example of that metaphysical reality did not change the fact that Christians did not reflect this union and needed to aspire towards it. Thus, when Chenchiah stated that Christianity was not a religion, he was choosing to move away from the first (traditional) theory of religion, one that commonly existed, towards a second (theological) view of religion as a Spirit-empowered transformation.

In view of contemporary theory, it is difficult to establish that two types of religion actually *exist*. Flood, for instance, is especially critical of quasi-theological religion, by which he means the strategy to view a common denominator across religions and substantively define religion outside cultural context.[21] Flood is particularly critical of John Hick, who negates the differences between religions to form his theory of religion: "to claim in a totalizing way that all traditions are paths leading to the same goal is to disclaim their uniqueness."[22]

Chenchiah, as we have seen, did not negate the differences between religions, and saw religion as legitimately existing, not just within its doctrinal affirmation but also within its contextual and experiential context—religions, especially the Indian religions, did satisfy. However, while religions existed as their own systems, religions also had an essential core—the desire for union with God. Here, Chenchiah expressed a substantive-relational theory, where true (often hidden) religion lay in the desire to access God. Thus, in Chenchiah, there was certainly an element of escaping the physical/phenomenological realities of religious discourse within the cultural

21. Flood, *Beyond Phenomenology*, 54–57.
22. Ibid., 56.

context—by appealing to a core and God. In that sense, he would be quasi-theological. However, Chenchiah also put this concept of religion alongside the more traditional concept of religion, where religion existed within culture. This kind of religion need not access its hidden core, and could sufficiently meet the needs of its adherents. As a result, Chenchiah's theology of religion could be theologically universalistic while also accepting religions in their own terms.

In this sense, Chenchiah's dual method, to view religion in two ways, provided the possibility for Christians to negotiate within the corruption of the world and the incorruptible life that Christians were called to. Chenchiah's dual theory of religion also allowed religion to be two things for a Christian: a public phenomenon within the rules of (secular) social sciences, as well as a theological category that applied to all action, even those that fall outside what is traditionally considered religious phenomena. His dual theory was clearly a reconstruction of religion from contemporary options, as well as a departure from existing theories.

As a result, even if we do not accept Chenchiah's theology of religion, his theological view of religion is congruous with the methodological call for Christian redescriptions of religion, and is not an approach to determine a universal essential religion in all cultures. A Christian classification of religion, such as Chenchiah's, allows a theory of religion to govern how Christians speak of (and engage with) the world. It can even be argued that the Christian sense of speaking of the world is to see all cultures from the point of view of their own religion, allowing their concept of religion to be reflected onto other cultures while also making their own associated value judgments.

Theology of Religion as Both Emic and Etic Discourse

Relatedly, Chenchiah used both emic and etic ways of talking about religion.[23] We saw in the introduction that theology relies significantly on the emic (insider) discourse. It was evident, as we saw in the previous chapter, that Chenchiah too operated within the emic discourse, particularly privileging both his conversion and his Indian-ness to formulate his theory of religion. However, there was also an etic (outsider) discourse of religion that emerged out of his emic approach. This etic discourse was applied to religions in general, especially when Chenchiah looked at the development of Hinduism and depicted the religions in India. Here he adopted a nonjudgmental (non-evaluatory) perspective to talk about

---

23. A deeper discussion of etic and emic is reserved for the next chapter.

religion, and was primarily concerned with looking at religion in its sociopolitical context.

Chenchiah dual theory can be seen as religion in two senses: the broad sense and the theological sense. It is however not uncommon to hear of a "double sense" of religion by theologians. For instance, Tillich speaks of religion in a "double sense," differentiating between the local symbols of religious experience that comprises of the narrow sense and the broader sense that embraces "every human attitude in relation to the Infinite."[24] Tillich's "double sense" is different from Chenchiah's dual theory in particular because there is little continuity between Chenchiah's two concepts of religion. Chenchiah operated with different presuppositions about each type of religion. He was able to function within either and even found positives in both. The traditional religion was discussed matter-of-factly, with critical comments made within the scope of traditional discourse. The true religion, like Christ, was of an entirely different genus. There were some continuity, some semblances of truth that had been passed down of old. However, the emphasis was largely on a radical revolution of something new—a literal new creation.

This interplay between the etic and emic approaches was Chenchiah's dual theory of religion in operation. How it can work out in a general theology of religion is discussed in the next chapter.

Sources of Theology: Bible and Religion in Chenchiah

Chenchiah's use of the Bible has been critiqued. The Gurukul Group, for instance, argues that Chenchiah offers no criteria to determine whether his new portrait of Christ is genuine or not, especially after rejecting the testimony of the Apostles and the Church. They find that Chenchiah rejected the biblical and apostolic traditions, and prioritized his own experience for theology. They take particular exception to Chenchiah's attack on the Church, on the New Testament and the authority of the apostles.[25] Particularly, they see in Chenchiah a hermeneutical shift: the moving from the priority of the apostles to understand Christ, to the priority of Indian philosophy.[26] Chenchiah, they argue, "wants to get rid of all tradition, creed, dogma and doctrine, and to build an Indian theology on an entirely new foundation."[27]

24. Tillich, *On Protestant Principles*, 248.

25. Gurukul Theological Research Group, *A Christian Theological Approach to Hinduism*, 52.

26. Ibid., 53.

27. Ibid.

Chenchiah's theological criterion, as we saw in the previous chapter, was that the believer must have a direct experience of God in Christ through the Spirit. Appasamy testified to this, and even commended Chenchiah for emphasizing the need for a direct experience of Jesus.[28] Appasamy recommended experience (*prathyaksha*) as a valid norm for theological thought, especially interpreting his theological method through Chenchiah's work.[29] However Appasamy was critical of the exclusive emphasis on experience and urged that experience needed to be corrected through the Word (*shabda*).[30] Yet, as we have seen, Chenchiah was not asserting a direct experience of God as the exclusive source of theology. Rather, he was emphasizing that it had to do with a *genuine* relationship with God. Chenchiah's experience of God as a criterion of theology was not to be equated with subjectivity. Chenchiah was certainly not calling for a mystical experience, like *bhakti*, as if to suggest that, through a deeper experience, more knowledge is gained. Another way of viewing "direct experience" is through the words of Fraser Mitchell, writing in 1947, who stated that "direct experience of God" is the call of scripture itself:

> we [must not] remain too tied to the Bible, which, we should always remember, points away from itself to the Person of whom it speaks. We must not substitute insistence on Bible-reading, however valuable such study may be, for the attempt to lead young people to wait quite simply and naturally upon God . . . What we desire for the young is experience; and direct experience of God seldom is mediated by book or in schools of any sort, as the whole Bible itself testifies. It comes to young and old in the concrete occurrences of their ordinary lives, and it is our task, whether as ministers or teachers, to create in the young—and keep alive in the older the expectancy that that is how experience of God will come to them in turn.[31]

In Mitchell's terms, the direct experience of God is not oppositional to scripture, but the very essence of a relationship with God.[32] However, for Chenchiah, this direct experience is also a call for religious struggle—the adventure of religion that calls for Yoga (especially Spirit Yoga) to bring to fruition in contrast to the entrapments the traditional religions place.

28. Appasamy, "The Christian Pramanas," 60–61.
29. Ibid.
30. Ibid., 66–67.
31. Mitchell, "Christianity in our Parishes," 125.
32. Perhaps the closest modern–day parallel of direct experience is with Pentecostal theology which too calls for a direct experience of God outside institutionalism.

Evaluation of Chenchiah's Theology of Religion

While it is unlikely that Chenchiah would ever agree to the importance of scripture as a whole, Chenchiah could have promoted a much higher value of scripture without compromising his theological stand on the priority of Christ.

We also see how Chenchiah's view of the Bible was related to his views of religion. Devasahayam observes that Chenchiah viewed the whole "Bible as a process of growth in religious understanding."[33] Chenchiah mentioned how the "Growth of religion from maturity to its perfection" was evidenced in the "texts of Scripture."[34] Thus Devasahayam calls this a "process framework,"[35] especially since the "gradual growth of religion" was expressed through a variety of religious phenomena that became an example of "the involutions of new stages of revelation."[36] This process framework was quite similar to Chenchiah's evolutionary understanding of religion.

A similar logic led Chenchiah to equate the Old Testament with the Jewish religion.[37] His rejection of OT was not a rejection of the OT *per se*, but a rejection of the normative nature of the OT for Indian Christian theology. Chenchiah believed that retrospective narratives were adopted by NT writers when looking at the OT. The same retrospective narratives, Chenchiah urged, needed to be applied to the Hindu scriptures and traditions. However, Chenchiah did not credit Judaism or Hinduism with superior knowledge or greater wisdom; it was an issue of what was more relevant in terms of a bridge from the past to the future. Importantly, both (all) past religions were to be judged by the new creation, namely Jesus Christ.

Nevertheless, one of the clearest ways in which we can see how Chenchiah erred was through his own hermeneutical criteria. In his critique of the Church, Chenchiah categorically rejected the Church, about which "the Master said so little," and instead preferred to talk only about the Kingdom.[38] Such logic, while commendable in drawing attention to the importance of the Kingdom of God, fails when applied to Chenchiah's own discourse of religion. Jesus never used the language of religion either. However, not once did Chenchiah critique the concept of religion on the same grounds that he critiqued the concept of the Church. This failure to account for the lack of religion in the Bible, suggests that Chenchiah, in this case, was largely react-

---

33. Devasahayam, "Role of the Bible," 98.
34. Chenchiah, "Notes By the Way," 439.
35. Devasahayam, "Role of the Bible," 98.
36. Ibid., 99.
37. See Chenchiah, Indian Christian theological Task, VIII," 88. Also a point made by Devasahayam, "Role of the Bible," 103.
38. Chenchiah, "The Church and the Indian Christian," 82.

ing to the world contextually, because religion was accepted as a universal category during Chenchiah's time.

Secondly, Chenchiah missed the point of Jesus' own words about the OT scriptures. Chenchiah rejected the OT as a norm for Indian theology. He equated OT with the Judaic religion and thus put it in the same category as Hinduism. Elsewhere, Chenchiah rejected fulfillment theology, saying that Jesus stood against all religions as the new revolution. Nevertheless, Jesus used an idea of "fulfillment" saying that he came not to reject the law, but to fulfill it,[39] which in its context suggests that he was referring to the OT scriptures. Jesus' idea of fulfillment is quite different from Chenchiah's, because Chenchiah wanted to project a break, while Jesus had suggested no such break with the OT. Chenchiah was exceedingly critical of fulfillment theology—he opposed any suggestion that religion could somehow lead to Christ. Jesus, however, used fulfillment language when referring to the Old Testament scriptures (and thus the Jewish law) and was less radical (in terms of breaking with the OT) than Chenchiah made him out to be. Chenchiah's norm of Christ, here, was selectively applied.

Religion and History: Evolution as Cosmographical Schema

We saw in the Introduction that a theology of religion would have a cosmographical schema, an assertion about cosmological universals that arise within emic discourse. For Chenchiah, the cosmographical schema depicted a God who was the creator and humanity the creation. For Chenchiah, this relation impacted the nature and destiny of both God and creation. Chenchiah agreed with Barth that there existed a huge divide between God and creation. Chenchiah offered that religion was the effort to bridge the gap between God and humanity. What Chenchiah added to this traditional schema was the evolutionary framework, where creation was shown to be in constant movement through evolution (not always in ascent). God, through the Spirit, had intervened in the history of creation with certain revolutions that caused the upwards leaps of evolution within creation. The best example of this revolution was Jesus, the new creation, who was God's ultimate answer to the quest of religion—namely, the union between God and man. Through Jesus and the Spirit, it was finally possible for humanity to evolve into a new species, the new creation. Clearly, Chenchiah's cosmological framework was not a simple historical evolutionism that witnessed the development of the concept of religion. Rather, it was a strongly metaphysical

---

39. Matt 5:17.

assertion that argued for a biological new creation in the literal sense.[40] Chenchiah does not differentiate between the new creation at the time of eschatology from the new creation at the time of regeneration. However, because for Chenchiah there are Christians who do not live as though they are "new creation," there is a possibility that for Chenchiah, "new creation" is both current and eschatological in that as individuals progress towards the new biological transformation, eschatology has already begun.

This biological transformation has made many of Chenchiah's critics uncomfortable. However, his biological view of new creation offers an example of how Christian theologians can genuinely make universal claims that attempt to be consistent with the knowledge that we know through science and through theology. I also argue that Chenchiah's use of evolution was not strong enough. His biological evolution was too restrictive and individualistic, and he would have benefited from a more social-evolutionary perspective that could have led him to be less aggressive against Western tradition and more supportive of the Church.

Critics of Chenchiah's Evolutionary Theory

Chenchiah's reliance on evolutionary categories has been generally criticized. For instance, the Gurukul Group feels that Chenchiah over-emphasized the biological process of new humanity: "when Mr Chenchiah speaks of this event as 'a biological process' he obscures its spiritual character. The word bios, generally, denotes animal life, and biological generation suggests animal (including human) procreation. But the matter is made worse when the author deliberately strips the new birth of its characteristic spiritual qualities by disregarding, and even speaking disdainfully of, repentance and faith. Thereby this spiritual event has been made really unspiritual."[41]

Similarly, Thangasamy states that in viewing "new creation" as a biological process Chenchiah "loses clarity and even plausibility."[42] Boyd believes that the "biological language" has rather "unfortunate Arian overtones."[43] Jathanna feels that Chenchiah's extensive use of evolutionary thinking was legitimate since it was part of the thinking of his contemporaries, yet Jathanna also feels that the use of evolutionary thinking makes "Chenchiah liable to the same criticism which he levelled against those who make an

40. Chenchiah, *Rethinking Christianity in India*, 57.

41. Gurukul Theological Research Group, *A Christian Theological Approach to Hinduism*, 63.

42. Thangasamy, *Theology of Chenchiah*, 19.

43. Boyd, *An Introduction to Indian Christian Theology*, 149.

alien thought-form the precondition for knowing Jesus."[44] Jathanna strongly disagrees with the exclusive use of evolutionary logic to understand Christ[45] and finds the overall evolutionary language "rather naive."[46]

Speaking in Chenchiah's defence, it is important to clarify his theological use of evolution. Critics are quick to reject Chenchiah's use of the biological process to describe salvation in Christ. However most can at least appreciate Chenchiah's softer (and contextually appropriate) use of evolution to show the development of religion. The use of evolution as development was quite common in Chenchiah's time (as we saw in Chapter Two), and is also common today.[47] For the most part, Chenchiah simply applied evolutionary theories to religion, much like the history of religions approach. Yet he also saw potential in Aurobindo's approach, that saw a teleological hope for human development.[48]

Wagner provides the most insightful critique of Chenchiah's views on evolution, though he overestimates the "naturalism" or "neonaturalism" in Chenchiah.[49] There was very little of naturalist thought in Chenchiah to begin with. He rarely addressed the direct findings of scientists and was instead satisfied by loosely calling religion a scientific experiment, aiming at similar results, without getting into what the scientific results really were. The neonaturalist discourse is more evident in Teilhard de Chardin, who adapted scientific theories in his book *The Phenomena of Man*, with only a final concluding comment on Christianity. In contrast, actual scientific evolutionary studies were either beyond the scope of, or irrelevant to, Chenchiah's theology.

Wagner correctly points out that Chenchiah viewed evolution within the eschatological schema, which is to say that Chenchiah reinterpreted Christian eschatological themes such as "Kingdom of God" and "new creation" within the frame of cosmic evolution.[50] It is here that Chenchiah's theory of religion is a cosmographical schema that includes creation and eschatological new creation. Yet Wagner finds Chenchiah's use of evolu-

44. Jathanna, *The Decisiveness of The Christ Event*, 414.

45. Ibid., 413.

46. Ibid., 391.

47. Barr notes how in contemporary theology "the idea of development of doctrine has a respectable and significant place in Christian theology." Barr, *Concept of Biblical Theology*, 99.

48. A more recent expression of religion as evolutionary religion is Bellah, "Religious Evolution," 358–74.

49. For a differentiation between naturalism and neo–naturalism, see Fulford, "Teleology without Tears," 77–94.

50. Wagner, *Erstgestalten einer einheimischen Theologie*, 110–111.

tionary religion problematic, especially since he opines that Chenchiah's development scheme is incongruous with his metaphysical scheme.[51] Wagner notes that Chenchiah's evolutionary theory of religion cannot address the problem of how Christ has begun a new life and yet the new life is somehow not yet realized.[52] If there is already a biological transformation, how is it that there is yet to be a transformation remaining? Chenchiah's evolutionism, Wagner believes, offers no solution to the apparent contradiction between the already and not-yet within Christian eschatology—ideas that scientific evolution could never address.[53]

On a personal note, Rajasekaran[54] points out that his uncle Chenchiah was troubled by "why the Sons of God like Jesus had not appeared and what has the Holy Spirit been doing all these twenty centuries?"[55] Rajasekaran suggests that Chenchiah offered that perhaps "the Christian has not yet done his part in the achievements of the new creation and that it is our business to decipher and appropriate from HIM the new power through the Yoga of the Holy Spirit."[56] Yet Rajasekaran goes on to state that Chenchiah remained dissatisfied with this answer.[57]

Contrary to the above, Chenchiah did have an answer to the now-and-not-yet contradiction, and it lay precisely in the evolutionary scheme. It was not enough for Chenchiah to see Christianity as a passing down or transferring of dogmas across generations. He specifically asserted that it was the Holy Spirit that was to be handed on, from person to person, and the particular role of the Holy Spirit was to create a new man. The failure of the Church to pass on the new man suggested, to Chenchiah, the need for a new method of passing down the Holy Spirit: his proposed method was the practice of Spirit Yoga within the Asrama context (an adaptation of Aurobindo's and C.V.V.'s yoga) as well as ancient forest dweller practices, though prioritizing Jesus and the Spirit. Thus, Chenchiah proposed that the Christian community needed Christianity to reach the Indian shores, and needed Indian Christians to learn from the best of the movements within contemporary Hindu religion to come up with a new way of passing down the Holy Spirit that could be shared with the world. Chenchiah thus suggested that the global Christian community needed Indian Christians, and

51. Ibid., 113.
52. Ibid.
53. Wagner, *Erstgestalten einer einheimischen Theologie*, 114.
54. Chakkarai's son and Chenchiah's nephew.
55. Rajasekaran, *Reflections on Indian Christian Theology*, 197.
56. Ibid.
57. Ibid.

thus now, in the fullness of time, humanity was at the cusp of making that evolutionary leap.

The positive in this kind of evolutionary thinking lies in theology taking evolution seriously, as an actual (not simply ideal) phenomenon for global discourse. An important weakness, which all Chenchiah's critics miss, is the overemphasis on an individualistic evolutionary theory, without exploring the possibility of social evolution. Both these ideas are discussed below.

A Defense of the Biological New Creation

In the Introduction, we noted how any integration of biology with religion—whether to say that religion is a region in the brain or showing how it impacts physiology—is doubtful because religion is a contextual construction. Nevertheless, Chenchiah's emphasis of the biological within his theory of religion, particularly his soteriology, offers a more integrated approach to theology, in contrast to a simple spiritualist approach. While Chenchiah offered no evidence to show how a person could become a "new man" in Christ, the theological reinterpretation to take "new creation" and "new man" to literally mean a new species is a bold step that takes evolution more seriously than philosophical/spiritual evolutionism.[58]

Unlike the spiritualist readings that look to the Holy Spirit working within the spiritual realm of a person, the possibility of biological or genetic transformation of a Christian when he becomes one with Christ cannot be overlooked. If the Christian religion is transformative, as Chenchiah argued that it must be, then it certainly could include a new biological life as well.

The New Testament has been seen to use "new creation" in two ways—soteriologically (related to the individual) and eschatologically (related to the end times).[59] While it can be argued that there is a biological re-creation in the eschatological new creation—as witnessed with the resurrection of Jesus—there is no overt evidence to suggest that a new biology occurs at the time of salvation. What can be argued is that salvation is a process, and that process involves not just the spirit of a human being but also the body. Looking at the theories of evolution—especially where change in behavior/lifestyle of a species can change its biological trajectory to adapt to new

---

58. For instance, Chenchiah says, "Jesus stands to man as man stands to animal... He transcends us as we transcend animals. Reason is our differentia, the Holy Spirit His." Chenchiah, "Jesus and Non-Christian Faiths," 60.

59. For discussion of various views related to "new creation," see Hubbard, *New Creation in Paul's Letters and Thought*.

environments—there could be more to evolutionary thought that warrants further theological attention. This is significant because most Christians, especially those who are critical of literalist readings of the Bible that give rise to young-earth science, still do not take evolution seriously enough. If indeed God did use evolution as a mode of creation, then how does it play out in all life, including theology, today? It is not enough to state that theology is a process, as if evolutionary mechanics only affect intellectual or spiritual reality.

Chenchiah not only views religion within the evolutionary schema but also sees the religious individual (the convert) within the evolutionary schema: the latter conceptual leap, while still needing further exploration and justification, at least attempts to take the material body seriously.

A Critique of the Limited Sense of Community, and Thus Social Evolution

Chenchiah missed the true implication of evolutionary theory by ignoring the social factors (of religion) within evolution. Chenchiah was so strongly against Western Church traditions that he failed to see any continuity between Indian Christian and Christian history. Furthermore, Chenchiah failed to note how within the social evolutionary framework the distinctly Christian community (those impacted by Jesus) could have been instrumental in the growth towards the future new man in Christ.

Appasamy makes this point by noting that Chenchiah did not have an answer to whether the saints in the past were new creations. Chenchiah had stated that "unfortunately Christ who has come into History remains solitary."[60] Yet Appasamy rightly critiqued that while Chenchiah had no problem in skipping 2000 years from Christ to find that Aurobindo and C.V.V. understood the truth, he wrongly ignored saints like Paul, Augustine, Francis of Assisi, Andrews, Sadhu Sundar Singh and Pandita Ramabai, who because of their devotion to Jesus could have been seen as the first types of new humanity, or at least as having arrived at an intermediate stage between man and new man.[61]

Appasamy's valid critique notwithstanding, there is a misunderstanding concerning Chenchiah's criticism of the Church. While the common belief is that Chenchiah rejected the Church, Chenchiah was still accepting of the concept of Christian community through the Kingdom of God and

60. Chenchiah, "Sri Aurobindo," 438.
61. Appasamy, "Who Is Jesus?" 76–77.

through the Asramas. This leads one to question what Chenchiah meant by Church and his dual theory of religion helps clarify just that.

Chenchiah was critical of the temple religion, the institutions of religion, especially the church that claimed that in it and through it salvation exists. He was critical of the Church as a center of power. He was critical of the abuse of power and of monopoly. He was critical of the dogmatic emphasis of the church, where the desire was to preserve doctrines and beliefs, rather than to preserve the true life to which it was supposed to testify. Such a critique is the critique of false religion, of temple religion. Chenchiah would have had a similar critique of the temples of Hinduism, and by extension, the mosques and gurudwaras of the world. It was not in the buildings that God resided, but in the Spirit. The moment the nomenclature of "Church" is replaced with Asrama, or even "Kingdom of God," there is less of a loss of the Church and more a change in the popular conception of the Church.

Nevertheless, Chenchiah wrongly interpreted new life in individualistic terms. The Spirit Yoga, for instance, affected only the doer and not the community around the person. The individual had to follow a certain path and only then could he or she gain new life. In contrast, Chenchiah failed to recognize any value in the community that extends beyond the nationalist and *swadesi* boundaries that he found himself in. In fact, there is much to be said in favor of a community of God working together to help each other become one with God, or even for a community to express different aspects of that oneness of God, and even, as a corporate body, be one with God. These ideas are not discussed much by Chenchiah across the global Church, but they could certainly be legitimate within Chenchiah's own understanding.

Then, pertaining to the scientific evolutionary theories, the Baldwin effect allows for cultural factors, especially learned behaviors, to affect the evolution of a species. While one must warn against an overreliance on Baldwin's theory, there is much in contemporary research within the evolutionary theory that links human culture (and thus religion) to the larger evolutionary scheme.[62] Baldwin's argument began with the observation that some subspecies, faced with conflict, gained new skills/behaviors (ontogenetic adaptations) outside their genes to enhance their chances of survival.[63] Furthermore, in some subspecies these new skills/behaviors became more effective through "social heritability," where the offspring would pick up these new traits through imitation and/or instruction in its "private family circle."[64] This social heritability could be maintained for long periods until

---

62. For instance see Richerson and Boyd, *Not By Genes Alone*.
63. Depew, "Baldwin and his many effects," 7.
64. Ibid.

the new skill/behavior became embedded as part of the genetic behavior of the species.[65] In effect, behavior and education—drawn within a community—is crucial for the biological evolution of a species.

Keeping in mind Chenchiah's own admission to the need of community, Baldwin's theory could be applied to Christianity. For instance, a member of the human species could gain access to this new Spirit-empowered knowledge, skill, or behavior (in this case the knowledge/power of Christ/Spirit), to begin to act differently from other human beings. Then, within a "private family circle"—whether Church, Kingdom of God or Asrama—these new behaviors/skills would be passed from generation to generation through imitation and instruction, though once again with the power of the Spirit, so that eventually more Spirit-filled human beings would be able to harness the power of Christ and Spirit in their lives. Eventually, the larger community would evolve into a new species that would be just like the God-man Jesus Christ. In effect, to call the Church the Body of Christ could also take on new significance.

Chenchiah was thus unnecessarily critical of the Church, which, as shown above, can be seen to function productively for the very biological evolution that Chenchiah wanted to promote. If the ultimate achievement of evolution happened within social participation, the role of the Church, both historic and contemporary, as a learning and behavior transforming community, would gain importance.[66]

Ultimately, while Chenchiah's evolutionary view of religion is simplistic, it takes a bold step that could actually lead to a stronger theological position and provide a synthesis of religion and theology, especially if theologians are able to overcome some of their biases against evolution.

Integrated Religion: Religion in the World

Earlier we saw that Chenchiah offered an integrated view of religion. One way this was expressed was by conceiving of a Christian as a person whose whole life is governed by the new religious transformation. The other way was to see true religion as an overarching system of transformation that transformed not only the individual but also the multiple cultures and

---

65. Ibid.

66. This is not to say that the Baldwin effect is the necessary motif to understand the nature of the Church. Rather, Chenchiah's own use of evolutionary scheme to understand and practice theology opens the avenues to look at similar schemes to gain richer clarity over complex issues.

religious traditions. This section addresses the strengths and weaknesses of this proposal.

Religion as an Integrated Life, Empowered by God

We have seen that Chenchiah's theology of religion was a critique of institutional rituals and dogmas. Much of the substructure that is usually associated with the phenomena of religion was deemed as a corruption of true religion, which was about the new creation, made possible through Christ and the Spirit. Similarly, Chenchiah was critical of *bhakti,* asserting that it achieved nothing in religion. In this sense, Chenchiah certainly does not deem religion to be a life for God *per se,* but more a life in relation to the God-man Jesus.

Chenchiah also offered a broader view of religion, conceived of as a transformed life, a life of new creation. While most of Chenchiah's work focused upon getting to the stage of new creation, there were hints at what that new creation would be like. Chenchiah was most like Gandhi in this respect, and we see it particularly in his positive description of Gandhi's *ahimsa,* which was not simply nonviolence but the force of a well-tempered and disciplined mind that faces up to the world of violence and hatred.[67] Like Gandhi, Chenchiah believed that religious transformation of the inner man would lead to the transformation of the outer world—where "religion and religious discipline and power are intended to build up free states, societies, and individuals."[68] Chenchiah himself urged Christians to remember how Gandhi embodied religion in his life and outlook to "create a unique political instrument."[69] It must be reiterated that unlike Gandhi, Chenchiah put Christ/Spirit at the center of that transformation, and thus Chenchiah offered a truly Christian theological adaptation of Gandhi.

We see something similar in Chenchiah's Asrama mode. It was to exist not simply as a community that was attempting unity with God for unity's sake, but also to challenge the caste and social structures, as a critique of priestly corruption and a rejection of the ascetic life that separated an individual from life. In another instance, Chenchiah commended a "social revolution" by linking religion to "patriotic endeavor."[70] A new community was

---

67. While this point is addressed in Chenchiah, "Religion in Contemporary India," 202, Minz emphasizes it in Minz, *Mahatma Gandhi and Hindu–Christian Dialogue,* 79.

68. Minz, *Mahatma Gandhi and Hindu–Christian Dialogue,* 79.

69. Chenchiah, "Christian Youth, Non-Christian Faiths," 452.

70. Chenchiah, "Indian Christian Politics," 325.

promoted that would express its "renunciation of caste by eating together, openly," would share income to help the needy, would devote themselves to the hard work of the production of food and clothing, would reject the economic hold of money, and would search for social harmony amongst the followers of various religions.[71] Such a project was clearly social. Yet Chenchiah still meant for this type of action to be a description of a new life, a new creation, especially as Chenchiah concluded the article by asserting that "we have to prepare the people for the changes" related to the "evolution of the world."[72]

All this to say, Chenchiah focused upon a transformation in and through religion rather than being preoccupied with how religion was distinct from nonreligion. Religion at its best was conceived in active (even adjectival) terms, as opposed to essentialist terms, to shape (and transform) the world. There was no separation between a religious and a political space. Rather, it was a religious power that informed/transformed the political space so that religious politics could exist, as well as religious commerce, religious ethics, religious education and so forth.

Interestingly, while Chenchiah rejected worship as the center of religion, his integrative view of religion is actually consistent with the broad view of worship as liturgical action. Chenchiah's "practice oriented" approach wanted to escape the mysticism of *bhakti*, yet his proposed actions were governed by theological meaning.

Chenchiah's theology of religion was integrative in that it extended beyond the scope of what was normally considered religion and extended to day-to-day common existence, confronting society both with foreign powers and internal evil. Thus, while the nationalist struggle took on a religious flavor, religion for Chenchiah was not just nationalism, but all of life, including what we eat, wear and do.

Positively, Chenchiah's theology of religion is helpful not simply because it rightly critiques the corrupt structures of negative religion, but also because it views religion as integrated with all life.

Theology Without Love: The System of Religion

There is, however, a significant failure in Chenchiah's theology of religion. Chenchiah's theology of religion lacked a fundamental appreciation of the cross. It thus remains as an impersonal system devoid of love or devotion. Chenchiah's religion as union emphasized primarily techniques for

71. Ibid.
72. Ibid.

realization and missed the passion that the incarnation implies. Similarly, the systems approach suggested that religion was more about human action and drew attention away from God's grace, potentially leading to an ungrateful religion without devotion. Both these ideas are dangerous for Christian theology, and point to a fundamental defect in Chenchiah's *theology* of religion.

The Gurukul Group is rightly critical of Chenchiah's disregard for atonement and justification by faith. They argue that Chenchiah replaces the centrality of the Gospel of atonement with the message of "a new cosmic energy."[73] This is not to forget that Chenchiah was attempting a corrective to the over emphasis of atonement by the traditional Christian missionaries and preachers of his time. Rajasekaran says that Chenchiah was not so much rejecting the cross—which Chenchiah did state was puzzling and absurd for Hindus—but that he was emphasizing the promise of salvation hereafter: "Other aspects of the life of Christ than that of the sacrificial lamb, were [far] more fascinating to Chenchiah . . . He [held] that construing Christianity as making laws, disobedience, sin, cross, propitiation, judgment misses the beauty and freshness of the Gospels. But poetry that stresses love, resurrection, communion, sonship gets us nearer to the Master."[74]

However Chenchiah's theology still failed to take into account Jesus' own assertions about the necessity and significance of his death and Chenchiah did not come to terms with Jesus' own grief/struggle with death. In effect, while in some matters Chenchiah's theology "is in agreement with Apostolic teaching," yet, because of its bias against atonement, his theology is "full of dangers and pitfalls," even to the extent that he "distorts the Gospel in a fatal way."[75]

The failure to emphasize the cross has a consequence in his theology of religion. Instead of religion being about the worship of God, or even a response to God, it becomes a system for union with God—a soteriology that rightly emphasizes the metaphysical dimensions of salvation without the love of God that gets you there.[76] Chenchiah does attempt to distinguish

---

73. Gurukul Theological Research Group, *A Christian Theological Approach to Hinduism*, 49–50.

74. Rajasekaran, *Reflections on Indian Christian Theology*, 15.

75. Gurukul Theological Research Group, *A Christian Theological Approach to Hinduism*, 62.

76. Here we can recount Boulton's view that God is against worship, and yet Boulton sees worship as an indispensable part of the current Christian world and the end of worship within the eschatological event. See Boulton, *God against Religion*, 6. Chenchiah in contrast rejects worship entirely as a lower stage of religious evolution.

religion from ideology, but still argues that "religion is realization."[77] The emphasis of a system is so strong in Chenchiah that we are left with a picture of religion, and Christianity, that is far removed from Christian witness. Jathanna notes that Chenchiah emphasized the system of religion so much that religion was more about a mechanical realization than about a right relationship with God, that is personal and transforming.[78] Jathanna adds, "it is not that Chenchiah is entirely wrong in attempting to develop certain useful techniques, and emphasizing the need for present experience, but that he does not sufficiently critically reflect on the issues of technique and realization from a Christian perspective, which would have given him a more balanced and dialectical view..."[79]

Chenchiah's lack of a theology of the cross naturally also leads to a lack of emphasis on devotion and worship. Due to his evolutionary soteriology, Chenchiah's theology of religion lacked the sense of love that led to the union between Man and God. It is not as if Chenchiah ignored God's love. He was aware that "God who loves us enough to intervene in a crisis has loved us enough to be Emmanuel—God with us."[80] Yet Chenchiah did not emphasize love, but focused on the effect of the incarnation on the "new evolutionary stage of man."[81]

We also see a difference between de Chardin and Chenchiah at this point. de Chardin integrated the Omega Point with Christianity by stating that, in Christianity, God was portrayed as uncompromisingly personal, both revealing himself and directing the universe (presumably within the evolutionary process).[82] de Chardin noted that the desire "to create to fulfill and to purify the world is, for God, to unify it by uniting it organically with himself."[83] Importantly, this principle of unity was governed by the value of love, where love was the ultimate unifying action within difference.[84]

Chenchiah, in contrast, portrayed the evolutionary goal of union with God in remarkably impersonal terms. Chenchiah's *mahashakti* in particular identified the power of God—for revolution as well as giving new capacity to humanity—and so the Holy Spirit seemed to be more like an energy to be harnessed. It is not surprising that Appasamy rhetorically asked whether

77. Chenchiah, "Sri Aurobindo," 438.
78. Jathanna, *The Decisiveness of the Christ Event*, 414.
79. Ibid.
80. Chenchiah, *Asramas*, 308.
81. Ibid.
82. de Chardin, *The Phenomenon of Man*, 320–21.
83. Ibid., 322.
84. Ibid., 323.

Chenchiah's God possessed "qualities of love and goodness which evoke a response from us and make us long for communion with Him?"[85]

Chenchiah's union with God was a metaphysical union and not a union in fellowship of love or friendship. To be fair, Chenchiah was aware of the notion of fellowship and was especially loving towards his Christian and non-Christian neighbors, throughout his life. For instance, in an editorial, Chenchiah urged the practice of the ethic of Christ.[86] In contrast to what he believed about the Jewish emphasis on law and justice, or even the Kantian moral imperative, Chenchiah offered that love was the very nature of Jesus.[87] This love was expressed when Jesus forgave his persecutors on the cross, an act that is heralded as love and blessing, yet note that this love was not directed to God, but to fellow human beings: "That love is powerful and potent beyond our petty reason has been demonstrated again and again. Yet we are afraid of God, Love and Saviors and do not give them a chance. Amidst greed and selfishness, ineptitude, moral degradation, one is proud that our high command tried and succeeded by applying Christ's and Gandhiji's doctrine of love to the worst spots of life."[88]

That sense of love could have only come from the sense of love one had received. Yet, either due to the oppositional context of the nationalist movement, or his critical stance towards mindless *bhakti* or even because of his attraction to the dispassionate method of Yoga, Chenchiah's evolutionary soteriology comes across as a system without passion or love, and thus also without devotion or gratitude for God's grace.

Another danger of a soteriology without the cross is the lack of emphasis on God's grace. The language of grace, very different from the language of God's power, shows the consequence of Chenchiah's system, which is not just without devotion but also without repentance and faith.

Jathanna strongly critiques Chenchiah's interpretation of repentance and faith as a "moral effort of man" as an "entirely alien interpretation," especially since Jesus himself stressed faith and repentance for the Kingdom of God.[89] Despite the advantages of the positive focus of Chenchiah's soteriology, Jathanna is still correct in pointing out that both the negative (repentance) and the positive (new life) "belong indissolubly together."[90]

---

85. Appasamy, "Who Is Jesus?" 73.
86. Chenchiah, "Editorial," 1–11.
87. Ibid., 1.
88. Ibid.
89. Jathanna, *The Decisiveness of the Christ Event*, 415.
90. Ibid., 416–17.

The necessity of repentance aside, a bigger problem confronts Chenchiah's theology of religion. Chenchiah was rightly critical of human action in religion and called for people to harness the cosmic energy of the Spirit. This effort was the true religion—the attempt to become one with God. Yet the irony becomes stark when he called faith and repentance as human effort to achieve this goal and yet offered Yoga as the alternative. Is not the harnessing of the Holy Spirit's power through Yoga a human action, and much more so than faith?

Despite his intentions, Chenchiah ultimately offered a salvation of works, where the goal of religion was achieved only through a series of actions on the part of the individual and God was (merely) an energy source to get one there. Chenchiah was more interested in highlighting the power to achieve the goal of true religion than in the process of becoming one with God, which remained primarily a human act.

CHENCHIAH'S THEOLOGY OF RELIGIONS

Chenchiah's theology of religion can also be seen through the strengths and weaknesses of his theology of religions. Positively, Chenchiah's theology of religions allowed for the supremacy of Christ as the basis of the equity of religions. Chenchiah was not interested in establishing Christian superiority over Hinduism, because he believed that Christ was superior to Christianity and all other religions in general.

In effect, in Chenchiah's common sense view of religion, all religions, including Christianity, were bound by the same process of degradation. The same dangers (and actual evidence) of corruption were expressed through history. This is a idea for a theology of religions because it allows for a shared space with people of other religions, especially through a similar sense of what is considered pure and impure in religion. Hindu thinkers like Aurobindo, Gandhi and others, critiqued priestly powers and archaic laws by emphasizing a deep spirituality. Clearly their ideas resonated across Indian society. Chenchiah, by putting Christianity under the same critique, allowed for a common platform of critiquing the evils of religion and commending its good. Chenchiah's position is a much-needed reference point when talking with people of other religions, especially those who share similar (substantive) theories of religion—the awareness that there is something deeper in religion that is pure, while its expression is often a corruption. This critique also allows for a positive cooperative element among religions, where, as Gandhi recommended, religions could work together because of shared concerns, for common purposes like nationalism, ethics and so forth.

Of course, at this point, a weakness of Chenchiah's theory of religion for his theology of religions was the predominantly Hindu engagement, especially in its emphasis of religion being about the union between God and man. This immediately cuts off Muslims from the dialogue/engagement table, a problem Chenchiah did not conceive of or address. Regardless, at least for Hindus, Chenchiah's approach was both nonaggressive and filled with potential.

Chenchiah's approach to other religions was further helped by his integrated view of religion, where the goal was not for a separate sacred space in culture, but a religious nature of culture. Chenchiah's theory of integrated religion brought religion to the center of society, much like how it was in the Bible and how it had been perceived (popularly) across Indian culture. Chenchiah's category of religion took into account both beliefs and actions, and thus did not prioritize belief or dialogue over actual engagement with others.

Furthermore, Chenchiah's theory of religion was not at the expense of one's identity, but was informed by a strongly particularlist (faith-based) point of view. Chenchiah's theory of religion, as we have seen, was not a secular philosophy but a religious theory, a theology, because of its emphasis on Jesus and the work of the Holy Spirit.

Regardless of possible modern-day accusations that this was an erroneous or oppressive depiction of the other religions, this way of looking at other religions (and even religion) can be viewed positively. In the language of Sumner, much of Chenchiah's dealing with the Hindu religion was a "retrospective narrative," especially with Christ gaining "final primacy."[91] For a Christian convert, a theologian, looking at religion need not be a quest for scientific objectivity; instead, it is natural and even warranted to look at all things through theological norms, which, in Chenchiah's case, was Christ.

Chenchiah thus engaged religiously with all life, including the interaction with religions. His Christian religious framework not only informed his theology of religions, but also his theology of politics, nationality, ethics and so forth. His mode of dealing with people of other religions like Hinduism was through retrospective narratives, since he prioritized Christ above all and did not seek to equate God with religion, of others or his own. The focus was on God and God's interactions with the world in multiple spheres, not simply on the so-called religious sphere. Insofar as God influences all

---

91. Sumner, *The First & the Last*, 174.

life, including politics, art and ethics, there was and would be a better standard for interaction with people who are not Christians.

The strength of this approach, especially in relation to other religions, is that it is a position of deep conviction. Even if people of other religions would not accept Chenchiah's positions, at least they could respect him. This again provides potential access to people of other religions.

However, Chenchiah seemed completely ignorant of the potential difficulties his theology of religion posed to his access of non-Christian religions. Chenchiah did not seem to realize that his strongly theological position, where everyone could gain access a new creation through Jesus Christ and his Spirit, could come across as patronizing towards the Hindu (non-Christian). As a Christian, I believe Chenchiah was on the right track and, in fact, had no other alternative in view of his sources of theology. However, for the high goals of interaction and engagement with non-Christians, he failed to realize that his very theological approach may make him ineffective by coming across as alienating. Had Chenchiah counted the cost of this approach, would he have still maintained his strongly theological stance? My studied opinion is that it is likely, because he clearly believed in the Christological and Pneumatological priority for salvation. Nevertheless, Chenchiah was closer to the exclusive and particularist points of view that he believed he was rejecting.

Another weakness in Chenchiah's theology of religions, perhaps the most fundamental one, was the lack of love as the driving force of the interaction. If interaction and unity was desired between groups of people, then God's loving initiative for the unity could have better informed Chenchiah's paradigm. Chenchiah did not sufficiently answer why Christians should care about non-Christians. His best answer was that true religion was the effort/longing for unity with God. Yet that does not answer why a Christian must leave his country, family, and comfort to help someone else to do the same. The idea that love is the driving force of God's mission, and thus our own mission is to tell others of God's love, is a factor missing in Chenchiah. This is disappointing yet unsurprising because there was no room for grace, mercy and devotion in Chenchiah's theology. His understanding of true religion was a system in contrast to other systems, which ultimately left Christians without any directive to love as they were loved.

SUMMARY OF THE CHAPTER

This chapter comes to an end with a few concluding remarks. Chenchiah's theology of religion is a combination of theory and theology. There are seven main ideas that can be derived from Chenchiah's theology of religion: 1) the dual theory of religion, that promotes looking at religion through common and broad senses; 2) the use of the emic and etic spaces; 3) the emphasis on Christ as norm for religion and religious experience; 4) the use of retrospective narratives, particularly where Christ-experience shapes the reading of any other narrative; 5) the (problematic) idea of evolution as the cosmographical schema for life and religion; 6) the related idea of religion as the revolution of transformation; and finally, 7) religion as integrated life.

As a methodological proposal, Chenchiah's theology succeeds. Particularly commendable is Chenchiah's emphasis on the dual theory of religion, the integrated religion and religion as emic discourse. Chenchiah's theology of religion is compatible with Balagangadhara's proposal that religion is meaningful action, particularly because it is expressed within a cosmic scheme that includes a sense of human nature and its destiny—both ideas were deeply embedded in Chenchiah's thinking.

Other aspects of Chenchiah's proposal have mixed results. For instance, Chenchiah adopted a subjective approach in his hermeneutics, that failed to account for the biblical witness in its totality. Similarly, Chenchiah's use of evolutionary theory is limited. He made an important suggestion for Christian theology, to bring the metaphysical (biological) question into Christian soteriological discourse. This, as I have suggested, is a much-needed corrective to spiritualist and psychological approaches to conversion and Christian discipleship. Unfortunately, Chenchiah did not push his evolutionary thinking to its logical conclusion and projected an individualistic approach rather than seeing evolution as social and organic. The latter corrective would have made him more appreciative of the Christian (Western) past.

Finally, as soon as we put Chenchiah's theology to use, to interpret what religion means for others, we run into a few problems. Fundamentally, the two errors are to view religion mechanistically as a system without love, and the other, emerging out of the lack of a theology of the cross, is that the system is a system of works without grace.

As it stands, while Chenchiah's theology of religion is a helpful and insightful way of looking at religion, it is not enough. We are thus left with an urgent need to supplement Chenchiah's theory and theology on several levels, from contemporary study as well as from broader biblical and theological discourse. Most of all, there needs to be a recovery of the aspect of love, honor and worship of God, as an important part of any Christian definition of religion.

5

A Critical Framework to Formulate a Theological Answer

INTRODUCTION

In the previous chapter we saw that Chenchiah is a helpful resource to answer the question "What is religion?" theologically. However, Chenchiah is not enough and there is the need to approach the question about religion with a contemporary theoretical, as well as biblical and theological perspective. Therefore, this chapter broadens the net to help us answer the question, "What is religion?"

Apart from Chenchiah's seven points,[1] I also have in mind Dubuisson and Balagangadhara's challenge,[2] that religion is a Christian construct to the extent that Christianity and religion are most alike in their tendencies to be belief-oriented, individualistic, universalistic, and antagonistic. In the previous two chapters, we saw how Chenchiah's view of religion helps address at least some of these challenges. In this chapter, I engage with secular theories of classification and integrated religion, along with biblical and theological religion. I show that to address the secular challenge facing religion, as well as the limitations of Chenchiah's theology of religion, a theological view of religion (which includes select secular, biblical, and theological sources) is needed.

---

1. As determined in the summary of the previous chapter.
2. As stated in the introductory chapter.

In this chapter, I look at two contemporary theories of religion, namely the contextual classification theory (from Russell McCutcheon) and the integrated religion theory (from Martin Riesebrodt). Next, I will interact with the concept of religion from a biblical perspective, particularly looking to broaden the understanding of religion as close to the textual intent as possible. Third, I draw a theological approach from the larger theological understanding that undergirds a theology of religion, and the concept of religion as worship from Augustine.

THEORY OF RELIGION: CONTEXTUAL CLASSIFICATION AND INTEGRATED RELIGION

In contemporary religious scholarship, there are several approaches to religion. However, we need to identify an approach that looks at religion in a manner consistent with and helpful for Christian theology. I isolate the contextual classification approach advocated by McCutcheon as a valid method for Christians to redescribe religion, and it is compatible with and rightly extends Chenchiah's theology of religion. In addition, I adapt Riesebrodt's interventionist theory of religion, which rightly draws attention to the God–human connection in religion.

Building a Theory of Contextual Classification

The contextual classification of religion views religion not as an essential "thing" but as a word that helps make linguistic and conceptual sense of culture.[3] Arnal recommends the use of 'religion' without reference to inherent content, as a descriptive or functional category that classifies culture rather than defines it.[4] Oftentimes definitions of religion rely on essentialism or substantialism, treating religion as if it was tangible and universal. In contrast, the aim of a classification is to label and categorize the things we see.[5] The classification approach views religion as a linguistic category that names various phenomena in taxonomies that are understandable to the one/community doing the naming.

From a study of McCutcheon, and Jonathan Smith who influenced him, we see that religion is a classified object, rather than an essential object

---

3. "Contextual classificatory" is a phrase I use to describe Smith and McCutcheon's ideas who emphasize the construction of a category in the context of academia.

4. Arnal, "Definition," 30–32.

5. See Smith's essay "A Matter of Class," 160–78.

that exists universally in the world. McCutcheon points out that the concept of religion is hardly universal. He opines that it is more useful as a category for the outsiders looking within than for the insiders using the word for themselves.[6] Even in cases where a community uses the concept religion or something similar, it is "intimately linked to a people's own self-description and self-identity."[7] For McCutcheon it is not surprising therefore that religion remains a slippery concept and "what counts as religion for one is hardly religion for another."[8] McCutcheon thus proposes that, "scholars of religion do not actually study religion, the gods, or ultimate concerns; rather, they use a folk rubric, 'religion,' as a theoretically grounded, taxonomic marker to isolate or demarcate a portion of the complex, observable behavior of biologically, socially, and historically situated human beings and human communities that talk, act, and organize themselves in ways that the scholar finds curious and in need of analysis."[9]

Smith adds that religions are not only "objects of classifications" but are also "powerful engines for the production and maintenance of classificatory systems."[10] Smith shows that classifications *in* religions are taxonomies that religions use to make sense of their world. Examples of such taxonomies are sacred/profane, pure/impure, true/false and the comparative ours/theirs, even "ours is like theirs."[11] However, there is also a taxonomy that is applied to the religions themselves, which Smith refers to as the classification *of* religions. Emerging from the scientific study of religions (*Religionswissenschaft*), and particularly from a university context, the classification of religions is expressed through taxonomies like primitive/modern, world/universal, nature/ethnic, theistic/polytheistic, etc.[12] These typologies are further extended to phenomena within classified religions, such as ritual/myth/ceremony, church/sect/cult, worship/practice and so forth.[13]

Relatedly, all classification is contextually driven by the community that does the classification.[14] This is to say, the contextual classification emerges from within the community, and in the case of religion, from the

6. McCutcheon, *Critics Not Caretakers*, 10–11.
7. Ibid., 11.
8. Ibid., 11–12.
9. Ibid., 11.
10. Smith, "Classification," 38.
11. Ibid., 38–39.
12. Ibid., 41–43.
13. Ibid., 43.
14. See for instance McCutcheon's essays on "Institutional Identity and the Significance of Theory," in McCutcheon, *Manufacturing Religion*, 192–213.

academic community. In the face of multiple definitions of religion, Smith explains: "'Religion' is not a native term; it is a term created by scholars for intellectual purposes and therefore is theirs to define. It is a second-order, generic concept that plays the same role in establishing a disciplinary horizon that a concept such as 'language' plays in linguistics or 'culture' plays in anthropology. There can be no disciplined study of religion without such a horizon."[15]

McCutcheon builds from this and argues that religion (like culture, art and so forth) is a word used for classification, which, while problematic, is still useful to help make (academic) sense of the world.[16] McCutcheon states,

> the study of religion ... is the disciplined inquiry of but one aspect of human cultural practices—an aspect identified, for the purposes of our study, by the definition we as scholars choose to use, a definition that suits our purposes and our curiosities. What unites us into this collective group ... is not only our shared curiosities, common tools, and agreed-upon standards of argumentation, but also the common institutional setting that draws us together, and to which our labors contribute. This setting is ... the public research university, an institution that has profound bearing on what ends up counting as the academic studying of religion.[17]

In effect, the word 'religion' is a term that is shaped (contextually classified) by the institutional setting, namely academia, for academic purposes.

The Insider/Outsider Approach to Religion

The contextual classification of religion can be further elucidated by the insider/outsider (emic/etic) approach to classification. McCutcheon asserts that theories are dependent not only on the context but also on the "interests that drive it."[18] He goes on to offer at least three different contexts of studying religion, namely theological, humanistic and human sciences (academic):

> theological studies of various sorts, housed in private and denominationally supported schools, which are aimed at

---

15. Smith, *Relating Religion*, 193–94.
16. McCutcheon, *Manufacturing Religion*, 210.
17. McCutcheon, *Studying Religion*, 71.
18. Ibid.

articulating, in a systematic and rational manner, the principles of the participant's viewpoint (whether that viewpoint is mainline or marginal, whether theologically liberal or conservative); humanist studies that, after comparative work uncovers deep similarities, understands diverse participant viewpoints to share universal values that are not necessarily apparent even to the participants; and those in the human sciences who understand all claims concerning the existence of such things as deep essences, self-evident meanings, and universal values to comprise an instance of data—whether that be claims concerning the existence of souls or the Human Spirit.[19]

Eliade's theory of religion is an example of the humanist approach, where the goal of the study of religion is to somehow improve the researcher and even humanity/society.[20] The theological approach, for instance expressed through Wilfred Cantwell Smith[21] or Paul Tillich,[22] is to prioritize the internal discourse of religion over the objective discourse, as well as make evaluatory remarks and value judgments. W. C. Smith, revealing his theological bent, says as much: "The end of religion, in the classical sense of its purpose and goal, that to which it points and may lead, is God. Contrariwise, God is the end of religion also in the sense that once He appears vividly before us, in His depth and love and unrelenting truth all else dissolves; or at the least religious paraphernalia drop back into their due and mundane place, and the concept 'religion' is brought to an end."[23]

Strenski is particularly critical of the theological approach and its encroachment on the theoretical study of religion. He critiques Green for trying to promote (unsuccessfully) Barth's theology of religion as a legitimate theoretical option for academia.[24] Strenski argues that "Barth's Christianity is too narrow and sectarian a starting point for the study of religion in our religious diverse nation and universities. Christianity, as well as Judaism, Islam, and such, are simply nonstarters when it comes to the foundations of the study of religion . . . Barth's concept of religion is, for one thing, theologically 'loaded' in a way that ipso facto disqualifies it and Barthian

---

19. McCutcheon, *Studying Religion*, 46.
20. See Eliade, "A New Humanism," 103.
21. See McCutcheon's critique of Smith in McCutcheon, *Manufacturing Religion*, 115.
22. See Smith's critique of Tillich in Smith, *Relating Religion*, 192–93.
23. Smith, *Meaning and End of Religion*, 201.
24. Strenski, "Why 'Theology' Won't Work," 31–44.

theology from any foundational role in the study of religion proper in a university."[25]

Similarly, Wiebe argues vehemently for a scientific view of the study of religion as opposed to a theological/ideological one.[26] Wiebe notes a sharp distinction between Christian theology and Christian religion, and says that theology is detrimental to religion.[27] Wiebe explains that his critique is against "theology that emerges as an academic/scientific discipline," attempting to legitimize the nonrevelation scientific method with revelation.[28]

McCutcheon, too, strongly opposes the mixing of worlds; of bringing humanist or theological methodologies into the academic study of religion. For him, theological methodologies are all too common, and should not be dominant in academia where the scientific methodology must be upheld. McCutcheon notes that since insiders usually go about their business, "fully immersed in their particular meaning/behavior world," the emic perspective (designated as insider) may actually be the outsider's *description* of the insider's voice: "the emic or insider perspective might better be understood as the outsider's attempt to reproduce as faithfully as possible—in a word, to *describe*—what might be considered to be the informant's own descriptions of his or her production of sounds, behavior, beliefs, meanings, institutions etc., should they offer such an account . . ."[29]

In contrast, McCutcheon contends that the etic perspective (designated as the outsider) refers to an observer's *redescription* of emic voices: "the etic perspective is the observer's subsequent attempt to take their own descriptive information (emic) and to organize, systematize and compare—in a word, to *redescribe*—it in terms of a system of the scholar's own making . . . What should be clear, then, is that the emic and the etic perspective are deeply intertwined."[30]

This is to say that while scholars of religion are urged to be faithful in adequately describing the emic perspective of religious communities/people, it is not enough. They also look to make connections beyond theology (of God's relevance to a community), to other issues like the nature of community itself.[31]

---

25. Ibid., 33.
26. Wiebe, *The Politics of Religious Studies*, 286.
27. Wiebe, *The Irony of Theology*, 174.
28. Ibid., 175.
29. McCutcheon, *Studying Religion*, 51.
30. Ibid.
31. Ibid., 56.

McCutcheon is arguing for the legitimacy of an academic method of religion, and he critiques theology in secular academia because it attempts to mix two distinct methodologies. The debate of whether we agree with the separation of theological methodology for secular academics or not, however, is not the focus of this study. Rather, the focus is on how theologians, writing/speaking within a theological space, should talk about religion.

McCutcheon, and others, can be seen to offer, through reverse logic, an approach to determine a theory of religion within the *theological* context. Wiebe for instance rightly argues that genuine Christian theology must prioritize faith and cannot look to exist, without conflict, within the objective scientific method that prioritizes reason.[32] Similarly, while McCutcheon states that emic perspectives are those by outsiders who attempt to describe the experiences of the actual participants, he does not discount the possibility that some participants (insiders) may want to enter the emic space to attempt descriptions for themselves and for others. The insider approach to religion allows Christians to understand themselves as a religion, and thus understand others (outsiders) from within that self-description. In effect, the correct space for developing a definition of religion for theologians is the theological space. Further, the norms of theology will help determine how the definitions are constructed and made relevant.

The God–Human Connection: Beyond Behavior and Discourse

While we can agree with McCutcheon that religion is a constructed category, it remains to be seen what shape the construction should take. Theological norms should guide theologians; however, there is also a need to be aware of theoretical standpoints that could be helpful for theological construction. One such theory of religion comes from Martin Riesebrodt, who offers an integrated view of religion and, more importantly, asserts that religion must be found in the God–human connection.

Riesebrodt takes into account the various problems within the theories of religion by offering a blended solution. He is aware of what he calls the postmodern critique of religion that correctly draws attention to the dangers of universalizing historically particularist ideas that lead to a misunderstanding of non-Western cultures.[33] However, dissatisfied with the postmodern critique,[34] he argues for a religion that is not simply a discursively produced concept (theology/doctrines/beliefs) but is a type

---

32. Wiebe, *The Irony of Theology*, 175–76.
33. Riesebrodt, *The Promise of Salvation*, 15.
34. Ibid., 15–19.

of meaningful action that exists in social action and relations.[35] Agreeing in principle with the classification approach, he nevertheless states that the "universal concept of religion represents a legitimate form of science fiction so long as it takes up fundamental facts of human action and social relations without making their specific shaping part of the definition."[36] Therefore, while "religion ... is not an empirically accessible object," it can only be studied "in its concrete forms and practices" such as "concrete actions, religious ideas, institutions, and communities—that is, historically and culturally concrete religions."[37]

Like Strenski's "common sense" starting point of religion, Riesebrodt too accepts an "everyday understanding of religion" to build a theory of religion.[38] In addition, Riesebrodt strongly emphasizes the meaning of and in religious action. However, Riesebrodt goes on to propose that religion is a type of social action that is differentiated for other types of social action—it is a complex of meaningful practices and actions which is situated in a systematic and specific web of meaning that is related to personal or impersonal superhuman powers.[39] This is to say that religion is differentiated from nonreligion by those actions that are related to superhuman powers and those that are not.[40] Founded on the premise that life is in perpetual crisis that is beyond the control of human beings, these religious actions are the culturally prescribed means to access superhuman powers for the promise of salvation that all religions naturally provide.[41] He states,

> Religion's promise ... remains astonishingly constant in different historical periods and cultures. Religions promise to ward off misfortune, to help cope with crises, and to provide salvation. Religions are less about 'the holy' than about blessings, salvation, and protection from misfortune, as well as about the providers and mediators of salvation. However, my theory does not represent an "essential definition" of religion. It does not seek to prove that all religions are "ultimately" the same, but rather to make it possible to compare them in relation to a structure of meaning that underlies them.[42]

35. Ibid., 21.
36. Ibid.,18.
37. Ibid.
38. Ibid., 74.
39. Ibid., 71–72.
40. Ibid.,171.
41. Ibid.,75, 181–82.
42. Ibid., xiii.

Riesebrodt identifies three types of religious practices, though he gives priority to the first one, namely "interventionist practices."[43] Interventionist practices refer to the actions of worship, and are further subdivided into four types of actions.[44] Actions that establish contact with superhuman powers—like prayers, chants, vows, sacrifices—are differentiated from actions that attempt to manipulate deities using magic or mantras.[45] Mystical trances and ascetic ecstasy are actions that suggest temporary interaction and are differentiated from actions that activate superhuman potential, such as self-empowerment and enlightenment.[46]

The second type of religious practices is the category of "discursive practices" which "hand down and revise religious knowledge concerning interventionist practices and stand in a dialectical relationship to that knowledge."[47] These are the theological voices in the religion, which are not the central feature of religion, but rather help interpret and explain the interventionist practices, which are.[48]

The third type of religious practices are the "behavior-regulating practices," which relate to the "reshaping of everyday life" and are concerned with the ethical behavior of the community.[49] Pertaining mainly to the do's and don'ts of a religion, like diet, hairstyle, and how to treat one another, they help regulate behavior. These practices can overlap with interventionist practices when, for instance, "intensive study of the sacred texts" is interpreted as a "form of religious service."[50] However, they are never in the same order as interventionist practices, which remain the "key to explaining religion."[51]

Riesebrodt notes that theories of religion tend to focus primarily on the latter two practices, either discursive or behavior regulating. A focus on the discursive (theology) leads to an emphasis on the doctrines of religion, which also leads to the privileging of the intellectual-cognitive side of religion.[52] A focus on behavior regulating practices leads to an emphasis upon

---

43. Ibid., 75.
44. Ibid.
45. Ibid.
46. Ibid.
47. Ibid.
48. Ibid., 86.
49. Ibid., 76.
50. Ibid.
51. Ibid., 76.
52. Ibid., 82.

the ethical subjectivist aspects of religion, where there is not much reflection on the modes of behavior or even on why something is being done.[53]

Riesebrodt recommends that a theory of religion must provide a "better connection between belief and practice."[54] His alternative is to privilege the interventionist practices, the actual worship of the community, as the focus of a theory of religion.[55] He does this for several reasons, not the least because this approach is neither functionalist nor essentialist. He opts for a focus on the worship of the community, because the most visible practices of the community are not in its theological ideals or even its ethical norms, but in the day-to-day interaction of life and superhuman powers.[56]

With this methodological reorientation, Riesebrodt asserts his cosmographical schema: humanity is confronted with unsolvable crises that require people to reach out to the promise of salvation offered in all religion.[57] This reaching out is played out in the worship of the community, best observed in the liturgy, which is broadly defined as the "institutionalized rules and scripts" that guide human interaction with superhuman powers, as it expresses and dramatises interventionist action.[58] Riesebrodt proposes that the liturgy, across cultures, is centerd on the expression of the need for salvation that is promised by religion.[59] Importantly, it provides a truer picture of what religion is:

> The meaning of religion, as expressed in the language of liturgies and prayer books, is clear ... And it is this language, not the language of the discourse of the intellectuals, that religious practitioners speak ... It is the language of liturgy that unites priests and laymen, intellectuals and farmers, workers and officials, and even doubters and unbelievers. Liturgies overlie subjective meanings in order to produce a generally binding symbolism and language that is recited, preached and sung. This language of liturgy is not the least of the things that every generation learns anew.[60]

Riesebrodt thus concludes that the center of all religion is the promise of salvation and the act of gaining access to that salvation. The other acts of

53. Ibid., 79–84.
54. Ibid., 82.
55. Ibid., 84.
56. Ibid., 92.
57. Ibid., 153.
58. Ibid., 84, 86, 117.
59. Ibid., 100.
60. Ibid., 117.

religion, the theological and the ethical, are only subsets of the primary act of religion as worship.

I find Riesebrodt's division of religion into three types of actions—interventionist, discursive and behavior regulating—useful for the Christian theological view of religion. Riesebrodt also rightly gives interventionist actions priority, stating that the center of religion lies in the worship of the community. Riesebrodt even allows behavior regulating practices to overlap with interventionist practices, especially if they are done in relation to the superhuman powers within the promise of salvation. Thus I offer that, using Riesebrodt's own logic, even discursive practices can be subsumed within interventionist practices, if the same principle that governs interventionist actions governs discursive (theological) action as well. Through this reassessment, doing theology can also be seen as an act of worship. Riesebrodt's view of liturgy or worship has to do with the practices associated with institutional meaning, especially the promise of salvation. Worship is that act which participates in the religious calling of the community, where contact is sought (and hopefully made) with the superhuman powers.

In Christian terms, Riesebrodt's theory of liturgy would mean instances where a Christian or a group of Christians participates in acts that are governed by the meaning of Christian sources/institutions. They would be geared to draw people towards God, so that they could gain access to salvation, implying a more sacramental idea. While attempting to access the promise of God's salvation, these acts would be repeatable, and be repeated. It is thus a positive view of religious action, and is determined by its conformity to institutional meaning.

Riesebrodt's theory allows for religions to be seen as holistic action that includes dogma, without giving dogma intellectual precedence. His integrated vision of religion offers Christian theologians a theoretical framework from which to understand religion. However, Riesebrodt's theory is not sufficient and a theologian must also look to biblical and theological witness to formulate a theology of religion.

Summary of Theoretical Discussion

We thus see three proposals from McCutcheon and Riesebrodt, which not only affirm Chenchiah's earlier hunch about religion, but clarify and extend it. We are offered not simply a dual theory of religion, but also a theory that suggests the possibility for the emic space to construct meaning. This allows a community to reshape the concept of religion to suit its needs. Chenchiah misses this latter aspect and largely constructs his theory of religion as an individual, and sometimes antagonistically against the larger Christian tradition. In fact, by prioritizing his own experience of Christ as the foundation for a theory of religion, Chenchiah loses out on the possibilities of using other Christian experiences of Christ. A more community oriented approach to theoretical and theological construction would certainly help.

Similarly, Chenchiah was on the right track when he suggested that religion was beyond doctrines, creeds and institutions. For Chenchiah, the connection with Christ and the Holy Spirit transformation were paramount. One can see how Riesebrodt's theory of "interventionist practices" would resonate with Chenchiah's own concern. However, Chenchiah rejected doctrines and behavior regulating practices in favor of direct experience. What Chenchiah failed to recognize was that the construction of creeds and the rituals of the institution could possibly be done through the larger rubric of interventionist practices. If all institutional actions were genuinely done in honor of God, and empowered by the Spirit to express the union between God and man, then we would have true religion—and true worship. To understand this concept of religion, and subsequently religion as worship, we turn to a biblical engagement.

BIBLICAL RELIGION: TRADITIONS AND BELIEFS IN RESPONSE TO GOD

We have already seen in the second chapter that there was a strong link between Christianity and the concept of religion, even if there was a significant divergence in its meaning after the Enlightenment. In this section we return to the foundational Christian text, to discover what reconstruction of the meaning of religion is possible within it, despite the lack of the word religion. In particular we look at how biblical scholars engage with the concept of religion, particularly in the Old Testament. Then, we turn to the New Testament to study the Greek words which have been translated as religion in English. Relatedly, we look at religion from the point of view of insiders (Jas 1:26–27) and of outsiders (Acts 17). The point that emerges is that religion, as seen from the Bible, is far from being an idealistic, belief-oriented concept. Rather, it is much more broadly conceived as an interplay of practices and belief, as determined by and in reverence to God.

Religion and Biblical Studies: History, Theology and Anti-institutionalization

In this section I look at biblical scholars who engage with the concept of religion. Two points emerge. First, it is best not to dichotomize between cultic practices and theological beliefs when thinking of biblical religion. Second, biblical religion exists in a dual mode, of being able to critique its own religious institutions (cultic practices) while still existing within a religious framework. Both ideas serve to inform the discussion we drew from Chenchiah, of religion as integrated action as well as religion as anti-institutional.

Historical and Theological Approaches to the Old Testament

Typically, biblical scholars have engaged with religion from either a historical or theological perspective. This is to say, scholars have focused on religion by focusing on the historical (visible) cultic practices of the community as seen through history. In contrast, other scholars have seen the religion of a community to mean the beliefs or doctrines of the community, as if the historical cultic practices were less important. A few recent scholars rightly see that there is no divide between the two and look for the theology of the community within the historical practices.

Over the past two centuries, the dominant way of looking at religion in the Bible has been through the history of religions approach, which has been expressed through the negation of the theological voices in the Bible. The history of religions approach, referred to as *Religionsgeschichte*, is associated with the coupling of the study of religions with historical criticism, to reconstruct "plausible understandings of ancient Israelite religion and early Judaism."[61] Mead asserts that the "ascendancy of [the history of religions] movement was accompanied by a corresponding decrease in scholarly attention to biblical theology."[62] In particular, Mead notes that the history of religions approach differed from the theological approach in three important ways. First, history of religions focused on the cultic practices as expressions of religious beliefs rather than on the content of the beliefs per se (theology).[63] Second, the method of the school was "developmental

---

61. Perdue, *Reconstructing Old Testament Theology*, 25.
62. Mead, *Biblical Theology*, 34.
63. Ibid., 35.

and comparative," aiming to study the evolution of those cultic practices.[64] Third, the research was descriptive rather than normative.[65]

Barr notes that there is some confusion regarding this use of religion as method, where the study of religion moves between "comparative religions," "history of religions" and the "scientific study of religion."[66] Regardless, these approaches are associated with objectivity and reject theological approaches to the Bible. Thus history of religions' scholars would reject attempts to see the biblical text in terms of its themes, theological assertions, or even progressive (teleological) history.

Zevit asserts that the Israelite religion is evident only in the culture and practices of a community.[67] He argues that the theological approach "tends to be synchronically flat" and incapable of understanding the real religion of the people of Israel.[68] In addition, Zevit attempts a study of Israelite religion from within its own context and through other surrounding religions.[69] Zevit goes on to identify certain key methods to address religion: "Israelite religion is most approachable through its manifestations in physical evidence in archaeological excavations that have uncovered cultic artefacts and cultic structures. Other sources of information are inscriptions and drawings found in excavations. All need interpretation, but each source can be interpreted only through the hermeneutics developed in the specialized discipline concerned with it, that is, archaeology and palaeography."[70]

Therefore for Zevit, the Bible is only one source of information, that too within the "historical-philological perspective."[71]

Martin Noth's *The Old Testament World* is another typical example of how OT scholars have used religion, where religion is a universal category that helps make the OT world clearer.[72] Noth identifies religion in a typically modern sense and proposes that the ancient Near East supplies ample religious source materials that help comprehend the "background for the Old Testament."[73] These source materials include religious texts used

---

64. Ibid.
65. Ibid.
66. Barr, *The Concept of Biblical Theology*, 100.
67. Zevit, *The Religions of Ancient Israel*, xiii.
68. Ibid.
69. Ibid., xiii, 23–27.
70. Ibid., 79–80.
71. Ibid.
72. Noth, *The Old Testament World*, 278.
73. Ibid.

within a cultic framework, such as hymns and prayers to the gods.[74] Even texts that are not overtly religious, like royal inscriptions, laws, epics, etc, are shown to "contain some material affecting the history of religion."[75] Archaeology draws attention to other religious source materials that aid in the "understanding of ancient religions."[76] These include the "remains of cultic structures, such as temples, and cultic equipment, such as altars . . . representations of deities . . . divine symbols etc."[77]

An alternative method to the history of religions approach is the biblical theology approach, which has "generally searched for a thematic unity in the midst of diversity in the canon along the lines of themes or traditions."[78] Mead notes that in the mid-twentieth century, which has also been referred to as the "golden age of biblical theology," the mood changed significantly towards theological approaches to the Bible.[79]

Gerhard von Rad, for instance, asserts that OT scholarship has abandoned the (false) opposition between the "religion of the prophets" and the "cultic religion of the priests."[80] This would suggest that the ideology (theology) of the prophets must be seen within the context of the cultic practices of the priests. Furthermore, von Rad goes on to distinguish the Israelite *religion* from other *religions* particularly through Israel's theology— "[Israel's] own peculiar religious ideas" that included "an entirely different *understanding* of the divine beneficent action."[81] von Rad also talks about the Israelite "faith" and how it interpreted (or even constructed) history.[82] In that sense, von Rad uses "faith" the way others would use "religious" history. In one instance, von Rad admits to the problem of religion, and states that there is no such thing as a "religion of Israel," by which von Rad means an abstracted faith entity: "A world of religious concepts later systematically arranged is of course an abstraction, for such a thing never existed in Israel in so complete and universal a way. So too the idea of a 'religion of Israel,' that is, the idea of the faith as an entity, appears more problematical still as a result of the investigation of the history of tradition in our own time

---

74. Ibid.
75. Ibid.
76. Ibid., 279.
77. Ibid.
78. Perdue, *Reconstructing Old Testament Theology*, 25.
79. Mead, *Biblical Theology*, 46.
80. Von Rad, *Old Testament Theology*, vol. 2, 5.
81. Ibid., 112.
82. Von Rad, *Old Testament Theology*, vol. 1, 105–15.

... Religious thought cannot be separated out from these traditions and represented thus in abstract."[83]

This statement, in the context of von Rad's critique of the dominance of the historical approach that discounts the theology of Israel, is a call for mutuality between theology and history.

Similarly, Walter Eichrodt clarifies that history has to do with the "genetic understanding of Old Testament religion in the interplay of historical forces" and theology "should illumine the entire dynamic content of the religion according to its internal structure."[84] To do this, theology "has no tools other than the history of religion . . . it proceeds from the same subjective presuppositions . . ."[85] Nevertheless, Eichrodt also argues for the need of the theological perspective "if one wants to penetrate to [the] center of the Old Testament, rather than remain on its periphery."[86] Thus, he calls for an understanding of the theology in the history.[87]

A stronger relation between theology and religion is seen in Brevard Childs. While his use of the word religion is negligible, there is a clear association between religion and theology, expressed in his canonical approach. He asserts that the canonical approach "reckons with the fact that Israel bore witness to its encounter with God in actual time and space, and yet registered its testimony in a text through a complex multilayered manner which far transcends the categories of ordinary historical discourse."[88] Thus, the two aspects of Israel's history and faith are "held together in a subtle balance within the shape of the canon."[89] For Childs, the cultic and legal stipulations are always put within a larger interpretative context, especially one that ultimately transcends cultic terminology.[90]

Barr is correct to note that OT theologies can also include "synchronic and holistic descriptions" and there is no need to assert that "history of religions" is more historical than "biblical theology."[91] The difference, Barr finds, is that the history of religions approach tends to focus on "all the forms and aspects of all human religions"[92] whereas "theology tends to be concerned

---

83. Ibid., 112.
84. Eichrodt, "Does Old Testament Theology," 27.
85. Ibid.
86. Ibid., 22.
87. Ibid., 28.
88. Childs, *Old Testament Theology*, 16.
89. Ibid.
90. Ibid., 89–90.
91. Barr, *The Concept of Biblical Theology*, 100.
92. Particularly with the discovery of the ancient Near East worlds and their

with the truth-claims of one religion and especially with its authoritative texts and traditions and their interpretation."[93] Nevertheless, OT scholars tend to over emphasize the difference between theological and historical approaches. When the concept of religion is used, it is either coupled with theology or with history. In addition, Barr also points out that the positive contribution theology makes is the recognition of the religious character of biblical study, especially in drawing attention to the factors in history that go beyond the social, economic and political forces.[94] Nevertheless, for Barr, a good theologian recognizes that social, economic and political forces do indeed influence the formation of theology. The religions approach, therefore, is more mindful of the historical forces, and the theological approach is more mindful of the ideology. For Barr, both must recognize each other's value.

This leads us to Velduis' caution that when looking at ancient cultures, religion must be viewed as something much broader and integrated, through real-world actions as well as through textual/academic reflection. His study of Mesopotamian religion offers a helpful paradigm of how history of religions could inform theological interpretations of biblical religion.[95]

What becomes evident is that a focus on either the cultic practices (historical) or the beliefs (theological) is too limiting and a view of religion as integrated is necessary. The historical and theological approaches should not be seen in opposition to each other. The OT shows a strong link between the cultic performance of the people of Israel and their beliefs. Both action and theology get importance in the scriptures.

Israelite Religion as Israelite Worship

The historical-theological approach has drawn out two further aspects when looking at OT "religion." The first is to see the Israelite cult as its worship. The second, which we will see in the next subsection, is to see the critique of religion from religion.

Albrecht Alt proposes that "the people of Israel came into existence because their tribes were united in the worship of the god Yahweh."[96] Alt goes on to call this worship the "religion of Yahweh."[97] Alt denies that the

significance as religions for understanding the Israelite religion.
  93. Barr, *The Concept of Biblical Theology*, 101.
  94. Ibid., 110.
  95. Veldhuis, *Religion, Literature and Scholarship*, 16.
  96. Alt, *Essays on Old Testament History*, 3.
  97. Ibid., 4.

cult defined the worship of Yahweh.[98] He offers instead a "primary relationship between the figures of the patriarchs and the cult of the gods of the Fathers," which links the revelation and the promise of Yahweh with posterity and Promised Land, as the key elements in the religion of Yahweh.[99] Alt notes that the OT writers "go out of their way to link the theme of the divine choice and promise" with their God.[100] Since God is shown to be the "guide and guardian,"[101] the cult is defined by the theology.

Augustine Pagolu has pointed out several problems in Alt's thesis,[102] but my point is to note Alt's equation of religion with the worship of the people of Israel. Pagolu himself identifies the 'patriarchal religion' in terms of its worship *and* cultic practices, as seen through the narratives.[103] Pagolu identifies patriarchal worship through altars, prayer, and pillars, while the cultic (religious) practices are evidenced through tithes, vows and purification.[104] Pagolu goes on to note that these acts of worship and cultic practices were linked to the Israelite belief in (and relationship to) their family God, to the extent that the cultic method and significance of their worship and practices were flexible.[105] Pagolu concludes that "the patriarchal religious practices are compatible with their worship pattern and their belief in a family God who went along with them wherever they went."[106] While confusion remains over worship and cult, the mixture of theology with practices leads to a concept akin to the "worship of the community," where belief in God governs the actions for God. This worship of the community is thus seen as its religion.

Religion against Religion in the Old Testament

The second aspect highlighted by the historical-theological approach is the critique of religion from religion. Childs sees no priority between the theology and the cultic practices of the people of Israel, because even the

---

98. Ibid., 6–10.
99. Ibid., 63.
100. Ibid., 64.
101. Ibid., 65.
102. Pagolu, *The Religion of the Patriarchs*, 16–18.
103. Ibid., 243.
104. Ibid.
105. Ibid., 243–46.
106. Ibid., 247.

prophetic critique of the priests is a religious critique.[107] Within this frame, Childs goes on to point out the "massive prophetic criticism of Israel's cult" from a theological standpoint of God's absolute sovereignty.[108] Examples of this are Isaiah's condemnation of "excessive cultic activity" towards a call for "justice" or Amos who "testifies that God hates feasts and sacrifices which do not affect the increase in justice."[109] Childs summarizes that "The chief theological point to be made is that the canon has contained within itself a major critique, not just of cultic religion, but of religion in general. The attack is grounded in a vision of God which renders totally inoperative all human response seeking to merit God's favor. The inability to respond to the will of a righteous and holy God serves to relativize all institutions of the covenant and throw Israel directly upon divine mercy."[110]

Childs thus correctly draws attention to the prophetic critique of religious systems, and also rightly notes that this is a religious critique.

Similar to Childs, Barr argues for a strong relation between theology and religion, noting there is need for coexistence.[111] Barr feels that the distinction between religion and theology is often simply a "trick with words" for "talking about God, witnessing to one's God, telling of his mighty acts, expounding Christology and the like, are not something other than religion: they are precisely what we mean by 'religion,' or at least part of it."[112] Barr notes for instance that Barth's critique of religion is itself a religious critique.[113]

Significantly, while theology was a part of the cultic performance of Israel, it was also the way the people of Israel were able to transcend their cultic activity and critique it. This critique was not purely a theological critique, but was seen as a (cultic) religious practice through the lives and words of the prophets. We see that though biblical writers were critical of those cultic practices that could have been understood as religious, they were also functioning within religion while doing so, implying a critique of religion from religion.

---

107. Childs states, "The prophets were not free-floating individualists, but usually belonged to a prophetic guild. Many of their well-known attacks on sacrifice and ritual ... appear now to be ad hoc formulations within an invective and directed to certain abuses, but were not ideologically based on an anti-cultic principle." Childs, *Old Testament Theology*, 173.

108. Childs, *Old Testament Theology*, 90.

109. Ibid.

110. Ibid.

111. Barr, *The Concept of Biblical Theology*, 139.

112. Ibid., 109.

113. Ibid.

From a theological standpoint, Tillich remarks that Christianity must hold on to the ambiguity of religion at precisely this point:

> The Christian message is the message of the end of religion; but as a message it is religious itself. Jesus did not announce the coming of a new religion, but he announced that the Kingdom of God, i.e. a 'new' all embracing reality is at hand. He minimized the laws of religion in the power of the Kingdom of God which was present in his person. Jesus emphasized the daily life duties over the ritual duties. He 'envisaged' the end of the temple and its cult. He attacked the representatives of religion and called secular people as disciples. He preached a God who is related to every act of our ordinary life, internal as well as external, and he devaluated the extraordinary acts of religion in the narrow sense. Since God was his only concern he had no religion besides his daily life.[114]

Thus Tillich urges that the Church must affirm "Divine Sovereignty over the institutions and doctrines of the Christian churches and protest against the attempts to bind the Christian message to the life and law of any historical Church."[115] At the same time, Tillich warns against a total negation that leads to complete emptiness of any "concrete content."[116] Only by holding faithfulness and critique together, Tillich suggests, can the true message of (Christian) religion be upheld.[117]

Returning to Chenchiah, we saw in the previous two chapters that Chenchiah's strong detraditionalization led him to prioritize history over beliefs and doctrines. In effect, his theory of religion, especially of true religion, promoted a transformed ethical life and not one that was held together by theology or even doctrinal truths. However, in relation to the Bible and theology, Chenchiah's view of integrated religion could have drawn more from biblical and theological witness. An integrated approach allows religion, drawn from the Bible, to be viewed as an activity, with religious effect being more important than the actual expression of religion in the cultural sphere. In addition, Chenchiah's critique of religion resonates with the prophetic critiques of temple religion. However, there is a sense of religion that Chenchiah misses. As we saw in the biblical discussion above, beliefs are as important as actions. This is to say, religion is a combination of beliefs and praxis, without the negation of either.

114. Tillich, "Protestant Principles," 248–49.
115. Ibid., 250.
116. Ibid.
117. Ibid., 250–51.

Word Study: Retranslating 'Religion'

We now move on to the New Testament, to study a few words related to religion. As I pointed out in Chapter One, there is no word like the English word for 'religion' in the biblical texts in their original languages. However, this has not stopped English translators, of either the LXX (especially in the Apocrypha) or the NT, from using 'religion' or "religious" to represent certain ideas. Keeping in mind that 'religion' is a category with a history, where current meanings cannot be imposed onto NT writers and readers, a reading of 'religion' at least as "tradition" (probably cultic) could be assumed. Buell finds that the original terms used for religion "are concretely related to how one lives and what one does" and so they "cannot be interpreted as only pertaining to belief or faith."[118] A more appropriate translation of these Greek words could be "practices, traditions" or "piety, being pious"—concepts that need not indicate an overarching idea that the modern word for religion suggests.

The most popular English translations of the OT do not have any mention of the word "religion." However, the English translations of the Septuagint (LXX) have a few references. For instance, Brenton's English translation of the LXX has the phrase "the *religious* of them" (2 Chron 5:6).[119] The Greek word in the LXX is φοβούμενοι, translated also as "the [God] fearing." In the Hebrew text, there is no idea of God-fearing or "fearing" and instead the "whole congregation" (וְכָל־עֲדַת) is implied. Similarly, the English translation of Prov 28:14 in the LXX refers to the man "who religiously fears," with the Greek word εὐλάβεια suggesting "Godly fear, reverence." However, in Hebrew, the word מְפַחֵד only suggests fear without a "religious" adjective.

In the Apocrypha, a few other words are used to suggest religion for English translators. In 1 Macc 1:43 we have the idea where the people "gladly adopted his *religion*; they sacrificed to idols and profaned the sabbath." Here, the word for religion is λατρεία, which can be translated as "service, worship, ritual duties." λατρεία is used again in 1 Macc 2:19 to show "everyone of them abandoning the *religion* of their ancestors." Second Macc 6:24 refers to "an alien *religion*" or even to "a strange religion," and uses the Greek word ἀλλοφυλισμὸν, which also possibly implies the adoption of "foreign customs."[120] In 3 Macc 1:3, "a Jew by birth who later changed his *religion* and apostatized from the ancestral traditions," is translated from the word

---

118. Buell, *Why This New Race*, 60.

119. The translations of the Greek words used here are drawn from BibleWorks 7.0, unless otherwise indicated.

120. Hastings, "Religion," 225. Hastings affirms that the thought of 'religion' in the Bible refers primarily to the "outward forms" rather than the "inner spirit."

νόμιμα, which suggests "statutes, laws, commandments," though the context suggests the cultic practices surrounding the law. Importantly, none of these words suggest a system of beliefs; rather they point to a combination of traditions and cultic practices. In fact, Boyarin rightly clarifies that when Ιουδαισμος appears in 2 Macc 8:14, "it doesn't mean Judaism the religion but the entire complex of loyalties and practices that mark off the people of Israel."[121] Boyarin adds that "Jewish writers do not identify themselves with and by that name at all, until . . . the nineteenth century."[122]

There are a few words that have been translated as religion or religious in the New Testament. For instance we have δεισιδαιμονεστέρους ("religious" in NRSV) is used in Acts 17:22 and δεισιδαιμονία ('religion' in NRSV), in Acts 25:19. Martin notes the debate among scholars over the meaning of this word and states that δεισιδαιμονία could mean either "religion/religious," "piety" or "superstition."[123] Thus, even if we were to interpret the word as religion, the sense of "traditions" rather than the sense of "belief in supernatural things" could be implied. However, a strong case has been made, especially by Barrett, to view δεισιδαιμονία negatively, as superstition,[124] or at least, as Martin would allow, for an intentional double meaning.

The other word translated as religion is εὐσέβεια which in its singular genitive form, the NRSV translates as 'religion' in 1 Tim 3:16, and as "godliness" in 2 Timothy 3:5. The singular dative form of εὐσέβεια is also translated as "godliness" in the NRSV (Acts 3:12, 1 Tim 2:2, 4:8, 6:6, 2 Pet 1:7). Judge comments that "godliness" is the more "common sense" interpretation of εὐσέβεια,[125] even as most other major English translations have chosen godliness over religion.

In John 9:31 θεοσεβὴς and in 1 Tim 2:10 θεοσέβειαν are used to give the sense of "God fearing." Both words come from θεοσέβεια, which became a common word for piety in early Christian writing. Barclay does not find much difference between θεοσέβεια and εὐσέβεια, saying that εὐσέβεια is right worship or "the rightness of the reverence, its freedom from superstitions and imperfections and improprieties" while θεοσέβεια can refer to the

---

121. Boyarin, "The Christian Invention of Judaism," 21.
122. Ibid.
123. Martin, *Inventing Superstition*, 5–8.
124. Barrett, *The International Critical Commentary*, 828–35.
125. Judge, *The First Christians in the Roman World*, 405.

"worship of God."[126] Early Christian writers began to use θεοσέβεια to refer to "true worship."[127]

Then there is λατρεία, which is translated as 'religion' in the Apocrypha (1 Macc 1:43 and 2:19), but is invariably translated as "service," "worship," or even "ritual duties" in the NT (Rom 9:4; Heb 9:1, 6). Betz finds that, in its verbal form, λατρεύω defines a service to God, emphasizing ritual worship and ethics, especially in contrast to "pagan polytheism."[128]

In addition, the Vulgate uses the Latin *religio* and its derivatives eight times—Acts 2:5; 10:2; 13:50; 26:5; Col. 2:18 and Jas 1:26–27, a fact which, to Griffiths, points to its lack of importance.[129]

Another word used in the NT to designate religion is θρησκεία, which is used in at least two separate ways. In one instance, in Acts 26:5, ὅτι κατὰ τὴν ἀκριβεστάτην αἵρεσιν τῆς ἡμετέρας θρησκείας ἔζησα Φαρισαῖος is translated as "that I have belonged to the strictest sect of our religion and lived as a Pharisee" by the NRSV. It can, in contrast, also suggest "our traditions." The other instance of θρησκεία is found in Jas 1:26–27. The words θρησκὸς and θρησκεία have meanings closer to ritual or even piety, but were translated in English to mean "religious" and "religion."

Evidently, biblical translators have incorporated concepts like worship, piety, and traditions under the umbrella term for religion and its derivative religious. It is also apparent that Bible translators have begun with a theory of religion that refers to religion as "worship, piety, and traditions." This uncritical theory of religion is rarely challenged and is instead used wholeheartedly by theologians.

Interestingly, despite the problems facing the concept of religion, Hans Dieter Betz makes a case for the use of the New Testament to inform academic definitions of religion.[130] He notes that "within the New Testament . . . several authors have made serious attempts to self-define Christian religion as they have understood it."[131] Which is to say, biblical authors not only express "their own religious experiences and ideas in their writings," they also look at their own religious experiences in an objective way as religion.[132] While Betz does agree that the exact concept of religion does not occur, he

126. Barclay, *New Testament Words*, 112.

127. Bertram, *"theosebes, theosebeia,"* in Kittel, *Theological Dictionary of the New Testament*, vol 1, 331.

128. Betz, "Christianity as Religion," 320.

129. Griffiths, "Religion," 672.

130. Betz, "Christianity as Religion," 315–44.

131. Ibid., 316.

132. Ibid.

finds that insofar as Paul views his 'worship in a 'polytheistic context'—for instance from the phrase, ὁ θεός, ω̣̃ λατρεύω "God, whom I worship" (Rom 1:9)—there is a sense that the concept of religion must also be drawn from biblical writers.[133] Betz brings his own sense of religion to prevail as he looks at the biblical text. However, he rightly notes how the text clarifies or even challenges his notion of religion. The concept of religion that emerges from Betz forms a theological construct to understand Paul and his context. Paul is seen as religious, and while promoting his religion he is also promoting clarity about religion. The concept of religion that Paul is shown to clarify is the Christian "tradition" of worship in a context where other traditions of worship exist.

Thus, a case can be clearly made that a 'biblical religion' can be conceived as including both about belief and action. While there is no word that denotes 'religion' in the sense of a 'system of beliefs and practices.' the words used to denote religion were used by practitioners who sought primarily to understand and promote a certain life with God. In fact, a broad use of 'worship' could just as well be a better translation for the words used for 'religion.'

Beyond Belief and Action: Religion for Insiders and Outsiders

Evident from the discussion so far is that the concept of religion is being broadened to include a strong performative aspect. This implies that visible acts that have their meanings drawn from God are also acts directed to God. As we saw in the previous section, each word that is translated as religion or religious in the Bible actually suggests something other than only a belief—it suggests an act or attitude expressed in action. It is thus unfair to label the biblical discourse in ideological/theological terms without taking into account the strong cultic framework that drew its meaning and purpose from that theology. Gealy rightly identifies religion in the Bible to mean practices of "(proper) religious observances or patterns of worship" as well as the "recognized structure of religious-ethical behavior," as opposed to its present meaning of "a system of doctrine, an organization, an approved pattern of behavior and form of worship."[134] He points to the alien nature of the concept of religion, by saying, "The infrequent use of 'religion' in the Bible is due to the fact that the concept of 'religion' is itself alien to the core of biblical thought [which employs faith]. The basic meaning of faith to the Hebrew is the concrete response of the whole man to God's call and obedi-

---

133. Ibid., 321.
134. Gealy, "Religion," 32.

ence to his command, not intellectual acceptance of a body of truth or even correct observance of special cultic acts. Primary for faith is man's relation to God, not his relation to faith structure or cult practice."[135]

Gealy goes on to assert that even though the concept of religion is alien to the Bible, there was an evident shift taking place from a Hebrew understanding of faith as the "concrete obedience of the whole man to God" to a more Hellenistic interpretation that focused on an "ecclesiastically approved system of doctrine, worship and behavior."[136] Notably, the recognition of the obedience to God as the marker of religion, and not the following of doctrines, is crucial here.

In this section I highlight two examples from the New Testament to clarify the above point. The first example depicts how a concept of 'religion' can be used for insiders namely in Jas 1:26–27. The second example explores the concept of 'religion' as applied to outsiders, in Acts 17:16–34. In both instances, the biblical text uses concepts that suggest that 'religion' (if we are to use this term) is something broader than simply belief or cultic practices. It suggests an integrated action that has its meaning from, and purpose towards, God.

Religion for Insiders: James 1:26–27

The sense of traditions above beliefs can be seen in Jas 1:26–27. It is quite intriguing and perhaps unfortunate, that modern day English Bible translators chose to translate the words θρησκὸς and θρησκεία found in this passage to "religious" and "religion." The ancient use of θρησκεία, as we have seen, suggested a meaning closer to ritual, traditions or even piety. Yet, even if we take the word as it has been translated, the emphasis of Jas 1:26–27 is still a focus upon religious action in honor of God rather than religious belief.

Huther, writing in the late 1800s, related Jas 1:26–27 to Jas 1:19, where James calls his brothers to be βραδὺς εἰς τὸ λαλῆσαι ("slow to speak").[137] However, significantly, Huther translated θρησκὸς as "serve God" and θρησκεία as "worship," so that his translation of Jas 1:26 read "If any one thinks to serve God, not bridling his tongue, but deceiving his heart, his worship is vain."[138] Huther argued that θρησκεία was not equivalent to εὐσεβεία as in 2 Pet 1:7, because θρησκεία referred to "external worship, the

---

135. Ibid.
136. Ibid.
137. Huther, *Critical and Exegetical Handbook*, 69.
138. Ibid.

manifestation of εὐσέβεια" without the "secondary idea of mere externality."[139] This distinction is important in that θρησκεία as an external εὐσέβεια could be the "outward act of εὐσέβεια" (where εὐσέβεια could be translated as piety), whereas "mere externality" could suggest that θρησκεία was referring to the externals of religion, like rituals, ceremonies, institutionalization and so forth.

More recently, the latter idea of θρησκεία being about the externals of religion has been suggested by Ropes who states that θρησκεία refers to "religious worship, especially, but not exclusively, external, that which consists in ceremonies."[140] Similarly, for Ropes, θρησκὸς suggests "given to religious observances."[141] Other modern interpreters also take this route, including Ralph Martin who adds that James condemns the "picture of the use of the tongue when it utters merely formal religious platitudes that have no substance evidenced by practical deeds."[142] Similarly Martin believes that, for James, θρησκεία had a sense of "worship and belief as expressed in religious observations or profession . . . when it fails to measure up to the standards set in verse 27."[143]

The problem with both Ropes and Martin is that they seem to give too much value to the word θρησκεία without considering a simple reading of the text. Their word study affects the theological meaning of the word, rather than the context of the sentence which determines the meaning of the word. For instance, Martin's view fails to take into account James' strong exhortation against uncontrolled speech. Similarly, Ropes admits that θρησκεία has a "considerable range of meaning," much like the English word "worship," yet he offers little application of this range of meaning in his interpretation.[144]

I find it reasonable to follow Huther, who believes that μὴ χαλιναγωγῶν γλῶσσαν αὐτοῦ (do not bridle their tongues) leads naturally to what θρησκεία would have meant to the readers, namely that James finds fault with those who equate zeal to speak as a sign of θρησκεία (which could read correctly as either "serving God" or 'worship').[145] This can be corresponded with θρησκείᾳ τῶν ἀγγέλων in Col 2:18, which interestingly and without controversy the NRSV translates as the "worship of angels." Furthermore, if we agree with Huther that 1:26 is related to 1:19, and all the more since

139. Ibid.
140. Ropes, *James*, 181.
141. Ibid.
142. Martin, *James*, 52.
143. Ibid.
144. Ropes, *James*, 181.
145. Ibid.

silence/self-control are themes spread across the Epistle, then it is perhaps more appropriate to think of Jas 1:26–27 as not being a study of true and false religion, as if James' purpose was to promote the understanding of the nature of religion. Rather, James must have been didactic, prodding his readers towards positive action/behavior, by showing negative action/behavior and positive action/behavior. Here too, true worship or even true service, would make ample sense.

However, there is another aspect of 'true religion' that merits more discussion. Judge relates this passage with the birth and development of the concept of religion within Christianity. Judge highlights two senses of religion: 1) the obsolete sense, where religion is the "practice of sacred rites and observances," and 2) the modern sense where religion is a "particular system in which the quest for the ideal life has been embodied."[146] This second modern sense, Judge argues, is a concept that is at the heart of Christianity: "any talk of Christianity in antiquity as one of a series of 'religions' is only possible through a historical muddle. Either it converts the ancient 'religions' (in the obsolete sense) into modern-style questing phenomena like Christianity, or it converts ancient Christianity into a ritually observant practice as though it belonged to some established culture as its sacred anchor."[147]

Judge illustrates this by looking at the word θρησκεία in 1 Tim 3:16. While acknowledging that the NIV takes the common sense meaning to suggest godliness, he still prefers the NRS translation that suggests not just religion but "our religion."[148] This is because the sense of θρησκεία is shown to be a 'credal function' unlike the typically cultic function of θρησκεία in other ancient traditions, here it is a quest "driven by doctrine."[149] Similarly, Judge asserts that James is using θρησκεία metaphorically and not in the sense of cultic worship which "transposes the term and challenges existing meanings and opens the way for 'religion' in its modern sense."[150] Furthermore, Judge notes the reinterpretation of λατρεία, a term usually reserved for sacrifices by priests, to mean the "worship in spirit."[151] A classic example being Rom 12:1–2, where Paul speaks of the transformed lifestyle as a λογικὴν λατρείαν (lit. spiritual sacrifice) which constitutes a kind of

---

146. Judge, *The First Christians*, 404.
147. Ibid.
148. Ibid., 405.
149. Ibid.
150. Judge, *The First Christians*, 406.
151. Ibid.

"spiritual worship."[152] Through each comparison, Judge wants to state that this moving away from cultic practices to a universal religious system that was cross-cultural and governed by laws beyond cultic practices, was the first sign of the emergence of the modern sense of religion. Judge concludes that Christianity is not a religion in the obsolete sense, but makes up its very essence in the modern sense: "So was Christianity a religion? Not at all, in the sense we give to that term with regard to ancient cultic practice. Yet it is of the essence of the idea as we now hold it, and which Christianity itself has created. It would be historically clearer, however, in either case, to analyze other cultural traditions first on their own terms."[153]

However, alternative readings to Judge are possible. They point to the more performative readings of the text. This occurs by seeing, firstly, that this passage is not about the definition of religion, but a didactic lesson for the Christian community. Secondly, the focus of the lesson is not simply theology but also theopraxis (godly action).

For instance, when looking at the text from a popular perspective, Watt focuses on the pastoral aspect of visitation. He implies that Jas 1:26–27 speaks directly to a society that "yearns for visitation in the outcry for substantial relationships and a more meaningful faith in this generation."[154] This bypasses the emphasis on understanding pure religion and draws attention to the "act" being recommended.

In addition, noted NT scholar Luke Johnson relates Jas 1:26–27 to the Hellenistic wisdom traditions, where virtue as well as mystery (in a cultic sense), were related to brevity in speech.[155] In that aspect, Johnson seeks to answer the question: "why and how should speech be connected to authentic religion?"[156] He points out the "religious" nature of taciturnity.[157] Johnson notes the contrast between James and the Hellenistic context by remarking upon James' relational reference of speech, where all human speech (and action) is qualified by God's speech (and action).[158] Johnson shows that while James was similar to Hellenistic tradition in connecting speech to virtue and character, unlike his Hellenistic counterparts, James'

152. Ibid.
153. Ibid., 408–9.
154. Watt, "Empowering the Laity," 5.
155. Johnson, *Brother of Jesus*, 157–64.
156. Ibid., 157.
157. Johnson for instance draws attention to the religious legitimization of silence in Hellenistic traditions by the Mystery cults as well as the Delphic Oracles. Johnson, *Brother of Jesus*, 162–64.
158. Ibid., 165–66.

judgment of speech was more severe, especially in contrast to the transcendental reference point.[159] Elsewhere, Johnson explains the contrast between foolish religion and pure religion, through how the measure of the world is contrasted by the measure of God: "Once more, we see the basic contrast between the measure of the world, revealed by a foolish religion that fails to control the tongue and indulges or deceives the heart, and the measure of God, revealed by a pure and undefiled religion that resists the measure of the world and shows its authenticity by giving gifts to the needy in the same way God gives them to all creatures."[160]

Here again, the question is not about what religion is, but rather whether the act is religious or not. The act, in verse 26 is controlled speech and in verse 27 is visiting orphans and widows. The religiosity of the act, in Johnson's terms, is determined by whether it corresponds to God or not.

Robert Wall provides another perspective. He proposes that 'religion' as used in James refers more to the "community's ethical performance rather than its cultic practice."[161] This, he argues, makes sense because "the normative role of the biblical Torah is to guide the sacred community within a profane world."[162] This is to say that the truth of religion would be measured in James not by its institutional norms and rituals but by the actual care it engenders for members of its community.[163] This however is different from inward and outward religion, an idea that Wall does not represent.

Thus, even false religion is judged by the failure of the character standard and not as a judgment of rituals or institutions of religion. The true 'religion' or 'worship' being implied would be, like Riesebrodt suggests, more than simply a discussion or an ethical practice but an actual connection with God, and an act of worship. It is in this sense, where an act is deemed true or worthy on the basis of whether it conforms to God's norms, that a translation for θρησκεία as a broad view of 'worship' (not in a simple cultic sense) is supported.

Religion for Outsiders: Traditional Readings of Acts 17:16–34

For a biblical view of how the category of 'religion' is used with outsiders, theologians have often looked at Acts 17:16–34 as a positive example of the Christian view of other religions. Here I look at the theology of religions

159. Ibid., 165.
160. Johnson, "The Letter of James," 189.
161. Wall, *Community of the Wise*, 100.
162. Ibid.
163. Ibid., 100–101.

that is derived from the passage and then show how a biblical rereading could provide a different interpretation of what religion could be.

Jacques Dupuis depicts an extremely positive picture of Acts 17:16–34. In his discussion of this passage, he points to Paul's "open attitude" towards Gentile religiosity.[164] He comments on how "affirmative" Paul is, and sees clear signs that God has manifested himself through 'nature' and the non-Christians having "a real relationship with God."[165] He notes, "Whatever be the exegetical problems raised by this passage—among others, concerning the Pauline or Lukan authenticity of the discourse—the message surely seems to be that the religions of the nations are not bereft of value but find in Jesus Christ the fulfillment of their aspirations. In comparison with what is offered in Jesus Christ, they seem very spare, but this does not prevent them from being a positive preparation for Christian faith."[166]

Ultimately, Dupuis proposes that in this passage the "Areopagus speech inaugurates a missionary strategy based on a positive approach to the religiosity of the Greeks."[167]

In contrast, Dean Flemming sees in this same passage "the content and method of missionary theologizing."[168] Flemming offers that though this speech affirms the Athenian's "religious aspirations" and "felt needs," Paul "is not simply identifying for them the God they had been honoring all along without realizing it."[169] Flemming continues, "their present condition of idolatrous ignorance must be corrected by a *true* knowledge of God through the proclamation of the gospel."[170] How different these two responses are in both content and tone! While Dupuis follows his agenda of affirming religious belief/systems, Flemming makes a subtle distinction and sees Paul affirming *only* their religious longings.

Ajith Fernando attempts to balance both the negative and the positive views of religion in his study of this passage. He strongly opposes pluralism and rejects the idea that all religions are equal and valid ways to God.[171] At the same time, he wants to be mindful of the positives of religion. Thus, using Paul's encounter with the people of Athens as a model,[172] he proposes

---

164. Dupuis, *Toward a Christian Theology of Religious Pluralism*, 49.
165. Ibid., 52.
166. Ibid., 49.
167. Ibid., 52.
168. Flemming, "Contextualizing the Gospel in Athens," 200.
169. Ibid., 203.
170. Ibid.
171. Fernando, *The Christian's Attitude toward World Religions*, 20–21.
172. For instance, Fernando defends his choice of Acts 17 by saying that "It gives

that non-Christian religions have "glimmerings of truth" and the point of contact for the Christian missionary is to meet non-Christian religions at their highest.[173] Fernando adds to this Paul's call for repentance.[174] The scope of this section limits us to only three aspects in Fernando's study.

Firstly, Fernando rightly depicts Paul as being "greatly distressed" (παρωξύνετο), even horrified, upon seeing the idols in Athens.[175] Yet, Fernando rejects the interpretation of δεισιδαιμονεστέρους as the negative "superstitious" in favor of the positive "religious," to mean people who respect or fear the supernatural.[176] There is an obvious contradiction—how does Paul feel such distress, even anger, upon seeing the idols, and yet commend the Athenians for their faith?

Fernando resolves this by saying that even though Paul was disturbed at first, "he did not show his provocation outwardly ... Instead, he said that he concluded from the observation that 'in every way [they] are very religious.'"[177] Furthermore, this "respect for the supernatural" was "implanted by God."[178] Therefore, Fernando asserts that Paul's first reaction was one that was tempered by a mellowed observation of true longings, that led him to make a controlled defence of the gospel.

Secondly, Fernando offers that the altar to the Unknown God is "evidence of unsatisfied longings."[179] Fernando states, "This altar was an admission by the Athenians that their knowledge of the supernatural was incomplete. Paul used this admission as a launching pad for his description of Jehovah God, who did complete everything. They set up their altar in an attempt to complete everything, but they did not known which god was able to do this. So he was described as unknown. Paul knew the God who completed everything without the assistance of any other gods. He introduced this God to the Athenians."[180]

Thus Fernando urges that, like Paul, we too "must look beyond form to the emptiness without God."[181] Evidently, in Fernando, a dichotomy

---

a most comprehensive description of Paul's attitude toward Gentile beliefs and his witness to Gentiles" and thus helps us relate to non-Christians. Ibid., 11–12.

173. Ibid., 51–52.
174. Especially in his chapter, "The Severe Side of the Gospel"; ibid., 57–67.
175. Ibid., 24–25.
176. Ibid., 39–40.
177. Ibid., 25.
178. Ibid., 40.
179. Ibid., 41.
180. Ibid.
181. Ibid., 43.

emerges between the form (religious rituals) and the longings (religious desire), where the longings are affirmed but not the ritualistic expressions of that longing.

A third aspect from Fernando is that he sees Paul's use of the Greek poets as an affirmation of at least some aspects of their system, and as a call to engage with them at their highest.[182] According to Fernando, Paul saw "*glimmerings of truth* in these systems that could be used to buttress his case for Christianity."[183] Fernando equates Paul's use of the poets as an approval, and furthermore a sign, that Paul is affirming the *best* ideas in the thought of the Athenians.

Ultimately of course Fernando is clear that no matter how much positive is found in other religions, they must come to the point of God's judgment and respond to the call for repentance.[184]

The theory of religion in play is that there were several religions in the Greco-Roman world, with Christianity being just one example. From Paul's point of view, Fernando would argue, Christianity was the true religion and the other religions are false. However, Fernando would add, they were not entirely false as there were several aspects in those religions that could be used as a points of contact for Paul's communication and evangelism.

Note also that there is a predominantly theological view of religion in play. Fernando compares the beliefs of the two groups, and not the practices. The judgment of Paul is a judgment of "true belief" (right knowledge). Similarly, a dichotomy exists between the rituals (expression) and the true longings (the point of contact).

Such a reading of the text is not surprising, especially since we have encountered a similar view from Chenchiah. Furthermore, Fernando's emphasis on "religious longings" is common to several contemporary theologians of religions.

Yet the question remains unanswered: is this reading of the text (and thus religion in the text) correct? As we will see, certain words and Paul's use of Greek thought allow for another possibility and it hinges on how we see Acts 17:16–34 in its larger literary context.

Religion for Outsiders: An Alternative Reading of Acts 17:16–34

For an alternative reading of Acts 17:16–34, especially in contrast to the traditional readings of the previous section, I draw attention to the literary

---

182. Fernando is clear that the entire system is not accepted by Paul; ibid., 91.
183. Ibid.
184. Ibid., 59.

A Critical Framework to Formulate a Theological Answer   251

context of the passage. Arguably, the literary context of Paul's speech is Socrates' speech to the Athenians,[185] found in Plato's *The Apology*.[186] Sandnes summarizes the similarities between Paul and Socrates in two ways and Johnson adds a third: 1) Paul's activity in the marketplace, is likened to Socrates; 2) Luke's use of the same world διαλεγομαι (dialogue) that was used for Socrates' activities; and 3) Socrates was charged for introducing foreign gods, just as Paul was.[187] Johnson further adds that Plutarch "in his treatise *On Being a Busybody* 2 (*Moralia* 516C) . . . refers to Aristippus picking up only 'seeds and samples' of Socrates' words,"[188] which is another accusation levelled against Paul.

With this as a literary context, we can proceed to the text. There are three key sections in this passage—Paul's entry into Athens, Paul's speech and the Athenian response.

Paul's Entry into Athens: Acts 17:16–21

Here we see the beginning of the encounter, where Paul and the Athenians are pitted against each other. Though Paul is clearly the observer, his perspective is held to be more "normative" (by Luke) than that held by the great Athenians. Hence, the judgment comes from Paul's point of view, despite Paul being on *trial*. In this section I highlight the meaning of certain words to emphasize that there is a negative view of Athenian 'religion' being depicted.

Verse 16: This passage is a continuation from the previous passage because Paul is shown to be waiting for them (αὐτοὺς), namely Silas and Timothy. Similarly, while in Athens, Paul's spirit was "irritated" or "greatly upset" (παρωξύνετο).[189] Johnson rightly notes that it was Paul's spirit and not the Holy Spirit that is said to be "irritated."[190] However this comment should not be seen as supporting Fernando's explanation of Paul's earlier irritation changing to a later (godly) acceptance. There is no textual evidence to suggest such a claim.

---

185. For further discussion of this point see Sandnes, "Paul and Socrates," 13–26.
186. Plato, *The Apology*.
187. Sandnes, "Paul and Socrates," 21; see also Barrett, *Acts*, 830.
188. Johnson, *Acts of the Apostles*, 313.
189. Johnson links the same term παρωξύνετο with Acts 15:39, found in Paul and Barnabes' dispute, and thus relates more closely with "angry" or even "outraged." Johnson, *Acts of the Apostles*, 312.
190. Ibid., 312.

It must also be noted that Paul was not alien to idolatry and foreign gods. He had recently seen enough in Philippi (Acts 16). It could be that Paul was angry with a city "full of idols," or perhaps the immorality associated with it. I suggest that Paul may have been disturbed when he saw idolatry in any city. However, I propose that the main reason Luke mentions this reaction is to present a negative picture of the Athenians.

Verse 17: The NIV and NASB translate διελέγετο as "reasoned," which indicates a positive picture of the communication. However, Barrett says that the word more strongly suggests "argued," and especially reminds us of the debate with the Jews in 17:2.[191] The passage also gives the impression that Paul debated in the market *because* he was so agitated/angry due to the idols, as the μὲν οὖν suggests. According to Johnson, the "debate" is a style associated with Socrates, an association "made more emphatic because of the μὲν οὖν."[192]

Verse 18: συνέβαλλον continues the argument/debate motif. Barrett is quick to point out that the word does not suggest politeness.[193]

Σπερμολόγος is a derogatory word for one who picks up scraps of information. Johnson translates it as "busybody," derived from the image of a bird picking up and dropping a seed (σπερμα), hence a "gossip" or a "peddler of second-rate religious opinions . . . which seems to be the sense here."[194]

Ξένων δαιμονίων, "strange gods/demons," though it is important to note that they are in the plural. As many scholars point out, the Athenians may have been confused, assuming that Jesus and resurrection (ἀνάστασιν) were two separate gods.[195] I say this because the confusion would have been all the more surprising, even amusing, for the Christian readers who were the implied readers of Acts. It surely does not portray Athenian knowledge in a good light.

Verse 19: Barrett rightly suggests that the interpretation of this scene depends on how we interpret ἐπιλαβόμενοι,[196] whether it was a "friendly inquiry or a trial?"[197] The Lukan context suggests that ἐπιλαβόμενοι means an arrest and/or aggression (cf. Luke 23:26; Acts 16:19, 18:17, 21:30). However,

---

191. Barrett, *Acts*, 828.
192. Johnson, *Acts of the Apostles*, 295.
193. Barrett, *Acts*, 830.
194. Johnson, *Acts of the Apostles*, 313.
195. Johnson in fact goes on to say that the "odd phrasing" of "Jesus and the resurrection" rather than the more common "the resurrection of Jesus" may have "given rise to the misapprehension about multiple deities." Johnson, *Acts of the Apostles*, 314.
196. Barrett, *Acts*, 831.
197. Johnson, *Acts of the Apostles*, 314.

scholars are also right in pointing out that Paul does not seem to be under any compulsion to stay in the end. Johnson believes that the "tone of the proceedings makes us think rather of a discussion than a formal hearing or trial."[198] Barrett does not gloss over the tension, especially because its relation to Socrates' trial, and states that Luke painted an "adversial" picture to suggest that Paul was possibly under a trial-like situation rather than free to come and go.[199]

Verse 20: This is a key verse that alludes to Socrates' trial, as parallels exist between the accusations against Socrates and Paul, as being teacher of ζενιζοντα τινα (strange things) and καινα διδαχηε (new things).[200] Johnson affirms that the Athenians were "open to instruction."[201] Though Barrett also wants to hold on to a positive picture of the "information seekers," he however allows for a negative picture in view of Josephus' negative description of such seekers in *Against Apion*.[202]

Verse 21: Witherington observes in this verse that Luke is *not* showing the Athenians to be "inquiring minds" or "noble seekers."[203] If we had any doubt over the nature of the Athenians, the implied author reaches out from this position (as he does through the "we" passages) and makes an out-of-the-narrative statement that negatively, even racially, describes the Athenians. This view, that the Athenians were idle busybodies, was not new. However, to be stated at this time in the narrative shows that Luke is making an important point. The Athenians were not in any sense described as the paragons of genuine listeners or seekers that Fernando and many theologians like Dupuis depict.

Paul's Speech: Acts 17:22–31

Much has been said about Paul's speech. Even Fernando through his study recognizes that the speech has a judgment motive running right through, which is to say that Paul is not simply affirming the Athenians, but contradicting them at each step. For Fernando this is bringing the Gentiles into the right knowledge, using their partially right knowledge as a "point of contact." However, the point that needs to be made is that Paul contradicts the Athenians and never affirms their traditions. Witherington sums it up well

198. Ibid.
199. Barrett, *Acts*, 515–16.
200. Johnson, *Sacred Pagina*, 314.
201. Ibid.
202. Barrett, *Acts*, 833.
203. Witherington, *The Acts of the Apostles*, 517.

by saying that Paul uses the familiar ideas in Athenian thought as "points of contact, to proclaim monotheism."[204] This is to say that Paul does not use the "points of contact" to affirm the Greeks but to judge them.

Verse 22: The choices available to interpret δεισιδαιμονεστέρους are either "religious" or "superstitious." As we saw earlier, Dupuis and Fernando use this word in a positive sense. Even Johnson prefers the positive, citing Josephus' *Against Apion* as proof that Athenian religiosity was common knowledge.[205] However, in the context of classical literature, and in view of Socrates' defence, the Athenians are not pictured in a positive light.[206] Of course, as we saw in the previous verse, Athenian idleness was common knowledge and so Luke is probably using δεισιδαιμονεστέρους as a literary device. Nevertheless, for Barrett, when this word is combined with Paul's disapproval of the idols, as well as seeing that in classical literature being superstitious was as bad as atheism (while the atheist did not believe in the gods, the superstitious ones made the gods evil), the negative meaning is most probably implied.[207]

Verse 23: Luke notes Paul's actions of walking and observing carefully (ἀναθεωρῶν) to highlight the Athenian lethargy and inactivity. Paul is the keener observer.

Ἀγνώστῳ θεῷ, to "the unknown god," could have referred to "everything else."[208] Regardless of whether this referred to only one God or many unknowns, it shows rather that the Athenians do not know, and Paul is the one who claims to be revealing the known God to them. Johnson rightly remarks that whom the Athenians unknowingly worship "is a rhetorical play on the 'unknown god' who is 'unknowingly worshipped.'"[209] This passage is again an allusion to the Socratic dialogue, where Socrates is shown to be the knowledgeable one in the crowd. However, Luke is also depicting Paul as being very unlike Socrates, because Socrates admits that "he knows that he does not know."[210]

---

204. Ibid., 518.

205. Johnson, *Acts of the Apostles*, 314.

206. Plato, *The Apology*. The text is from a pro-Socrates perspective and Socrates is shown to be pleading for the Athenians to show good sense, but they continue in their lack of knowledge.

207. Barrett, *Acts*, 835.

208. For discussion on the Unknown God see Witherington, *The Acts of the Apostles*, 521–23.

209. Johnson, *Acts of the Apostles*, 315.

210. See especially Socrates' famous illustration of Delphi's Oracle in Plato, *Dialogue*.

Verses 24–26: The speech goes on to illustrate who this God is and we see a play between Paul's God and Athenian traditions. Paul confronts idolatry with the doctrine of creation. There are also echoes of Isaiah which suggest that the speech is not entirely Hellenist.[211] The contrast between the lifeless idols and the living (especially in view of the resurrection) God is striking, especially in relation to other Pauline letters (cf. 1 Cor 8:4, 12:2).

Verse 27: While this is often used as a verse to show how non-Christian religions can find God, I suggest that it is blindness that is emphasized here. ψηλαφήσειαν αὐτὸν καὶ εὕροιεν "grope and find him" is not necessarily a positive image. In the context of the passage (and the audience), it denotes a negative way of finding God.[212] Barrett shows that, in Stoic belief, God is not far off. Yet the uncertainty implied in the search for this "near" God, in Luke's construction, "does not represent its successful conclusion is certain."[213]

Verses 28–29: Scholars' views on Paul's use of Greek authors usually is that he highlights the best of Greek tradition,[214] or that Luke is showing that Paul is well-versed with Greek traditions and thus is a model for us.[215] However, the Aratus quotation "we are his offspring" is in the context of Zeus, of who the poet says, "him do we mortals never leave unnamed."[216] In the context of the "known–unknown" discussion, Paul is more likely setting the stage for the naming of the unknown God.

Verses 30–31: Fernando joins many scholars who rightly point out that this is ultimately a Christian message because of its call to repentance in view of the coming judgment by "the man"—the man who the implied readers would know to be Jesus. Johnson adds that "the ignorance of the Jews who rejected the Prophet Jesus (Acts 3:17; 13:27) . . . is applied to the erroneous conceptions of the divine rampant in the Gentile world."[217] This is important because neither the Jews nor the Gentiles are given inherent epistemological certainty. Note furthermore that the judgment ἔστησεν ἡμέραν has legal overtones, possibly continuing the debate motif.

---

211. See, Fudge, "Paul's Apostolic Self-Consciousness at Athens," 193–98. He shows parallels between Isaiah 42 and Isaiah 49 as found in the LXX with Paul's speech.

212. ψηλαφήσειαν in Greek literature, according to Barrett, alludes to the blinded Cyclops "as he tried to lay hands on Odysseus and his men," which suggests the "unlikelihood of success." Barrett, *Acts*, 845.

213. Ibid., 844.

214. Fernando, *The Christian's Attitude toward World Religions*, 52.

215. Flemming, "Contextualizing the Gospel in Athens," 207.

216. Aratus, *Phaenomena*.

217. Johnson, *Acts of the Apostles*, 317.

Athenian Response: Acts 17:32–34

The Athenian response, I argue, is the key point of the passage, especially seen in line with the previous events of the chapter. Regardless of Paul's efforts, the Athenians remain sceptical and even mock Paul and the gospel. Thus the implied author Luke would clearly want his implied readers to side with Paul and reject the Athenian response.

Verse 32: ἐχλεύαζον is to "make fun of," "sneer at," while ᾽ακουσόμεθα has legal "hearing" overtones. Both of these reactions are negative, unlike Fernando's view that at least the second is positive. It is also remarkable that this occurs after Paul's mention of the resurrection of the dead, after ἀνάστασιν has been clarified.

Verse 33: While many scholars hesitate to view this passage as a trial setting because Paul leaves the Areopagus unharmed, the fact is that the word ἐξῆλθεν (came out) can suggest both that Paul "came out" or that he "escaped." There are evidences of both meanings in Lukan writings: simply leaving/departing (Acts 2:1; Acts 14:20; Acts 15:40; Acts 18:23) and more aggressive departure/escape (Luke 4:35; Luke 17:29 and Acts 16:18, 19). Johnson suggests that there could be possible echoes of Luke 4:30, "where Jesus passes through his would-be murderers after the speech in Nazareth, but it is a faint one at best."[218]

Verse 34: In continuation with the Lukan style of entry–exit narratives, this passage too ends with a list of believers, though certainly much less than in Berea (from the same chapter).

Acts 18:1: "After this" changes the tone of the text, and we see finally a new section. Through the above notes I argue that the Athenian discourse in Acts 17 does not show Athenians or their religiosity in a positive light. In fact, the focus is as much on the negative perceptions of the Athenians as on Paul's true message. The critique of the Athenians lies on their cultic practices that included idolatry. Also to be noted is that Paul finds the Athenian "unknown God" problematic. The overall negative tone of this passage suggests that the Athenians, who pride themselves on their knowledge, are shown to have value *only* in an aspect that is unknown to them, that needed Paul to reveal. Furthermore, this knowledge of the true God which Paul brings is not a belief about the true God, or even a correct view about that true God, but actual knowledge/connection with God. Much like Riesebrodt's interventionist practices, Paul is not concerned with correct Athenian knowledge about God as much as their actual knowledge of God. The Athenian traditions and religiosity are shown to be folly and wrong in

---

218. Ibid.

contrast with Paul's correct knowledge and actions. If indeed Paul is critiquing the Athenians' worship, and thus their religion, Paul is in effect promoting Christian worship and thus the Christian religion.

Summary of Biblical Discussion

Thus we see that while there is the idea of true worship as godliness (piety), true worship is also the worship of the true God. From the textual discourse, we see that the word translated as religion has broad meanings, which include piety and traditions. However, what makes Christian piety and traditions unique is their truth as governed by how they correspond to God and God's revelation, and not to their own standard.

Similarly, in the theology of religions derived from Acts 17, it is not the religious longings of the Athenians that is to be commended. What must be weighed is their actual knowledge of God expressed through a different cultic practice (no idolatory). As Paul indicates, this knowledge is not simply beliefs but is expressed through a critique of the false cultic practices (the wrong way of worshiping the true God), in favor of right worship.

As a result, a biblical view of religion certainly focuses on the cultic practices of people. However, it transcends a purely cultic or even theological approach, to enquire about the real contact with God. The real contact with God, in line with the other words designated as religion, suggests a broad view of worship. This is to say that contact with God is contained within the correct behavior towards the true God. Thus, though the Bible depicts an awareness of other cults, as a worship metaphor, the only true worship that is commended is one that is rightly (through actions and belief) directed to God. We see again that Chenchiah, failing to emphasize truth, misses out on the biblical dimension of integrated religion and direct experience of God.

THEOLOGICAL RELIGION

Drawing from the Bible, but also moving beyond the text to the theological context, I now draw out a theological basis to answer the question "what is religion?" First, I adapt McCutcheon's theory to show that it is consistent with an insider theological method. This is also shown to be consistent with Chenchiah's proposal. I also show the value of the contextual classification approach, by arguing that the Christian definition of religion is by nature a Christian construct. In this regard, Dubuisson and Balagangadhara are shown to be right, at least for Christians, as the concepts of religion and

Christianity are linked. However, the limited theological vision of Dubuisson and Balagangadhara shows that their view of Christianity is reductionist and stereotypical. In contrast, a broader theological view of religion, drawn from the discussion above, but also from the cosmographical schema and Augustine's thought, is proposed.

Theological Method that Prioritizes the Insider

Looking for the theological approach to religion, we are able to see some consistencies with McCutcheon and Riesebrodt. In particular, there is a strong call from theologians to prioritize the insider (confessional) voice while doing theology.

Theologian John Webster points to the conventions that have become dominant in modern-day scholarship, conventions that he argues are culturally determined.[219] The methodology of academia today privileges a certain kind of knowing and working; it is an "anthropology of enquiry" which emphasizes "intellectual selfhood," and is bound by "the most potent moral and spiritual ideals of modernity."[220] In contrast to this social learning pattern, Webster offers a theological method that privileges God in the process of human discourse: "The distinctiveness of Christian theology lies ... in its invocation of God as agent in the intellectual practice of theology. In order to give account of its own operations ... Christian theology will talk of God and God's actions. Talk of God not only describes the matter into which theology enquires but also, crucially, informs its portrayal of its own processes of enquiry."[221]

Webster highlights two principles that result in bringing God into the process of knowing. The ontological principle is that God is not a hypothesis but "the reality which actively constitutes and delimits the field of theological activity."[222] The noetic principle asserts that theology is not simply about God as object but also directed *by* God as subject: "theology is [not] governed by a doctrine of Scripture of revelation, but something prior to both, namely this: the 'object' to which the theologian's gaze is directed is inalienably subject ... the object of theology is nothing less than the eschatological self-presence of God in Jesus Christ through the power of the Holy Spirit. Theology is oriented to this active presence, and its enquiries

---

219. Webster, *Confessing God*, 14.
220. Ibid.
221. Ibid., 25.
222. Ibid., 26.

are both materially and formally determined, borne along and corrected by that presence."[223]

Webster suggests that this way of knowing challenges academic knowing, and goes on to make a case of how theology has a legitimate place in the university. While arguing for the legitimacy of theology in academia is not the concern of this dissertation, that God is both the object and the directing subject of theological inquiry is an important assumption being made in this study. To this I would add Gutierrez's assertion that theology is not simply the reflection of God and his works, but is also work in response to God.[224] In this sense, theology is certainly a "second order" activity (an etic voice) that observes the words and works of God and the people who claim to know him. However, it is also a "first order" activity in both academic and experiential senses (an emic voice), where the experience of faith in God directs the manner, purpose and content of theological reflection.[225]

To this extent, Grenz is right in asserting that to determine what constitutes theological thinking, the chief sources of theology must include scripture, the past and present Christian tradition, and the culture that scripture and tradition are found in.[226] However, to the extent that a balance of sources is sought to be achieved, it can be said that Christian tradition has not always been unanimous.

Hans Frei provides a helpful taxonomy of the different theological attempts to view culture and Christian tradition.[227] Type I is the discourse that subjects Christian discourse to cultural philosophical frameworks, where nothing in Christianity is legitimate if it does not conform to external principles of assessment. Type V is at the other extreme, that gives exclusive authority to tradition and does not allow any dialogue with culture, and cannot be judged at all by cultural criteria. Type II, III and IV are the attempts at a balance. Type II offers primacy to a cultural principle, like existentialism, and looks at theology from that framework. Type III tries to draw equally from tradition and culture, without giving primacy to either. Type IV, and the approach that I adopt in this dissertation, asserts a primacy for theological tradition, with openness to culture. As Ford explains: "Type 4 gives priority to Christian self-description, letting that govern the applicability of general criteria of meaning, truth and practice in Christian theology, yet nevertheless engaging with a range of disciplines

223. Ibid.
224. Gutierrez, *A Theology of Liberation*.
225. Grenz, *Theology for the Community of God*, 11.
226. Ibid., 21.
227. Frei, *Types of Christian Theology*.

and with other worldviews and theological positions in ad hoc ways ... It is 'faith seeking understanding,' basically trusting the main lines of classic Christian testimony to God and the Gospel, but also open to a wide range of dialogues—not least because God is seen as involved with all reality."[228]

The emphasis on the theological space to determine the theological discourse is sometimes charged as fideism, where subjectivity replaces reasonable and critical thinking. Bernard Lonergan vociferously argues against fideism stating that theological method, even while governed by God, is critical and intellectually sound. He suggests eight functional specialities for doing theology—research, interpretation, history, dialectics, foundations, doctrines, systematics and communications.[229] These functional specialties are grounded in Lonergan's four levels of consciousness, which are the way human beings grow in knowledge, namely experience, understanding, judgment and decision. The point here is that, for theological discourse, one cannot abandon the normal way human beings learn and know. However, for theologians, there is a special method employed to these ways of knowing. While Lonergan's work is complex and extensive, my concern here is to see how his method helps in formulating a theological discourse for understanding religion.

There are three proposals that make Lonergan's method theological. First is his call for faith as the controlling framework to view the world. Lonergan asserts that scientific/theoretical knowledge offers one way of looking at the world, while faith offers "another kind of knowledge," reached through "God's love flooding our hearts."[230] In effect, the scientific mind works with one horizon, while the mind converted in love transcends to another horizon while continuing to use scientific discourse and processes: "Without faith, without the eye of love, the world is too evil for God to be good, for a good God to exist ... faith and progress have a common root in man's cognitional and moral self-transcendence ... Faith places human efforts in a friendly universe; it reveals an ultimate significance in human achievement; it strengthens new undertakings with confidence. Inversely, progress realizes the potentialities of man and of nature; it reveals that man exists to bring about an ever fuller achievement in this world; and that achievement because it is man's good also is God's glory."[231]

228. Ford, *Shaping Theology*, 16.

229. Lonergan devotes a chapter to each of his functional specialties in his *Method in Theology*. See Lonergan, *Method in Theology*. Ogilvie provides a helpful summary in Ogilvie, *Faith Seeking Understanding*, 121–39.

230. Lonergan, *Method in Theology*, 115.

231. Ibid., 117.

Second, this converted self allows the individual to be more authentic. Lonergan's call for authenticity is in stark contrast to the religious studies methodology that distances personal moral life from scholarship. For Lonergan, moral life and decisions are necessary for the theologian to better use the functional specialties.

The third call within dialectics is the necessity to make responsible judgments and not simply leave research to gathering and assessing data. Any theological proposal, even definition, must lead theologians to act in one way or another, to decide on the goodness and value of the proposal. This third aspect, of making responsible decisions/judgments, is also improved with authenticity: "[with] the discovery of oneself as a moral being, the realization that one not only chooses between courses of action but also thereby makes oneself an authentic human being . . . there emerges in consciousness the significance of personal value and the meaning of personal responsibility."[232]

Thus, in contrast to the positions of the academic study of religion, theologians are bound by a different method to look at the world. In view of the 'theological' space for understanding religion, theologians *should not be* purely objective and descriptive. Theologians *must be* involved with the broader issues that include political and social (and theological) agendas. Theologians are 'religious devotees' who look at religion as a self-description, as much as something to be studied and used for *religious* purposes. In addition, a theologian must look to prioritize theological sources when interpreting knowledge of the world. While various theological traditions may do it differently, a broadly defined evangelical method would include the prioritization of the Trinitarian God, especially of Jesus and the Holy Spirit, in both theological concepts and actual experiential reality, as epistemic principles. Similarly, a theologian would seek to make a connection between his or her personal life in their academic or nonacademic life. It is precisely these connections that makes a theology of anything, including a theology of religion, possible.

Theological Method for the Contextual Classification of Religion

Over the last few chapters I have shown that religion as a category changed in meaning over time, and that Chenchiah's category of religion was not only an expression of traditional religion but a moving away from it. This suggests that the concept of religion changes depending on who (or which community) is defining it. Denise Buell is right in saying that "What

232. Lonergan, *Method in Theology*, 38.

counts as Christian has always been a matter of negotiation, argument, and revision."[233] Thus, Christians need not be bound by certain descriptions of what they are supposed to be and can reinterpret their own traditions and definitions. In the evangelical tradition, the norms of scripture give direction to any such redescription. While we need not be committed to the essential existence of religion as an ontologically real entity in culture, we can be committed, as Christians, to formulating a view of religion that is both consistent with our theological norms as well as validly (once again in view of our theological purposes) describes the world that we live in. In this sense, the theological classification of religion encourages the use of emic (insider) space to develop a theology of religion. As a result, what is considered religion, and subsequently Christianity, are open for reclassification within a valid theological method.

For theologians, the contextual classification view of religion, along with the insider/outsider view of religion, is a useful approach for understanding "what is religion." The classificatory view does not commit to a particular meaning of religion, but remains an approach by which to understand religion. Similarly, the insider voice allows theologians to approach religion from a faith perspective, in a theological context. McCutcheon's opposition to theology in the religious studies landscape need not affect the theologians, who intentionally look to make broad connections between their world and the world beyond. McCutcheon states that theological viewpoints presume that religious experience, rituals and spirituality "gain meaning by reference to something that lies outside historical change," namely God, or the sacred.[234] The reference to an external reality is certainly a given in theology, and correctly describes how theologians will determine the meaningfulness of religious activity in view of God and God's creation. Furthermore, the emic perspective, even though it is described as the outsider looking into a community, also allows the insider to relate with outsiders through a common language. Unlike McCutcheon's view that the insiders mostly only experience their reality without wanting to reflect upon it, Christian theologians have the task of both experiencing their spiritual reality as well as thinking about and seeking to communicate it. Thus it remains the valid starting point for theological description and redescription as well.

We can recount Grenz's assertion that theology is a second-order activity that, as an interpretative exercise, reflects on God and his works/words rather than being the "first–order" commitments and experiences of

---

233. Buell, "Why This New Race," 24.
234. McCutcheon, *Critics not Caretakers*, 86.

the Christian community.[235] Webster too shows that theology exists as both second-order description of faith and first-order religious experience. This is evident in Webster's depiction of God as both the object and the directing subject of theology, to the extent that words about faith that are said in the context of faith become confessional faith statements. Christians can exist within the duality of rational objectivity and faith-oriented subjectivity.

Chenchiah, as we have seen, addresses religion as a convert, and especially uses retrospective narratives to look back at his Hindu heritage. Similarly useful is Chenchiah's emphasis on the dual theory of religion. Religion viewed in a common sense way, as well as religion viewed as a specifically Christian activity, are positive ways forward for Christian theologians to understand religion—both as insiders and outsiders.

Thus, when what we see in this section and Chenchiah's view are combined, we are able to make the following assertions about our approach to religion. We agree that religion is a Christian construction, though the Christian religion is better served by being constructed within theological norms. In addition, unlike the objective study of religion, the Christian community must approach religion in two ways—from within faith (emic) and also from outside it (as etic). Similarly, our theology is a description of our religion as well as a religious action.

Cosmographical Schema: Religion and Meaning

According to Dubuisson, religion is a cosmographical schema equivalent to the Christian construct. As an example, Dubuisson cites Christian anthropology,[236] though it obviously extends to all assertions about reality including God, humanity, sin, salvation and eschatology. Balagangadhara similarly call this a configuration of learning, the way the West orders its reality.[237] Others may even call this "worldview," a concept which Balagangadhara says is equivalent to "religion."[238] It is important to restate that Dubuisson and Balagangadhara are critical of secular theories of religion that subconsciously (and uncritically) derive from Christian discourse. However, they say nothing about a Christian's own conception of religion. It is in this context that we even began to construct a theology of religion and looked at how the scriptures would define the religion. In this section,

---

235. Grenz, *Beyond Foundationalism*, 17.
236. Dubuisson, *The Western Construction of Religion*, 38.
237. Balagangadhara, *The Heathen in His Blindness*, 463.
238. Ibid., 392.

we look at the cosmographical schema of Christian drawn from Chenchiah, and the Christian conceptions of universal truth that pertain to religion.

From theological discourse, any number of cosmic statements can be the matrix around which the concept of religion could operate. For instance, the God and humanity divide, holiness and sin, God the creator and sustainer of the world, the coming again of Jesus, and so on. Undergirded by these theological statements, the shape of religion would be further fine-tuned.

Chenchiah's theology of religion related religion to action in response to the cosmic crisis that divided humanity from God, and when Chenchiah identified the need to access God to bridge this gap. Chenchiah also prioritized the *act* of religion as experimentation for union rather than the dogmas or the ethical demands. This is reminiscent of Riesebrodt's priority of the interventionist practices over the discursive (theological).

However, Chenchiah's careless use of evolution makes his cosmographical schema hard to accept for modern Christian theologians. As we mentioned earlier, a more rigorous thinking on the mechanisms of evolution within the Christian schema may result in a richer understanding of the way God deals with his creation through evolution. The main argument in favor of this position is that if indeed God used evolution as his method for creation, then it is difficult to presume that he has suddenly stopped this evolutionary method all of a sudden in his current dealings with his creation. However, Chenchiah's assertion of evolution, while a theological construction, remains loaded in favor of a theological position that is not entirely consistent with scripture. To view the new creation solely in biological terms is to fail to come to terms with the other aspects of "new creation" that are outside biology. While Christians are wrong to ignore physical regeneration, to prioritize it above all else is also a folly, and not entirely necessary for a theory of religion.

However, the cosmographical scheme that Chenchiah offered is an important insight into using Christian schema for a theology of religion. For instance, the use of the Barthian "God and humanity divide" was seen as a problem that religion sought to solve. Similarly, Chenchiah's view of looking at the incarnation as the way of transforming the question of religion, was also a strongly Christological reinterpretation of theory. For Chenchiah, the Christological solution of "true" religion bridged the gap between God and humanity through the incarnational mode of "new creation"—the focus being on the actuality of the new creation rather than simply the belief in it. This theological reorientation is much needed and helpful for theologians even today.

A Critical Framework to Formulate a Theological Answer   265

Furthermore, we have already seen that the biblical view of religion was much more integrated with beliefs and actions. There is a danger, therefore, to view cosmographical schema in an ideological or worldview sense. There is enough in Christian discourse, even using Chenchiah, to suggest that the cosmographical schema that Christian theologians operate with is not simply a theological belief that governs actions, but an actual connection with God who determines which action is religious or which is not. To outsiders, this God-talk would look like dogmatic theology, but from an insider's point of view, it is an actual act of worship. Riesebrodt's theory of religion suggests that interventionist actions are those actions that function within crisis of humanity and the promise of salvation. Christian belief extends beyond the promise of fulfillment. Thus for Christians, the cosmographical schema can and must involve not just the idea of crisis but also, because of the belief in a true and living God, the actual hope for fulfillment.

The Christian view of religion agrees that there is a duality between God and creation, opposition even. In this sense, Barth, Chenchiah and several other theologians are correct to say that God is against religion.

However, with the Christological (incarnational) and Pneutamatological (postpentecostal) events, we see that duality is not an end in itself. The division that exists does not mean that the division remains. The divide of Christianity must be seen within God's attempt at reconciliation. It is not enough to point to a conflict. Any Christian theology of religion must also include the act of God sending his Son, and the Son becoming a human being, so that human beings can be like God the Father. The theological discourse that God reconciles, saves and glorifies, may be missed by secular scholars when looking at Christianity. However, within the emic discourse, it must not only be emphasized, but also prioritized. This idea must pervade our concept of religion.

The universalization of this schema would be oppressive if done in the guise of secular academics. However, as Christians make sense of their world, it is not only natural but theologically necessary for Christians to prioritize a Christian conception of the world. Thus, to see the world in conflict with God, and to see the effort of religion to solve it, is a valid view of religion.

Therefore, even without Chenchiah's biological overtones,[239] Christians can find a model for the reconception of religion within the Christian cosmographical schema. If religious life is life that is lived by a person transformed by the Holy Spirit, then religion describes all aspects of life in this

---

239. Though I have suggested earlier that the biological overtones need not be thought of as negative.

world that lead the person towards that transformed living and expressions of transformed living. Moreover, the transformation is being affected until the final day, when the transformation will be complete.

The key missing feature in Chenchiah's cosmographical schema, which Riesebrodt captures, is the emphasis of religion as the promise of *salvation*. This salvific idea is almost entirely missing in Chenchiah, and is more fully developed in an early Christian theologian, to whom we now turn.

Redescribing Religion as Worship: An Augustinian Approach

What we have seen so far is that the concept of religion has been clarified to include the concept of worship. This leads to the question "What is worship?" From the earlier biblical discussions, worship consisted of the cultic acts that derived their meaning and value from theology. In addition, seen from Riesebrodt's theoretical framework, worship is not simply the meaning making activity, but the promise of salvation. This salvation is believed to be an *actual* salvation, for Christians. In effect, worship is the worship of God, implying that a Christian way of looking at religion can be to see how it not only derives its meaning from God but is also directed to God.

The need for an integrated view of religion that takes into account a cosmographical narrative that is consistent with biblical discourse paves the way for a more positive view of religion as worship, an idea expressed by early Christian theologians, and particularly by Augustine. Augustine's conception of religion is integrated with life—as we observed through the discussion by Chenchiah and the discussion this chapter on biblical religion—but also offers a language of religion as worship that provides a positive view of God and people.

While religion defined as worship was not the only definition used by early Christian writers, it was popular. Prior to Augustine, even Clement, Justin and Origen used θεοσέβεια to denote true worship.[240] Furthermore, in the *The Epistle to Diognetus*, θεοσέβειαν των Χπριστιανων (in I,i) can mean worship or piety of Christians,[241] even though Meecham translated θεοσέβειαν των Χπριστιανων as "religion of Christians."[242]

When Augustine viewed religion as worship, he also clarified its usage. Due to the prevailing ambiguity of the word, Augustine preferred to use *religio* in a qualified sense to mean exclusively the "religion which binds us

---

240. Bertram, "Theosebes, theosebeia."
241. Buell, *Why This New Race*, 30.
242. Meecham, *The Epistle to Diognetus*, 75.

to God alone."²⁴³ Augustine thus conceived of religion as an *activity* that could be positive, to the extent that the "Christian religion" was the "one saving and true religion," and the true way of worshipping the true God.²⁴⁴ Augustine did not attempt to define religion as a category outside the worship of God, such as religious disposition or even belief systems. Rather, his focus on religion was consistently to view life as an act of worship that included sacrificing to and honoring God.

There were two aspects of worship within Augustine's view of religion. One was that of the worshipper, which included the sacrifices, the attitudes and the honor that the individual or community brought to God. The other was the true God, who gave meaning and value to that act of worship. An example of this double view of worship in religion was seen when Augustine narrated the story of Marcus Regulus.²⁴⁵ Regulus was a Roman general who was captured by his enemies, the Carthaginians, and then sent back to Rome as a representative to negotiate the exchange of prisoners. If Regulus was unsuccessful, he was bound by an oath to his gods, that he would return to his captors to most likely be killed. In the end, the Romans refused to agree to the Carthagnian demand, and Regulus, bound by his oath to the gods, returned to die a painful death.²⁴⁶ In Augustine's retelling, Regulus' act is "most noble," an act of virtue made "for the sake of religion" that reminds that "he worshipped the gods diligently, and faithfully kept the oath that he had sworn by them," even if it was also "worthless" and brought him "no profit."²⁴⁷

A more negative example of Roman religion is found in Augustine's critique of the Roman games, which were also an act of religion, but this time of a shameful disgrace.²⁴⁸ Augustine noted that the "propitiation to such deities was so wholly wanton, impure, immodest, wicked and unclean" and was "inimical and detestable to true religion."²⁴⁹

While the critique of false religion is obvious, Augustine was also not entirely appreciative of the Regulus type of religion either. Augustine noted that Regulus was not a false worshipper, for he kept his oath faithfully.²⁵⁰ Nevertheless, Augustine saw in Regulus a distinction between the worship-

---

243. Augustine, *The City of God*, X/1, 393.
244. Ibid., IV/1, 143.
245. Ibid., I/15, 23–26.
246. Ibid., 23–24.
247. Ibid., 25, 23.
248. Ibid., II/27, 90.
249. Ibid.
250. Ibid., I/24, 37.

per from the (false) object of worship. Even though Regulus was faithful to his oath, his oath was sworn to "false gods."[251] In contrast, Augustine was able to project Christianity as "our most wholesome religion," because there was no such dichotomy.[252] True worship would not simply be an ethical lifestyle; it would also need the true God to make it entirely true. Thus, unlike the false worship of the Romans and other pagans, Augustine called for the highest virtue (even more than Regulus) for Christians because of the reality of the Christian God.[253] Though Regulus' religion had much to commend, it remained false because it had false gods while the truth of the Christian religion stood out because of the true God.

Augustine was not talking about other religions being false, as Griffiths believes. Griffiths rightly points out that for Augustine, *religio* meant worship, yet Griffiths misleading states that Augustine's view of religion suggested that there could be "true and many false religions."[254] Augustine had famously stated: "religion is to be sought neither in the confusion of the pagans, nor in the offscourings of the heretics, nor in the insipidity of schismatics, nor in the blindness of the Jews, but only among those who are called Catholic or orthodox Christians, that is, guardians of truth and followers of right."[255]

Yet this is not an idea that suggested that other "religions" were false. The plurality of false religions suggests that there were many wrong "religions," implying our modern category of religion. However Augustine's focus was not on socioethnic or doctrinal alternatives to Christianity, but on the kind of worship. For Augustine, the expression of true religion was found in righteousness and godliness, in honour of the true God.[256] False religion was that which was identifiably immoral, but furthermore, despite examples of moral Regulus, false religion was any worship of a false God. True religion was to be found when both the act of worship and the object of worship were true.

Augustine offered a clear statement of the relation between religion and the worship of God in the review of his *De Vera Religione* (On True Religion): "I wrote a book *Concerning True Religion* in which I argued at great length and in many ways that true religion means the worship of the one true God, that is, the Trinity, Father, Son and Holy Spirit. I pointed out

---

251. Ibid.
252. Ibid., I/15, 25.
253. Ibid., I/24, 37.
254. Griffiths, "Religion," 672.
255. Augustine, "Of True Religion," in Burleigh, *Augustine: Earlier Writings*, 231.
256. Augustine, *The City of God*, II/28, 91.

A Critical Framework to Formulate a Theological Answer 269

how great was his mercy in granting to men by a temporal dispensation the Christian religion, which is true religion, and how man is to adjust his life to the worship of God."[257]

Augustine defined true religion as "the way of the good life," where God (and only God and not his creation) was acknowledged and worshipped in "purest piety."[258] True religion was also linked to a life governed by God and directed by him. One way this was achieved was by seeing Jesus as both the one to whom sacrifices were made, and the one on whom the Church would pattern how sacrifices were made: "He is both the priest who offers and the sacrifice which is offered; and He intended that there should be a daily sign of this in the sacrament of the Church's sacrifice."[259]

Enigmatically, Augustine went on to add that "what is now called the Christian religion existed of old and was never absent from the beginning of the human race," suggesting that true religion existed even before it was called Christian.[260] Yet, this was because Augustine believed that the earlier sacrifices of "holy men of old were the many and various signs of this true sacrifice, which was in this way prefigured in many things," to the further extent that "all false sacrifices have yielded" to the supreme and true sacrifice of Christ.[261]

While doctrine (right belief) was important for Augustine, it was not exclusively so. In an indictment against hypocrisy, Augustine made a strong link between doctrine and the practice of the sacraments:

> However philosophers may boast, anyone can easily understand that religion is not to be sought from them. For they take part in the religious rites of their fellow citizens, but in their schools teach divergent and contrary opinions about the nature of their gods and of the chief good, as the multitude can testify . . . Innumerable heresies that turn aside from the rule of Christianity testify that men are not admitted to sacramental communion who think and endeavor to persuade others to think otherwise of God the Father, of his wisdom and of the divine gift [the Holy Spirit] than as the truth demands. So it is taught and believed as a chief point in man's salvation that philosophy, i.e., the pursuit of wisdom, cannot be quite divorced from religion, for those

---

257. Augustine, "Retractations," I, xiii, in Burleigh, *Augustine: Earlier Writings*, 218.

258. Augustine, "Of True Religion," in Burleigh, *Augustine: Earlier Writings*, 225.

259. Augustine, *The City of God*, X/20, 422.

260. Augustine, "Retractations" I, xiii, in Burleigh, *Augustine: Earlier Writings*, 218.

261. Augustine, *The City of God*, X/20, 422.

whose doctrine we do not approve do not share in our sacramental rites.[262]

For Augustine, God was more than a belief but an actuality, and religion was transformative of the entire person.[263] This life was hardly theoretical alone; it required discipline and practical concern. If God did exist and was active, as Augustine interpreted God to be, then Augustine's theology of worship rightly called everyone to whole-life worship. Interestingly, the kind of worship was not as important for Augustine as the worship of God who was true. Therefore, for Augustine, belief *and* sacraments (rituals) went together. The idea of worship was not simply in some acts localized within certain spaces, but was much broader and included all life and people. Augustine admitted to the dual emphasis of religion, that it must include the worship of God and "is to be observed in human relationships, affinities and friendships of every kind."[264] Which is to say, the concept of religion "does not escape ambiguity when used in discussing the worship of the deity; for we cannot strictly speaking say that *religio* means nothing other than the worship of God, since we should then be unjustifiably disregarding the sense in which the word applies to the observance of duties in human relationships."[265]

While there were ethical, theological and cultic components in religion, Augustine would promote a greater metaphysical dimension where acts of religion, in honor of a true God, were deemed worthy or unworthy by God. This view of worship was also a broad view in that it extended beyond a simple cultic expression within a religious space, to the assertion that all life was to be lived in honor of God.

It must be noted that Aquinas (interpreting Augustine) emphasized that religion was only about God and nothing else, including our neighbor.[266] However, Aquinas was making this point to emphasize that God must be the sole focus of worship, not the worship of anything else, a point which Augustine would also agree with. It must be added that Aquinas' view of religion was similar to that of Augustine's, especially when Aquinas equated religion to a life of worship: "it belongs properly to religion to show honor to

---

262. Augustine, "Of True Religion," in Augustine, *Earlier Writings*, 230.

263. See for instance, the idea of using the five senses "to believe and praise the works of God, to cultivate love of God, to seek tranquillity of thought and action, and to know God." Ibid., 279.

264. Augustine, *The City of God*, X/1, 392.

265. Ibid.

266. Aquinas, "Question 81.1: Of Religion," in Aquinas, *Summa Theologica*, 1523.

God," and furthermore "all those things through which reverence is shown to God belong to religion."[267]

In addition to all this, it must be noted that Augustine's view of religion, even worship, was rooted in the concept of love. Augustine made it a point to relate "pure religion" with "sincere love to God and our neighbor."[268] Speaking on "the true worship of God," Augustine used Christological-sacrificial language to emphasize the connection between worship and love.[269] Augustine stated, "To Him, we owe the service . . . whether this be expressed through certain sacraments or performed within our own selves . . . Our heart is His altar when we lift it up to Him. The priest Who pleads for us is His only-begotten Son. We sacrifice bleeding victims to Him when we strive for His truth even unto blood . . . [through religion] we approach Him through love . . ."[270]

Furthermore, this love was not simply devotion to God, but extended to a missional calling, where the love of God was related to the command to "encourage his neighbor to love God."[271] James Smith draws attention to the importance of love in Augustine's vision of religion by saying that, for Augustine, "religion is at root a question of love."[272] Smith notes that Augustine sees love Christologically—where Christ determines not only the centrality of love but also the right manner of love.[273] Thus, the motivation of religion and the manner of religion are both love.

The question that needs to be answered is, "what is gained by viewing religion as worship," especially since Chenchiah strongly rejected any worship or even *bhakti* motifs to his view of religion. I pointed out in the previous chapter that a serious lack in Chenchiah's view of religion was the idea of relating to God in love. Chenchiah's view of religion was more like a system of transformation that relied more on power (*shakti*) than on grace. Not surprisingly, there was no need for the cross in Chenchiah's theology.

Augustine's theology, in contrast, held to the view that religion needed to be integrated with life (as Chenchiah would also agree), but Augustine also offered a view of religion that was more consistent with the Christian schema that prioritizes the love of God through the cross. This love, being the centerpiece of the Christian understanding of God, gives shape not

---

267. Ibid, 1533.
268. Augustine, "On Free Will," in Burleigh, *Augustine: Earlier Writings*, 207.
269. Augustine, *The City of God*, X/3, 394–96.
270. Ibid., 394–95.
271. Ibid., 396.
272. Smith, *Introducing Radical Orthodoxy*, 110.
273. Ibid., 112–13.

only to what religion should be like, but why the religious person must be religious.

The lack of love leads to a lack of clarity over the need for the reaching out to non-Christians. Naturally, scholars like Dubuisson and Balagangadhara find Christian religion to be antagonistic and divisive. Dubuisson and Balagangadhara are right in pointing to the conflicts that Christianity presupposes, conflicts that naturally reflect in Christian ideas of religion. There is a duality between God and creation, sin and salvation, etc. However, an important theological reorientation is reconciliation. The dualities in Christianity, whatever they be, are not meant to remain in contradiction. There is a strong sense that they are meant to be bridged; conflicts are meant to be resolved.

With the emphasis on love, a redescription of what religion is, an expression not just of what humanity must do, but also an expression of why humanity must do, is held together. Religion must always be a human act. Nevertheless, as humans act, they act in response to a God who loved. Plus, humans act because they too love God and their neighbor. The key conflict, between God and humanity, that has so strongly reflected in Christian conceptions of religion, as well as in the division between authentic religion versus the inauthentic cultic practices, are not intended to be eternal divides. With the incarnational principle (that in Jesus, God became human), and the pneumatological principle (that the Holy Spirit descended to stay on earth), ideas that we have seen reflected in Chenchiah, Christian theology of religion must rightly lead to the desire for and the act of reconciliation of differences, within the individual as well as between communities (even between Christians and non-Christians). Viewing religion as worship, the antagonistic associations with the Christian conception of religion can be revised, at least by Christians themselves.

Furthermore, such a Christian theology of religion will also lead to a positive theology of religions (hope for others). Being Christlike, in Augustinian terms, is not just a transformation into a new creation, but also a transformation in a new relationship. This relational angle better serves Christians wanting to promote a relevant theology of religions, one that is both consistent with Christian discourse and correctly missional. These Christian truisms, largely missing in Chenchiah's scheme, become necessary for a more contemporary missional theology of religions, and thus, worship, an act of love and devotion to God, becomes a central idea that redefines what religion is, and how Christians should relate with people from other religions.

The significance of this Augustinian vision of religion as worship, especially loving worship, is that religion is not a system. True religion is not about following rules or principles, or having the correct beliefs, but about having the right relation with the true God and his people.

SUMMARY OF THE CHAPTER

While we can agree with McCutcheon that religion is a constructed category, and also with Riesebrodt that religion has to do with the "promise of salvation" we add that religion for Christians is constructed through Christian methodology. Further, in view of Riesebrodt's promise, religion is that actual connection between humanity and God. Riesebrodt rightly asserts that religion is not simply the cultic expression (behavior regulating) or the discourse (the theology/beliefs), but the promised connection with God. What Riesebrodt fails to highlight for Christian concerns is that, for Christians, the connection with God occurs (or must occur) in all its discourse (theology) as well as in its behavior regulating practices (cultic rituals). In fact, insofar as all acts are done in honor of God, all such acts are religion.

In this chapter I presented the critical framework to formulate a theology of religion. I began with McCutcheon's classification theory of religion, arguing that it allows for a Christian construction of religion. Similarly, I showed how Riesebrodt's theory served two functions. It provided a way for theologians to adapt their view of an integrated religion, one that was also consistent with biblical witness. Though Christian theologians may find Riesebrodt's claims limited, a theologian is not bound by those limitations and can be more explicit about the reality of God and salvation.

To this discussion, I added a study of biblical sources and views of biblical scholars. I showed that the Bible did not in fact have any word that resembles the modern view of religion, but that a broad concept of worship was a valid way of looking at the words translated as "religion." I also showed, using the works of various biblical scholars that the biblical view of 'religion' was not purely belief oriented, individualistic or necessarily antagonistic. Rather, religion in the Bible was both belief *and* practice oriented, and was thus integrated with life. Chenchiah's concerns are yet again shown to have been on the right track, though his rejection of belief is shown to be a significant flaw.

The theological approach drew attention to the theological method. The contextual classification position was supplemented with a discussion on theological method, particularly looking at the work of scholars like John Webster, Bernard Lonergan, and Hans Frie. Through this I suggested that the theological priority for intellectual reasoning about religion was warranted. This was also consistent with Chenchiah's promotion of the insider view of religion. Similarly, I agreed that religion, and thus Christian religion, would have a universal cosmographical schema, one that prevents the Christian religion from being simply a matter of individualism. At this point, the limited usefulness of Chenchiah's cosmographical schema is evident because, even though he emphasized that religion had to do with a crisis between a real God and people, the mode of reconciliation was individualistic. Chenchiah however was on the right track when viewing religion as an activity.

I then moved to Augustine, who offered additional clarity on the shape of Christian religion. Through Augustine I showed that integrated religion, the cosmographical schema, and even the defence against antagonism, could be responded to by relating religion to a broad view of worship. What I ultimately argued for in this chapter was a definition of religion that emphasized a loving relationship with God. The answer to the question, "What is religion," included that "religion is worship." Thus, I argued that while the theological view of religion as worship—an integrated life, a life devoted to God—was within the scope of Chenchiah's vision, it was also an important corrective to Chenchiah's theology of religion. With this in view, we are ready to conclude this study with a theological answer to the question, "What is religion?"

6

Conclusion

What Is Religion? A Theological Answer

> ... *true religion means the worship of the one true God, that is, the Trinity, Father, Son and Holy Spirit.*[1]

REVIEW

The title of this study calls for a theological answer to the question, "What is religion?" However, the scope has been much larger than just defining the word religion and significant gains have been made in the process: a) a diagnosis of the definitional problem in a theology of religions; b) the clarification of a method of theology of religion; c) a history of the concept of religion in both Western and Indian contexts; d) a substantial study of the Indian theologian Chenchiah that drew out aspects about religion that had never before been observed in his writings; and e) a unique theology of religion that draws from secular, biblical and theological sources.

To address the question, I had to first establish that there was indeed a problem with the concept of religion; a problem that necessitated serious attention from theologians. Most theologians had not thought there was any need to define religion, let alone define it theologically. In this study, I have

---

[1] Augustine, "Retractations," I, xiii, 218.

argued that if theologians of religions want to address religion, they also need to be aware of the object of their study, namely what religion is.

I also argued for the necessity of a theology of religion, which is a theological definition of religion. Such a definition potentially affects what we think of religion, how we relate to religion, and how we relate to others to whom the concept is applied. The theology of religion that we developed drew from theological and extratheological sources. I showed that a theology of religion—to understand what the category of religion means theologically— is an urgent need in the Indian context, where the concept of religion is so important. To that extent this study moves the theological discussion to address that need. I argued that one way Christians, especially in the Indian context, could start developing their theology of religion is to employ the thought of Indian Christian theologians.

We then looked at the development of the concept of religion in history. The purpose was twofold. First, to note the relation between religion and the Christian context in which the concept of religion emerged. Second, to identify the key concepts of religion during Chenchiah's time. It became evident that the concept of religion had a colorful history, where it had moved from being considered an *activity* in response to God, to becoming a concept associated with beliefs and experience.

We also considered Indian thinkers like Aurobindo, Vivekananda, Gandhi and Ambedkar. In the context of the reform/revival movements of Hinduism, their theories of religion displayed similarities as well as sharp differences. Curiously, Aurobindo and Vivekananda offered theological (ideological) views of their religion, while Gandhi and Ambedkar offered more "integrated" views of religion, that delved into how religion could help the nation. Chenchiah was influenced by both perspectives.

I also showed the prominence of evolutionism in the study of religion, and drew particular attention to how both Christian theologians and Hindu thinkers used evolutionary thinking to address religion. Evolutionism also played a key role in Chenchiah's theology of religion.

In addition, I reviewed the theological views of religion prevalent during the time of Chenchiah, particularly focusing on discussions concerning religion at the world missionary conferences. We saw that a range of Christian thinkers fell between the two views—negative and positive—concerning religion. Chenchiah, we saw, attempted to offer both a negative and positive view of religion in his own theology.

My chapter on Chenchiah's theology of religion observed how a combination of theoretical and theological thinking contributed to a unique theology of religion. Several key points emerged in his theology of religion. Religion was dealt with in two separate ways. Chenchiah recognized religions as they were commonly understood through rituals and traditions. However, he was also aware of a deeper meaning of religion, one that was best achieved through the coming of Christ as man. There was thus a traditional view of religion that Chenchiah dialogued with, along with a theological definition that drew from an understanding of Christ. This I showed to be Chenchiah's dual theory.

Chenchiah also addressed religion as a convert, an insider. This is significant because he did not attempt to look at Hinduism from an objective point of view, on its own terms, but was aware of how any understanding of Hinduism was shaped by his understanding in Christ.

Chenchiah strongly used evolutionary logic for his thinking about religion. He argued that Christ's incarnation, through the Spirit, offered a new impetus—a revolution—to allow religion to transcend its limitations (and potential) to become a new creation (with new potential). This view of religion began with the correctly acknowledged crisis between God and humanity, which was *resolved* in the incarnation, and made available, through the Spirit, to all people. Chenchiah believed that there were movements within Hinduism (and possibly other religions) that were aware of this true religion, but only Christ was the source of actually achieving it. In that way, Chenchiah not only imposed his theological framework on other religions, but also on evolutionary religion itself.

Another important contribution that Chenchiah made to the theological discussion concerning religion was the critique of institutions, while appealing for an actual religious transformation (new creation). This, from historical context, was shown to be detraditionalism. However, Chenchiah's contribution was that the temple (institutional) and the ascetic/mystical (pure) religions were both criticized. Neither ritualistic religion nor *bhakti/mystic* religion was true religion. True religion, for Chenchiah, lay in the actual transformation of the individual in Christ, through the Holy Spirit, and living that transformed life in this world, which included the quest for Indian independence in a Spirit-transformed way.

Chenchiah's theology of religions—his attempt to relate his faith with the faiths of other non-Christians—was curiously missional, in that he was concerned with helping others know and experience Christ's transformation. At the same time, his theology of religions was not devoid of mutuality, one that he himself claimed to have experienced between Hindu and Christian thought. Regardless of evangelical hesitation in Chenchiah's use of Hindu sources, there remained a strong theological (Christological) priority in Chenchiah that invariably looked at Hinduism from Christian points of view, making him more "evangelical" than others have given him credit for.

In the evaluation chapter, it was evident that most scholars either misunderstood Chenchiah's view of religion, or deemphasized it. Nevertheless, there were certain weaknesses in Chenchiah's theology of religion. Significantly, his evolutionary thinking promoted an individualistic religion that failed to recognize evolution within a social (and thus, ecclesial) context. However, most significantly, his evolutionary religion was a depersonalized system that was shown to be devoid of love, a key component in Christian theology. As a result, his theology of religion, while offering Jesus as its basis, failed to come to terms with the cross and Jesus' own motivation to lay down his life for others.

The fifth chapter aimed to supplement (even correct) Chenchiah's theology of religion, with a critical and theological framework for developing a contemporary theology of religion. I drew from secular scholars, particularly McCutcheon and Riesebrodt. Using McCutcheon's contextual classification of religion I showed how religion was a category constructed by a community for contextual purposes. Similarly, the agenda of the community would determine the shape of the religion. While Chenchiah rightly constructed religion from a Christian theological framework, his construction was largely individualistic.

As Christian theologians, as insiders of the faith, we as a Church could discourse with the category of religion, yet our categories would still be shaped by our faith. This view was shown to be consistent with the faith-first theological method promoted by many theologians, like Webster and Lonergan. Chenchiah's prioritization of the Christian faith was also shown to be consistent with this, and to be a preferred method for constructing the meaning of religion.

Through an extended biblical discussion, we saw that religion was integrated with life, better thought of not simply as beliefs but as practices governed by truth. This allowed a conception of religion as worship, for the actions governed by truth-claims were not in the abstract but directed by God and for God. The retranslation of certain words interpreted as religion confirmed this claim. The biblical discussion also showed how it was possible to exist within religion and yet also critique religion, functioning within a dual approach to religion. Religion must critique itself, identifying the corruptions within, while also focusing on the truth of religion, which is founded not in the acts of religion, but in the true God.

I also showed that while Christianity was a cosmographical schema, it was neither individualistic nor antagonistic, particularly because of its view of worship and love.

A new view of religion, actually a recovery of an older view, was achieved through reviewing the work of Augustine. Religion as worship of the true God was the new language of religion that was proposed as both an addition and corrective to Chenchiah.

RELIGION IS . . .

We are now ready for a theological statement about what religion is. The goal of defining and thus constructing the meaning of religion, especially from theological sources, is called a theology of religion. Theology of religion is the discipline that draws attention to the need for clarity about what religion is, and also identifies and analyzes the sources used for constructing and using such definitions. Theology of religion differs from a theology of religions, the discipline that seeks to relate one religion to another. However, they are related since the theology of religion helps identify what a religion is (and is not), so that a theology of religions can meaningfully engage with that which falls under the definition of religion. The point of this study has been that, for theologians who seek to interact with people of other faiths, of other religious dispositions, it is important to understand what religion is in the first place.

Not surprisingly, after this study, the answer to the question "what is religion" is complex and is addressed at two levels. At one level, the question "What is religion?" must be addressed from a theoretical standpoint. From here, the answer is that *religion is a linguistic construct that is useful for the community (that constructed or adapted the concept) to make sense of the world*. This is the classification theory of religion, where religion is neither universal nor does it point to an essential action or experience that is evident across cultures. Religion is simply a word used by scholars, and now in popular jargon, to denote several kinds of actions and phenomena. This construct of religion is influenced by enlightenment thinking, especially in that there is an effort made to separate religious action and beliefs from nonreligious (secular) action and beliefs. Nevertheless, insofar as this concept of religion is recognized to be a linguistic construct, it avoids the universalizing tendency of enlightenment thinking and draws attention to the contextual history of the construction.

This theory of religion is significant for Christian theologians because, as Chenchiah rightly asserts, there is a difference between Christ and religion. Christ, for Christians, is living, essential, foundational and absolute. Religion, in contrast, is just a word that Christians have used to classify their own experiences in relation to the experiences of others. This separation between the absolutely real and the constructed concept is a fundamental theoretical standpoint that I have been arguing for in this paper, and affirm at the end.

With this in mind, the other level that the question "what is religion" can be answered is from the theological standpoint. Applying a theological method to the definition of religion, we are left with the following answer: *religion is a theologically constructed category for Christians to classify their unique experience of God and the unique outworking of that experience in the world.* In effect, this is a contextual classification theory. As the classification theory asserts, religion, like culture, art, politics, is only a word that orders the world, and does not actually represent it. However, this linguistic construction is not ideology-free and is largely determined by the context and concerns of the community using the category to talk about religion. For Christian theologians, speaking from and to a theological context, Christian theologians (should) intentionally bring in Christian presuppositions to the discussion about religion. To the extent that religion is constructed by the Christian community, the concept of religion will not only have Christian influence but will also have a Christian purpose.

Nevertheless, this two-level answer is not sufficient. The changing meanings of religion force Christians to be more precise in the contemporary setting. Christian religion need not be synonymous with modern religion, and a Christian redescription of religion (a theology of religion) using Christian tradition (biblical and historical) can be attempted. The classification theory of religion allows Christians to redescribe what religion is today. Yet, even as Christians exist in the world and use the world's language, a dual approach towards religion is adopted—one that views oneself as the true religion while also seeing one's own religion as one among many religions.

Thus, a Christian theologian of religions adopts a dual theory approach to religion, asserting that religion is two things simultaneously. First, religion is what it is commonly understood as in contemporary context, much like an etic (outsider) perspective. Second, religion is a theological category that makes sense to those who share a common faith experience and tradition, an emic (insider) perspective.

In the first instance (etic), the theologian enters the global academic/popular discourse with the view that religion is a linguistic construct and is thus able to dialogue with any of the various definitions of religion available. A definition of religion could be that religion is the collection of rituals and beliefs of a community directed towards a supernatural power, so that the adherents can gain access to a better life on earth or at least hope for a better one beyond death. Similarly, Hiebert's multidimensional definition, or even a generic "family resemblance" definition, could suffice.

This view of religion would classify, though not exclusively, the typical actions and beliefs—actions such as prayer, fasting, or pilgrimage, and beliefs about God, cosmos or salvation. One can be open to considering a broader view of religion here, where the concept of religion could extend beyond the boundaries of God and the supernatural to worldviews and ideological commitment. However, I still emphasize, following Chenchiah and Riesebrodt, that religion, even in its theoretical (etic) sense, has to do with a crisis that needs supernatural power, and does not include atheistic or political ideology. In other words, religion is not passionate commitment to any community or cause. Rather, a religion is a religion when a community is involved in the effort to solve a human crisis with supernatural assistance.

The second (emic) instance is where it gets more interesting and valuable for the Christian theologian of religions. While on one level, religion is what is commonly understood, on another level, religion is a combination of a religious view *of* the world and religious actions *in* the world, all directed in honor of God. This is theological religion.

One aspect of theological religion is that, like a worldview, it makes universal claims; there is a cosmographical schema in place. The theological presuppositions within the Christian view of religion must include the conflict between God and humanity. In that sense, religion is a human activity in response to God's activity, in the context of God's reconciliation of humanity to himself. For Christians, several universal assertions are made—God created the world; human beings are created in the image of God and yet have fallen and are in need of salvation; all creation exists to honor God; and Jesus' incarnation as a historical event with universal significance, etc. Such universalizations are natural within the emic discourse; they are faith statements that emerge from the genuine trust/faith in the narrative and through personal experience. Such universalist discourses can and must be open to challenge, especially from other Christian emic discourses. Only then would the blindsidedness of worldly interpretations, that influence the supposed "biblical" interpretations, be revealed. Yet, that does not change the fact that Christian theologians must continue to make universal statements and also explore the implications of those universalist (emic) claims.

The universalizing of religion must further be expressed through the all-encompassing nature of the Christian religion, both historically and theologically. We find that, seen through the Christian tradition, both biblical and historical, a strongly practical-performative view of religion rather than a purely theoretical/dogmatic view, is proposed. Thus, all action that relates to God, in either positive or negative ways, is seen as religious. Even the classification of religion, when done within the mode of religious action, is also religious, much like doing theology is praxis. Religion must be shown as performative, a religious act, where reading/interpreting the text and formulating doctrines is as much a part of Christian worship (religion) as participating in communion. Similarly, when eating, drinking, bathing and all other *mundane* activities of daily existence are brought into the purview of religious life, then all things become religious.

Furthermore, worship, especially broadly conceived, is a good example of such an internal redescription of religion. All this is done through a theological-insider discourse, especially prioritizing Christology and Pneumatology for a particularly reconciliatory motif. While worship as a concept gives to religion the focused emphasis of its relationship to God, liturgy as worship provides cultural rootedness to the otherwise ephemeral concept of worship. The emic voice must hold onto the view that all activity is ultimately potentially religious. If religion is to be viewed as worship, then the controlling framework is that there is no space outside the scope of religion. Theologians do not look for religion in certain aspects of society, or in beliefs or even worldview. Rather theologians are to see the world as a canvas for religion. Thus, religious politics would be the worship of God through politics, and religious art would be the worship of God through art. Such an integrative view of religion is more in line with the biblical discourse and can help us assess and construct relations with "religions."

The category of religion, conceived theologically as worship, holds that all actions determined by the theological framework as religious actions, are a response to God. Thus there is no distinction made between cultic acts and theology. The Christian acts (viewed as forms of worship) are expressed in internal and external, discursive and practical, ways. The internal worship is that which pertains to the transformation of the individual and community, through participation in the life of the (local) Church. The focus of these actions involve the personal discipline of quiet times, prayers, fasts and celebrations, as well as the corporate disciplines of churchgoing, tithes, baptism, communion, festivals and so forth. The goal of each of these acts, sometimes called rituals, is to strengthen the individual and community, by expressing the goals of salvation already received, though now in greater measure. However, this activity of religion must also include all aspects of life, rather than simply those activities that are deemed religious *a priori*. Thus, politics, art, and the day-to-day tasks of common living, can take on a religious tone when viewed within the framework of worship—acts that are directed by God and devoted to God.

Another aspect of theological religion would be the religious critique of religion. Much like what Chenchiah urged Indian Christians to do, to reject temple and ascetic forms of religion for a real experience of God and fellowship with humanity, so also must there be a sense of detraditionalization in the Christian theological religion. Our critique of religion must be a critique firstly of our own fallacious institutions, even false doctrines and systems. Only then can we critique similarly corrupt and fallacious institutions and systems of non-Christians.

Finally, it is here that we also perceive the distinction between true and false religion. True religion, seen as worship, and in the Augustinian sense of true worship of the true God, is the right behavior as determined by God, directed in honor and love of the true and living God. Any action that fails one or both of these criteria is false worship, and thus false religion. True religion is not that it is more evolved or even more correct, but that there is a real connection with the only true God. Note that this is a theological definition, meant for insiders. The missiological value of talking the language of judgment to non-Christians is not discussed at this point. Nevertheless, Christian theologians of religions must operate with the sense of not just what religion truly is, but also what true religion is.

If true religion is the true worship of the true God, and false religion is the wrong kind of worship or the worship of the wrong God, what then is nonreligion? I assert that, theologically, there is no sphere outside religion. If a person chooses to operate outside the bounds of God, that person may *think* they are outside religion. Nevertheless, their life is a testimony of false religion (again, this is speaking from the Christian theological standpoint). Whether a life is directed to God or not, theologically speaking God remains the reference point for all life. Hence, there is no place that a Christian can say God is not involved, for at all times God is either being rejected or accepted.

IMPLICATIONS FOR A THEOLOGY OF RELIGIONS

Finally, what are the implications of this view of religion for a theology of religions? At least three remarks can be made. Firstly, we can deemphasize the view that religions are ethno–spatial entities and thus we need not try to find God's presence, or prove God's absence, within them. Religion can be seen as a constructed category, which suggests that communities are constantly reshaping what is considered to be religion and what is not. Furthermore, it is not surprising that "interreligious dialogue" has not achieved much in India, and is met with suspicion from other religions. The Christian theological bias is quite evident from the outset, from the definition of what religion is and what is not. Any attempt to construct a category of religion that is not a Christian construct enters into the realm of humanist religion or academic religion. Such methodologies are legitimate within their own spheres and have their own norms. However, a Christian theology of religion must use its own norms. The Christian construction is valid and necessary, so also the Christian concern to interact with other religions on Christian terms. The necessity to reform how the dialogue takes place still exists, but reliance on Jesus Christ and the Spirit must not be lost.

Secondly, any observation of religion must be identified within the dual rubric of objective (etic) religion and theological (emic) religion. Objective religion is the supposed shared space of how people view religion. Some may believe that religions do exist and they could happily apply the category of religion to themselves, others may not. The dual theory will allow us to discourse with both kinds of people, largely because we are governed by the contextual classification theory of religion—namely, theological religion.

An example of the shared space in operation is through the critique of religion. It is not uncommon to hear from various religions that religious structures, institutes and beliefs are corrupt. As Christians, we can share in that space and critique that which is worthy of critique, even the corruptions within Christianity. Here, Chenchiah's critique of temple religion and ascetic religion is especially valuable.

Another example of the shared space in operation is through the emphasis on action, much like the ethical-praxis approach for a theology of religions. The ability to work together for social or pro-nation causes is commendable and recommended. It is also possible because of an objective view of religion that uses mutual categories of religion. Chenchiah illustrates this by his involvement with Indian nationalism.

Thirdly, the theological perspective offers an integrated view of religion. Conceived as worship, all action is religious if done in honor of God. The theological view of religion, while prioritizing a Christian view of religion, still views praxis and love from within the frame of worship, to interact not only within the Christian community but also with those outside the Christian community. Hence, all interactions with the world are within the rubric of worship—out of our love for God. In that sense, while the content of our religious deliberations will be different within different contexts, our attitude will remain within the attitude of love and devotion to God, and the love of fellow human beings. All interactions with the world, in all realms, will be religious acts of bearing witness to the godly transformation hopefully evident in Christians, as well as a service modeled on how Christ served. While the internal acts are focused upon the inner transformation of the individual and the Church, the external acts would be focused on the transformation of culture and the world.

Bibliography

Abbott, Lyman. *The Evolution of Christianity.* Boston: Houghton, Mifflin, 1892.
Abraham, K. C. "Interpreting Christian Social Ethics in Modern India: A Comparative Evaluation of the Implications of the Theological Writings of Chenchiah and M. M. Thomas." PhD diss., Princeton Religion Research Center, 1978.
Adams, Robert Marrihew. "Faith and Religious Knowledge." In *The Cambridge Companion to Friedrich Schleiermacher,* edited by Jacqueline Marina, 35–51. Cambridge: Cambridge University Press, 2005.
Adamson, James. *The Epistle of James.* New International Commentary on the New Testament. Grand Rapids: Eerdmans, 1983.
Adinarayan, S. P. "Sri P. Chenchiah: An Appreciation." *Guardian,* June 25, 1959, 197.
Albuquerque, Teresa. "The Role of the Christians in the National Struggle for Freedom." In *They too Fought for Freedom—The Role of Minorities,* edited by Asghar Ali Engineer, 194–210. Gurgaon, Haryana: Hope India Publications, 2006.
Aleaz, K. P. *Dimensions of Indian Religion: Study, Experience and Interaction.* Calcutta: Punthi Pustak, 1995.
———. *Religions in Christian Theology.* Kolkata: Punthi Pustak, 2001.
———. *Theology of Religions: Birmingham Papers and Other Essays.* Calcutta: Moumita, 1998.
Allen, Douglas. "Phenomenology of Religion." In *Encyclopedia of Religion,* edited by Lindsay Jones, 10:7086–101. 2nd ed. Farmington Hill, MI: Thomson Gale, 2005.
Alles, Gregory D. "Otto, Rudolf." In *Encyclopedia of Religion,* edited by Lindsay Jones, 10:6928–31. 2nd ed. Farmington Hill, MI: Thomson Gale, 2005.
Almond, Philip C. *The British Discovery of Buddhism.* Cambridge: Cambridge University Press, 1988.
———. "Wilfred Cantwell Smith as Theologian of Religions." *Harvard Theological Review* 76 (1983) 335–42.
Aloysius, G. *Nationalism without a Nation in India.* New Delhi: Oxford University Press, 1998.
Alt, Albrecht. *Essays on Old Testament History and Religion.* Translated by R. A. Wilson. Oxford: Basil Blackwell, 1966.
Alves, Rubem. *What Is Religion?* Translated by Dan Vinzant. Maryknoll, NY: Orbis, 1984.
Ambedkar, B. R. *Annihilation of Caste: With a Reply to Mahatma Gandhi.* 3rd ed. (1944). Online: Part 1 in: http://wcar.alrc.net/mainfile2.php/Documents/76/ Part 2 in:

http://wcar.alrc.net/mainfile2.php/Documents/77/ [Website: World Conference against Racism, 2002.]

Ambedkar, B. R. *The Buddha and His Dhamma*. Unpublished text provided by Eleanor Zelliot as prepared by Vasant Moon, 1956. Online: http://www.columbia.edu/itc/mealac/pritchett/00ambedkar/ambedkar_buddha/index.html#index [pdf available from http://pdfcast.org/pdf/the-buddha-and-his-dhamma-by-dr-b-r-ambedkar#]

Anderson, Gerald H., editor. *Asian Voices in Christian Theology*. Maryknoll, NY: Orbis, 1976. Online: http://www.questia.com/PM.qst?a=o&d=99352531.

Antes, Peter. "Religion: Study of Religion." In *The Encyclopedia of Christianity*, edited by Erwin Fahlbusch et al., 4:575–76. Translated by Geoffrey W. Bromiley. Grand Rapids: Eerdmans, 2005.

Appasamy, A. J. "The Christian Pramanas or the Norms of Theological Thought." *Indian Journal of Theology*, March 1953, 1–8. Reprinted in *The Christian Bhakti of A. J. Appasamy (A Collection of His Writings)*, edited by T. Dayanandan Francis, 56–69. Madras: CLS, 1992.

———. "Pramanas." *Pilgrim* 82 (June 1949) 13–15. Reprinted in *The Christian Bhakti of A. J. Appasamy (A Collection of his Writings)*, edited by T. Dayanandan Francis, 51–55. Madras: CLS, 1992.

Aragon, Averell U. "Toward an Asian Evangelical Theology of Religions." *Journal of Asian Mission* 2 (2000) 25–41.

Aratus. "Phaenomena." In *Callimachus, Hymns and Epigrams. Lycophron. Aratus*. Translated by A. W. Mair and G. R. Loeb. Classical Library 129. London: Heinemann, 1921. Online: http://www.theoi.com/Text/AratusPhaenomena.html.

Ariarajah, Wesley S. "The Impact of Interreligious Dialogue on the Ecumenical Movement." In *Pluralism and the Religions: The Theological and Political Dimensions*, edited by John D'Arcy May, 7–21. Herndon, VA: Cassell, 1998.

Asad, Talal. *Genealogies of Religion: Discipline and Reasons of Power in Christianity and Islam*. Baltimore: Johns Hopkins University Press, 1993.

Augustine. *The City of God Against the Pagans*. Edited and translated by R. W. Dyson. Cambridge Texts in the History of Political Thought. Cambridge: Cambridge University Press, 1998.

Aurobindo. *Essays: Ideals and Progress*, 2nd ed. Calcutta: Arya, 1922.

———. *The Renaissance in India*. Pondicherry: Sri Aurobindo Ashram Trust, 1918.

———. *The Superman*. Pondicherry: Sri Aurobindo Ashram Trust, 1920.

———. *The Synthesis of Yoga*. Pondicherry: Sr. Aurobindo Ashram Trust, 1988.

Azariah, V. S. "The Communal Award," *Guardian*, 8 September 1932, 368.

Baago, Kaj. *The Movement around Subba Rao*. Bangalore: Society for the Understanding of Christ, 1968.

Bagchi, Reeta. *Mahatma Gandhi and Dr. B. R. Ambedkar on Islam and Indian Muslims*. Delhi: B. R. Publishing, 1998.

Baillie, John. *The Interpretation of Religion: An Introductory Study of Theological Principles*. Edinburgh: T. & T. Clark, 1929.

Balagangadhara, S. N. *"The Heathen in His Blindness . . .": Asia, the West and the Dynamic of Religion*. Studies in the History of Religions 64. Leiden: Brill, 1994.

Baldwin, James Mark. "A New Factor in Evolution." *The American Naturalist* 30 (June 1896) 441–51.

Barclay, William. *New Testament Words*. Philadelphia: Westminster, 1964.

Barnes, Michael. *Theology and the Dialogue of Religions*. Cambridge Studies in Christian Doctrine. Cambridge: Cambridge University Press, 2002.
Barr, James. *The Concept of Biblical Theology: An Old Testament Perspective*. Minneapolis: Fortress, 1999.
Barrett, C. K. *Acts*. Vol 2. International Critical Commentary. Edinburgh: T. & T. Clark, 1998.
Barth, Karl. *Church Dogmatics*. Translated and edited by G. W. Bromiley and T. F. Torrance. Edinburgh: T. & T. Clark, 1975.
———. *The Epistle to the Romans*. Translated from the 6th edition by Edwyn Hoskyns. London: Oxford University Press, 1972.
———. *Göttingen Dogmatics: Instruction in the Christian Religion*. Vol. 1. Edited by Hannelotte Reiffen. Translated by Geoffrey W. Bromiley. Grand Rapids: Eerdmans, 1991.
———. *The Humanity of God*. London: Collins, 1971.
———. *The Knowledge of God and the Service of God According to the Teaching of the Reformation: The Gifford Lectures Delivered in the University of Aberdeen in 1937 and 1938*. Translated by J. L. M. Haire and Ian Henderson. London: Hodder & Stoughton, 1938.
———. "Questions which 'Christianity' Must Face." *The Student World* 25 (1932) 93–100.
Basu, Shamita. *Religious Revivalism as Nationalist Discourse: Swami Vivekananda and New Hinduism in Nineteenth-Century Bengal*. New Delhi: Oxford University Press, 2002.
Bayly, Chris. *Origins of Nationality in South Asia: Patriotism and Ethical Government in the Making of Modern India*. New Delhi: Oxford University Press, 1998.
Beaglehole, J. H. "The Indian Christians—A Study of a Minority." *Modern Asia Studies* 1 (1967) 59–80.
Bearce, George D. "Intellectual and Cultural Characteristics of India in a Changing Era, 1740–1800." *Journal of Asian Studies* 25 (November 1965) 3–17.
Beard, Mary, John North, and Simon Price. *Religions of Rome: Vol. I: A History*. Cambridge: Cambridge University Press, 1998.
Bellah, Robert N. *Beyond Belief: Essays On Religion in a Post-Traditionalist World*. Berkeley: University of California Press, 1991.
———. "Religious Evolution." *American Sociological Review* 29 (1964) 358–74.
Berger, Peter L. "Some Second Thoughts on Substantive versus Functional Definitions of Religion." *Journal for the Scientific Study of Religion* 13 (1974) 125–33.
Bernhardt, Reinhold. "Religion: Theological Factors." In *The Encyclopedia of Christianity*, edited by Erwin Fahlbusch et al., 4:576–78. Translated by Geoffrey W. Bromiley. Grand Rapids: Eerdmans, 2005.
Bertram, Georg. "*Theosebes, theosebeia*." In *TDNT*, 3 (1965) 123–28.
Betz, Hans Dieter. "Christianity as Religion: Paul's Attempt at Definition in Romans." *Journal of Religion* 71 (1991) 315–44.
Beyers, Jaco. "What Is Religion? An African Understanding." *Hervormde Teologiese Studies* 66 (2010). Online: http://www.hts.org.za/index.php/HTS/article/view/341.
Bianchi, Ugo. "History of Religions." In *Encyclopedia of Religion*, edited by Lindsay Jones, 6:4060–68. 2nd ed. Farmington Hill, MI: Thomson Gale, 2005.

Bloch, Maurice. "Religion and Ritual." In *The Social Science Encyclopedia*, edited by Adam Kuper and Jessica Kuper, 732–36. 2nd ed. London: Routledge, 1999.
Boulton, Matthew Myer. *God against Religion: Rethinking Christian Theology through Worship*. Grand Rapids: Eerdmans, 2008.
Bowie, Fiona. *The Anthropology of Religion: An Introduction*. Oxford: Blackwell, 2000.
Boyd, Robin. *Introduction to Indian Christian Theology*. Delhi: ISPCK, 1969.
———. "The Philosophical context of Indian Christian Theology with Special Reference to P. Chenchiah." In *Indian Voices in Today's Theological Debate*, edited by Horst Bürkle and Wolfgang M. W. Roth, 47–69. Lucknow: Lucknow, 1972.
Boyarin, Daniel. *Border Lines: The Partition of Judaeo-Christianity*. Divinations. Philadelphia: University of Pennsylvania Press, 2004.
———. "The Christian Invention of Judaism: The Theodosian Empire and the Rabbinic Religion." *Representations* 85 (2004) 21–57.
———. "Rethinking Jewish Christianity: An Argument for Dismantling a Dubious Category (to which is Appended a Correction of my *Border Lines*)." *Jewish Quarterly Review* 99 (2009) 7–36.
Boyer, Ernest Jr. "'What is Religion?': Shaftesbury, the German Enlightenment, and Schleiermacher." ThD diss., Harvard Divinity School, 2002.
Boyer, Pascal. *The Naturalness of Religious Ideas: A Cognitive Theory of Religion*. Berkeley: University of California Press, 1994.
Braaten, Carl E. "The Christian Faith in an Inter–Faith Context." *Dialog: A Journal of Theology* 43 (2004) 233–37.
Braley, Joshua. "Bringing God to Mind: Christian Theology in the Light of the Critical Study of Religion." PhD diss., Graduate School of Vanderbilt University, 2006.
Braun, Willi. "Religion." In *Guide to the Study of Religion*, edited by Willi Braun and Russell T. McCutcheon, 3–18. London: Continuum, 2000.
Bremmer, Jan. "Secularization: Notes Toward a Genealogy." In *Religion: Beyond a Concept*, edited by Hent de Vries, 432–37. Future of the Religious Past. New York: Fordham University Press, 2008.
Brockman, David R. "Turning to Religious Others: Visions and Blindspots in Modern Christian Reflection About Non-Christians." PhD diss., Southern Methodist University, 2006.
Brown, Giles. "The Hindu Conspiracy, 1914–1917." *Pacific Historical Review* 17 (1948) 299–310.
Brown, Peter. *Religion and Society in the Age of Saint Augustine*. New York: Harper & Row, 1972.
Bruteau, Beatrice. *Evolution toward Divinity: Teilhard de Chardin and the Hindu Traditions*. Wheaton, IL: Theosophical Publishing, 1974.
Buell, Denis Kimber. *Why This New Race: Ethnic Reasoning in Early Christianity*. New York: Columbia University Press, 2005.
Burleigh, J. H. S. *Augustine: Earlier Writings*. Philadelphia: Westminster, 1953.
Burnaby, John. *Amor Dei: A Study of the Religion of St. Augustine*. Hulsean Lectures for 1938. London: Hodder & Stoughton, 1938; reprinted, 1947.
Byrne, Peter. "Religion: Definition and Explanation." In *International Encyclopedia of Social & Behavioral Sciences*, edited by N. J. Smelser and P. B. Baltes, 13060–62. Oxford: Pergamon, 2001.

Cabezón, José Ignacio. "Identity and the Work of the Scholar of Religion." In *Identity and the Politics of Scholarship in the Study of Religion*, edited by José Ignacio Cabezón and Sheila Greeve Davaney, 43–60. New York: Routledge, 2004.
Cairns, D. S., editor. *World Missionary Conference, Edinburgh 1910: Report of Commission IV: The Missionary Message in relation to Non-Christian Religions*. Edinburgh: Oliphant & Revell, 1910.
Calvin, John. *Institutes of the Christian Religion*, vol. 1. 2 vols. Edited by John T. McNeill. Translated by Ford Lewis Battles. Louisville: Westminster John Knox, 2006.
Capetz, Paul E. "'A Seed of Religion': A Study In The Theologies of Calvin and Schleiermacher." PhD diss., University of Chicago Divinity School, 1996.
Capps, Walter H. *Religious Studies: The Making of a Discipline*. Minneapolis: Fortress, 1995.
Chakrabarty, Bidyut. *Social and Political Thought of Mahatma Gandhi*. Routledge Studies in Social and Political Thought 43. London: Routledge, 2006.
Chandra, Bipan et al. *India's Struggle for Independence: 1857–1947*. New Delhi: Penguin, 1989.
Chatterjee, Partha. *Nationalist Thought and the Colonial World: A Derivative Discourse?* London: Zed, 1986.
Chethimattam, J. B., editor. *Unique and Universal: Fundamental Problems of Indian Theology*. Bangalore: Dharmaram College, 1972.
Chetsingh, R. M. "The State and Conscience." *Guardian*, 1 October 1942, 46–49.
Childs, Brevard S. *Old Testament Theology in a Canonical Context*. Philadelphia: Fortress, 1986.
Chenchiah P. "The Challenge of Modern Hinduism to the Finality of the Christian Gospel." *Guardian*, 5 September 1940, 565–66.
———. "Christ and Hinduism." *Guardian*, 22 March 1945, 91–92.
———. "The Christian in a Hindu Environment." *Guardian*, 9 February 1950, 84–85; 16 February 1950, 100–101.
———. "Christian Youth, Non-Christian Faiths and Indian Culture." *Guardian*, 27 July 1939, 452–53; 3 August 1939, 468–70.
———. "Christians and Yoga: A Study of the Technique of Realisation in Relation to the Aims and Objects of Christianity." *Guardian*, 23 March 1944, 136–37; 30 March 1944, 149–50; 6 April 1944, 162–63; 13 April 1944, 174–76; 20 April 1944, 186–87.
———. "Christianity and Hinduism." *NCCR* 48 (March 1928) 119–38.
———. "The Concept of Time in Religion." *Guardian*, 29 June 1939, 388–89; 6 July 1939, 404–5.
———. "Conversions and Colleges." *Guardian*, 2 March 1944, 100–102.
———. "The Cross and Resurrection." *Guardian*, 26 February 1959, 7; 16 April 1959, 124.
———. "Dangers Ahead." *Guardian*, 23 October 1958, 427–28; 30 October 1958, 436–37.
———. "The Dilemma and Dialectic of Religions." *Guardian*, 8 June 1944, 268–69; 15 June 1944, 280–81; 22 June 1944, 293–94; 29 June 1944, 302–3; 6 July 1944, 306–7.
———. "Dr. Kraemer, Inter-Religious Co-operation and Syncretism." *Guardian*, 29 March 1951. 152–53.
———. "Editorial." *The Pilgrim* 8 (1 March 1949) 1–5.

———. "Editorial Notes." *The Pilgrim* 8 (2 June 1949) 1–12; 8 (3 September 1949) 2–4; 8 (4 December 1949) 2–9; 9 (1 March 1950), 1–12; 9 (2 June 1950) 1–11; 9 (3 September 1950) 1–8; 9 (4 December 1950) 1–6; 10 (1 March 1951) 1–5; 10 (4 December 1951) 1–8; 11 (2 June 1952), 1–8;

———. "Essentials of Christianity." *Guardian*, 10 August 1933, 378; 17 August 1933, 389; 31 August 1933. 413; 7 September 1933, 424; 14 September 1933, 438; 21 September 1933, 449; 28 September 1933, 461; 5 October 1933, 472; 9 November 2011, 533.

———. "Evangelism in Free India." *Guardian*, 16 August 1956, 326–27; 23 August 1956, 337–38.

———. "The Future of Christianity in India." *Guardian*, 23 February 1928, 88–92; 26 June 1941, 292–93; 3 July 1941, 304–5; 10 July 1941, 316–17.

———. "The Holy Spirit: Meaning and Significance of Christianity: Bible Studies." *Guardian*, 30 June 1932, 252; 14 July 1932, 276; 21 July 1932, 287; 28 July 1932, 300; 11 October 1932, 323.

———. "In Relation to Hinduism." *The Jerusalem Meeting of the International Missionary Council*, March–April 1928, 294–95, 313–16.

———. "Indian Christian Politics: The Communal Way and the Way of the Ideal." *Guardian*, 4 October 1945, 315–17; 11 October 1945, 325.

———. "Indian Christian Theological Task: Review and Restatement." *Guardian*, 2 January 1947, 6–7; 9 January 1947, 20–21; 16 January 1947, 29–31; 23 January 1947, 44–45; 30 January 1947, 57–58; 6 February 1947, 67–68; 13 February 1947, 77–79; 20 February 1947, 99–100; 6 March 1947. 110–12.

———. "Indian Christians and Co-operation with Non-Christians." *Guardian*, 24 April 1958, 165–67; 1 May 1958, 175–77.

———. "The Indian Situation." *Guardian*, 1 May 1941, 196–97.

———. "The Kingdom of God in India." *Guardian*, 4 May 1939, 260–61.

———. "Master C. V. V. of Kumbakonam and Briktha Rahitha Tharaka. Raja Yoga: A Study of Recent Religious Development in India." Guardian, 14 October 1943, 484–85; 21 October 1943, 497–98; 28 October 1943, 509–10.

———. "My Search for the Kingdom of God." *Guardian*, 8 February 1951. 65–66.

———. "Problems of Conversion in New India: A Plea for Rethinking on Both Sides." *Arunodayam*, April 1954, 9–12; May 1954, 9–10.

———. "Problems of the Indian Christian Community." *Guardian*, 22 January 1942, 28–30; 29 January 1942, 40–42; 5 February 1942, 52–53.

———. "Professor Kraemer and Syncretism." *Guardian*, 19 April 1951, 188–89; 26 April 1951, 200–201.

———. "The Prospects of Christians in India." *Guardian*, 14 August 1958, 328–29; 21 August 1958, 336–37.

———. "The Psychology of the Hindu Mind and the Presentation of the Christian Message." *The Pilgrim* 8 (March 1949) 11.

———. "Religion in Contemporary India." *Guardian*, 24 November 1938, 740–42; 1 December 1938, 756–57.

———. "Religions and the World." *Guardian*, 27 November 1952, 383.

———. "The Religious Situation in India." *Guardian*, 9 August 1956, 314.

———. "Reviews: Professor Radhakrishnan and a Parliament of Religions." *The Pilgrim* 9 (4 December 1950) 20–21.

———. "Revolution in Mission." *Guardian*, 11 July 1957, 274–75.

———. "Samapada Chaturanga: Theology: Religion." *The Pilgrim* 9 (2 June 1950) 31–33.

———. "Science Serves a Better World." *Guardian*, 16 October 1958, 416–18.

———. "Sri Aurobindo—His Message." *Guardian*, 9 September 1943, 424–25; 16 September 1943, 437–38.

———. "The Theological Task in India." *NCCR* 63 (February 1943) 63–65.

———. "Who Is Jesus? A Study of Jesus in Terms of the Creative Process." *Guardian*, 29 July 1943, 352–53; 5 August 1943, 364–65; 12 August 1943, 377–79; 19 August 1943, 389–92.

Chowdhry, D. A. "Communal Award," *Guardian*, 22 September, 1932, 392.

Chung, Paul. "Karl Barth and Inter-Religious Dialogue: An Attempt to Bring Karl Barth to Dialogue with Religious Pluralism." *Asia Journal of Theology* 15 (2001) 232–46.

Cicero. *De Natura Deorum*. Translated by H. Rackham. Loeb Classical Library. Cambridge: Harvard University Press, 1967.

Cox, Jeffrey. *Imperial Fault Lines: Christianity and Colonial Power in India, 1818–1940*. Stanford: Stanford University Press, 2002.

Crockett, Clayton. "On the Disorientation of the Study of Religion." In *What Is Religion? Origins, Definitions and Explanations*, edited by Thomas A. Idinopulos and Brian C. Wilson, 1–14. Studies in the History of Religions 81. Leiden: Brill, 1998.

D'Costa, Gavin. "Christian Theology and Other Faiths." In *Companion Encyclopedia of Theology*, edited by Peter Byrne and Leslie Houlden, 291–313. London: Routledge, 1995.

———. *Christian Uniqueness Reconsidered: The Myth of a Pluralistic Theology of Religions*. Maryknoll, NY: Orbis, 1990.

Danz, Christian. "Glaube in der multireligiösen Gesellschaft: Zur Bildungskompetenz evangelischen Glaubensverständnisses." *Hervormde Teologiese Studies* 63 (2007) 207–20.

Davies, Douglas J. "The Theology of Religion." in *Religious Studies and Theology: An Introduction*, edited by Helen K. Bond et al., 7–30. New York: New York University Press, 2003.

Dornakal, V. S. "The Bishop's Letter." *Dornakal Diocesan Magazine*, September 1942, 2.

DeBie, Linden J. *Speculative Theology and Common-Sense Religion: Mercersburg and the Conservative Roots of American Religion*. Eugene, OR: Pickwick Publications, 2008.

Deol, Harnick. *Religion and Nationalism in India: The Case of the Punjab*. Routledge Studies in the Modern History of Asia 8. London: Routledge, 2000.

Devanandan, P. D. "After Tambaram—What? An Indian Christian Layman's Point of View." *Guardian*, January 26 1939, 42–43.

Devasahayam, V. "Role of the Bible in the Writings of Pandipeddi Chenchiah: Its Authority, Interpretation and Relation to Hindu Scriptures." ThD diss., Senate of Serampore College, 1988.

Devashayam, D. M. and A. N. Sudarisanam, editors. *Rethinking Christianity in India*. Madras: Sudarisanam, 1938.

Di Noia, J. A. "Pluralist Theology of Religions: Pluralist or Non-Pluralist?" In *Christian Uniqueness Reconsidered: The Myth of a Pluralistic Theology of Religions*, edited by Gavin D'Costa, 119–34. Faith Meets Faith Series. Maryknoll, NY: Orbis, 1990.

———. "Religion and the Religions." In *The Cambridge Companion to Karl Barth*, edited by John Webster, 243–56. Cambridge Companions to Religion. Cambridge: Cambridge University Press, 2000.

Dorrien, Gary. "The 'Postmodern' Barth? The Word of God As True Myth." *The Christian Century*, April 2 1997, 338–42.

Dubuisson, Daniel. *The Western Construction of Religion: Myths, Knowledge, and Ideology*. Translated by William Sayers. Baltimore: Johns Hopkins University Press, 2003.

Dupuis, Jacques. *Jesus Christ at the Encounter of World Religions*. Translated by Robert R. Barr. Maryknoll: Orbis Books, 1989.

Durkheim, Emile. *The Elementary Forms of Religious Life*. Translated by Karen E. Fields. New York: Free Press, 1995. French orig., 1912.

"Editorial: The Tambaram Conference—Some Impressions." *Guardian*, 19 January 1939, 19.

"Editorial." *The Examiner*, 24 May 1930.

Eichrodt, Walter. "Does Old Testament Theology Still Have Independent Significance within Old Testament Scholarship?" In *Old Testament Theology: Flowering and Future*, edited by Ben C. Ollenburger, 21–32. Sources for Biblical and Theological Studies 1. Winona Lake, IN: Esenbrauns, 2004.

Eldridge, Michael. "Philosophy as Religion: A Study in Critical Devotion (Socrates, Spinoza, John Dewey)." PhD diss., University of Florida, 1985.

Eliade, Mircea. "Paul Tillich and the History of Religions." In *The Future of Religions*, edited by Paul Tillich and Jerald C. Brauer, 31–36. New York: Harper & Row, 1966.

Elm, Susanna. "Orthodoxy and the True Philosophical Life: Julian and Gregory of Nazianzus." In *Cappadocian Writers. Other Greek Writers: Papers presented at the Thirteenth International Conference on Patristic Studies Held in Oxford 1999*, edited by M. F. Wiles and E. J. Yarnold, 69–85. Louvain: Peeters, 2001.

Farquhar, J. N. *The Crown of Hinduism*. London: Oxford University Press, 1913.

Fitzgerald, Timothy. "Religion, Philosophy and Family Resemblances." *Religion* 26 (1996) 215–36.

———. *The Ideology of Religious Studies*. New York: Oxford University Press, 2000.

———. "Experience." In *Guide to the Study of Religion*, edited by Willi Braun and Russell T. McCutcheon, 125–39. London: Continuum, 2000.

———. *Discourse on Civility and Barbarity: A Critical History of Religion and Related Categories*. Oxford: Oxford University Press, 2007.

Flemming, Dean. "Contextualizing the Gospel in Athens: Paul's Areopagus Address as a Paradigm for Missionary Communication." *Missiology: An International Review* 30 (2002) 199–214.

Flood, Gavin. *Beyond Phenomenology: Rethinking the Study of Religion*. London: Cassell, 1999.

Ford, David. *Shaping Theology: Engagements in a Religious and Secular World*. Oxford: Blackwell, 2007.

Frazer, James G. *Psyche's Task: A Discourse Concerning the Influence of Superstition*. 1920. Reprinted, New York: Cosimo, 2007.

Frei, Hans. *Types of Christian Theology*. Edited by George Hunsinger and William C. Placher. New Haven: Yale University Press, 1992.

Frykenberg, Robert. "The Emergence of Modern 'Hinduism' as a Concept and as an Institution." In *Hinduism Reconsidered*, edited by Gunther D. Sontheimer and Hermann Kulke, 82–107. New Delhi: Manohar, 1991.

Fulford, K. W. M. "Teleology without Tears: Naturalism, Neo-Naturalism, and Evaluationism in the Analysis of Function Statements in Biology (and a Bet on the Twenty-first Century)." *Philosophy, Psychiatry & Psychology* 7 (March 2000) 77–94.

Gairdner, W. H. T. *"Edinburgh 1910" An Account and Interpretation of the World Missionary Conference*. 2nd ed. Edinburgh: Oliphant, Anderson & Ferrier, 1910.

Gandhi, M. K. *An Autobiography: Or the Story of My Experiments with Truth*. Translated by Mahadev Desai. Ahmedabad: Navajivan, 1927. Reprinted, 1984.

———. *Hindu Dharma*. 1978. Reprinted, New Delhi: Orient Paperbacks, 2005.

———. *Speeches and Writings of M. K. Gandhi*. Madras: Natesan, 1922.

Gealy, Fred D. "Religion." In *The Interpreter's Dictionary of the Bible*, edited by George Arthur Buttrick, 4:32. Nashville: Abingdon, 1962.

Geertz, Clifford. *The Interpretation of Cultures: Selected Essays*. New York: Basic Books, 1973.

Gerish, B. A. and Sergio Sorrentino. "Schleiermacher, Friedrich." In *Encyclopedia of Religion*, Edited by Lindsay Jones, 12:8159–67. 2nd ed. Farmington Hill, MI: Thomson Gale, 2005.

Gilkey, Langdon. "Plurality and Its Theological Implications." In *The Myth of Christian Uniqueness: Toward a Pluralistic Theology of Religions*, edited by John Hick and Paul F. Knitter, 37–50. Faith Meets Faith Series. Maryknoll, NY: Orbis, 1988.

Gill, Jerry H. "Faith Not without Reason: Kant, Kierkegaard and Religious Belief." In *Kant and Kierkegaard on Religion*, edited by D. Z. Phillips and Timothy Tessin, 55–72. New York: St. Martin's, 2000.

Gorringe, Timothy. "Gandhi and the Christian Community." In *Indian Critiques of Gandhi*, edited by Harold G. Coward, 153–69. SUNY Series in Religious Studies. Albany: SUNY Press, 2003.

Green, Garrett. "Challenging the Religious Studies Canon: Karl Barth's Theory of Religion." *Journal of Religion* 75 (1995) 473–86.

Grenz, Stanley. *Theology for the Community of God*. Nashville: Broadman & Holman, 1994.

Grieve, Gregory Price. *Retheorizing Religion in Nepal*. Religion/Culture/Critique Series. New York: Palgrave Macmillan, 2006.

Griffiths, Paul J. "An Evangelical Theology of Religions." In *No Other Gods Before Me? Evangelicals and the Challenge of World Religion*, edited by John G. Stackhouse Jr., 163–70. Grand Rapids: Baker Academic, 2001.

Griffiths, Paul J. "Religion." In *Dictionary for Theological Interpretation of the Bible*, edited by Kevin Vanhoozer, 672–75. Grand Rapids: Baker, 2005.

Griffiths, Paul J. "Introduction." In *Philosophy of Religion: An Anthology*, edited by Paul J. Griffiths and Charles Taliaferro. Blackwell Philosophy Anthologies 20. Malden, MA: Blackwell, 2003.

Gupta, Amit Kumar. "Defying Death: Nationalist Revolutionism in India, 1897–1938." *Social Scientist* 25 (September–October, 1997) 3–27.

Gurukul Theological Research Group. *A Christian Theological Approach to Hinduism: Being Studies in the Theology of A. J. Appasamy, V. Chakkarai and P. Chenchiah*. Madras: Christian Literature Society, 1956.

Gutierrez, Gustavo. *A Theology of Liberation: History, Politics and Salvation*, edited and translated by Sister Caridad Inda and John Eagleson. Maryknoll, NY: Orbis, 1973.

Gyger, Pia. "The Religions and the Birth of a New Humanity." In *Pluralism and the Religions: The Theological and Political Dimensions*, edited by John D'Arcy May, 90–96. London: Cassell, 1998.

Hallencreutz, Carl F. *Kraemer Towards Tambaram: a Study in Hendrik Kraemer's Missionary Approach*. Lund: Gleerup, 1966.

Halyburton, Thomas. *Natural Religion Insufficient; and Revealed Necessary to Man's Happiness in his Present State*. Edinburgh: Pr. by the Heirs and Successors of A. Anderson, 1714.

Harrison, Peter. *'Religion' and the Religions in the English Enlightenment*. Cambridge: Cambridge University Press, 1990.

Hastings, J. "Religion." In *A Dictionary of the Bible*, edited by James Hastings, 4:225. 1920. Reprinted, Peabody, MA: Hendrickson, 1988.

Hawley, John Stratton. "Naming Hinduism." *Wilson Quarterly* 15 (Summer 1991) 20.

Heehs, Peter. "Nationalism." In *Studying Hinduism: Key Concepts and Methods*, edited by Sushil Mittal and Gene Thursby, 265–77. London: Routledge, 2008.

Hefner, Philip. "Editorial: What Is Religion to Do?" *Zygon* 41 (2006) 501–04.

Heim, Mark S. *The Depth of the Riches: A Trinitarian Theology of Religious Ends*. Grand Rapids: Eerdmans, 2001.

Hick, John. *God Has Many Names: Britain's New Religious Pluralism*. London: Macmillan, 1980.

Hick, John, and Paul F. Knitter, *The Myth of Christian Uniqueness: Toward a Pluralistic Theology of Religions*. Faith Meets Faith Series. Maryknoll, NY: Orbis, 1986.

Hiebert, Paul G. *Cultural Anthropology*. Philadelphia: Lippincott, 1976.

Hivner, Richard Leroy. "The Christian Society for the Study of Hinduism, 1940–1956: Interreligious Engagement in Mid-Twentieth Century India." DLitt et Phil diss., University of South Africa, 2011.

Hobsbawm, E. J. *Nations and Nationalism since 1780—Programme, Myth, Reality*. 2nd ed. The Wiles Lectures Given at the Queen's University of Belfast. Cambridge: Cambridge University Press, 1992.

Hocking, William Ernest. *Re-thinking Missions: A Laymen's Inquiry After One Hundred Years*. New York: Harper & Brother Publishers, 1932.

Hodgson, Peter C. *Hegel and Christian Theology: A Reading of the Lectures on the Philosophy of Religion*. Oxford: Oxford University Press, 2005. Online: http://www.questia.com/PM.qst?a=o&d=110131555.

Hubbard, Moyer V. *New Creation in Paul's Letters and Thought*. Society for New Testament Studies Monograph Series 119. Cambridge: Cambridge University Press, 2004.

Hunsinger, George. "Postliberal Theology." In *Cambridge Companion to Postmodern Theology*, edited by Kevin J. Vanhoozer, 42–57. Cambridge Companions to Religion. Cambridge: Cambridge University Press, 2003.

Huther, J. E. *Critical and Exegetical Handbook to the General Epistles of James, Peter, John and Jude*. Translated by Paton J. Gloag et al. 1883. Reprinted, Winona Lake, IN: Alpha, 1979.

Idinopulos, Thomas A. "What Is Religion?" *Cross Currents* 48 (1998) 366–80. Online: http://www.crosscurrents.org/whatisreligion.htm.

Idinopulos, Thomas A., and Brian C. Wilson, editors. *What Is Religion? Origins, Definitions and Explanations.* Studies in the History of Religions 81. Leiden: Brill, 1998.

Ingham, Kenneth. *Reformers in India 1793–1833: An Account of the Work of Christian Missionaries on Behalf of Social Reform.* Cambridge: Cambridge University Press, 1956.

James, William. *The Varieties of Religious Experience: A Study in Human Nature.* Centenary Edition. 1902. Reprinted, New York: Routledge, 2002.

Jathanna, Origen V. *The Decisiveness of the Christ-Event and the Universality of Christianity in a World of Religious Plurality: With Special Reference to Hendrik Kraemer and Alfred George Hogg as well as to William Ernest Hocking and Pandipeddi Chenchiah.* Studien zur interkulturellen Geschichte des Christentums 29. Bern: Lang, 1981.

———. "The Madras Rethinking Group and Its Contributions to the Development of Indian Christian Theology." *Religion and Society* 44 (September 1997) 82–83.

Job, G. V. "The Christian Movement in India." In *Rethinking Christianity in India*, edited by D. M. Devashayam and A. N. Sudarisanam, 1–46. Madras: Sudarisanam, 1938.

Johnson, Luke Timothy. *Brother of Jesus, Friend of God: Studies in the Letter of James.* Grand Rapids: Eerdmans, 2004.

———. "The Letter of James." In *The New Interpreter's Bible*, edited by Leander Keck, 12:189. Nashville: Abingdon.

———. *The Acts of the Apostles.* Sacred Pagina. Collegeville, MN: Liturgical, 1992.

Jones, Kenneth W. *Socio-Religious Reform Movements in British India.* New Delhi: Cambridge University Press, 1994.

Jordens, J. T. F. *Gandhi's Religion: A Homespun Shawl.* London: Macmillan, 1998.

Joseph, P. Varghese. *Indian Interpretation of the Holy Spirit: An Appraisal of the Pneumatology of Appsamy, Chenchiah and Chakkarai.* Dehradun/Delhi: New Theological College/ISPCK, 2007.

———. "The Pneumatology of Pandipeddi Chenchiah: A Critical Appraisal." *Doon Theological Journal* 2 (2005).

Judge, E. A. *The First Christians in the Roman World: Augustan and New Testament Essays.* Edited by James R. Harrison. Wissenschaftliche Untersuchungen zum Neuen Testament 229. Tübingen: Mohr/Siebeck, 2008.

Kant, Immanuel. *Critique of Pure Reason.* Translated by Werner S. Pluhar. Indianapolis: Hackett, 1996. Online: http://www.questia.com/PM.qst?a=o&d=97885105.

Karkkäinen, Veli-Matti. *An Introduction to a Theology of Religions: Biblical, Historical and Contemporary Perspectives.* Downers Grove, IL: InterVarsity, 2003.

———. *Trinity and Religious Pluralism: The Doctrine of the Trinity in Christian Theology of Religions.* Aldershot, UK: Ashgate, 2004.

Kim, Heung Gyu. "Prolegomena to a Christian Theology of Religions." PhD diss., Southern Methodist University, 1998.

King, Richard. *Orientalism and Religion: Postcolonial Theory, India and 'The Mystic East.'* London: Routledge, 1999.

———. "Orientalism and the Modern Myth of 'Hinduism.'" *Numen* 46 (1999) 146–85.

Kittel, Gerhard Friedrich, and Geoffrey William Bromiley, editors. *Theological Dictionary of the New Testament.* 10 vols. Grand Rapids: Eerdmans, 1985.

Knitter, Paul F. *Introducing Theologies of Religions.* Maryknoll, NY: Orbis, 2003.

Knopf, D. "Hermeneutics versus History." *Journal of Asian Studies* 39 (1980) 495–505.

Kohn, Hans. *A History of Nationalism in the East*. London: Harcourt, Brace, 1929.

Kolarz, Walter. "Religion and Communism in Africa." *Heythrop Journal* 3 (1962) 219–31.

Krech, Volkhard. "From Historicism to Functionalism: The Rise of Scientific Approaches to Religions around 1900 and Their Socio-Cultural Context." *Numen* 47 (2000) 244–65.

Krüger, Horst. *Indian Nationalists and the World Proletariat: The National Liberation Struggle in Indian and the Labour Movement before 1914*, translated by Renate Sarma. New Delhi: Indian Council of Historical Research, 2002.

Kumar, Nigel. "Communalism and Nationalism: Lessons from the Indian Christian rejection of the 'Communal Award' in 1932." In *Indian and Christian: Changing Identities in Modern India*, edited by Cor Bennema and Paul Joshua Bhakiaraj, 155–73. Bangalore: SAIACS, 2011.

———. "Ritual Is not Religion: Exploring Balagangadhara's Proposal for Understanding the East." *ARC* 37 (2009) 237–46.

Küng, Hans. "What Is True Religion? Toward an Ecumenical Criteriology." In *Toward a Universal Theology of Religion*, edited by Leonard Swidler, 231–50. Faith Meets Faith Series. Maryknoll, NY: Orbis, 1987.

Kunin, Seth D., editor. *Theories of Religion: A Reader*. Edinburgh: Edinburgh University Press, 2006.

Lactantius. *Divine Institutes*. Translated by Anthony Bowen and Peter Garnsey. Liverpool: Liverpool University Press, 2003.

Lai, Pan-Chiu. "Barth's Theology of Religion and the Asian Context of Religious Pluralism." *Asia Journal of Theology* 15 (2001) 247–69.

Larbeer, Mohan P. *Ambedkar on Religion: A Liberative Perspective*. New Delhi: ISPCK, 2003.

Larson, Gerald James. "Scholarship on Religion and Communities of Faith." *Journal of Hindu–Christian Studies* 20 (2007) 30–34.

Lash, Nicholas. *The Beginning and the End of 'Religion'*. Cambridge: Cambridge University Press, 1996.

LaSor, William Sanford, David A. Hubbard, and Frederick W. Bush. *Old Testament Survey: The Message, Form and Background of the Old Testament*. 2nd ed. Grand Rapids: Eerdmans, 1996.

Lauer, Quentin. "Hegel, G. W. F." In *Encyclopedia of Religion*, edited by Lindsay Jones, 6:3892–95. 2nd ed. Farmington Hill, MI: Thomson Gale, 2005.

Lemche, Niels Peter. *The Old Testament between Theology and History: A Critical Survey* Louisville: Westminster John Knox, 2008.

Lin, Jan van. *Shaking the Fundamentals: Religious Plurality and Ecumenical Movement*. Church and Theology in Context 36. Amsterdam: Rodopi, 2002.

Lindbeck, George. *The Nature of Doctrine: Religion and Theology in a Postliberal Age*. Philadelphia: The Westminster Press, 1984.

Little, Dale W. "The Significance of Theology of the Holy Spirit for Theology of Religion and for Theology of Mission in the Writings of Lesslie Newbigin and Clark Pinnock." PhD diss., Trinity Evangelical Divinity School, 2000.

Lonergan, Bernard. *Method in Theology*. New York: Herder & Herder, 1972.

Lorenzen, David N. *Who Invented Hinduism? Essays on Religion in History*. New Delhi: Yoda Press, 2008.

Macnicol, Nicol. "Hinduism and Christianity: Some Points of Contact and Divergence." *Expository Times* 36 (1925) 323–26.
Madan, T. N. "Hinduism: An Introductory Essay." In *The Hinduism Omnibus*, edited by Nirad C. Chaudhuri et al., xi–xxxvi. New Delhi: Oxford University Press, 2003.
Madan, T. N. *Modern Myths, Locked Minds: Secularism and Fundamentalism in India*. New Delhi: Oxford University Press, 1998.
Madden, Frederick Eliot. *The Dominions and India since 1900*. Edited by John Eliot Darwin. Westport, CT: Greenwood, 1993.
Mallampalli, Chandra. *Christians and Public Life in Colonial South India, 1863–1937: Contending with Marginality*. New York: Routledge Curzon, 2004.
Dhavamony, Mariasusai. *Christian Theology of Religions: A Systematic Reflection on the Christian Understanding of World Religions*. Studies in the intercultural history of Christianity 108. Frankfurt: Lang, 1998.
Martin, Dale B. *Inventing Superstition: From the Hippocratics to the Christians*. Cambridge: Harvard Unviversity Press, 2004.
Martin, Ralph P. *James*. Word Bible Commentary 48. Waco, TX: Word, 1988.
Marx, Karl. *Early Writings*. Translated by Rodney Livingstone and Gregor Benton. London: Penguin Classics, 1992.
Masih, Y. *Introduction to Religious Philosophy*. Delhi: Motilal Banarsidass, 1971.
Masuzawa, Tomoko. *The Invention of World Religions: Or, How European Universalism Was Preserved in the Language of Pluralism*. Chicago: University of Chicago Press, 2000.
McBride, James. "Tillich in an Alice-in-Wonderland World." *Christian Century*, June 3–10, 1987, 516–17.
McCormack, Bruce L. "Revelation and History in Transfoundationalist Perspective: Karl Barth's Theological Epistemology." *Journal of Religion* 78 (1998) 18–38.
———. "The Unheard Message of Karl Barth." *Word & World* 14/1 (1994) 59–66.
McCutcheon, Russell T. "The Category 'Religion' in Recent Publications: A Critical Survey." *Numen* 42 (1995) 284–309.
———. *Critics not Caretakers: Redescribing the Public Study of Religion*. SUNY Series: Issues in the Study of Religion. Albany: SUNY Press, 2001.
———. "A Default of Critical Intelligence? The Scholar of Religion as Public Intellectual." *Journal of American Academy of Religion* 65 (1997) 443–68.
———, editor. *The Insider/Outsider Problem in the Study of Religion: A Reader*. London: Cassell, 1999.
———. *Manufacturing Religion: The Discourse on Sui Generis Religion and the Politics of Nostalgia*. New York: Oxford University Press, 1997.
———. "Redescribing 'Religion' as Social Formation: Toward a Social Theory of Religion." In *What Is Religion? Origins, Definitions, and Explanations*, edited by Thomas A. Idinopulos and Brian C. Wilson, 51–71. Studies in the History of Religions 81. Leiden: Brill, 1998.
———. *Studying Religion: An Introduction*. London: Equinox, 2007.
McDermott, Gerald R. *Can Evangelicals Learn From World Religions? Jesus, Revelation & Religious Traditions*. Downers Grove, IL: InterVarsity, 2000.
McGrath, Alister. *The Passionate Intellect: Christian Faith and the Discipleship of the Mind*. Downers Grove, IL: InterVarsity Press, 2010.
Mead, James K. *Biblical Theology: Issues, Methods and Themes*. Louisville: Westminster John Knox, 2007.

Meecham, Henry G. *The Epistle to Diognetus: Greek text with introduction, translation and notes*. Manchester: Manchester University Press, 1949.

Milbank, John. "The End of Dialogue." In *Christian Uniqueness Reconsidered: The Myth of Pluralistic Theology of Religions*, edited by Gavin D'Costa, 174–91. Faith Meets Faith Series. Maryknoll, NY: Orbis, 1990.

Minz, Nirmal. *Mahatma Gandhi and Hindu-Christian Dialogue*. Bangalore: CISRS, 1970.

Mitchell, Fraser W. "Christianity in Our Parishes." *Expository Times* 58 (1947) 123–26.

Mohanty, Jitendra Nath. *Reason and Tradition in Indian Thought: An Essay on the Nature of Indian Philosophical Thinking*. Oxford: Clarendon, 1999.

Moraes, Frank. *Jawaharlal Nehru: A Biography*. Mumbai: Jaico, 2007.

Müller, Max. *India: What Can It Teach Us?* London: Longman, Green, 1883.

Murphy, Tim. *Representing Religion: Essays in History, Theory and Crisis*. London: Equinox, 2007.

Nanda, B. R. *In Search of Gandhi: Essays and Reflections*. New Delhi: Oxford University Press, 2004).

Nehru, Jawaharlal. *The Discovery of India*. New Delhi: Oxford University Press, 1983.

Nicholson, Hugh. "Comparative Theology after Liberalism" *Modern Theology* 23 (2007) 229–51.

Niles, D. T. *From Edinburgh to Tambaram*. Tellippalai: ACM, n.d.

Niles, Damayanthi. "The Study of Popular Religions and Our Theological Task." *Asia Journal of Theology* 18 (2004) 212–19.

Nongbri, Brent. "Paul Without Religion: The Creation of a Category and the Search for an Apostle beyond the New Perspective." PhD diss., Yale University, 2008.

Noth, Martin. *The Old Testament World*. Translated by Victor I. Gruhn. Philadelphia: Fortress, 1966.

Oberoi, Harjot S. *The Construction of Religious Boundaries: Culture, Identity, and Diversity in the Sikh Tradition*. Chicago: University of Chicago Press, 1994.

Oddie, Geoffrey A. "Constructing 'Hinduism': The Impact of the Protestant Missionary Movement on Hindu Self-Understanding." In *Christians and Missionaries in India: Cross-Cultural Communication since 1500*, edited by Alaine Low and Robert Eric Frykenberg, 155–82. Grand Rapids: Eerdmans, 2003.

Oddie, Geoffrey A. *Imagined Hinduism: British Constructions of Hinduism, 1793–1900*. New Delhi: Sage, 2006.

Ogilvie, Matthew C. *Faith Seeking Understanding: The Functional Specialty 'Systematics' in Bernard Lonergan's 'Method in Theology.'* Milwaukee: Marquette University Press, 2001.

Ohki, Hideo. "On the Meaning of Transcendence." In *What Asian Christians are Thinking: A Theological Source Book*, edited by Douglas Elwood, 147–58. Quezon City: New Day Publishers, 1976.

O'Toole, Roger. *Religion: Classic Sociological Approaches*. McGraw-Hill Ryerson Series in Canadian Sociology. Toronto: McGraw-Hill Ryerson, 1984.

Otto, Rudolf. *The Idea of the Holy: An Inquiry into the Non-Rational Factor in the Idea of the Divine and Its Relation to the Rational*. Translated by John W. Harvey. London: Oxford University Press, 1923. Reprinted, 1958. Online: http://www.questia.com/PM.qst?a=o&d=7672652.

Paden, William E. "Before 'The Sacred' Became Theological: Rereading the Durkheimian Legacy." *Method & Theory in the Study of Religion* 3 (1991) 10–23.

Pagolu, Augustine. *The Religion of the Patriarchs*. Sheffield: Sheffield Academic, 1998.
Pal, Bipin Chandra. *An Introduction to the Study of Hinduism: A Study in Comparative Religion*. Calcutta: Gupta, 1908.
Pals, Daniel L. "Is Religion a Sui Generis Phenomena?" *Journal of the American Academy of Religion* 55 (1987) 259–82.
Pandey, Gyanendra. *The Construction of Communalism in Colonial North India*. New Delhi: Oxford University Press, 1990.
Panikkar, Raimon. *The Intrareligious Dialogue*. Rev. ed. Mahwah, NJ: Paulist, 1999.
Patton, William, editor. *The Authority of Faith: International Missionary Council Meeting at Tambaram, Madras, December 12 to 29, 1938*. Tambaram Series 1. London: Oxford University Press, 1939.
Pelikan, Jaroslav. *The Christian Tradition*. Vol. 5, *Christian Doctrine and Modern Culture (since 1700)*. Chicago: University of Chicago Press, 1989.
Pennington, Brian K. *Was Hinduism Invented? Britons, Indians, and the Colonial Construction of Religion*. Oxford: Oxford University Press, 2005.
Perdue, Leo G. *Reconstructing Old Testament Theology: After the Collapse of History*. Overtures to Biblical Theology. Minneapolis: Fortress, 2005.
Pinnock, Clark H. *A Wideness in God's Mercy: The Finality of Jesus Christ in a World of Religions*. Grand Rapids: Zondervan, 1992.
Plato. *The Apology*. Translated and Introduction by Benjamin Jowett (1871). Internet Sacred Text Archive, 2010. Online: http://www.sacred-texts.com/cla/plato/apology.htm.
Preus, Samuel J. "Zwingli, Calvin and the Origin of Religion." *Church History* 46 (1977) 186–202.
Puniyani, Ram. *Religion, Power and Violence: Expression of Politics in Contemporary Times*. New Delhi: Sage, 2005.
Race, Alan. *Christians and Religious Pluralism: Patterns in the Christian Theology of Religions*. London: SCM, 1983.
Rad, Gerhard von. *Old Testament Theology*, Vol 2 - *The Theology of Israel's Prophetic Traditions*. Translated by D. M. G. Stalker. New York: Harper & Row, 1965.
Radhakrishnan, S. *The Hindu View of Life: Upton Lectures Delivered at Manchester College, Oxford, 1926*. London: Allen & Unwin, 1927.
———. "The Indian Approach to the Problem of Religion," *Philosophy East and West* 9 (1959) 36-38.
Rajagopalan, Swarna. "Secularism in India: Accepted Principle, Contentious Interpretation." In *The Secular and the Sacred: Nation, Religion, and Politics*, edited by Willian Safran, 241–58. London: Cass, 2003.
Rajasekaran, V. C. *Reflections on Indian Christian Theology*. Madras: CLS, 1993.
Rajshekar, V. T. *Mahatma Gandhi & Babasaheb Ambedkar: The Verdict of History*. Bangalore: Dalit Sahitya Akademy, 1989.
Ramnath, Maia. "Two Revolutions: The Ghadar Movement and India's Radical Diaspora, 1913–1918." *Radical History Review* 92 (Spring 2005) 7–30.
Reardon, Bernard M. G. *Religious Thought in the Nineteenth Century: Illustrated from Writers of the Period*. Cambridge: Cambridge University Press, 1966.
Richards, Glyn. *Towards a Theology of Religions*. London: Routledge, 1989.
Richerson, Peter J., and Robert Boyd. *Not by Genes Alone: How Culture Transformed Human Evolution*. Chicago: University of Chicago Press, 2005.

Riesebrodt, Martin. *The Promise of Salvation: A Theory of Religion*. Translated by Steven Rendall. Chicago: University of Chicago Press, 2010.

Rives, James B. *Religion in the Roman Empire*. Blackwell Ancient Religions. Malden, MA: Blackwell, 2007.

Robertson, S. "Religion as Life-Sustaining: A Pluralistic Perspective." *Religion and Society* 51 (March 2006) 1–20.

Röhr, Heinz. "Bhakti and Christian Faith—according to Rudolf Otto (1869–1937)." Translated by Michael Vogt. *Journal of Religious Culture* 14 (1998) 1–10.

Ropes, James H. *A Critical and Exegetical Commentary on the Epistle of St. James*. International Critical Commentary. Edinburgh: T. & T. Clark, 1916.

Rüpke, Jörg. "Roman Religion." In *The Cambridge Companion to the Roman Republic*, edited by Harriet I. Flower, 180–95. Cambridge: Cambridge University Press, 2004.

Sabatier, Auguste. *Religions of Authority and the Religion of the Spirit*. Translated by Louise Symour Houghton. New York: McClure, Phillips, 1904.

Saler, Benson. *Conceptualizing Religion: Immanent Anthropologists, Transcendent Natives and Unbounded Categories*. Studies in the History of Religions 56. Leiden: Brill, 1993.

Salmond, Noel A. *Hindu Iconoclasts: Rammohun Roy, Dayananda Sarasvati, and Nineteenth-century Polemics Against Idolatry*. Waterloo, ON: Canadian Corporation for Studies in Religion, 2004.

Samson, Paul R., and David Pitt, editors. *The Biosphere and Noosphere Reader: Global Environment, Society and Change*. London: Routledge, 1999.

Sandnes, Karl Olav. "Paul and Socrates: The Aim of Paul's Areopagus Speech." *Journal for the Study of the New Testament* 50 (1993) 13–26.

Sarkar, Sumit. *Modern India: 1885–1947*. New Delhi: Macmillan, 1983.

Schineller, J. P. "Christ and Church: A Spectrum of Views." *Theological Studies* 37 (1976) 545–66.

Schleiermacher, Friedrich. *On Religion: Speeches to Its Cultured Despisers*. Translated by John Oman. Louisville: Westminster John Knox, 1994.

Schloss, Jeffrey, and Michael J. Murray, editors. *The Believing Primate: Scientific, Philosophical and Theological Reflections on the Origin of Religion*. Oxford: Oxford University Press, 2009.

Schott, Jeremy M. *Christianity, Empire and the Making of Religion in Late Antiquity*. Philadelphia: University of Pennsylvania Press, 2008.

Schwartz, Seth. *Imperialism and Jewish Society, 200 B.C.E. to 640 C.E.* Jews, Christians, and Muslims from the Ancient to the Modern World. Princeton: Princeton University Press, 2001.

Schwöbel, Christoph. "Particularity, Universality, and the Religions: Toward a Christian Theology of Religions." In *Christian Uniqueness Reconsidered: The Myth of Pluralistic Theology of Religions*, edited by Gavin D'Costa, 30–46. Faith Meets Faith Series. Maryknoll, NY: Orbis, 2000.

Scott, Charles Newton. *The Religions of Antiquity as Preparatory to Christianity*. London: Smith, Elder, 1914.

Seal, Anil. *The Emergence of Indian Nationalism: Competition and Collaboration in the Later Nineteenth Century*. New Delhi: Chand, 1971.

Selvanayagam, Israel, editor. *The Multi-Faith Context of India: Resources and Challenges for Christians*. Bangalore: BTTBPSA, 1993.

Sen, Amartya. *Identity and Violence: The Illusion of Destiny*. London: Penguin, 2006.
Sen, Indira, editor. *Sri Aurobindo on Yoga*. Pondicherry: Sri Aurobindo Ashram Trust, 1980.
Seth, Sanjay. "Rewriting Histories of Nationalism: The Politics of 'Moderate Nationalism' in India, 1870-1905." *American Historical Review* 104 (February 1999) 95-116.
Sethna, K. D. *Teilhard de Chardin and Sri Aurobindo: A Focus on Fundamentals*. Varanasi: Bharatiya Vidya Prakash, 1973.
Seung, T. K. "Kant, Immanuel." In *Encyclopedia of Religion*, edited by Lindsay Jones, 8:5076-81. 2nd ed. Farmington Hill, MI: Thomson Gale, 2005.
Sharpe, Eric J. *Comparative Religion: A History*. London: SCM, 1975.
———. *Faith Meets Faith: Some Christian Attitudes to Hinduism in the Nineteenth & Twentieth Centuries*. London: SCM, 1977.
Sherry, Patrick. *Religion, Truth and Language-Games*. London: Macmillan, 1977.
Singh, Karan. *In Defence of Religion and Other Essays*. New Delhi: Vision Books, 1978.
———. "The Hindu Renaissance." In *Freedom, Progress & Society: Essays n Honour of Professor K. Satchidananda Murty*, edited by R. Balasubramanian and Sibajiban Bhattacharyya, 1-8. Delhi: Motilal Banarsidass, 1986.
Singh, Narendra. *A Christian Theology of Religions: Recovering Dialectical Method*. Bangalore: SAIACS Press, 2005.
Smart, Ninan. "Meaning in Religion and the Meaning of Religion." Colloquium paper, University of Lancaster (December 1969) Online: http://www.ucalgary.ca/~hexham/courses/courses-2007/rels-379/readings/smart-religion.html.
Smith, Huston. *Why Religion Matters: The Fate of the Human Spirit in an Age of Unbelief*. New York: HarperCollins, 2001.
Smith, James K. A. *Introducing Radical Orthodoxy: Mapping a Post-secular Theology*. Grand Rapids: Baker Academic, 2004.
Smith, John E. "Philosophy: Philosophy of Religion." In *Encyclopedia of Religion*, edited by Lindsay Jones, 10:7113-22. 2nd ed. Farmington Hill, MI: Thomson Gale, 2005.
Smith, Jonathan Z. *Imagining Religion: From Babylon to Jonestown*. Chicago Studies in the History of Judaism. Chicago: University of Chicago Press, 1982.
———. "Religion, Religions, Religious." In *Critical Terms for Religious Studies*, edited by Mark C. Taylor, 269-84. Chicago: University of Chicago Press, 1998.
———. "Classification." In *Guide to the Study of Religion*, edited by Willi Braun and Russell T. McCutcheon, 35-44. London: Continuum, 2000.
Smith, Wilfred Cantwell. *The Meaning and End of Religion: A New Approach to the Religious Traditions of Mankind*. New York: Macmillan, 1963.
Smith, William Robertson. *Religion of the Semites*. 1894. Reprinted, Piscataway, NJ: Rutgers, 2002.
Southwold, Martin. "Buddhism and the Definition of Religion." *Man* 13 (1978) 362-79.
Speer, Robert E., editor. *The Christian Life and Message in Relation to Non-Christian Systems: Report of the Jerusalem Meeting of the International Missionary Council, March 24-April 8, 1928*. London: Oxford University Press, 1928.
Srivastava, R. S. "The Integralist Theory of Evolution." In *The Integral Philosophy of Sri Aurobindo: A Commemorative Symposium*, edited by Haridas Chaudhuri and Frederic Spiegelberg, 133-42. London: Allen & Unwin, 1960.
Stokes, Gale. "How Is Nationalism Related to Capitalism? A Review Article." *Comparative Studies in Society and History* 28 (1986) 591-98.

Strenski, Ivan. "On 'Religion' and Its Despisers." In *What Is Religion? Origins, Definitions and Explanations,* edited by Thomas A. Idinopulos and Brian C. Wilson, 113–32. Studies in the History of Religions 81. Leiden: Brill, 1998.

———. *Thinking about Religion: An Historical Introduction.* Malden, MA: Blackwell, 2006.

———. "Why 'Theology' Won't Work." In *Religious Studies, Theology, and the University: Conflicting Maps, Changing Terrain,* edited by Linell E. Cady and Delwin Brown, 31–44. Albany: SUNY Press, 2002.

Sumner, George R. *The First & the Last: The Claim of Jesus Christ and the Claims of Other Religious Traditions.* Grand Rapids: Eerdmans, 2004.

Sugirtharajah, Sharada. *Imagining Hinduism: A Postcolonial Perspective.* New York: Routledge, 2003.

Taylor, Mark C. "Defining Religion." *Chronicle of Higher Education* 51 (2004) B4.

Teilhard de Chardin, Pierre. *The Phenomenon of Man.* Translated by Bernard Wall. London: Collins, 1959.

Tennent, Timothy C. *Christianity at the Religious Roundtable: Evangelicalism in Conversation with Hinduism, Buddhism and Islam.* Grand Rapids: Baker Academic, 2002.

Thangasamy, D. A. *The Theology of Chenchiah: With Selections from His Writings.* Bangalore: CISR, 1966.

Thapar, Romila. "Imagined Religious Communities? Ancient History and the Modern Search for Hindu Identity." In *Cultured Pasts: Essays in Early Indian History,* 965–89. New Delhi: Oxford University Press, 2000.

Thomas, Abraham Vazhayil. *Christians in Secular India.* Cranbury, NJ: Associated University Presses, 1974.

Thomas Aquinas, Saint. "Question 81.1: Of Religion." In *Thomas Aquinas: Summa Theologica: Complete English Edition in Five Volumes,* vol. 3. Translated by Fathers of the English Dominican Province. Rev. ed. Allen, TX: Christian Classics, 1948.

Thomas, George. "Christian Indians and Indian Nationalism, 1885–1950: An Interpretation in Historical and Theological Perspectives." PhD diss., University of Hamburg, 1979.

Thomas, H. G. "Christian Leaders of Madras and the Crisis." *Guardian,* 3 September 1942. 414.

Thumma. Anthoniraj. *Dalit Liberation Theology: Ambedkarian Perspective.* Delhi: ISPCK, 2000.

Tice, Terrence N. "Schleiermacher Yesterday, Today and Tomorrow." In *The Cambridge Companion to Friedrich Schleiermacher,* edited by Jacqueline Marina, 307–18. Cambridge Companions to Religion. Cambridge: Cambridge University Press, 2005.

Tillich, Paul. *The Future of Religions.* Edited by Jerald C. Brauer. New York: Harper & Row, 1966.

———. *The New Being.* 1950. Reprinted, Lincoln: University of Nebraska Press, 2005.

———. *Theology of Culture.* New York: Oxford University Press, 1959.

———. *What Is Religion?* Translated by James Luther Adams. 1969. Reprinted, New York: Harper, 1973.

Troeltsch, Ernst. *The Social Teaching of the Christian Church.* Vol. 2. London: Allen & Unwin, 1931.

Tylor, E. B. *Primitive Culture.* London: Murray, 1871.

Varughese, T. P. "Christology in the Writings of Pandipeddi Chenchiah and Raimundo Panikkar: An Indian Evangelical Assessment." PhD diss., Westminster Theological Seminary, 1998.
Varughese, V. S. "Cultural Disorganization among the Adivasis: A Study of the Paniyas of Wynad." *Religion and Society* 44 (June 1997) 83–106.
Veer, Peter van der. *Religious Nationalism: Hindus and Muslims in India*. Berkeley: University of California Press, 1994.
Veeraraj, Anand. *Green History of Religion*. Bangalore: Centre for Contemporary Christianity, 2006.
Vivekananda, Swami. *The East and the West*. 6th reprint. Calcutta: Advaita Ashrama, 1963.
———. *The Chicago Addresses*, 11th ed. Calcutta: Udbodhan Office, 1945.
———. *The Complete Works of Swami Vivekananda*. Vol. 2. Calcutta: Advaita Ashrama, 1963.
Wach, Jaochim. "The Place of The History of Religions in the Study of Theology." *Journal of Religion* 27 (1947) 157–77.
Wagner, Herwig. *Erstgestalten einer einheimischen Theologie in Sudindien: Ein Kapitel indischer theologiegeschichte als kritischer Beitrag zur Definition von "einheimischer Theologie."* Veröffentlichungen zu Mission und Ökumene. Munich: Kaiser, 1963.
Waller, James, Mary Edwardsen, and Martinez Hewlett. "Evolution: Evolutionism." In *Encyclopedia of Religion*, edited by Lindsay Jones, 5:2913–17. 2nd ed. Farmington Hill, MI: Thomson Gale, 2005.
Watson, Thomas. *Popular Evidences of Natural Religion and Christianity*. London: Longman, Hurst, Rees and Orme, Paternoster-Row, 1805.
Ward, Marcus. *Our Theological Task: An Introduction to the Study of Theology in India*. Madras: CLS, 1946.
Weber, Bruce H., and David J. Depew, editors. *Evolution and Learning: The Baldwin Effect Reconsidered*. Cambridge: MIT Press, 2003.
Weber, Max. *The Protestant Ethic and the Spirit of Capitalism*. Translated by Talcott Parsons. First published in 1930 by Allen and Unwin. London: Routledge Classics, 2001.
Webster, John. *Confessing God: Essays in Christian Dogmatics II*. London: T. & T. Clark, 2005.
Weiner, Myron. "The Struggle for Equality: Caste in Indian Politics." In *The Success of India's Democracy*, edited by Atul Kohli, 193–225. Contemporary South Asia 6. Cambridge: Cambridge University Press, 2001.
Whaling, Frank. "Indian Christian Theology—The Humanity of Christ and the New Humanity." *Scottish Journal of Theology* 31 (1978) 319–33.
———. "Religion, Theories of." In *Blackwell Encyclopedia of Modern Christian Thought*, edited by Alister McGrath, 547–53. Oxford: Blackwell, 1993.
———. "Theological Approaches." In *Approaches to the Study of Religion*, edited by Peter Connolly, 226–74. London: Continuum, 1999.
Whaling, Frank, editor. *Contemporary Approaches to the Study of Religion*. Berlin: Mouton, 1985.
Whitehead, Alfred North. *Religion in the Making*. Lowell Lectures 1926. 7th ed. New York: World, 1971.
Wiebe, Donald. *The Politics of Religious Studies: The Continuing Conflict with Theology in the Academy*. New York: St. Martin's, 1999.

———. *The Irony of Theology and the Nature of Religious Thought*. Montreal: McGill-Queen's University Press, 1991.

Wilson, John F., and Thomas P. Slavens. *Research Guide to Religious Studies*. Chicago: American Library Association, 1982.

Witherington, Ben III. *The Acts of the Apostles: A Socio-Rhetorical Commentary*. Grand Rapids: Eerdmans, 1998.

Wolfart, Johannes C. "Postmodernism." In *Guide to the Study of Religion*, edited by Willi Braun and Russell T. McCutcheon, 380–95. London: Cassell, 2000.

Woodhead, Linda and Paul Heelas, editors. *Religion in Modern Times: An Interpretative Anthology*. Oxford: Blackwell, 2000.

"World Missionary Conference—Notes from Reports of Groups." *Guardian*, 5 January 1939. 8–13.

Wynn, Mark. "Religious Language." In *Companion Encyclopedia of Theology*, edited by Peter Byrne and Leslie Houlden, 413–32. London: Routledge, 1995.

Yong, Amos. *Beyond the Impasse: Toward a Pneumatological Theology of Religions*. Grand Rapids: Baker Academic, 2003.

———. *Discerning the Spirit(s): A Pentecostal-Charismatic Contribution to Christian Theology of Religions*. Journal of Pentecostal Theology Supplement Series 20. Sheffield: Sheffield Academic, 2000.

Zaehner, R. C. *Evolution in Religion: A Study in Sri Aurobindo and Pierre Teilhard de Chardin*. London: Oxford University Press, 1971.

Zeldin, Mary-Barbara. "The Religious Nature of Russian Marxism." *Journal for the Scientific Study of Religion* 8 (1969) 100–111.

Zevit, Ziony. *The Religions of Ancient Israel: A Synthesis of Parallactic Approaches*. London: Continuum, 2001.

Zimand, Savel. *Living India*. New York: Longmans, Green, 1928.

Index

Abbott, Lyman, 65
abolition of religion, 65, 88, 101
Abraham, K. C., 43, 165
academia/academic (study of religion), 2, 9, 14–15, 121, 220–25, 235, 241, 258–59, 261, 280, 283
action as religion, 216, 226–31, 235–36, 238, 242–46, 263–65, 270, 278–84
action as ritual, 20–22, 235, 242, 246, 282
Albuquerque, Teresa, 108, 113
Aleaz, K. P., 2, 37
Aloysius, G., 76–77, 86
Alt, Albrecht, 235–36
Alves, Rubem, 14
Ambedkar, B. R., 49, 77, 82, 86–89, 116, 162, 164–65, 276
Appasamy, A. J., 46, 120, 123–24, 131, 200, 207, 213–14
Aquinas, Thomas, 271
Asad, Talal, 6
ascetic religion, 154–55, 168, 180, 184, 197, 284
Asrama, 121, 139, 141, 154–59, 183–84, 197, 205, 208–10
Augustine, 36, 52–53, 101, 207, 220, 258, 266–75, 278, 283
Aurobindo, 49, 68–69, 73, 79–82, 116, 125, 127, 141, 144–45, 172, 174–75, 177, 193, 195, 204–5, 207, 215, 276
Azariah, V. S., 105–6, 109–10

Balagangadhara, S. N., 9–10, 17–24, 35, 47, 52, 218–19, 258, 263–64, 272
Baldwin, James/Baldwin effect, 62, 208–9
Barnes, Michael, 27, 29
Barr, James, 204, 232, 234–35, 237
Barrett, C. K., 240, 251–55
Barth, Karl, 34, 50, 97–102, 115–16, 134–35, 147, 163, 179, 180–81, 202, 223, 237, 264–65
Basu, Shamita, 70, 72–73, 81, 90
belief/belief-oriented (religion as), 5, 20–25, 47, 55, 60, 64, 66, 86, 156, 190, 195, 219, 228, 230, 239–40, 242–44, 248, 250, 255, 257, 265, 267, 270, 273
Bellah, Robert, 58, 60, 204
Bergson, Henri, 125, 176–77
Bernhardt, Reinhold, 37
Betz, Hans Dieter, 241–42
bhakti, 59, 83, 85, 143, 157–59, 168, 190, 200, 210–11, 214, 271, 277
Bloch, Maurice, 4
Boyarin, Daniel, 240
Boyd, Robin, 41–42, 118, 125, 133, 176–77, 203
Braaten, Carl, 30–31
Buddhism, 1, 5, 7–8, 13–14, 25, 34, 89, 149–50, 155, 158, 160, 162, 178
Buell, Denise, 239, 262, 267

Calvin, John, 53–54, 101
Chakkarai, Vengal, 110–11, 114–15, 119, 205

Index

Chenchiah, Pandipeddi, iv–v, vii–x, 2, 35–36, 40–50, 54, 65–66, 69, 74, 79, 81–82, 86, 92, 96–97, 104, 116–220, 229–31, 238, 250, 257–58, 262–66, 271–79, 281–82, 284
Childs, Brevard, 236–37
Chowdhry, D. A., 112
Christian/Christianity, 1, 7–8, 17–28, 34, 38, 40–65, 70–73, 85, 90–129, 136–39, 141, 144–47, 150–230, 238, 241, 245–46, 250, 258–59, 262, 265, 268, 270, 272, 278, 284
Cicero, 51
classification theory (and religion), 32, 47–48, 194, 198, 219–22, 226, 258, 262, 273–74, 278–81, 284
colonialism, 10, 70
communal/communalism, 74, 76–77, 104, 106–13, 122, 186
cosmographical schema, 18, 24, 47, 81, 116, 202, 204, 218, 228, 258, 263–66, 274, 278, 281
cult/cultic practices, 31, 38, 69, 143, 221, 232–47, 256–57, 266, 270, 272–73, 282
culture/cultural, 2, 4, 6–22, 29–35, 43–47, 50–55, 60–77, 82, 89, 93, 101–8, 113–14, 121–25, 127, 142, 162–63, 168, 170, 197–98, 208–9, 216, 220–26, 232, 235, 238, 245–46, 258–59, 260, 262, 279–80, 282, 284

Daly, Mary, 28
Darwinian evolution, 62, 173, 176
Datta, S. K., 109
Davies, Douglas J., 39–40
de Chardin, Teilhard, 63, 125, 172, 176–77, 204, 213
Devasahayam, V., 44, 117–18, 121, 124–25, 129, 185, 201
dharma, 11–12, 70, 73, 85, 143, 158, 160–61, 186
dual theory (and religion), 46, 54, 133–34, 150, 168, 179–82, 190, 195–99, 208, 218, 229, 231, 240, 263, 267, 270, 277–78, 280, 284

Dubuisson, Daniel, 10–11, 13, 17–18, 24, 35, 47, 219, 258, 263–64, 272
Dupuis, Jacques, 25–26, 38–40, 248, 253–54
Durkheim, Emile, 66

Edinburgh Missionary Conference, 50, 92–93, 96, 103
Eichrodt, Walter, 234
Eliade, Mircea, 223
emic. See Insider.
Enlightenment, 10, 33, 45, 53–55, 59, 186, 227, 230, 279
etic. See Outsider.
evolution/evolutionary theory (and religion), 5, 29, 55, 61–65, 74, 78–82, 90, 93, 97, 102, 116, 125, 135–38, 142–45, 149–50, 154, 158, 16–68, 172–79, 185, 191, 193, 195–97, 199–214, 218, 232, 264, 276–78

false religion, 3, 52, 180, 208, 245, 247, 268, 269, 283
Family resemblance, 7, 8, 45, 175, 280
Farquhar, J. N., 91, 172, 177–78
Fernando, Ajith, 248–51, 253–56
Fitzgerald, Timothy, 8, 10, 16, 87
Fleming, Dean, 248, 255
Flood, Gavin, 13, 197
Frazer, James, 64
Frei, Hans, 259
Frykenberg, Robert, 67

Gandhi, M. K., 49, 75–77, 82–89, 93, 106–8, 116, 120, 125, 142–43, 153, 162, 164–65, 175, 177, 193, 210, 214–15, 276
Geertz, Clifford, 6, 45
Golwalkar, M. S., 77
Green, Garrett, 100, 223
Grenz, Stanley, 259, 263
Griffiths, Paul J., 25, 33–35, 241, 268
Gurukul Group, 134, 193, 199, 203, 212
Gutierrez, Gustavo, 259

Hallencreutz, Carl F., 96

Hampson, Daphne, 28, 132
Harrison, Peter, 10, 53–55, 59
Heehs, Peter, 67–70, 76–77
Heim, S. Mark, 27
Hick, John, 25, 28, 197
Hiebert, Paul, 6–7, 280
Hindu/Hinduism, 1–2, 7, 12, 14, 22, 25–27, 35, 40–42, 46, 49, 59, 65–94, 101, 105, 107, 109–19, 124–45, 153–67, 170–93, 198, 201–2, 205, 208, 212, 215–17, 263, 276–77
Hocking, Ernest William, 94, 103
Hogg, A. G. 103–4, 154
humanist/humanism (and religion), 71, 95, 112, 147, 165, 176, 194, 222–24, 283

Indian Christian, 49, 67, 69, 78, 104–33, 137, 139, 141, 154, 158, 161, 167, 172, 175, 176–77, 182, 185, 187, 190, 201, 203, 205, 207, 210, 212, 276, 282
Indian theology, viii, 49, 122, 125, 173, 199, 202
insider/emic, 47, 117, 161, 169, 198–99, 202, 218, 222, 224–25, 229, 258–59, 262–65, 274, 277, 280–84
integrated religion, 48, 66, 85–86, 120, 138, 142–43, 159, 195, 206–20, 225, 229, 231, 235, 238, 243, 257, 265–66, 272–74, 276, 278, 284
Islam/Muslim, 19, 25–26, 34, 60, 67, 69, 72–77, 86, 105, 107, 109, 120, 145, 162, 178, 185–86, 188–89, 208, 216, 223

James, William, 64
Jathanna, O. V., 41, 43–44, 101–2, 118–21, 125, 127, 172, 194–95, 203–4, 213–14, 294
Jerusalem Missionary Conference, 25, 28, 50, 93–101, 119, 163, 170–71
Jones, Rufus, 94–95, 163, 171,
Joseph, P. Varghese, 136
Josephus, 253–54

Kant/Kantian, 56–57, 123, 214
Karkkäinen, Veli-Matti, 25–26, 39
King, Richard, 10, 50, 157
Knitter, Paul, 25, 37
Kraemer, Hendrik, 92, 94, 96, 101–3, 134, 152, 154, 163, 184
Küng, Hans, 28, 38
Kunin, Seth D., 3–7, 64, 163

Lactantius, 51–52
Lash, Nicholas, 4, 12
Lindbeck, George, 29
Lonergan, Bernard, 260–61, 274, 278
Lorenzen, David, 67

Macnicol, Nicol, 91, 94
Mallampalli, Chandra, 92, 108, 109
Marx/Marxian 65–66, 74, 100
Master C.V.V., 127, 141, 144–45, 175
Masuzawa, Tomoko, 25
McCutcheon, Russell, 9, 15, 47, 220–25, 229, 257–58, 262, 273, 278
McGrath, Alister, 32
Mead, James K., 231, 233
Miller, William, 118, 124
Mitchell, Fraser, 200
Mohanty, J. N., 124
Müller, Max, 90
Muslim. See Islam.

nationalism/nationalist, 6, 48–50, 66, 69–79, 86, 92, 95, 101–21, 124, 142–43, 163, 165, 185–87, 211, 214, 216, 284
Nehru, Jawaharlal, 77–78, 143, 162, 164–65
Niles, D. T., 92–93, 96, 101
Noth, Martin, 232

Oberoi, Harjot S., 67
Oddie, Geoffrey, 12, 67, 70
Otto, Rudolf, 55, 58–59
outsider/etic, 47, 117, 161–63, 198–99, 218, 222, 224, 259, 262–63, 280–81, 284

Pagolu, Augustine, 236
Pandey, Gyanendra, 76–77

Paul, K. T., 96, 109, 111
Pennington, Brian K., 67
Pieris, Aloysius, vii–viii
pluralism/pluralist, 21, 26, 37–39, 84–85, 190, 248
pramanas, 124, 131, 200
pure religion, 44, 194, 246–47, 271

Race, Alan, 26
Rad, Gerhard von, 233–34
Radhakrishnan, S., 162, 187
redescribe/redescription (religion), 15, 47–48, 198, 220, 224, 262–63, 266, 272, 280, 282
Regulus, Marcus, 267–69
religio, 20–22, 34, 45, 50–53, 82, 241, 267–68, 270
Riesebrodt, Martin, 1, 220, 225–30, 247, 256, 258, 264–66, 273, 278, 281
ritual, 8, 13, 18, 20, 22, 142, 146, 155, 157–58, 166, 221, 237–39, 241, 243
Ropes, James H., 244
Roy, J. J. M. Nichols, 111–12
Roy, Ram Mohan, 71, 145, 175

Sabatier, Auguste, 61
Saler, Benson, 8
Samartha, Stanley, 27, 31–32
Saraswati, Dayanand, 72
Sawarkar, V. D., 77
Schleiermacher, Friedrich, 57–58, 61, 101
Sen, Amartya, 14
Sen, Keshub Chandra, 71
Sharpe, Eric, 73, 90–93, 96, 102
Singh, Sadhu Sundar, 114, 207
Smart, Ninian, 13
Smith, Huston, 4
Smith, James, 271
Smith, Jonathan Z., 15, 31, 45, 50–51, 53, 59, 220–23
Smith, Robertson, 60
Smith, Wilfred Cantwell, 9, 37, 39, 223
Socrates, 21, 25, 251–54
spirituality, vii, 2, 5, 68, 82, 86, 160, 164, 165, 215, 262

Strenski, Ivan, 7, 15–16, 46, 64, 223, 226
Sugirtharajah, Sharada, 2
Sumner, George, 29, 132, 216
sycretism/syncretist, 184, 187, 193

Tambaram Missionary Conference, 50, 92–93, 96–97, 101–4, 119–20, 151, 180
temple religion, 44, 154–55, 158, 164, 168, 184, 194, 208, 238, 284
Thangasamy, D. A., 42, 118–19, 125, 203
theological method, 2, 29, 36, 49, 116, 123–24, 200, 218, 258–62, 274, 278, 280
theology of religion, vii–ix, 1–2, 24, 26, 31, 35–50, 86, 97, 101, 104, 117, 134, 141, 161, 168–72, 177, 179, 182, 185–86, 190, 192–95, 198–99, 202, 210–23, 229, 261–62, 264–65, 272–80, 284
theology of religions, vii–ix, 2, 25–48, 127, 141, 185–86, 189–90, 195, 215–17, 247, 257, 272–73, 275, 277, 279, 283, 284
Thomas, Abraham, 104
Thomas, George, 105–6, 113–14
Tillich, Paul, 31–32, 199, 223, 238
traditio, 20–21
tradition (and ritual), 9, 11–13, 20–21, 38–39, 51–54, 60, 69, 143–44, 146, 166, 180, 230, 233–34, 239–46, 255, 259, 277
Troeltsch, Ernst, 37, 61
true religion, 1, 3, 17, 24, 34, 47, 53, 55, 57, 82, 84, 88, 95, 143, 150, 152–59, 168–72, 179–84, 190, 193–94, 197, 199, 209–10, 215, 217, 230, 238, 245, 250, 265, 267–70, 273, 275, 277, 280, 283
Tylor, E. B., 5, 64

unbelief (religion as), vii, 101, 103
universal religion, 8–9, 59, 71, 82, 102, 111

Vivekananda, Swami, 49, 69, 73, 81–82, 85, 116, 125, 145, 162, 193, 276

Wagner, Herwig, 118–25, 133–34, 172, 194–96, 204, 205
Ward, Marcus, 123, 129
Weber, Max, 66
Webster, John, 258–59, 263, 274, 278
Whaling, Frank, 3, 37–38, 139, 176
Whitehead, Alfred North, 3
worldview, 15, 19, 22–24, 32, 133, 260, 263, 265, 281–82

worship, 22–23, 34, 36, 47–48, 51–54, 84, 91, 116, 143, 146, 148, 166, 185, 211–13, 218, 220–21, 227–30, 235, 236, 239, 240–47, 254, 257, 265–75, 278, 282–84

yoga, 79, 81, 127, 131–32, 138–44, 152, 154, 156–61, 166–67, 185, 196, 205
Yong, Amos, 27, 39

Zimand, Savel, 75

www.ingramcontent.com/pod-product-compliance
Lightning Source LLC
Chambersburg PA
CBHW071156300426
44113CB00009B/1225